WORKS BY
ZHU YONGXIN
ON
EDUCATION

History of Chinese Ancient Educational Thought

ZHU YONGXIN

New York   Chicago   San Francisco   Athens   London
Madrid   Mexico City   Milan   New Delhi
Singapore   Sydney   Toronto

ISBN   978-0-07-183819-1
MHID   0-07-183819-8

e-ISBN   978-0-07-183820-7
e-MHID   0-07-183820-1

McGraw-Hill Education books are available at special quantity discounts to use as premiums and sales promotions or for use in corporate training programs. To contact a representative, please visit the Contact Us pages at www.mhprofessional.com.

Contents

Listen to the Voice
of the Masters

Bathed in a five-thousand-year civilization
I approached the masters of education
Amidst the voluminous books
I listened to the voice of their wisdom

I listened to Confucius. His "No Child Left Behind" speech created a precedent for private schools; "By nature, people are similar, but later practice makes them different" spreads the meaning of learning; and his "Never be content with your study; never be impatient with your teaching" guided generations of teachers.

I listened to *Records of Education* (*Xue Ji*), in which little more than 1,000 words, ranging from "influence the people and form moral customs through education" to "give priority to education in building up a country and governing its people"; from "help both the good students and the slow ones"; and from "teaching is learning" to "prevent evil before it is manifested" and "the timeliness of instruction, just when it is required," revealed the great significance of education.

I listened to Han Yu, who said, "Progress in studies comes from diligence and is failed by indolence; success comes from forethought, while thoughtlessness leads to failure." He also said, "Where there is the doctrine, there is my teacher, so pupils are not necessarily inferior to their teachers." His essay "On Teaching" has become the motto of countless teachers.

I listened to Zhu Xi. His *Bailudong Academy Rules* were the regulations for the management of schools in ancient times. *Zhu Zi's Learning Methods* are still popular today. The famous Goose Lake Monastery Debate is still remembered by intellectuals.

I listen to the masters, review the creation and change of the imperial college system, and lament on the features and contributions of the academies. I hope that time-honored educational thinking can keep developing and become timeless.

Preface

It is known to all that China's ancient culture shone with great splendor and that this is closely related to its cultural inheritance of education. The Chinese nation has long cherished the tradition of education, and its educational thoughts are characterized by the long history and valuable influence of China's ancient education through successive generations.

This book describes the origin and development of ancient China's educational thoughts, clarifies the main attributes and theoretical basis of these thoughts, and introduces ancient China's conception of moral education, teaching theories, guidance for teachers, reading methods, the imperial examination system, academies of classic learning, elementary education, and so on by subject. In this way, the book presents the evolution of ancient China's educational thoughts and their profound influence on later generations from different perspectives, striving to objectively exhibit a full view of the history of ancient China's educational thoughts.

Unlike ordinary writings on the history of ancient China's educational thoughts, this book adopts a thematic, rather than a chronological, approach to introduce the educational thoughts of different ancient Chinese educators. It attaches importance to the basic attributes of ancient Chinese educational thoughts, discusses the similarities and differences between ancient Chinese and Western educational thoughts, and provides a deep analysis of some important educational issues.

This book has been translated into Korean and Japanese successively. Korean and Japanese cultures have a deep relationship with Chinese cultural traditions, since they are Asian countries and their educational thoughts are similar. This book is now translated into English to present it to Western readers. This book aims to point out misperceptions that readers from English-speaking countries may have had regarding ancient China's educational thoughts so that they can be corrected and the exchanges of Chinese and Western educational thoughts can be further enhanced.

As I pointed out in this book, Chinese educational thoughts cherish common customs, morality, harmony, and the collective, whereas Western educational thoughts attach importance to divinity, material gain, competition, and individuality. At present, given the increasingly frequent exchanges and conflicts among different groups and nations, I believe that only the promotion of communication can lead to the integration of ideological thoughts, and only the power of education can create a harmonious world.

Zhu Yongxin
October 28, 2014, Beijing

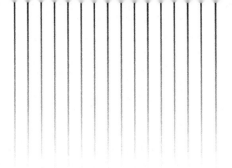

Introduction

Why Do We Need a History of Educational Thought?

In the study and review of the historical course of education, people are always most concerned with the significant events in the history of education, the development of decisive or groundbreaking educational systems, and the educational laws and policies that have influenced the developmental process of education. However, they do not take the thoughts of some of history's great educators as seriously. In fact, in the long history of human civilization, both the occurrence of educational events and the formation of educational systems have been affected to varying degrees by the thoughts of educators. To some extent, it can be said that the educators of any time elaborate on topics already discussed by past educators and have dialogues of the soul with great educators of the past.

Therefore, an in-depth analysis of and intensive research on the educational thoughts of past great educators are of great significance and play an important role in our understanding of the educational development process and our grasp of the developmental laws of education. It is safe to say that in the history of world civilization, the thoughts of these great educators have developed colorful and diverse forms of ideological content and are rare treasures for the further promotion of the development of education. Further research and analysis of these educational thoughts, and sublation on this basis, will facilitate current educational work.

1

The Nature and Characteristics of the History of Educational Thoughts

1. The Nature of the History of Educational Thoughts

The history of educational thoughts, as a discipline that systematically and comprehensively studies the educational ideas, theories, and thoughts of the great domestic and foreign educators of both ancient and modern times, is drawing more and more attention. However, depending on the specific area of theoretical study, different scholars have different views on the subjects of the history of educational thoughts, and they propose a number of different interpretations and explanations of "educational thoughts." Some representative viewpoints are as follows.

Educational thoughts are the "rational understanding of educational phenomena," which mainly include educational proposals and educational theories. They are roughly divided into two groups: the first group is more sporadic and consists of less ideological education systems, such as people's preliminary views, ideas, proposals, requirements, and recommendations about education or certain aspects of education; the second group is more systematic and consists of rigorous educational thoughts, such as people's educational theories and educational doctrines proposed through in-depth exploration, repeated testing, and improvements made on the basis of the summarization of predecessors' experience.[1]

Zhang Binxian and Chu Hongqi stated in *A History of Western Educational Thoughts*:

> Whatever the form of the specific result of an educational thought (that is, views, opinions, doctrines, or theories), in essence, educational thoughts are the rational understanding of educational phenomena. In other words, although educational thoughts are the results of our understanding of the world of education, such understanding is neither emotional and intuitive, nor vague and uncertain, nor arbitrary and improvised. In this sense, educational thoughts are different from discussions of, feelings for, and the experience of educational phenomena and educational issues. As a product of human rationality, educational thoughts are our grasp of educational phenomena by the use of certain concepts and scopes. They are the results of contemplative activities and are established in some forms or expressed in some ways.[2]

Some scholars define educational thoughts as "people's understanding and generalization of a variety of educational phenomena and objective laws, which include some educational theories, as well as experience and points of view from educational practices." It has also been pointed out that educational thoughts are "designed to answer how educational work should conduct arguments on and answer questions about educational methods for the various issues raised." Educational theories explore educational issues as objective matters, and address 'what education is,' whereas educational thoughts answer 'how to educate.'"[3]

It is safe to say that these above-mentioned understandings of educational thoughts are reasonable and correct, but different scholars' different perspectives, depths of understanding, and expressions result in differences in the understanding of educational thoughts.

Literally, thoughts refer not only to thinking and ideas, but also to the system of certain views, concepts, and ideas held by a particular class or political party. Mao Zedong said, "The accumulations of perceptions will develop into rational knowledge, which is thought."[4] In his view, thoughts are humans' rational knowledge.

Based on the original meaning of thoughts and other scholars' understandings of educational thoughts, we believe that educational thoughts are the awareness and perception of educational phenomena and educational issues formed on the basis of educational practices under the social conditions of a certain historical era. Thus, the history of educational thoughts is a discipline that studies the generation, changes, and laws of development of educational thoughts. Obviously, as with any ideology, educational thought is also a process of historical development, and this process also has a certain regularity. After continuous reflection, supplementation, research, and analysis by educational thinkers and researchers, a content-rich educational system was gradually formed, thus establishing the history of educational thoughts as a discipline.

The history of domestic and foreign educational thoughts is the historical process of studying the generation, formation, development, and evolution of domestic and foreign educational thoughts in ancient and modern times, and is based on research and summarization of past educational thinkers' thoughts. Thus, education is defined by its historical nature and historical characteristics.

First, the formation and development of educational thoughts is subject to the impact and constraints of historical conditions. The education of each age is closely linked to the society of the age and is subject to the impacts and constraints of the political, economic, and cultural conditions of the age. Educational thought is people's awareness and perception of educational phenomena and issues under certain social conditions, which determines the close link between educational thoughts and the social and historical conditions of each era. Hence, the content of an educational thought is determined by the social and historical conditions of the time, and it varies based on different social and historical contexts.

From a vertical perspective, all countries have experienced different historical courses, resulting in different schools of educational thought. The historical development of Western educational thought can be roughly divided into the following stages: ancient Greek and Roman times, the Renaissance of the late Middle Ages, and the development of modern society from the seventeenth century onward. During this process, several types of educational thoughts were formed and developed, such as orators' education, scholastic education, religious educational reform, Pan-Intellectualism, the education of gentlemen, liberal education, the "new education," progressive education, and eternal education. Among these, dozens of educational theories and schools developed into educational systems, while the formation of these educational theories and schools was closely related to prevailing social and historical conditions and therefore subject to the impacts and constraints of the various conditions of the age in which they were formed. For instance, the thoughts of progressive education and "new education" were closely related to the social and economic changes in Europe and the United States in the early nineteenth and twentieth centuries, respectively. During these times, Europe and the United States were experiencing chaotic economies, political instability, and class antagonism, among other problems. This led to a focus on two basic tasks for European and American education. One was to develop somewhat educated and well-trained workers with some initiative and creativity, individuals who could "not only create profits for the bourgeoisie, but would not disturb the tranquility of the bourgeoisie."[5] The other was to cultivate leaders and ruling elites that were loyal to the interests of their class, with a wide range of knowledge and a pioneering spirit. In order to meet the needs of society at the time, the thoughts of progressive education and "new education" criticized traditional educational theory and methods, and advocated a new form, content, and methods of education, which came into being during this period and became part of the wide-ranging social reform movement in both Europe and the United States.

From the perspective of the development of Chinese educational thoughts, China experienced three historical stages: ancient, modern, and contemporary times. In each period there emerged many educational theories and schools, as well as trends, such as Confucian education, Taoist education, Mohist education, science education, Westernized education, reform education, civilian education, and life education. Similarly, the formation of these educational theories and thoughts was also subject to the different levels of development and social background of different periods in China's history. For example, in the late Spring and Autumn and early Warring States Periods in ancient China, the thoughts of Confucian education and Mohist education reflected the social needs of the early transitional period from slavery to the feudal system, and reflected the progressive trend that impacted "the Official School" and led to the development of private school education.

From a horizontal perspective, educational thoughts during one specific historical period also show a plural characteristic. Usually there is one dominant school of educational thought, supplemented by various nonmainstream schools. In most cases, the dominant school of educational thought is suited to the social and historical development of the time and meets the needs of the political and economic development of the time. Otherwise, it could never be recognized and accepted by the society, let alone play a leading role. For example, during the Renaissance period in the West, center stage was given to the people, rather than God, as had been the case during the medieval period. The greatness of being human and the concept of "free will" were stressed. Emphasis was given to the earthly life and comforts of man. Humanistic education and scientific knowledge were promoted. Friedrich Engels had this to say about this historical event: "It was the greatest progressive revolution that mankind has so far experienced, a time which called for giants and produced giants: giants in power of thought, passion, and character, in universality and learning."[6] Therefore, to meet the needs of social development, criticisms were made of scholasticism and emphasis was placed on the all-round development of humankind. People advocated for expanding the school curriculum and subject scope and using new educational ideals and approaches, which led to the emergence and prosperity of humanistic educational thought.

Humanistic educational thought played a dominant and leading role during the Renaissance and contributed significantly to the transformation of educational thinking and an improvement in educational quality. Subsequently, the scholasticism featuring the dominant theology of medieval times faded. During the Renaissance, there were other emerging schools of educational thought, including utopian socialist educational thought, early-stage scientific educational thought, and the educational thought manifested in the religious reform led by Martin Luther. But their influence was smaller than that of humanistic educational thought.

Another example can be found in ancient Chinese society, where Confucianism played a dominant role among all schools of educational thought. This was because Confucian educational thought was compatible with the needs of the feudal political and economic organizations of the time. Further, the basic spirits and principles of Confucianism emphasized linking culture and education to politics and economics, and Confucian educational thought advocated the practice of "reciting instead of creating; believing and worshiping the ancient sages." These views were helpful for gathering and cementing the wisdom of the ancient Chinese sages, culture, and traditions. Confucian educational thought was deeply rooted in the national conditions of China with the purpose of disseminating national culture to all social classes. Confucian educational thought also developed according to changes in social conditions and corrected itself during its historical course. The reason Confucian educational thought maintained its dominant position among all schools was because it is compatible with the needs of social and educational development in China. At that time, the Legalist, Taoist, and Mohist schools of educational thought were incompatible with the needs of social and historical development in China and were therefore unable to gain the attention and support of the ruling class.

Second, the historical aspect of the birth and development of any educational thought is reflected in its historical inheritance. Friedrich Engels said, "The philosophy of every epoch, since it is a definite sphere in the division of labour, has as its presupposition certain definite intellectual material handed down to it by its predecessors, from which it takes its start."[7] He also said, "The ideologist dealing with history then possesses in every sphere of science material which has formed itself independently out of the thought of previous generations and has gone through an independent series of developments in the brains of these successive generations."[8] During the developmental course of the study of the phenomenon and nature of education, there exist the same phenomena. The educational thought of every epoch is the fruit of rational thinking about the educational experiments and experiences of the epoch and new insight into its regularities, all of which have been handed down to future generations as historical and ideological materials. When future educators are studying the educational phenomena and nature of their own epoch, they need to draw lessons from the materials that have been passed down to them by their predecessors and inherit and reform them according to their own social conditions and characteristics. Therefore, connections are created between old and new educational thoughts to shape a relationship of inheritance.

The reason inherent connections are created between the educational thoughts of different times and societies is that, under different social conditions and in different times, although education has its own characteristics and patterns, their essential characteristics, which determine the basic nature of all human activities and human relationships, are already shaped, cemented, and formalized on the day of the birth of education.[9] Regardless of the time, the basic components of education always include educators and students, as well as the purpose of education, content of education, and methods of education. This has ensured that education has had some steadily maintained characteristics during its development, which means that education is based on such elements for its existence and expansion into different societies. This is why successors can learn from the fruits of their predecessors and make them into their own tools and materials. This is how human societies have inherited, updated, and developed toward the ultimate truth.

2. The Nature of Educational Thoughts

In the previous section, we analyzed the nature of educational thought. From the analysis and observations of the development of Chinese and foreign educational thoughts, we can clearly see that educational thought has the following characteristics.

1) Practicality

During the developmental course of both Chinese and foreign educational thoughts, many educators have shaped their own schools of educational thoughts on the foundation of their practical experiments and activities. These individuals are not only great educational philosophers and theorists but also great practitioners, including the ancient Chinese sage Confucius. He started his private teaching career at the age of 30 and spent most of his lifetime and energy teaching his apprentices and collecting and sorting ancient archives and documents. He taught more than 3,000 apprentices, among whom were 72 brilliant minds who had special skills or talents. Based on his extensive practices, Confucius brought forward many unique propositions and ideas, including knowledge regarding the function, purpose, content, morals, principles, and approaches of education.

Confucius made a great contribution to educational development, which has had profound implications for the educational histories of both China and the world. Taking the ancient Roman educational philosopher Quintilianus as another example, Quintilianus began his teaching career in AD 58. Later on, he created the Institutio Oratoria in the Latin and Greek languages with funding provided by the state. He taught there until he retired in AD 90. His teaching career lasted for more than 20 years. His book *De Institutione Oratoria* was based on his practical teaching experiences. In it he summarized his working experiences in the educational field and provided his own insights into and opinions on the purpose and function of education, oratory education, teaching philosophy, and teachers, which facilitated the development of education in the Roman Empire. We can cite numerous examples from both Chinese and foreign educational histories.

Educational practices are the source of and foundation for the creation of educational thought. Without practical work, educational thought can be thought of as a river with no water or a tree with no roots. Educational thought is based on educational activities. Educational thought also affects and regulates educational activities to some degree, sometimes positively and sometimes negatively.

2) Nationality

Every nation has its own living space, its own sphere of history and culture, its own social, economic, and political systems, and its own educational traditions and characteristics with their own national features. The educational thoughts of great educators are also shaped by the factors mentioned above and have the hallmarks of national identity. For example, Confucian educational thought advocates the ideas of respecting teachers, moral education, teaching according to students' aptitudes, and combining learning and thinking. All of these ideas have become fine traditions in Chinese educational history. Compared with other nations in the world, China's educational ideas have their own national characteristics. Let us take the scholastic educational thought of Western Europe for another example.

In the Middle Ages, the church controlled the entire society and had a penetrating influence on education. Under such circumstances, scholastic educational thought, with its characteristic strong religious features, was born. In terms of educational purpose, scholastic educational thought advocated using education to serve the church and theology and to foster devout Christians and priests; in terms of educational content, the main materials were the Bible and other works of theology; in terms of moral education, the focus was again on theology. We can say that the theology-centered scholastic educational thought comprehensively and decisively affected education in medieval times and played a significant role in the history of Western educational thought. During the hundreds of years of development afterward, theological education penetrated Western educational activities and thoughts to varying degrees, distinguishing them from Chinese educational thought.

3) Class Nature

Thought as a form of ideology has associations with class. In terms of the relationships among the political system, economic structure, and educational system, the type of education is decided by the dominant political and economic institutions of a society. Therefore, educational thought is subject to the constraints of the thought and economic foundation of the ruling class. Only when education meets the goals of political and economic development in certain societies, and satisfies the interests of the ruling class, can it be accepted and recognized. This means that educational thoughts must be in line with the interests of the ruling class. Educational thoughts that are against the interests of the ruling class are supplanted, struck down, and do not have the opportunity of becoming mainstream thoughts.

Class is also an important feature of educational thought. For example, in the Han Dynasty, the great educator Dong Zhongshu advocated the Three-Quality Theory and promoted the three cultural policies of worshiping only Confucianism, opening schools, and focusing on official selection through examinations. He also had his own opinions on teaching and moral cultivation. Undeniably, his thought and political proposals were very important for the educational development at the time. However, we should also understand that all such proposals were to serve the ruling class of the feudal society. He made Confucianism a theology and a tool to rule the people mentally to safeguard the feudal order.

As another example, the modern educator Xu Teli came up with many theories on the function and policy of education, teaching, and teachers. As a proletarian revolutionary and educator, his thoughts were based on Marxism, Leninism, and Mao Zedong Thought. They were based on the interests of the masses to promote social and educational development in China.

4) Patterns

According to dialectical materialism, the creation and development of all things, including educational thoughts, have certain patterns. First, in terms of the scope of educational thought, these patterns cover the function, position, policy, purpose, content, and methods of education, as well as teachers, students, and educational management. It was on these foundations that Chinese and foreign educators have shaped their own schools of educational thought through research and exploration.

The developmental course of educational thought has undergone the stages of partial to comprehensive development, from inferior to in-depth, and from simple to sophisticated. Only by looking at such patterns can we understand the educational thought of a particular educator in a systematic, comprehensive, and objective way.

Why Do Teachers Need to Study Educational Thoughts?

One Western scholar has said, "History can make a young man into an old man without wrinkles or white hair, give him the experiences possessed by an older man without causing disease or inconvenience to him, and enable him to make reasonable predictions of the future." This indicates the importance of learning and understanding history to the development of humankind. As a teacher who undertakes teaching as a profession, you must understand education, especially the educational experiences of others. And one good way of achieving this is to study the history of educational thought. Ancient sages have said, "History makes a wise man." Teachers must study the history of educational thought to understand the present and future of educational development and assimilate the educational thoughts of great educational minds in history. Only by doing so can they learn the essence of education from others and use it as their own, avoid making mistakes through blind explorations, and improve their teaching capabilities and quality. The significance of learning the history of educational thought can be illustrated in the following ways.

1. Learning the History of Educational Thoughts Can Help Teachers Expand Their Knowledge Base

The impact a teacher has on his students should not be limited to one specific subject. The teacher must have a broader view of knowledge. The history of educational thought can help teachers understand many of the works of great educators, including knowledge of the educational conditions of different countries and different historical periods, as well as the unique political, economic, and cultural features associated with them. We can learn a great deal about philosophy, politics, and religion when learning about the methods of great educators. For example, in the Song Dynasty, Neo-Confucianism theorist Zhu Xi not only discussed general education, but also shared his views on how to read in his work *Master Zhu's Way of Reading*. He suggested that one should read step by step, examine the text carefully, read it and contemplate it, learn from it, make more effort, and keep reading it. As for teachers, when studying the educational thought of Zhu Xi, it is beneficial to study his reading methods.

For another example, when studying the educational thoughts of Augustine and Aquila, one can understand the conditions of society at the time, dominated by theology in the medieval period, and some of the religious and philosophical issues of the time, from the transitions from patristic philosophy to scholasticism and from nominalism to Realism. Teachers can learn much when studying the thoughts of ancient educators in a systematic way.

2. Learning the History of Educational Thoughts Can Improve Teachers' Theoretical Knowledge

All teachers accumulate their own experiences during teaching. But personal experiences are far from enough. One must be in touch with one's emotional experiences, which means one must learn from the experiences and theories of others. The subject of the history of educational thought can help teachers to achieve knowledge because this subject is based on the personal experiences of many great educators and summarizes all the practical work of these great educators. Further, the experiences of these educators have become theories. Studying the history of educational thought is a great help for improving the theoretical knowledge of teachers.

3. Learning the History of Educational Thoughts Can Improve Teachers' Practical Teaching Skills

In the subject of the history of educational thought, we come to understand the theories of great educators. For example, we can learn educational principles and approaches from the practical experiences of our predecessors, including the concepts of teaching students according to their needs, combining learning with thinking, inspiring new thinking, taking gradual steps, and putting theories into practice. We can also learn many moral educational principles and approaches, such as upholding your moral principles in practice, reflecting upon yourself, and correcting your errors. All these experiences may be learned, understood, and accepted by teachers. Teachers can apply such principles to their own teaching practices to improve their results. Thus, by studying the theoretical experiences of predecessors, teachers can avoid making the same mistakes. They can use the experiences of their predecessors to significantly improve their teaching abilities. Some teachers have said they "should have read" of certain theories after seeing the fruits of studying them. And they are right.

4. Learning the History of Educational Thoughts Can Help Teachers Understand the Patterns of Teaching and Education

As mentioned above, we know that educational thought has its own unique patterns. In fact, such patterns are the topics of many educators when discussing and studying the basic elements and nature of education. Only by mastering the patterns of education can a teacher achieve a successful teaching career. By learning the history of educational thought and understanding the explorations of our predecessors in terms of the patterns of education, we can learn from their findings, apply their theories by combining them with our own experiences, and further study the patterns of education to ensure success.

5. Learning the History of Educational Thoughts Can Enhance Teachers' Sense of Responsibility

During the development of education throughout history, there have been many great educators who have provided not only unique theoretical perspectives but also valuable material for thought on the development of education. These great educational thinkers were also admirable teachers. They worked diligently and selflessly. They devoted their entire lives to the cause of education. When teaching, great educators were better than their contemporaries in many areas and set a good example for all the teachers.

The modern Chinese educator Yang Xianjiang is a good example. He started his teaching career in 1917 after graduating from a normal university. He upheld his communist beliefs and made great contributions to the proletarian educational cause. After the National Revolution failed in 1927, he fled the country. But he did not give up on his educational career and wrote a book entitled *A Brief History of Education*. Later on, he was monitored and persecuted by the Japanese police. So he returned to Shanghai, where he continued to write and translate educational books and finished the book *Guidelines of New Education*. He died from disease in Tokyo on August 9, 1931, at the age of 36.

For another example, the famous Soviet humanist educator Vasyl Olex-androvych Sukhomlynsky spent his career as an elementary school teacher in a rural area from the age of 17 until his death. During his entire teaching career, he devoted all his love to his students. To realize his educational dream, he became headmaster of Bovleksh Middle School. Meanwhile, he passed on his teaching experiences to his peers. He also wrote more than 40 books on education, including *One Hundred Suggestions to Teachers* and *Bovleksh Middle School*. All his books have had a profound impact on the development of education throughout the world and have encouraged the development of the educational philosophies of other educators. All of these great and noble educators with strong morality and character have selflessly contributed to the development of education. They are the role models for all teachers. Learning the history of educational thought can help teachers improve their sense of responsibility and mission and improve their own qualities and ethics. The stories of these great educators can be lessons for teachers to learn from. History's great educators can inspire teachers to seek truth and achieve greatness.

6. Learning the History of Educational Thoughts Can Help Teachers Achieve Educational Innovation and Shape Their Personal Teaching Philosophy and Style

We have mentioned that the birth and development of educational thought has the feature of inheritance. Any school of educational thought is not born out of nothing. Instead, it is built on the research of predecessors. In the twenty-first century, the content, method, form, and administration of education must meet the needs of the times and social development. Many traditional educational philosophies can no longer meet such demands. Therefore, fresh educational thinking and ideas are urgently needed. And today's teachers undoubtedly have an important role to play in this process. Teachers must have their own voices to reflect on educational thinking. They must understand and study the works of others on educational philosophies and determine their advantages and weaknesses in order to shape their own ideas and theories according to actual conditions. The works of many brilliant teachers have proven the importance of this point.

How Should Teachers Learn the History of Educational Thoughts?

It is said that "sharp tools make good work." Learning the history of educational thoughts and mastering scientific learning methods are similarly necessary to produce good teaching. In this regard, the following issues merit our attention.

1. Upholding the Principle of Realism and Dialectics

The dialectical materialism and historical materialism of Karl Marx provide the master guidebook for studying the history of educational thought. We should uphold a dialectical and realistic approach when dealing with the thoughts of any educator. We need to analyze the specifics of every issue and learn from both their positive and negative features. We should not be single-minded. Rather, we should take a comprehensive approach. Not every great educational philosopher is right or wrong on everything. He may be right or wrong during one specific historical period or under certain conditions. With changes in time and social conditions, his theories might come to have an opposite meaning. For example, Confucian educational thought has played an important role in China. And many of these views are still accepted and applied by educators today. However, we can also see the shortcomings of his theories. In terms of the purpose of education, Confucius advocated that "talents should be selected to serve as imperial officials" and "to never give up on old traditions."

We can also now see incorrect ideas in the philosophies of Augustine in medieval times. In Western Europe, many inaccurate theories prevailed, including obscurantism, asceticism, corporal punishment, and disdain for Greek and Roman academics, which were to some extent influenced by Augustine. However, we cannot say that the educational philosophies of Augustine are totally valueless. He advocated that secular knowledge can be used by the Christian faith and advocated that the Church in the medieval period should preserve ancient classics. And his views on the educational activities of convent schools were also positive and progressive. When assessing the educational philosophy of one educator, we must uphold the realistic and dialectical approach. We cannot approve or disapprove of all of his ideas.

Educational thought is the product of long-time human activities and the fruit of human wisdom. It has continuity and respects no borders. Therefore, when developing educational thought in China, we need to pay attention to the educational philosophies of Western educators and apply their theories according to our own national conditions. In terms of modern and contemporary educational ideas, we need to assess them scientifically and modify them to suit our own national conditions of education. We should absorb the positive attributes of their theories and make them part of our own educational thought system. Of course, the history of educational thought to some extent reflects the will of the ruling class. Therefore, when studying Western educational philosophies, we need to understand the capitalist class nature of such theories and uphold our own principles in criticizing them. In another aspect, the development of educational thought has historical connections and patterns. Therefore, there is also continuity and connections among different theories. When studying the history of educational thought, we must connect the theories of different educators from different times and countries, make careful comparisons and analogies, and find the differences and similarities to help us understand the patterns of the educational thought and better understand various schools of educational thought.

2. Upholding the Principle of Putting Theory into Practice

Putting theory into practice is the basic method for learning any subject. To master the history of educational thought, one should read books carefully, use the basic theories and knowledge of the subject, and master the educational theories of great educators. However, when studying theories, teachers must put all valuable educational thought into practice according to the needs and conditions of their teaching and study the history of educational thought with regard to questions they have raised during their practice. During the learning process, they should use all educational theories and philosophies to examine the problems they face in practice. By using the method of putting theory into practice, teachers can understand and master educational philosophies and use the theories of predecessors to solve the problems they have faced in the practice of teaching. This is one of the main purposes for learning the history of educational thought.

3. Adopting the Method of Combining Learning with Thinking

Confucius said, "Learning without thought is labor lost; thought without learning is perilous." When learning, one must think as well. When learning the history of educational thought, on one hand, you have to read and understand the history of educational thought and master the educational experiences and findings of one's predecessors; on the other hand, one must ensure that teachers take the initiative to think independently and use their creative thinking as the tool for analyzing and solving problems. This is an important task for learning the history of educational thought. At present, China is facing a transitional period in educational reform. We need to reform our education to meet the needs of our times, in terms of the value, purpose, content, methods, and tools of education. Therefore, teachers must combine learning with thinking, not get stuck in existing ideas and theories, and take the lead to explore new territories of educational thought.

4. Advocating Reading the Original Works of Great Educators

In many of the textbooks on educational thought, the authors introduce the philosophies of individual educators in separate chapters to organize the theories of both ancient and modern and both Chinese and foreign educators. By studying these theories in this way, teachers can systematically master the philosophies of great educators. However, this also presents the problem that teachers' thinking might be influenced and even dictated by the existing theories and philosophies of the researchers, which is not helpful for teachers in making new explorations into the original thinking of great minds. Therefore, teachers must read some original works by great educators when studying the history of educational thought and studying from textbooks. This is helpful for better understanding the philosophies of great educators and inspiring new thinking among teachers to shape new opinions and theories.

The history of educational thought is a systematic subject. It discusses not only the views of educators on education but also the social context and theoretical foundations that affected the thinking of these educators, including philosophy, religion, psychology, and physiology. Therefore, if teachers have a large pool of knowledge in these areas, it will be helpful for them in understanding the educational philosophies of great educators.

The teachers need to develop their own methods, habits, and conditions for learning while following the above-mentioned suggestions in studying the history of educational thought. It was said in ancient times that "there is no universal method for learning." I believe that teachers must pay attention to learning and do their job diligently. Only in this way can they master this subject. And mastering the history of educational thought will greatly improve their job performance.

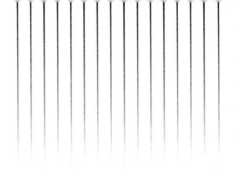

1

The Origin and Development of China's Ancient Educational Thought

More than a million years ago, China was already populated by primitive people. Correspondingly, primitive education began to take shape. In the process of conquering nature, our ancestors passed on their experience to subsequent generations, and thus we see primal education taking shape. Whether our ancestors were thinking about their educational behavior consciously or unconsciously, primitive educational thought was emerging. Although we cannot speak with our ancestors or speculate on their educational thinking, we can glimpse ancient education by means of archeological studies. The advent of written language and school has enabled us to grasp the origins of ancient educational thought.

The Origins of Ancient Educational Thought

Ancient educational thought in China can be dated back to the Yin and Zhou Dynasties, when examples of the earliest written language appeared. By this time, the educational system and the teaching of the Six Arts[1] had almost reached maturity, laying the groundwork for the birth of new educational thought. Since political thought was intrinsically linked with education, and there was no differentiation between officials and teachers before the Western Zhou Dynasty, ancient educational thought was always blended with political, military, and philosophical thought, rather than being an independent theoretical form.

The earliest educational thought can be examined through selected materials from books like the *Book of Documents* (the *Shangshu*, one of the Five Classics of ancient Chinese literature), the *Book of Changes*, the *Book of Poetry*, and *The Rites of Zhou*, among others. But the one which is most thorough and representative is the discourses of Duke Zhou.

Duke Zhou, with surname Ji, given name Dan, and a further name Shudan, was the fourth son of King Wen and the brother of King Wu of the Zhou Dynasty. He helped King Wu to destroy King Zhou of the Shang Dynasty and was honored as a founding hero. After the death of King Wu, he helped King Cheng to rule the country and made great contributions to the establishment and consolidation of the Zhou Dynasty. His deeds were written in history as "continuing the cause of King Wen, performing the duty of a king, and administering affairs of the state."[2] Although Duke Zhou did not write any works on educational issues, his thoughts on education still hold a special status in the history of educational thought in China because of the status of the Western Zhou Dynasty and the contributions he made to the dynasty.

1. Stressing the Political Function of Education

Duke Zhou emphasized the political function of education, considering education an important tool for ruling and reassuring people, as well as for changing manners and customs. He held that only when people were educated would they not cheat each other or break the law. "The ancients would persuade, protect, and educate each other so that there was no cheating or fraud."[3] If people were not educated as Duke Zhou described, it was felt that resistance and resentment would sprout in people's hearts and curses issue from people's mouths, thus endangering the social order.

To educate the people and make them abide by societal norms, Duke Zhou proposed the idea of "Yi Education." He said, "Now that we are unable to make contact with the outside, we shall carry out the Yi Education and teach our people the virtues of King Wen."[4] "Yi" means norms or principles. "Yi Education" thus means educating people to behave well and abide by desired norms. During his reign, supported by the efforts of Guoshu, Hongyao, Sanyisheng, Taidian, Nangong Kuo, and other excellent ministers, King Wen's virtues were taught to the people, making them well behaved and helping them to live contently. Therefore, after Duke Zhou gained political power, he emphasized the education of survivors from the Yin Dynasty. He once advised Kangshu,

"You are just a young man bearing a heavy burden. Since our king is endowed with the protection of the survivors from the previous dynasty, you have to help the king to realize God's mission and transform the people to live a new life."⁵ He asked Kangshu to honor his destiny and help King Cheng to educate the survivors from the previous dynasty to become "new people." Punishment and education were the two tools the ruling class used to maintain social order. But Duke Zhou advocated that "morality should be promoted and punishment carried out cautiously." He advised that moral education should come before punishment, focusing on the political function and the psychological effect of education. He said:

> The judicial officers ruled the people with fair punishment and taught them morality through education. With the king's virtues shining on all corners, all people are honoring their moral cultivation. In this way, the country can maintain the justness of punishment and promote desired norms when governing the people.⁶

These words mean that when a judicial officer taught people to abide by the law and honor moral integrity, there would be no punishment for crimes. If the king ruled with virtue and the ministers judged fairly, making the politics just and the glory of morality shine on all corners, all people would make their living according to the principles of moral education. Therefore, punishments would be handed out pursuant to the law, and people would comply with governance and take delight in obeying the law. In contrast, if education were neglected and punishment abused, with slaughter happening at will, people's resentment would be provoked.

Duke Zhou's emphasis on the political function of education greatly influenced the later ages, forming a basic character of China's ancient education. In later generations, the Confucian idea of "governing the country by virtue," the idea of "establishing education before government and carrying out governance," and "education as the only way to develop good virtue," as described in *The Records on the Subject of Learning*, Dong Zhongshu's concept of "education as the basis of governance," and Wang Anshi's view of "political education as a must" were all ideas built on Duke Zhou's thoughts.

2. Stressing the Modeling Significance of the King

In *Shangshu: Announcement of the Duke of Shao*, advice is given for the young King Cheng from Duke Zhou, which meant that King Cheng was expected to have the virtues of the saints and set examples for his people to follow and abide by the law. Duke Zhou held that the virtues, ambitions, and behaviors of the king had significant physical and psychological influence on the people he ruled. If the king possessed saint like virtues, his people would comply with the law self-consciously, thus spreading good virtue. Conversely, if the king was immoral and committed bad deeds and abuses, his people would feel resentful and would be likely to offend against the law.

Shangshu: Against Luxurious Ease was also advice for King Cheng from Duke Zhou. It discussed the social education influence of the king's behavior on his people, demonstrating the relationship between people's crimes and the king's immorality. For example, this text holds that the king should not focus on seeking pleasure but know the efforts of agricultural harvesting and the hardships of his people. It praises King Zhongzong of the Yin Dynasty because "he could treat the endowed throne seriously and discreetly, rule the people with honesty, and distance himself from luxurious ease in order not to neglect governance," all of which were reasons why he ruled the country successfully for 75 years. And so did King Wen, who achieved the goal of reassuring his people and reclaiming lands in good order. Kind, merciful, modest, and respectful, he reassured the people and cared for orphans and widows. Working from morning until sunset, he devoted himself to social harmony and did not even take the time to eat meals. Because of his kindness, modesty, respect, and good deeds, which set examples for the people, the people could live and work in peace and contentment and render the king's grace to orphans, widows, and other people in need. According to the above stories, Duke Zhou continuously advised King Cheng to follow the model of King Wen and other wise kings, and encouraged him to comply with rules respectfully and contemplate his faults. Duke Zhou advised King Cheng to use the power of his throne seriously and work with the people prudently, in good faith, and with honesty. King Cheng was advised to guard against luxurious ease and weak governance.

Because they started from the educational function of the king's deeds, Duke Zhou and other influential thinkers focused on the exemplifying significance of the ruler and requested the ruler to influence the people with his own virtue. This thinking is reflected in the *Book of Poetry* and the *Book of Changes*. For example, the *Book of Poetry* says that "once you follow the steps of King Wen, all the country will trust you,"[7] and "the king's virtue wins the trust of his people and the people follow his moral deeds."[8] The *Book of Changes: Lin Gua* says, "The subject is advancing. Through his firm correctness there will be good fortune." This means that when the king is ruling the country, his mind should be with the people. Continuing to do this will bring good fortune to the country. Gao Heng made a note on the above saying, "Inspired by reading the remark of the advancing intuition in the *Book of Changes*, the king's ambition and deeds should be upright in order to influence his people." The concepts of stressing the king's exemplifying significance and advocating the influence of people by the king's upright deeds were later developed by Confucius and Mencius as an important part of Confucian moral education. For example, Confucius said, "If the ruler does righteous deeds, the people will voluntarily follow even without order; otherwise, the people will resist, and even compliance will be forced by order." Wang Anshi said, "Those who teach should be good models." These thoughts can be dated back to Duke Zhou's views.

3. Stressing the Educating Function of Art

Artistic education in ancient China began with the rites of religious activities and the songs and dances of primitive society. Until the Western Zhou Dynasty, artistic education focused primarily on learning the Six Classics and the Six Arts, especially poetry and music.

The teaching of poetry and music has played a significant role in Chinese culture since ancient times. *Shangshu: Canon of Shun* recorded a dialogue between Shun and Kui:

> The Emperor said, Kui! You are appointed to manage the musical education of the young people, making them straight and mild, generous and prudent, righteous but not rude, simple but not arrogant. Poetry can be used to express ideals, and songs are for emotions. Sing in tune and play the musical instruments to the note. The well-proportioned symphony of the eight instruments can help people to communicate with the gods and nature in harmony (这里少一句话的翻译).

In this dialogue, Shun asked Kui to educate the youth with music and develop them into people who are straight and mild, generous and prudent, righteous but not rude, and simple but not arrogant. Duke Zhou also taught poetry and music in person, laying the foundation for China's ancient artistic education. The *Book of Poetry* is a representative work of poetry education and is the earliest collection of poetry in China. It was the classic that Confucians used to educate people. Although it was expanded and revised over a long period of influence, the contribution of its creation and the revisions made by Duke Zhou cannot be neglected. According to research, 31 pieces of work in *Sacrificial Odes of Zhou* in the *Book of Poetry* were written or revised by Duke Zhou. In addition, "Shadbush" in *Minor Odes of the Kingdom*, as well as "Odes of Zhou and the South" and the "Odes of Bin" (a kind of local music) in the *Book of Poetry* may also be works written or revised by Duke Zhou.[9] The educational function of these poems is obvious, as described in "Shadbush" from the *Minor Odes of the Kingdom*:

> The flower of Shadbush with its torus is dazzlingly beautiful. In the world now, brothers treat each other better than anyone else. The greatest concern

between brothers is the threat of death. Even when one has died and been buried in the wilderness, his brothers will make every effort to search for him. If one is troubled like the wagtail trapped in the land, his brothers will hurry to help him. In contrast, his so-called good friends cannot offer any help but a deep sigh. Even though brothers may quarrel with each other at home, they can unite together to withstand insult from outside. But even if one has many good friends, his friends cannot offer any favor when he is trouble.

This is a poem advising that brothers should love and care for each other. Duke Zhou also focused on collecting folk poems and songs, which he used as tools to admonish the ruler. Ban Gu, a historian in the Han Dynasty, held that Duke Zhou took the responsibility to collect folk songs, writing, "In early spring, when the people were scattered in the fields to work, the envoys would shake bells to collect songs along the road, which would then be presented to the officials. The officials then chose suitable melodies to match the words of the songs and performed them before the king in order to inform him of the public voice." "July" from the "Odes of Bin" in the *Book of Poetry* was selected by Duke Zhou to be performed at court. This piece reflects on the starvation and exploited status of the people:

In July, the Fire star starts to set in the west, and the weather starts to cool down. In September, women start to make clothes. In November, the north wind starts to blow. In December, the days become chilly. Without either fine clothes or poor clothes to defend against the cold, how can one live through the end of the year?

Duke Zhou presented this poem to King Cheng to inform him of the difficulties of agriculture and the hardships faced by ordinary people,[10] encouraging the king to understand his people and guard against luxurious ease while ruling the country.

Duke Zhou also contributed to the promotion of musical education. Though the *Book of Music* has been long lost, and thus it is not known whether Duke Zhou made any additions to this book, it is believed to have recorded music and dances created by Duke Zhou. "The Ancient Music" in the *Annals of Lv* says, "After King Wu succeeded to the throne, he led several troops to conquer Yin. Before the troops arrived at the capital of Yin, King Zhou of Yin had been failed in Muye by the elite soldiers of King Wu. When returning to his capital, King Wu offered up the captures in the imperial ancestral temple, reported the number of enemies killed, and appointed Duke Zhou to create the music of 'Great Wu.'" "Great Wu" was a large-scale song and dance in the Western Zhou Dynasty that represented the prosperity at the beginning of the

Zhou Dynasty. As a part of musical education, it is a required course when studying the civilization of the Western Zhou Dynasty.

The theory and practice of Duke Zhou's attention to the educational function of the arts greatly influenced later generations. For example, Confucius advocated that "a person's accomplishment starts from the learning of poems, becomes independent from the learning of rites, and finishes by the learning of music."[11] He held that poems could arouse people's moral emotion and music could enable people to accomplish moral cultivation. In the Ming Dynasty, Wang Yangming advocated that poetry and music education could cultivate students' emotions, self-control, and morality, keeping them from the erosion of "evils."[12]

Duke Zhou's analysis of moral education and his emphasis on education for the king by special teachers also had influence on later generations, among which the most directly and significantly affected person may be Confucius. His greatest ideal was to carry out "Duke Zhou's classics" and recover the rites of the Zhou Dynasty. His educational thought was inspired by Duke Zhou to a great extent. Since Confucian educational thought symbolizes China's educational thought directly, it is clear that Duke Zhou's educational thought and its status in the history of China's ancient education thought are undeniably significant.

Two Miracles: Confucius and *The Records on the Subject of Learning*

In the history of both China's and the world's educational thought, there are two magnificent miracles. These are the first true educational thinker in the world, Confucius, and the first true volume of educational literature, *The Records on the Subject of Learning*.

The Educational Thought of Confucius

Confucius (551 to 479 BC), whose personal name was Qiu and whose courtesy name was Zhongni, came from Zouyi in the state of Lu (today's Qufu in Shandong). He lost his father at the age of 3 and his mother at the age of 17. He started to teach at about 30 and from then on devoted his life to education for more than 40 years. Although he had been engaged in politics several times during his lifetime, he never stopped teaching. It is said that he had 3,000 disciples and cultivated 72 brilliant talents.

The greatest contribution Confucius made to education was to establish private schools and advocate the concept of "education for all."[13] This proposition of education for all fully manifested the humanistic and democratic elements of Confucian educational thought, paving the way for cultural devolution and education popularization, which was an epoch-making reform in China's educational history.[14]

Although private teaching had existed before Confucius, its scale and influence cannot be compared to that of Confucius. Confucius' concept of "education for all" broke the limitation of "learning authorized by the government" and created educational opportunities for the lower classes. This not only was beneficial in raising the educational level of the whole society but also promoted the rise of the earliest intellectual class in China.[15]

Confucius not only proposed the idea of "education for all" but also implemented it. He claimed that any person who sent him a loaf of dried pork could be accepted as his disciple.[16] Therefore, disciples could join Confucius regardless of their nationality, class, property, or age. For example, coming from all corners of the country, there were Yan Yuan and Ran Qiu from the state of Lu, Gongye Chang from the state of Qi, Zizhang from the state of Chen, Zigong and Zixia from the state of Wei, Sima Geng from the state of Song, Ziyou from the state of Wu, Gongsun Long from the state of Chu, and Qin Zu from the Rong People in the state of Qin. With regard to class and property status, there were Nangong Jingshu, Sima Niu, and Meng Yizi from noble families; Zigong from a rich business family; Yan Yuan, who lived in a slum with inadequate access to food and water;[17] Zilu, who was a countryman from Bian County;[18] Zhonggong, who was deprived of accommodation;[19] Yuanxian, who "lived in a fully stocked hut with grassy roof, worn wooden door, mulberry shoot–made hinges, two rooms with urn-made windows, and mud-patched wall cracks, which leaked on rainy days, but was enough for him to play musical instrument in;"[20] Zeng Shen, who dressed in rags; Min Ziqian, who dressed in clothes made of reed catkins; and Gongye Chang, who was once in prison. Confucius embraced all kinds of disciples. With regard to age, there were Qin Shang, who was four years younger than Confucius, and also Gongsun Long, who was 53 years younger than him. There were fathers and sons attending the same school, such as Yan Yao and Yan Yuan, as well as Zeng Dian and Zeng Shen. There were also brothers receiving education at the same time, such as the Meng Yizi and Nangong Shi brothers. Although there were also people who felt that "Confucius' students were too varied," accepting all of these students reflected his idea of "education for all" and the practice of his ideal to "love all walks and befriend all humane people."

Confucius' promotion of "education for all" is intrinsically linked to his deep understanding of humanity. He proposed a simple humanistic proposition: "Human nature is similar; it is practice that makes humans move apart." He held that people's natures are similar to each other, and that differentiation at a moral or intellectual level is the result of education. Starting from this theory, he maintained that all people could renew and enhance themselves through education. Therefore, education for all should not be just a possibility but a necessity. This proved true. The disciples mentioned above, who had different family backgrounds and intellectual foundations, all became talents and even famous elites under the education and guidance of Confucius, who believed in "being tireless in teaching."[21]

Starting from the thesis that "human nature is similar; it is practice that makes humans move apart,"[22] Confucius stressed the significant influence of education on people's development, forming China's Confucian tradition of emphasizing education and creating the precedent for "mass education."

Among Confucius' ideals, achieving harmony between learning and behaving was the highest goal. "Promoting learning and cultivation together, Confucius taught his students knowledge from books and knowledge of behavior and effectively formalized China's philosophical style of stressing awareness of life and the world."[23] Reflected in the educational content, this style pays attention to the specific principles of daily life and the realization of a perfect personality. "Shu Er" in *The Analects of Confucius* elaborated on the basic requirements of Confucius for his students:

Aspire to the Way, align with virtue, abide by benevolence, and immerse yourself in the arts.

The "Way," "virtue," and "benevolence" are all key concepts that Confucius used to describe morality and breeding. One should aspire to the Way, align with virtue, abide by benevolence, and then start the learning process step by step, hence recreating oneself among the arts of rites, music, archery, charioteering, literature, and mathematics. "Xue Er" in *The Analects of Confucius* states, "A young man should serve his parents at home and be respectful to elders outside his home. He should be earnest and truthful, loving all, but become intimate with his innate good-heartedness. After doing this, if he has energy to spare, he can study literature and the arts." Thus Confucius based education on the cultivation of specific behavioral habits, which had from the beginning revealed the difference from the ancient Western educational style, which considered recognition of the supreme conceptual world as the educational ideal. Even the so-called Six Classics and Six Arts were designed to further cultivate and foster both, a perfect personality and good behavioral habits. In "Jingjie" from the *Book of Rites*, Confucius says

If they show themselves men who are mild and gentle, sincere and good, they have been taught from the *Book of Poetry*. If they have a wide comprehension of things, and know what is remote and old, they have been taught from *Shangshu*. If they are large-hearted and generous, open and honest, they have been taught from the *Book of Music*. If they are pure and still, refined and subtle, they have been taught from the *Book of Changes*. If they are courteous and modest, grave and respectful, they have been taught from the *Book of Rites*. If they suitably adapt their language to the things of which they speak, they have been taught from the *Spring and Autumn Annals*.

As an outstanding educator, Confucius acquired plenty of valuable educational experience during his lifetime and summarized a set of principles and methods based on educational practice, such as the combination of learning and thinking, the enlightenment of thinking, the exemplification of one's own behavior, and an individualized method of instruction. These are the essential components of Confucius' educational thought, which directly influenced the formation and development of the principles and methods of both ancient and modern China's educational thought.

Compared to Western educators throughout history, it is not difficult to see that Confucius is no less brilliant, whether in educational practice or theoretical establishment.

In the West, the first significant educational thinker was Pythagoras of ancient Greece (580 to 500 BC). Like Confucius, Pythagoras also recruited disciples and gave lectures. He once recruited 300 disciples in Croton and formed a teaching club. Therefore, he was called by Hegel "the first people's teacher" in the West. However, the teaching club he established was primarily a religious and political association. This organization held religious rites every day and held regular gatherings and sacrificial ceremonies in a temple. Pythagoras and his disciples were also the earliest scientists in ancient Greece, achieving brilliant results in mathematics and astronomy. Music, arithmetic, geometry, and astronomy were the four required courses in Pythagoras' teaching club. As opposed to Confucian education, which prioritized morality, Pythagoras emphasized science. Music was not primarily used to edify or cultivate, but to reflect a kind of harmony, which was considered one of the attributes of the cosmos. Pythagoras even equated the distance between the celestial bodies to the ratio of octave, fifth, and fourth, which reflected his endeavor to analyze problems from a scientific perspective, even when there was no scientific basis. Pythagoras was clearly a philosopher and a scientist, and as an educator, he set up a teaching club and was devoted to the recruitment of disciples and teaching. However, he was actually not an education thinker, as he did not systematically elaborate on the internal laws of education. In this regard, he lagged far behind Confucius.

After Pythagoras, Socrates stood out among Western educators. He was born 10 years after and died 80 years after Confucius' death. As with Confucius, he elaborated on the theories of his predecessors without creating original works of his own ideas. His philosophical and educational ideas were scattered throughout dialogues in the works of Plato and the *Memorabilia*, written by Xenophon. Unlike Confucius' method of recruiting disciples and establishing schools, Socrates viewed society as the lectern and argued with people in markets, gyms, squares, workshops, and stores about various philosophical questions. In terms of educational methods, the greatest contribution made by Socrates was his approach of passing on knowledge and morality.

Socrates held that the teacher's task was not creating and transmitting the truth, but to be a "midwife," eliciting new thoughts and helping people to discover the truth in their own hearts. Based on this idea, he often used the question-and-answer method of teaching with his disciples, proposing a question and then leading them to answer. If the answer was wrong, he would not correct them immediately or point out the mistake, but would ask additional questions to clarify the correct answer. This is the famous "Socratic Method."

Socrates once said, "I am not a teacher of knowledge but a midwife who elicits knowledge." Therefore, his method is also called the "elicitation method" or the "midwife method." It does not teach ready-made answers but deepens the students' cognition continuously through the process of exposing their thinking contradictions. In this way, students are taught how to think and the right way to obtain knowledge.

The question-and-answer method that Confucius used to teach his disciples is by no means inferior to Socrates'. Confucius not only clearly proposed an enlightening method of teaching but also applied it to his teaching practice: "If a student is not eager, I will not teach him; if he is not struggling with the truth, I will not reveal it to him. If I lift up one corner and he cannot come back with the other three, I will not do it again." As recorded in the *Analects of Confucius*, the questions he asked his disciples were as many as over a hundred and focused on such topics as benevolence, rites, politics, filial piety, knowledge, and nobility. Following the principle of enlightenment and the method of individualized instruction, Confucius employed various strategies when asking his questions. "Yan Yuan" in the *Analects of Confucius* records a dialogue which is similar to the Socratic Method:

Zi Zhang asked what a *shi* (scholar) should be like, that he may be called "distinguished."
    Confucius said, "What do you mean by 'distinguished'?"
    Zi Zhang replied: "It means to be heard of through the state, and to be heard of through the clan."
    Confucius said, "This is fame, not being distinguished. One who is distinguished has an upright character and loves justice. If you listen carefully to what people say, observe their facial expressions, and are careful to be humble to them, you will be distinguished in your town and distinguished in your clan. As far as 'fame' is concerned, if you put on a show of goodness but do otherwise, and are not the least bit bothered by doing so, you will indeed be 'famous' in your town and 'famous' in your clan."

For his disciple's question, Confucius did not answer directly, but posed another question to let the disciple think for himself. He then affirmed or negated the disciple's idea. Though the record might have omitted some of the process, the above method of Confucius has the same substance as Socrates'.

Socrates also touched upon theories of education, acknowledging morality as knowledge and the accessibility to knowledge and morality through education. But unlike Confucius' intensive and systematic analysis of education's internal laws, most of Socrates' theories fell into the scope of educational philosophy.

Through this brief comparison, it can be seen that the origins of Chinese and Western education have their own characteristics and merits. Ancient Western education focused primarily on science, while ancient Chinese education focused primarily on ethics. Ancient Western education focused on speculation on educational philosophy, while ancient Chinese education focused more on the internal law of education. However, in terms of educational practice and theories, as well as the breadth, depth, and system of educational thought, Confucius surpassed both Pythagoras and Socrates. In terms of influence of educational thought, Confucius as "the teacher for thousands of generations" was more outstanding as an educator who had an unsurpassable influence on later generations. Confucius deserves to be considered the first educational thinker in the world.

Educational Thought in *The Records on the Subject of Learning*

The Records on the Subject of Learning is one article in the *Book of Rites*. The *Book of Rites* is also called the *Book of Rites of Junior Dai*, in which Junior Dai refers to Dai Sheng, the nephew of Dai De of the Western Han Dynasty. Both Dai De and Dai Sheng were pioneers of the Western Han Dynasty's science of rites. Dai De was a learned scholar in the Imperial College during the period of Emperor Xuan of the Western Han Dynasty, who collected 85 works about China's ancient rites to form the *Book of Rites of Senior Dai*, of which 39 survive today. According to research, *The Records on the Subject of Learning* in the *Book of Rites* compiled by Dai Sheng was written by Yue Zhengke of the School of Zisi-Mencius in the late period of the Warring States, who also wrote the *Great Learning*.

The Records on the Subject of Learning is a monograph focusing on the subject of education. Although there are only 1,229 characters in it, it has rich content with detailed and well-organized discussion of topics ranging from the function of education to the assumptions of the education system, from the success-and-failure law of education to the mutually beneficial and valuable relationship between teachers and students. In particular, its research on the success-and-failure law of education concisely portrays the basic law of school education, which can be seen as a general outline of school education. It says:

> The rules aspired to in the Great Scholar were the prevention of evil before it was manifested, the timeliness of instruction at the moment it was required, the ability of lessons to adapt to circumstances, and the good influence of example to parties observing one another. It was from these four things that the teaching was so effectual and flourishing. Prohibition of evil after it has been manifested meets with opposition and is not successful. Instruction given after the time for it is past is carried out with difficulty. The communication of lessons in an undiscriminating manner and without suitability leads to injury and disorder and fails in its object. Learning alone and without friends makes one feel solitary and uncultivated with but little information as to why. Friendships of festivity lead to opposition to one's master. Lack of respect for the teachers' lecturing leads to the neglect of one's learning. These six things all tend to make teaching vain.
>
> When a superior man knows the causes that make instruction successful and those that make it of no effect, he can become a teacher of others.

This passage elaborates on the basic laws of school education in four aspects. First, the preventive function of education: to prevent students' misbehavior before it happens, thus nipping the misbehavior in the bud. If the misbehavior is forbidden after it has happened, the bad habit will have been formed and is hard to correct. Second, the timeliness of education: given the chance, education should be conducted in the moment. If guidance is not given at the best time, the opportunity will be missed and the efforts will be wasted, thus making achievement rare, even with arduous work. Third, the gradual progress of education: educate according to the level of the students' physical and psychological development and their existing knowledge. Without sound order and systematic teaching materials, it will be difficult for education to achieve its desired effect. Fourth, the interactive nature of education: mutual study among students makes the best of each of them, giving play to collective education. If one encloses himself when studying and lacks the help of his teacher and friends, he will not acquire knowledge easily; if he makes friends with inappropriate people, he will be accompanied by students who misbehave and then disobey the instruction of their teachers and elders; if he associates with these students all day long and talks frivolously, he will desert his study. As a teacher, only when he knows the reason for the success and failure of education and masters the internal law of education can he be qualified for his work.

The Records on the Subject of Learning is also significant for expounding on the school system. It can be said that *The Records on the Subject of Learning* first proposed the prototype of the educational system, including the, organizational, scheduling, and examination systems. It states:

> According to the system of ancient teaching, for families, there was the village school; for neighborhoods, there was the xiang (庠); for larger districts, there was the xu (序); and for the capitals, there was the college.
>
> Every year students entered the college, and every second year there was a comparative examination. In the first year it was seen whether the students could punctuate the texts of the classics and distinguish their ambitions; in the third year, they were reverently attentive to their work and determined what companionship was most pleasant to them; in the fifth year, they extended their studies and sought the company of their teachers; in the seventh year, they discussed the subjects of their studies and selected their friends. They were now said to have made some small achievements. In the ninth year, when they knew the different classes of subjects and had gained a general intelligence, were firmly established and would not fall back, they were said to have made grand achievements. After this, the training was sufficient to transform the students and to change (anything undesirable in) manners and customs. Those who lived near at hand submitted with delight, and those who were far off thought (of the teaching) with longing desire. Such was the method of the Great Scholar; as is said in the *Note*, "The little ant continually exercises the art (of amassing)." This could be used as clarification.
>
> At the commencement of teaching in the Great College, (the masters) in their skin caps presented the offerings of vegetables (to the ancient sages) to show their pupils the principle of reverence for them, and made them sing (at the same time) the (first) three pieces of the Minor Odes of the Kingdom, as their first lesson in the duties of officers. When they entered the college, the drum was beaten and their satchels were opened that they might begin their work reverently. The cane and thorns were there to secure in them a proper awe. It was not until the time for the summer sacrifice was divined that students were inspected in order to give enough time to develop their ambitions and to give composure to their minds. They were continually under inspection, but not spoken to in order to keep their minds undisturbed. They listened, but they did not ask questions, and they could not transgress the order of study (imposed on them). These seven things were the chief regulations in the teaching. As it is expressed in the *Note*, "In all learning, for he who would be an officer, the first thing is (the knowledge of) business; for scholars, the first thing is the directing of the mind."

The first paragraph above proposes the assumption of the educational system being established from central to local locations according to the administrative system. This assumption is actually the prototype of China's ancient educational system, which had been followed by the feudal ruling class since the Han Dynasty.[24] The second paragraph discusses the examination system: the learning content and requirements were regulated according to different educational stages, and the teaching effects were tested regularly. The third paragraph first discusses the "rites of the Great Scholar," that is, the opening ceremony of the college. During this ritual, the minister of education would lead all teachers and students wearing skin caps in offer vegetables to worship the ancient sages, showing their respect for teaching principles. It then discusses the supervisory system, putting forward the requirements for the time and methods of educational supervision.

Further, *The Records on the Subject of Learning* proposed valuable suggestions on issues of developing the merits and correcting the defects of the learner through teaching the restraint, cultivation, relaxation, and enjoyment of learning, as well as the mutual benefit for teachers and students.

Viewing *The Records on the Subject of Learning* from the scope of the global history of education, we can draw the conclusion that this work is truly a miracle of education. Many Westerners consider *Institutio Oratoria*, written by Marcus Fabius Quintilianus, the ancient Roman educator, to be the first educational treatise. For example, *The History of Education*, written by N. A. Konstantinov, states, "In the history of education, this is the earliest work that has close connections with school practice."[25] In terms of the history of Western education, this is in line with reality. Before Quintilianus, neither Pythagoras nor Socrates created any works; *The Republic*, written by Plato, is first a political treatise; although Aristotle had written plenty of works, he did not write about education; *Orator*, written by Marcus Tullius Cicero, primarily discusses orators and only minimally discusses education; *Institutio Oratoria*, by Quintilianus, was the quintessence of the author's 20 years' teaching experience, in which the first, second, and twelfth volumes discussed general issues of education. But if considered in the scope of the global history of education, the claim that *Institutio Oratoria* is the first true treatise on education is biased.

First, in terms of time, *The Records on the Subject of Learning* was completed during the late period of the Warring States (about 300 BC), while Quintilianus lived from AD 35 to 100, and *Institutio Oratoria* was written after Quintilianus retired at the age of 50. Therefore, *The Records on the Subject of Learning* was written approximately 300 years before *Institutio Oratoria*. As for John Amos Comenius, the Czech educator who was crowned as "the father of modern pedagogy," his representative work, *The Great Didactic*, was written 1,800 years after *The Records on the Subject of Learning*.

Second, in terms of content, although Quintilianus' *Institutio Oratoria* discusses in detail the functions and three stages of school education (primary, literature, and rhetoric school), the progressive stages of learning (imitation, taking in theoretical instruction, and practice), the emphasis on individualized teaching according to students' personality and age, and the requirement of teachers' integrity and ability, it primarily discusses the education of orators and the micro-matters of teaching. *The Records on the Subject of Learning* combines the macroscopic, mid-level, and microcosmic matters of education in the discussion, which provides a more comprehensive and systematic discussion than *Institutio Oratoria*. However, undeniably, the discussion of the micro-matters in *Institutio Oratoria* may be more comprehensive and intensive than that of *The Records on the Subject of Learning*. Therefore, each has its own merits.

Third, in terms of influence, Quintilianus' *Institutio Oratoria* cannot be compared with *The Records on the Subject of Learning*. After the appearance of the latter, it has appeared in various forms since the Eastern Han Dynasty, reaching more than 140 modern times, and having a far-reaching influence on China's ancient education. As modern scholar Wang Shunan said, "This *Note* was among the educational materials of the three sacred kings. According to the account of Confucians since the Zhou and Qin Dynasties, the scale of the primary and middle school and of the college, the time schedule of schooling, and the teaching method are all recorded in the book. Thus the education strategy for the people of previous kings can be researched, and the school education methods of Eastern and Western countries today can be proved to be similar with each other. Therefore, it is a necessary book for teachers to refer to."[26] Japanese scholar Takeshi Taniguchi also expounded on the influence of *The Records on the Subject of Learning* on Japan's education: "*The Records on the Subject of Learning* is the earliest classic education treatise in China, which has been highly respected in Japan's ancient academic field. When reading educational theories and books of educational practice written by outstanding Japanese educators, such as Ansai Yamazaki, Sokou Yamaga, Heishu Hosoi, and Ekiken Kaibara, we can find passages related to *The Records on the Subject of Learning* and the vigorous spirit embodied in it. The significant influence of this famous book on the history of Japan's education is rarely seen."[27] Relatively speaking, although Quintilianus' *Institutio Oratoria* also had a great influence and was considered the culmination of educational practice in ancient Rome, "laying the foundation for the development of educational theories since the Renaissance,"[28] it was rediscovered in 1416 after having been lost for over 1,300 years. Further, its handing-down time was 1,700 years less than that of *The Records on the Subject of Learning*; thus its scale of affecting time and space was far less than that of *The Records on the Subject of Learning*. Therefore, *The Records on the Subject of Learning* deserves to be considered the first education treatise in the world.

The Development Track of Ancient Educational Thought

China's ancient educational thought has lasted for thousands of years. Throughout history, there appeared four times of climax for the contention of a hundred schools of thought, promoting the development of academic and educational thought of the time. There are rich connotations in China's ancient educational thought. Apart from different educational trends at different stages and times, there are also regional differences, such as differences in regional cultural education during the Spring and Autumn Period and the Warring States Period, the cultural education of Zoulu (today's Zou City in Shandong Province), Sanjin (three ancient states in today's Shanxi Province), Yanqi (today's Hebei and Shandong Provinces), and Jingchu (today's Hubei Province); ethnic differences (the education dominated by the Han culture and the ethnic minority groups); and subject distinction, with education for the upper classes, officials, and nobility versus education for the lower classes). Hereafter, the four times' "contention of a hundred schools of thought" will be described as the historical clue, dividing the development of ancient educational thought into four periods.

1. Educational Thought in the Pre-Qin Period

The Pre-Qin Period generally refers to the Yin and Zhou Dynasties, as well as the Spring and Autumn Period and the Warring States Period before the establishment of the Qin Dynasty in 221 BC. It was the period during which ancient Chinese society changed from a slavery to a feudal system, with the realms of politics, economics, culture, education, and even natural science changing significantly. Thinkers from different classes and hierarchies expressed their own ideas and conducted discussions in order to solve diverse problems occurring in the social sphere, bringing about the academic prosperity of the "contention of a hundred schools of thought."

In terms of cultural education, there appeared a new pattern in the Pre-Qin Period, that is, academic devolution, the rise of the scholarly class, the decline of official education, and the rise of private education. The "contention of a hundred schools of thought" originated from a debate between the schools of Confucius and Mo-tse, which also promoted the development of educational thought into an unprecedentedly active period.

The Confucian School was established by Confucius and succeeded mainly by Mencius and Xuncius. It was not only a noted school of thought in the Pre-Qin Period, but also the largest influence on national thought throughout ancient society in China. The Confucian School stressed the significance of education, considering that education has the function of transforming society and renewing people. For example, Confucius said, "If you govern the people legalistically and control them by punishment, they will avoid crime but have no personal sense of shame. If you govern them by means of virtue and control them with propriety, they will gain their own sense of shame and thus correct themselves."[29] He stressed the function of education, which cannot be replaced by punishment.

Mencius also considered education as the main tool to advocate a "benevolent government": "Good government does not win over the people so much as good instruction. Good government is feared by the people, while good instruction is loved by them. Good government gains the people's wealth, while good instruction gains their hearts."[30] As for *The Records on the Subject of Learning*, it proposed more precisely the propositions of "education as a must for edification" and "education as the basis of governance."

The Confucian School stressed moral education, which was considered the fundamental element of education. Confucius proposed the view that "a noble man is a man of virtue" and "the noble man concerns himself with the fundamentals; once the fundamentals are established, the proper way appears,"[31] which highlighted the supremacy of morality.

Mencius stated more directly, "Establish Xiang, Xu, Xue, and Xiao, all those educational institutions, for the instruction of the people. The name Xiang indicates nourishing as its object, Xiao indicates teaching, and Xu indicates archery. By the Xia Dynasty, the name Xiao was used; by the Yin, that of Xu; and by the Zhou, that of Xiang. As to the Xue, they belonged to the three dynasties, and called by that name. The object of them all is to illustrate human relations."[32]

With regard to human relations, "Between father and son, there should be affection; between sovereign and minister, righteousness; between husband and wife, attention to their separate functions; between old and young, a proper order; and between friends, fidelity."[33] These tenets are the basis of the ethics in feudal society.

Xuncius also emphasized the cultivation and practice of morality, considering the "cultivation of a person" with "moral virtues" as the highest state of moral education.[34] The Confucian School also had great achievements in expounding on the content, principles, and methods of education.

With its founder, Mo Di, the Mohist School represented the small producers of the handicraft industry. During the Spring and Autumn and the Warring States Periods, both the Confucian and the Mohist Schools were claimed to be "noted schools." The core of the Mohist thinking system was "to love each other distinctly and to benefit each other mutually."[35] Thus, on education, it advocated cultivating "virtuous men" and "tolerant men" who could manage the state affairs and benefit the people and also love all and benefit each other mutually. Based on the principle of "benefiting all," Mohism stressed the succession of practical techniques and made outstanding breakthroughs in scientific technical education, such as geometry, optics, mechanics, acoustics, and machine manufacturing, which not only realized the initial leap from industrial techniques to scientific theory in ancient China but also commenced the history of China's ancient science and technology education. Further, Mohism's moral evaluation approach of "examining the combination of a person's motivation and his behavior," the learning attitude of "doing things according to one's ability" and "concentrating on the fundamentals while restraining the incidentals," the educational art of "reflecting a substance through its conception" and "evaluating the categories and discovering the reason," and the theory of stressing the influence of environment to "form a habit" are also unique in the history of China's educational thought, certainly having significant influence.

The Legalist School was named for its advocacy of political reform and legal institutions. At the beginning of the Spring and Autumn Period, Duke Huan of Qi appointed Guan Zhong to implement political reform, which led to the advent of legalists on the political stage. Thereafter, the Legalist School was represented by Li Kui, Wu Qi, Shen Buhai, Shen Dao, Shang Yang, and Han Fei. The educational thought of the Legalist School was to replace the special form of school education, private education, with social education, proposing the ideas of "educating by law" and "learning from government officials" in order to counter the traditional idea of "educating by rites" and "learning from Confucian scholars." Therefore, carrying out legal education was the dominant feature of Legalist educational thought. The apparent fault of Legalist educational thought was to overemphasize the function of legal institutions so that the significance of education was neglected. Han Fei also directly admitted this point, saying, "If there is a failing son, his parents getting angry at him, and he does not repent; his neighbors blaming him, he remains indifferent; his teachers teaching him, he does not change. With the three good aspects of his parents' love, his neighbors' help, and his teachers' wisdom crowning him, he is not touched at all and refuses to mend his ways. Until one day local officials perform their official business with weapons, searching for evildoers, he becomes scared and finally changes his bad habits and misbehaviors."[36] All edification was eclipsed before punishment. The extreme of this kind of thought was cultural tyranny, which was once embodied in the behavior of "burning books and burying scholars" in the Qin Dynasty. Of course, there were also some merits in Legalist thought, such as the emphasis on the selection and cultivation of practical talents, vocational and technical education, and the examination of learning. Its emphasis on legal institutions also complemented the Confucian tradition of stressing edification, viewing it as an important element to maintain social stability.

Daoism was founded by Laozi (named Li Dan) in the Spring and Autumn Period and succeeded by the School of Emperor Huang and Laozi in Jixia

Academy, represented by Zhuang Zhou in the Warring States Period and Tian Pian from the State of Qi. Based on the social and political ideal of "small country with small population," Daoism proposed the idea of "detaching from the sacred and smartness," "simplicity," "detaching from desires," and "wu-wei (no deliberate action)", advocating natural education to shed the shackles on individual freedom. Founder Laozi said, "Man takes his law from the Earth; the Earth takes its law from Heaven; Heaven takes its law from the Dao. The law of the Dao is its being what it is."[37] The significance of education lies in promoting the whole of a human's natural character, enabling people to get rid of all the troubles in social life and to return to the state of wu-wei in their natures.

Further, there were also educational views promoted by the School of Yin-yang, the School of Names, the School of Diplomacy, the Miscellaneous School, the School of Agriculture, the School of Military, and the School of Minor Talks, among others. Their discussions, together with the educational thoughts of Confucianism, Mohism, Legalism, and Daoism, formed the colorful and diverse trend of educational thought in the Pre-Qin Period. The educational thought of the Pre-Qin Period made significant contributions to the formation and development of China's educational thought.

2. Educational Thought in the Period of the Qin, Han, and Six Dynasties

The Period of the Qin, Han, and Six Dynasties included many dynasties, such as the Qin Dynasty, the Han Dynasty, the Three Kingdoms Period, the Eastern and Western Jin Dynasties, and the Northern and Southern Dynasties. This period lasted for more than 800 years, from the establishment of the Qin Dynasty in 221 BC to the perishing of the Southern Dynasty of Chen in 589 AD. It can be divided into two stages: the Qin and Han Period, when the unified and powerful centralized feudal monarchy was established, developed, and gradually consolidated, and the Six Dynasties, when the second major abruption and period of mass chaos in China's history appeared. In the Wei, Jin, and Northern and Southern Dynasties, there appeared the second "contention of a hundred schools of thought" in China's academic history.

After the unification of China by the First Emperor of Qin, the first feudal monarchy in China's history was established. An official teaching system in politics was established, and in cultural education, the policies of standardizing the form of writing, ethical regulations, measurement, and the establishment of one highest authority were promoted, all of which had great influence on later generations. At the beginning of the Han Dynasty, the School of Emperor Huang and Laozi mediated the transformation from the legal education system of the Qin Dynasty to the moral education system of "dominant Confucianism." After

Dong Zhongshu proposed the cultural education policy of "rejecting all schools but Confucianism," the ethical politics in ancient education were formalized. Elaborated by Dong Zhongshu, Confucian ethical education with a core of three cardinal guides (the emperor sets the example for his ministers, the father for his son, and the husband for his wife) and five virtues (benevolence, righteousness, propriety, wisdom, and trustworthiness) became more systematic and more theoretical, with more absolutism and more mystery.

Educational causes in the Han Dynasty saw new exploitation and development. First, the official education system was established and improved, with the teaching system being composed of the Imperial College, the Palace School, the Hongdumen School, and the County School, the learning and teaching in the feudal office, and the teaching content of the classics. Second, private education flourished and prospered. There was enlightenment education mainly in the Shuguan (the ancient primary school), ordinary classics study mainly in village schools, and special classics study mainly in Jinglu or Jingshe (the ancient college with stored books), which developed into Shuyuan (academy) education following the Tang and Song Dynasties. Third, the system of talent selection through recommendation and examination appeared and was carried out, forming the pattern for the development of official schools to cultivate talents, the emphasis on examinations to select talents, learning of Confucian classics to cultivate talents, and the exclusive selection of Confucian intellectuals, which had a direct influence on the generation of the imperial examination. The development of education fostered a generation of outstanding education thinkers, among whom the most prominent ones were Dong Zhongshu and Wang Chong.

Dong Zhongshu, honored as the "Confucius of the Han Dynasty," inherited the moral governing tradition of Confucianism, emphasizing the social and political functions of education. His three major proposals for cultural education—the rejection of all schools but Confucianism, the appointment of outstanding teachers and the establishment of the imperial college, and the emphasis on examinations to select talents broadly—were adopted by the emperor and became the foundation for the cultural education policy of the Han Dynasty. Based on the theory of "three classes of human characters," Dong Zhongshu held that sages could not be named, nor could shallow people, but only the "characters of ordinary people" could "be changed by education, thus leading to sound behaviors."[38] In terms of moral education, the content of the three cardinal guides and five virtues, as well as the principles and methods of moral education, first proposed by Dong Zhongshu also had a significant impact, the latter including the advocating of righteousness and awareness of the right way, not scrambling for benefit, blaming oneself more and others less, accumulation from small to greatness, and accumulation from tiny trifles to become notable.

Wang Chong of the Eastern Han Dynasty proposed a unique educational theory to refute the learning style of superstition and blind worship of the ancient sages prevalent at that time. He affirmed the significance of environment and education in cultivating people, advocating that "people should first be educated in school and then be restrained by the law."[39] He objected that "people are born to have knowledge," proposing the idea of "knowing through learning, learning in order to know, and knowing by asking."[40] He also held that "a person with knowledge is a person with power,"[41] which might be the most primitive expression of the saying "knowledge is power," expressed 1,500 years before Sir Francis Bacon (1561 to 1626) immortalized these words. Wang Chong opposed mechanical study, emphasizing the combination of learning and practice; he objected to the learning method that advocated blind belief in the teacher and worshiped the ancients, but advocated the exploration learning style of "asking questions when having doubts" and "verifying the truth."[42]

There were other important ancient books, including *Lv's Commentary on History*, *Huainanzi*, *FaYan* (*The Records of Judgment Principles*), *The Records of the Grand Historian*, *XinYu* (*Essays of New Ideas*), *XinShu* (*The Book of Newly Collected Essays*), *BaiHuTongDeLun General Views*, *Hanshu* (*The History of the Han Dynasty*), *ShuoYuan* (*Historical Anecdotes*), *ShenJian* (the political and philosophical ideas of Xunyue), and *Taiping Jing* (a classic of Daoism). Each discussed educational issues to different degrees and enriched the educational thought of this period. During the period of the Northern and Southern Dynasties, the nation was in turbulence and the regime changed frequently; the noble class grabbed valuables; metaphysics was prevalent; the official school was periodically razed or abolished, while the private school prospered; and the pattern of "the contention of a hundred schools of thought" appeared. In terms of educational thought, the three areas of talent education, metaphysical education, and family education were most prevalent. "Heroes emerged in troubled times." During this period, the society in want of talents not only cultivated talents practically but also provided talent education theoretically. For example, in *Advice to My Son*, author Zhuge Liang says, "You have to learn to acquire intelligence. You cannot enrich your knowledge without learning, and without ambition you cannot accomplish your study." He proposed the talent education thought that one should base talent on learning and start with setting an ambition. The *Records of the Figures*, written by Liu Shao, systematically discuss the categories and the cultivation, appointment, and identification of talents, making a significant treatise on talent education theory.[43]

The metaphysics of the Wei and Jin Dynasties were a special philosophical thought trend based on the thought of Laozi and Zhuangzi. The metaphysicians were mostly the "famous scholars" at the time, including He Yan, Wang

Bi, Ji Kang, Ruan Ji, Xiang Xiu, Pei Wei, Guo Xiang, and Zhang Zhan. Although the metaphysicians had no interest in general education principles or the internal laws of education, they broke fresh ground with opposition to traditional Confucian educational thought. For example, Ji Kang refuted the Confucian ethical codes and classics education tartly in *On the Theory of Natural Learning*, stating, "Now if we take the palace in which political and educational affairs are taught as the house in which the coffin is put, take the reading of classics as nonsense, take the Six Classics as the weeds in deserted fields, and take righteousness as smelly carrion, those who read the classics will feel dizzy, who abide by the courtesy of bowing will have a hunchback, who wear the formal dress with rank-revealing patterns will suffer from cramp, and who talks about ritual system will have tooth decay. Then they will dump all those above and restart by following everything in the world. Therefore, although one may never be tired of learning, he will also make mistakes. So one can know that those days when Confucianism was not learned may not be long nights, and the Six Classics may not be the sun."

"Passing ethical codes" was to break the old, while "letting nature be" was to set up the new. The metaphysicians held that the biggest mistake of Confucian ethical codes was to depress the personality and damage the natural development of people. Therefore, the key to education was to free the personalities of the educated ones to let them develop naturally. The highest ideal of metaphysical education was cultivating the "supreme people," who "had culture inside, stuck to their simplicity, had no guilt inside and no disappointment when handling common affairs outside, made no friend for benefits, took no position for ranks, learned lessons from the past and the present, and wiped out lusts."[44] In the history of Western education, the French philosopher Rousseau (1712 to 1778) was the first to claim the educational idea of going "back to nature," saying in *Emile* that "Everything is good when it leaves the hands of the Creator; everything degenerates in the hands of man." Although the view of Ji Kang and other metaphysicians could not be compared with the natural education theory of Rousseau, they proposed the educational idea of "letting nature be" over 1,600 years earlier, which should be considered a major reform in the world's history of educational thought.

The family education of this period cannot be neglected, either. The most accomplished text on this topic was the *Admonitions for the Yan Clan*, written by Yan Zhitui, consisting of 20 chapters. The text elaborates roundly on the meaning of education and general issues of family education in terms of establishing oneself in society, managing a household, handling social affairs, and learning. Yan Zhitui emphasized that family education must be carried out as early as possible, holding that "young children can concentrate their mind; when they grow up, they will be distracted easily. Therefore, education should be carried out early, before missing the best opportunity."[45] He not only criticized the education method of "love without instruction" but also opposed the physical punishment of "abusing the kindred." However, he advocated being "strict while amiable,"[46] that is, combining strictness with love. He also discussed the specific teaching content of family education, such as the emphasis on language, morality, and determining one's ambition, and the instructional method for children's learning, such as "reading in person," "diligent learning," "cherishing time," and "exchanging views with others." His theory of family education had significant influence on later generations and was crowned as the "principle of family education" and the template for the book of family education by the later feudal scholar-officials whose theories of family education were influenced by his work. No wonder it was said that "family education originated from this,"[47] and "among the Six Dynasties, the family education of Yan Zhitui was most honored and passed on for the longest time."[48] Further, in the period of the Wei and Jin Dynasties and the Six Dynasties, Buddhist education, Daoist education, and ethnic education also struck fresh notes.

3. Educational Thought in the Period of the Sui, Tang, and Song Dynasties

The Period of the Sui, Tang, and Song Dynasties refers to the four periods of the Sui Dynasty, the Tang Dynasty, the Five Dynasties, and the Northern and Southern Song Dynasties. This period lasted for about 700 years, from the establishment of the Sui Dynasty in AD 581 to the perishing of the Southern Song Dynasty in AD 1279. It was a time when ancient China was united again after a long period of fracture. During this time, cultural education was unprecedentedly prosperous and the third "contention of a hundred schools of thought" in the academic realm appeared.

In the Period of the Sui, Tang, and Song Dynasties, the educational cause developed further with several new features. After the Hongdumen School (an artistic specialty) in the Han Dynasty, the Sui Dynasty established a school of calligraphy, mathematics, and music; the Tang Dynasty carried out vocational training in Sitiantai (the ministry of astronomy), Taipusi (the ministry of horsemanship), and Taiyueshu (the ministry of music). All these promoted the standardization of specialty education and vocational education in ancient China. The Imperial Examination system was founded and gradually completed in the Sui and Tang Dynasties, and the Academy of Classical Learning system was developed and gradually improved in the Tang and Song Dynasties, having significant influences in the ancient education of China.

During this period, advancements in educational thought were quite active, with the establishment of numerous schools and development of various ideas. Han Yu was devoted to maintaining the tradition of Confucianism, proposing the educational tenet of "knowing the education for the ancient kings." In his article "On the Teacher," he discussed teaching issues in terms of the functions, tasks, and selection standards of teachers, as well as the teacher–student relationship. As the first famous work concentrating on teacher issues, the article proposed some noted ideas that have lasted until the present day, such as "all scholars must have teachers," "teachers are to be passing on the truth, teaching courses, and clearing up the students' confusion," "a student may be better than his teacher, and a teacher may not be more worthy than his students," and "there are sequences in gaining knowledge, and different people who learn different skills have their own advantages." His article "Explaining Questions About Learning" is an educational essay that has beautiful words and profound meaning. In the form of dialogue, it concentrates on learning issues, and the words "one's learning is accomplished because of diligence and deserted because of idling about; the success of one thing lies in repeated thinking but is destroyed by random deeds" became a popular quotation. His work *Ode to Zichan's Maintenance of the Village School* had a positive impact on promoting local education. His theory of "three classes of human nature" elaborated on the significance of education in people's development, having great influence on later generations.

The Period of the Song Dynasties witnessed the peak of the development of China's ancient educational thought. Fan Zhongyan and Wang Anshi, who were educational reformers, advocated education in practical statecraft and actively proposed to reform the educational system, content, and method, trying to change the vicious circle of cultivating, selecting, and appointing talents into a virtuous one. Although their education reform movement ended in failure, some of their achievements persisted in different ways, and their influence on the education of the Song Dynasties cannot be underestimated. Further, the famous maxim on behavior of Fan Zhongyan of "being concerned about people before people have worries, and having enjoyment after all the people are happy," and Wang Anshi's admonition article, "Shangzhongyong" ("Pity for Zhongyong"), have become important education materials passed on to later generations.

Hu Yuan endeavored to realize the reform ideals of Fan and Wang. More precisely, his practice and theory of education reform enlightened Fan and Wang's proposition of macro education reform. His idea of "departmental teaching" and the system of distinguishing major and minor subjects were conceptualized over 400 years earlier than those of the developed countries in the world. His teaching methods, such as self-study guidance, intuitional instruction, game teaching, and field inspection, were also unique, breaking conventional regulations.

The Neo-Confucianism of the Song Dynasties was divided into four schools, including the Lian School (led by Zhou Dunyi), the Luo School (led by Cheng Yi and Cheng Hao), the Guan School (led by Zhang Zai), and the Min School (led by Zhu Xi), among which the "Cheng-Zhu Neo-Confucianism" represented by Cheng Yi, Cheng Hao, and Zhu Xi was most influential and formed the ideological system of Neo-Confucian education. In terms of the purpose of education, Cheng-Zhu Neo-Confucianism explicitly proposed the guideline that "the sages' words are to educate people to keep to nature and eliminate human desire,"[49] and affirmed the significance of education in cultivating talents, unifying ethics, changing temperament, rectifying people's minds, and beautifying customs. In terms of the content of education, Cheng-Zhu Neo-Confucianism created the pattern of comparing the "Four Books" (*The Great Learning, The Doctrine of the Mean, The Analects of Confucius,* and *Mencius*) with the Five Classics, contributing to crucial differences in the pattern of the educational content in later feudal society in ancient China. In terms of moral education, Cheng-Zhu Neo-Confucianism advocated fostering the "sage" who could "make his heart sincere, cultivate his moral character, rectify the mind, and regulate the family, country, and the world," and reach the moral realm where people were "equally virtuous with heaven and earth, detached from material desire, fair-minded, brilliant but conniving, impartial, and following the doctrine of the mean,"[50] through cultivation methods, such as setting one's ambition, showing respect, being honest, refreshing the mind, having few desires, rectifying one's behavior during youth, and being cautious.

In terms of educational theory, Cheng-Zhu Neo-Confucianism further deepened the education principles of "teaching according to different individuals, enlightening while guiding, progressing gradually, reviewing to gain new knowledge, and combining the learning of extensive and specialized knowledge." The reading method of Zhu Xi also made important contributions to ancient educational theory. No matter what the society at the time or in the later generations, the educational thought of Cheng-Zhu Neo-Confucianism, which was established as the official educational thought dominating the later feudal society of ancient China soon after the death of Zhu Xi, had a large impact.

Countering Cheng-Zhu Neo-Confucianism, the Mind Philosophy represented by Lu Jiuyuan stands out. Based on the fundamental proposition of Mind Philosophy that "the universe is my mind, and my mind is the universe," and "the mind is the reason,"[51] Lu Jiuyuan held that the purpose of education was "cultivating oneself through the enlightenment of his mind" and "the purpose of the ancestors teaching people was to set the mind, cultivate the mind, and restore the lost mind... With maintenance and irrigation, it is the path of learning and the method of acquiring morality."[52] Based on this theory, the "perfect man," with excellent virtues, and the "super man," with independent spirit, were cultivated. In terms of moral education, the Mind Philosophy of Liu Jiuyuan elaborated on the process of moral education: "'Lv (履; manner) shows us the foundation of virtue; Qian (谦; modesty), its handle; Fu (复; restoration), its root; Heng (恒; constancy), its solidity; Sun (损; harm), its cultivation; Yi (益; benefit), its abundance; Kun (困; difficulty), its exercise of discrimination; Jing (井; limitation), its field; and Xun (巽, container), its regulation.' ...The nine diagrams are the essential elements for the cultivation of a noble man, which are arranged in the above order and are all indispensible."[53]

In terms of teaching, different from the Cheng-Zhu Neo-Confucianism view of "reading extensively before returning to simplicity," Lu Jiuyuan advocated "enlightening people's minds before extensive reading,"[54] and proposed specific principles and methods, such as the independent spirit, exchanging and arguing different views, and rethinking. The main features of Lu Jiuyuan's educational thought were once summarized by saying that it advocated the overall instead of separate understanding, it "respected inside morality" instead of "pursuing the outside knowledge," it was the exploration of the inside to introspect instead of the experience of the outside, it advocated independent thinking instead of blind faith in books and sages, and it emphasized practice instead of the inconsistency between words and deeds.[55] The first three points grasp the main features of the difference between the education of Mind Philosophy and Neo-Confucianism.

The Utilitarian School, represented by Chen Liang and Ye Shi, opposed not only Cheng-Zhu Neo-Confucianism but also the Mind Philosophy of Lu Jiuyuan. At the same time criticizing the hollow talk about life and morality of both the Neo-Confucians and the Mind Philosophers, it established an educational theory that emphasized practical use, utility, and genuine abilities. The Utilitarian School advocated the educational purpose of learning to meet practical needs and understanding truth to handle affairs accordingly, the educational concept of attaching equal importance to history and arts and focusing on truth and reality, and the educational principles and methods of "boldly criticizing and creating, as well as studying rigorously and arguing with teachers and friends." These tenets became the theoretical origins of the educational thought of the early enlightenment thinkers of the late Ming and early Qing Dynasties and the academic nourishment for the sinology masters of the Qing Dynasty, adding to the glory of the development of China's ancient cultural education.

4. Educational Thought in the Period of Yuan, Ming, and Qing

The Period of Yuan, Ming, and Qing included the three dynasties of Yuan, Ming, and Qing and lasted for over 560 years, from the perishing of the Southern

Song Dynasty by the Yuan Dynasty in 1279 until the Opium War of 1840. During this period, society was in a state of great reform, with all academic thoughts remaining active, forming the fourth "contention of a hundred schools of thought" in the history of academic thought in ancient China. The education system in the Period of Yuan, Ming, and Qing basically followed that of the Han and Tang Dynasties, but also proposed certain new features as well, one of which was the increase in social education. Although ancient educators in China had long before proposed the idea of social edification, it was not until the Yuan Dynasty that it was truly put into practice. The community school and temple school of the Yuan Dynasty were the typical social education institutions. In Zhiyuan Twenty-fifth Year of the Period of Kublai Khan (1288), the Yuan government formally released the edict to "Set every 50 of the villages in all the counties as one community, and for each appoint a community head who is aged and familiar with agricultural issues. . . . Set one school in every community, appoint teachers who have good knowledge of the classics, and allow children to study there in slack farming seasons. Recommend that the government examine those who are accomplished at their study."[56] Centered on the activities of the Confucian Temple with the popularization of Confucianism ethics as the purpose, the temple school provided a form of social education. In this period, another feature of education was that the government further enhanced the control of school education and the imperial examination, carrying out feudal absolutism in cultural education.

In terms of educational thought, there was an intense anti-Neo-Confucianism inclination in the Ming and Qing Dynasties, and educational thinking trended toward developing individuality and advocating practical learning. Succeeding and developing the views of Lu Jiuyuan's Mind Philosophy, Wang Shouren proposed the teaching theory of "externalizing morality" and the moral education view of "unifying knowledge and action." In terms of children's education, he opposed teaching methods that destroyed children's natures, such as "urging children to learn how to punctuate and demand that they be decent and restrained" and "lashing and binding them like they are prisoners." He proposed methods such as induction, enlightenment, and ironical persuasion, which conformed to children's characters of "enjoying themselves and fearing restraint and inspection," to "let the children's desire to learn bud"[57] like the flowers and trees moistened by showers and breezes. In terms of course design, he held that the combination of reading and composing verses, as well as learning etiquette, complied with the natural physical and psychological development of children.

Born two years before the death of Wang Shouren, Li Zhi was also one of the pioneers who opposed Neo-Confucianism. He objected publicly to the blind worship of Confucius and proposed strongly to learn from the books of

Shen Buhai and Han Feizi. In terms of educational thought, his main contribution was to propose the teacher–student relationship view of "the teacher as a friend" and to advocate for women to take part in education,[58] which he personally practiced. The relationships between him and his students were presented as "learning with the same method and sharing joys and sorrows," like they were kin. When he lectured in Macheng, he also recruited female students publicly, challenging conventional views, as well as feudal ethical codes.

In the joint period of the Ming and Qing Dynasties, Huang Zongxi was the first scholar to propose a relatively systematic and completely democratic educational thought in the modern sense in ancient China. Starting from a foundation in democratic politics, he strongly rebuked the eight-part essay of the imperial examination, a literary composition prescribed for the imperial civil service examinations, known for its rigidity of form and poverty of ideas. To combat the absolutism and prerogatives of feudal education, he designed a schooling system to popularize education, which was a system including the Meng School (primary school), County School (middle school), Imperial College (college), and Academy (graduate college), which together formed the prototype of the modern schooling system.

Another famous education thinker at the time was Wang Fuzhi, who had abundant written works and profound knowledge. He viewed education as one of the three guidelines of "wealth, military force, and intelligence" to strengthen a country, holding that the reason for the perishing of the Ming Dynasty was the "decline of education" and the "loss of intelligence."[59] Based on the theory of human character that "one's character is gradually formed as time goes by," he emphasized that one's character could be fostered if not yet fully formed and could be changed if already formed, thus revealing the significant impact of education on people's development. The educational principles and methods he proposed, such as the important link between learning and thinking, instruction according to students' abilities and opportunities, an emphasis on actions in teaching, the combination of enjoyment and encouragement in learning, and consistency in teaching, epitomized the essence of China's ancient education and created new ideas.

Another noteworthy school of education in the Period of Ming and Qing was the Practical Education School, represented by Yan Yuan and Li Gong. Opposing Neo-Confucianism in the Song and Ming Dynasties, which advocated studying mechanically, Yan Yuan and Li Gong proposed education through "practical learning" and "practical use," spearheading the new orientation for China's ancient educational approach to practice. In terms of the purpose of education, Practical Education stood for training the talents who had "practical statecraft" to "benefit the people" and "serve the people." In terms of educational content, Practical Education claimed to set "practical writing," "practical action," "practical substance," and "practical use" as its principles, and emphasized artistic, physical, natural scientific, and labor education. In terms of educational method, Practical Education opposed sitting still for empty talk, instead advocating acting and arguing, considering that "learning and teaching should emphasize talking for 10 or 20 percent of the time and acting for 80 or 90 percent of the time." This was the prototype of the concept of "concise instruction and frequent practice" found in modern teaching theories.

Practical Education broke through the conventional regulations of Confucianism in terms of educational content and method, as well as the shackles of thousands of years of feudal education, predicting to a certain extent the inevitable generation of modern scientific education and labor education. In other words, Practical Education reflected the citizen stratum's desire in the period of capitalism germination in ancient China, thus having a fundamental influence on the content reform of modern education.

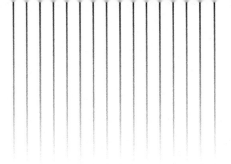

2

The Main Features of China's Ancient Educational Thought

China's ancient educational thought was developed in the special ecological environment of ancient China's space and time. To authentically master the main features of China's ancient educational thought and gain an understanding of its development, one has to analyze the special ecological environment of the time in detail.

Although China's ancient educational thought belongs to the past, its modern significance should not be neglected. As history instructs, if its penetrating power and potential influence or its inertial mechanism and regenerative capacity are neglected, modern education will lose its frame of reference and will hardly be able to move ahead.

The Ecological Environment of Ancient Educational Thought

From the perspective of cultural ecology, the ecological environment is one of the key elements impacting cultural categories. The ecological environment is composed of the geographical environment of a culture or nation, the material production methods of the culture or region, and the established social organizing forms of the culture or region. In ecological environments, differences in geographical environments often lead to differences in production methods, which then lead to differences in social organizing forms. The natural condition of a temperate continental climate determined the dominant natural economy of agriculture in China, and the advantage of its agricultural production method has fostered China's patriarch-centered system. The ancient educational thought that developed in this ecological environment was undoubtedly branded with the mark of Chinese characteristics. Therefore, we will first analyze this special ecological environment.

1. A Semi-Enclosed Continental Environment

As distinguished from the temperature zone and littoral zone, China belongs to the temperate continental zone. Unlike the tropical and frigid zones, because of its moderate climate, the temperate zone provides sound production and living conditions, making it a possible origin for the world's civilizations. Just as Hegel said, "The reason why the real stage of history is the temperate zone, specifically the northern temperate zone, is that there, the earth forms a continent, which, as the Greek people have said, has a broad chest."[1]

China, located in the warm temperate zone in the East Asian continent's temperate zone, generated the earliest civilization in the world because of its advantaged geographical environment. Unlike those in oceanic nations, our ancestors had been living on the East Asian continent since time immemorial, of which the eastern region borders the sea, which was difficult to cross, the northwestern region spans the boundless Gobi desert, and the southwestern region is home to the precipitous Tibet Plateau. Because of the difficulty of land and sea transportation in ancient times, there formed a semi-enclosed geographical environment that was open to the inside roundly and broadly while being relatively isolated from the outside. Because of this geographical environment, Chinese culture has been contained within a huge "harbor" for thousands of years,[2] forming a so-called isolating mechanism of culture. Therefore, the continuity of China's ancient culture was maintained without any cultural tragedies, such as the ruin of Indian culture by the invasion of Aryans, the Hellenization of Egyptian culture due to the capture of Egypt by Alexander the Great, and the interruption of Roman culture by the assault of the Germanic tribes.[3]

This semi-enclosed continental environment had important influences on cultural education in ancient China. Due to the development of China's ancient culture in this huge harbor and the scarce knowledge of the outside world for the ancient Chinese, our ancestors always took their own country as the mainstay of the world with intense national self-consciousness. The ancient Chinese believed that they were at the center of the world; hence they had the saying that "China is the center of the world" and considered surrounding areas as "Siyi" (backward foreign ethnic groups from different places) and "Manmo" (reckless tribes). The obsessive self-consciousness of the continental nation also brought with it the nostalgic feeling that "the moon is brighter in my hometown" for the Chinese nation, highlighting the patriotic inclination emphasized in China's ancient educational thought. In *The Valuable Admissions of Pitirim Sorokin*, Lenin revealed the internal relations between the "isolating mechanism" of culture and patriotism. He said, "Patriotism is one of the extremely ingrained sentiments, formed by the mutual isolation of separate motherlands for hundreds and thousands of years."[4] The famous Southern Song Dynasty poet Lu You said in one of his verses that "seeing Venus put away her light at night, I yearn to sacrifice myself for my country but suffer from the lack of a battlefield." Gu Yanwu, a philosopher from the early Qing Dynasty and the later Ming Dynasty, said that "every man alive has a duty to his country." These passages reflect the intense passion of patriotism in ancient China.

2. Natural Economy of Agriculture

Continental nations can be divided into three types: desert continental (mid-Asia, with a pastoral economy), prairie-forest continental (Eastern Europe, with an agricultural nomadic economy), and great river continental, represented by China. The great river continent offered people flat land, a warm climate, and abundant water, providing advantageous conditions for our ancestors to develop intensive agricultural production. The archaeological exploration of Wuxian in Jiangsu and Banpo in Xi'an manifested this as far back as seven or eight thousand years ago. People planted millet in the Yellow River basin and rice in the Yangtze River basin based on local conditions, thus establishing China as the earliest agricultural country in the world. After our ancestors developed an agricultural society focused on a planting economy following the economic stage of hunting and gathering, farming began to be taught. For example, *Baihu General Views* recorded that "People in ancient times all ate the meat of beasts. Till the time of Shennong when the population increased, without enough beasts, Shennong followed the conditions of the weather (the heaven) and geographical position (the earth) and created plowing tools, teaching people the work of farming." The *Book of Changes: Xici* also said, "After the death of Fuxi, Shennong rose. He cut wood as Si (a primitive shovel) and baked to bend the wood as Lei (a primitive plough), teaching all people to use them." The agricultural production method of the natural economy exerted a direct influence on the social organizing system and thought patterns.[5]

First, agriculture takes land as its primary production material. But the quantity of land is limited, and once occupied, it will be possessed for a long time, while its protection, the plough work, and the planting and harvesting of crops cannot be completed by an individual. Therefore a small group that is long-lasting and stable must be established as the basic unit of work, of which, undoubtedly, the most satisfying one is family based. Hence, preserving the family benefit as well as the harmony and solidity of the family unit became the supreme tenet for these small groups. Since the family is the core of economic and social life, other groups are often considered families, and even the whole country can be seen as a family. Therefore, the family is the epitome of the country, and the country is the magnification of the family, thus forming "familism."

Second, agricultural work was conducted with one family as the basic unit. Therefore, in ancient China, society was composed of thousands of similar but extremely separate villages and towns that had few commodity exchange relationships with one an other. As water resources were the lifeline of agriculture, treating water sources and building large-scale water irrigation systems were prerequisites for a farming nation to survive. Facing the overwhelming power of nature, our ancestors could not survive individually but had to cooperate as a large group and build water conservancy projects to defend against droughts and floods. At the same time, "to effectively manage these projects, an organizing net covering the entire country or at least the important population centers in the country should be established; therefore, those who controlled this organization were always tactfully preparing to enforce the supreme power."[6] The organizer and commander worked in mass collaboration, then became the absolute monarch. The first absolute monarchy in China's history, the Xia Dynasty, was founded by Qi, son of the Great Yu, who led in controlling water. Hence, on one hand, an attachment psychology that sought protection and emphasized authority had been formed; on the other, a collective awareness of mutual coordination had also been formed. This produced an important influence on China's ancient educational thought.

Third, in the process of agricultural production, due to the fragile nature and slow growth of crops, farmers had to follow older farming methods and experiment cautiously, without any breakthroughs. If a small technical improvement was attempted, a long period of starvation might occur if it did not work, which threatened people's survival. Mr. Liang Qichao once discussed the exploring and adventurous characters uniquely possessed by oceanic nations: "Trying to have a view of the sea, one may suddenly feel that he has surpassed all the tiredness in the world, and his behavior and mind will have obtained boundless freedom. Although navigators are ultimately pursuing profit, they have to set aside gains and losses at the beginning and venture their life and possessions on a single stake, taking on all challenges. Therefore, the longer one has been on the sea, the braver and nobler his spirit will be. This is why coastal people have been more active and ambitious than inland peoples since ancient times."[7] Farmers working in the fields had neither the possibility nor the necessity to conduct adventures like this. For them, following the experience of their ancestors could offer them adequate food and clothing, while innovative endeavors might lead to no harvest at all. Naturally, this led to an attitude and behaviors of precaution, respecting ancient ways while neglecting the present and resisting change, the habits of handling matters prudently, with rare displays of passion and extreme doings.

Fourth, in the process of agricultural production, crops grow slowly over a long period. There are many steps in farming, including sowing, weeding, fertilizing, irrigating, preserving, reaping, and storing, all of which are time-consuming and arduous tasks. Therefore, ancient agricultural community members were required to have tough willpower, treating every step of production with extreme patience and perseverance. The Chinese traditions that advocate diligence, tenacity, and patience are inevitably related to this characteristic. The learning beliefs of "practice making perfect" and "working with perseverance" emphasized in China's ancient educational thought also originate from this.

Fifth, during agricultural production, the land as the means of production was imperative. To plant crops, people had to stay and live by a fixed plot of land for a long period of time. To attach their descendants to the land, agricultural society emphasized the worship of ancestors, encouraging people to succeed to the land of their ancestors and take care of their ancestors' tombs on inherited land. Ancient agricultural society stressed attachment to one's native land and an unwillingness to leave it, as well as the views of "no far-away traveling when one's parents are still alive" and "well-being at home but difficulty in journey." As long as they could make a living, members of an agricultural society generally would not leave their hometown. This long-term settled life formed a consciousness of eternity and sense of history, creating the popular sayings in agricultural society, "There are farmers but no officials lasting for a hundred years," "A man making a fortune because of official works will last for only a second, while a man getting rich from farming works hundreds of thousands of years," and "The predecessors plant a tree for future generations to enjoy shade." These sayings reflect the consciousness of eternity and historical sense of ancient Chinese agricultural society. The extraordinary prosperity of ancient China and the tradition of teaching historical knowledge emphasized in educational thought were also related to the characteristics of the agricultural society.

Sixth, in the process of agricultural production, agricultural nations need not only fixed settlements, but also a regular farming schedule, so ancient agricultural societies pursued a static and stable situation, fearing wars, chaos, and change. Once wars started, not only would there be conscription of soldiers and requisition of grain, but farming work would also be impacted, threatening people's living. The highest requirement of China's farmers was having ample food and clothing as well as a peaceful life. Therefore, among the vocabulary of the Chinese, to move meant the advent of disasters, and stillness meant tranquility and peace. The value of upholding stillness while restraining movement represented the Chinese psychological attitude of pursuing peace, moderation, and stability, while detesting turmoil and conflict, fostering the sluggish psychology of making concessions to avoid trouble and drifting through life. The traditions of preferring harmony to competition and preferring stillness to movement were also represented in China's ancient educational thought.

Seventh, in the process of agricultural production, the productivity of land was limited, and if the planting method of shifting agriculture was not adhered to, the productivity of the same piece of land would decline after several cycles of cultivation. Apart from the busy farming season, members of the agricultural society usually had a slow pace of life. With no entertainment available to married couples, they had active sexual lives. Moreover, due to the demand for population and the value of human resources in agricultural society, the birth of children became an important part of life. To feed a large population with limited land would, of course, cause a situation of insufficiency. Hence, the values of diligence, thrift, leisure, and serenity were accepted by people.

3. Patriarchal Society with the Family and Country as a Whole

The absolute advantage of the agricultural production method fostered the development of ancient China as a country with a very unusual social and political system and social organizing form—a patriarchal society encompassing the family and the country as a whole, having significant influence on the historical development of the Chinese nation as well as the formation and development of China's ancient educational thought.

Unlike the revolutions of ancient Greece and Rome, in which the slavery democratic party overthrew the clan aristocracy, changing from a system of family slavery into a system of labor slavery and building up the "city-state" country, in the process transforming a primitive society into a slavery society, in ancient China, clan leaders were transformed directly into slaveholders, changing the family slavery system into a clan slavery system and building up the "home-state" country. Hence, the disintegration of the clan society was insufficient, as the patriarchal system and corresponding ideology and thinking patterns were based on principles of blood relations; the paternal parent being the center and the legal wife's first son being the heir, left over from clan society, were maintained and followed continuously.

The reason that the patriarchal system was not significantly threatened or destroyed is related to the agricultural natural economy of ancient China. The agricultural natural economy provided abundant nutrients for the patriarchal system, making the soil rich for the survival of the system. In the natural economy, society functioned with the family as the basic unit and villages and small towns in which "the crowing of cocks and barking of dogs can be heard while people are completely isolated from each other all their lives." Each village and town was formed by a clan, or family, group, and small towns were usually named "Zhangjiazhai Village" or "Lijiazhuang Village." Based on this, society and the country were also constructed on the model of a "family," forming a patriarchal society for the family and the country as a whole, and "syncretism of emperor and father." This organizational form was one of the main reasons that ancient Chinese society remained stable for such a long period of time, developing only gradually. Ancient Chinese society had the following features.

First, the patriarchal society for the family and the country as a whole was a society with males as the center. Under this patriarchal system, the male parent was the core of the family; he was not only the symbol of the power of the family, but also the possessor of the family wealth. A parent with this supreme status might even determine the death of his family members according to his own intentions. After the death of the male parent, an heir had to be selected from among all the male descendants of the father. Therefore, only by giving birth to male children could the family line continue generation after generation in order to "succeed the ancestors" and "continue the family line." Only by giving birth to male children could one be said to have accomplished the supreme "filial piety" and receive the greatest "blessing," living up to the expectations of one's ancestors. There were also economic reasons for males to be seen as the center of the family and society. Mr. Fei Xiaotong once analyzed that, "'To raise sons for old age' is one vital part in a small-scale peasant economy. In a paternal society, the daughter would be married to become a labor production unit of another family, while the son would marry one wife to gain labor for his own production unit."[8] Governed by this concept, the central social status of males was further consolidated, while at the same time there was a trend that women were excluded from social and cultural education. A woman "should obey her father before marriage, her husband after marriage, and her son following her husband's death." Women had the status of an accessory and were the lowest stratum of society. In ancient educational thought, the views that "innocence is the virtue of women" and "women and inferior men are hard to get along with" reinforced the general view of women in society.

Second, patriarchal society with the family and the country as a whole was a society with a strict hierarchy. In ancient China's patriarchal society, a person's status was determined by his blood relations and his seniority in the clan, while in the country, the regulation among officials was decided according to their ranks. In a clan, the father was the supreme power. In *Shuo Wen Jie Zi*, a Chinese dictionary of words and expressions, "father" is defined as "the one who sets the rules. As the head of a family, he leads the family and educates the children. The character *fu* (father) is written like a hand holding a cane." Its meaning was not limited to biological relationships between parents and children, but also included the sense of ruling and power. Therefore, in the *Book of Rites*, it was said, "A house

cannot have two masters, nor can a country have two emperors." The administration system of the country was seen as the magnification of the administration
of a household, in which the emperor possessing absolute power was called the
"father of the country," while the ministers were called the "family retainers." "If
the emperor orders the minister to die, the minister will become disloyal if he
resists; if a father orders his son to die, the son will fail his responsibility of filial
piety if he resists." Therefore, the most important task for a man in ancient China
was to make clear his specific status in a strictly regulated hierarchical society
and to learn to obey his superiors and elders absolutely. This social order with
strict hierarchy was the so-called definition of "human relations (according to
the feudal ethics)," and the clarification of human relations was the fundamental
purpose of education in ancient China. The specific educational content included
the three cardinal guides and five virtues, as well as benevolence, righteousness,
and morality. These were considered the key aspects of "human relations."

Third, ancient China's patriarchal society with the family and the country as
a whole was a society with obligations as a fundamental component. Suiting the
strict hierarchical system and its corresponding power structure, the concept
of obligations was unilaterally and severely twisted by the ruler's emphasis on
absolute obedience of the lower classes to the honored classes, for example, the
minister to the emperor, the wife to the husband, the servant to the master, and
the inferior to the superior. Therefore, "once born, a person was surrounded
by a net of obligations; he had to fulfill the obligations corresponding to his
status when interacting with his siblings, parents, spouse, family, society, the
emperor, and the country, according to the hierarchical structure of junior to
senior, distant to close, son to father, and minister to emperor. Then, as a reward
for meeting his obligations, he would obtain his own right. Of course, he also
required obedience from his inferiors."[9] Obligations as the fundamental aspect
of ancient China's patriarchal society had notable positive and negative effects.
Their positive effects can be defined by a sense of loyalty to one's country, its
people, and its history, with the typical behaviors being repaying the country
with supreme loyalty, scarifying to achieve virtue, fighting for the right of the
people, and enjoying an unimpeachable reputation. However, obligations could
also be interpreted as blind loyalty and filial piety to one's emperor and one's
father, as well as the brutal devastation of humanity, with typical examples being
"keeping the nature and eliminating human desire" and "starvation being far
less important than saving of one's integrity." It can be said that China's ancient
education was ultimately the education of obligations.

Fourth, ancient China's patriarchal society with the family and the country
as a whole was a society that valued blood relations. The substance of this
patriarchal society was to establish a person's interpersonal relationships by
blood, and then determine his political, social, and economic status in society,

which was inherited through his ancestors generation by generation. The high value of blood relations in ancient China's society was reflected typically in the appellations for kinfolk. For example, in English, a person calls his father's elder brother, his father's younger brother, and his mother's brother by the same word, "uncle"; his father's sister, his paternal uncle's wife, his maternal uncle's wife, and his mother's sister by the same word, "aunt"; his father's father and his mother's father by the same word, "grandfather"; and his father's mother and his mother's mother by the same word, "grandmother." But in ancient China, a whole set of auxiliary appellations was created to further specify the type of blood relation, such as Biao, Tang, Zeng, Xuan, Yuan, Wai, Yuan, Xian, Qin, Gan, Ji, and Hou. The emphasis on blood relations led to and expanded on the intense family awareness that "a person from outside my clan is a person with different intentions." For example, one may refer to his teacher as Shifu (teaching father), his friends as brothers, his leaders as parentlike chiefs, his countrymen as siblings, and his team as a large family. Since human relations and saving face were important principles in the interpersonal communication within a clan, the Chinese psychology of valuing human relationships and saving face are also related to this. In China's ancient educational thought, the tradition advocating the concept of "treasuring harmony" and "seeing the world as one family" is also the revelation and reflection of this family awareness.

As mentioned earlier, in the ecological environment composed of China's semi-enclosed continental environment, the agricultural natural economy, and the patriarchal society with the family and country as a whole, the cultural soil was built for the survival and development of the Chinese nation, while the ancient educational thought born and bred by this cultural soil obviously reflected these unique aspects.

The Main Features of China's Ancient Educational Thought

When analyzing the main features of China's ancient educational thought, as well as understanding the cultural soil and ecological environment that it depends on, we must also view it from the perspective of the world's educational thought history. Further, as the soul of educational thought is its educational values, the main features of China's ancient educational thought are essentially the educational values of the thinkers and even the whole nation at the time. Therefore, by understanding ancient educational values, we can understand the main features of ancient educational thought.

1. Emphasizing Secularity While Neglecting Divinity

China's ancient educational thought emphasized the secular function of education, while Western educational thought emphasized divinity. Therefore, the emphasis on the secular instead of the divine was the first important feature of China's ancient educational thought, as well as "the first significant difference between the thinking patterns reflected from the origins of Eastern and Western educational thought."[10]

The ancient Greek philosopher Socrates firmly believed that God was the creator and dominator of the world, and that God had created humans and "given humans souls" to make humans superior to other animals. Believing that people might go to hell after death, he sincerely and thoroughly described the experience of a soul in hell. Quintilianus of ancient Rome pointed out in *Institutio Oratoria* that, "If the universe is ruled by divine guidance, the country should be governed by kind people. If our souls come from heaven, we must make every effort to obtain virtue in order not to reduce ourselves to the slavery of worldly pleasures."[11] Therefore, he regarded the orators he cultivated as "people sent from God to do credit for the world."[12] In the Middle Ages, as the emphasis on divinity became more intense, religious education requested people to be the tools carrying out God's will, keeping the Last Judgment in mind at all times. The splitting off of religious sects, the religious wars, and the persecution of the pagans gave full play to divinity in education. Until modern times, when secular education gradually became a reality, religious education emphasizing divinity was still an indispensible part of Western education.

In comparison, in China, only Duke Zhou in the Yin and Zhou Dynasties made use of people's primitive religious awareness, proposing the views of "punishment from God" and "performing the punishment of heaven." Actually, Duke Zhou himself was not convinced of the existence of a god or gods; he simply used the concept of god to enhance the power of punishment. Since the time of Confucius, China's educational thought has followed the path of secularity. Confucius said not to talk about extraordinary things, feats of strength, disorder, or spiritual beings,[13] setting an example of the rational attitude of Confucians. As for the religious activities of worshipping ghosts and gods, although Confucius did not clearly object, his statements that "worship the ancestors as though the ancestors really exist, and worship the gods although the gods really exist,"[14] "one who has not made the issues of people clear should not talk about the issues of ghosts," and "one who does not understand living matters has no way to know matters about and after death"[15] revealed his doubt about the reality of ghosts and gods. For Mencius, though heaven was sometimes considered the dominator, with a will and a personality, it was actually imaginary instead of an absolute heaven, which was sacred and could not be offended. As he said, "Disasters caused by nature (heaven) can be escaped, but there is no way to escape the evils done by people themselves,"[16] "Opportunities of time endowed by heaven are not equal to the advantages of the situation afforded by the earth, and the advantages of the situation afforded by the earth are not equal to the unity arising from the accord of men."[17]

"A person's weal and woe are caused by himself."[18] Therefore, in terms of social and political views, Mencius underlined that heaven was not the key element determining people's will: "The reason why King Jie and King Zhou lost their country lay in their loss of the people; the reason for their losing the people lay in the failing of the people's hearts. To conquer the world in the right way is to conquer the world through winning the people's favor. To win the people's favor in the right way is to win their hearts."[19] In terms of educational views, he emphasized that one should "introspect first when meeting failures" and "afflict his will and tire his body" instead of placing all hope in mysterious heaven-born knowledge. The Confucian tradition of stressing the secular rather than the divine has become a feature of Chinese culture that cannot be neglected. Just as Lin Yutang said in *My Country and My People*, "Nothing is more striking than the Chinese humanist devotion to the true end of life as they conceive it, and the complete disregard for all theological and metaphysical fantasies extraneous to it....There is no doubt that Chinese people are in love with life, in love with this earth, and will not forsake it for an invisible heaven. They are in love with life, which is so sad and yet so beautiful, and in which moments of happiness are so precious because they are so transient. They are in love with life, with its kings and beggars, robbers and monks, funerals and weddings, births and sicknesses, glowing sunsets and rainy nights, and feast days and wine-shop fracases."[20] In the history of China's education, though Buddhism had a certain influence, it never assimilated the Confucian views of education; its practice, which was free from vulgarity, was not accepted by the majority of the people.

In summary, China's ancient educational thought emphasized the secular while neglecting the divine, stressing the nurture of people in secular social life and advocating the cultivation of people with an ethical spirit to serve the political and economic facets of society. Instead of setting detachment from worldly affairs as the purpose of education, China's ancient educational thought presented a spirit of entering into society positively.[21]

2. Emphasizing Morality While Disdaining Material Gain

China's ancient educational thought emphasized the ethical principles of education, while Western educational thought emphasized the principles of material gain. Therefore, the emphasis on morality and disdain of material gain forms the second important feature of China's ancient educational thought.

Western utilitarianism was first advocated by Bentham, but its spirit originated with Socrates, who stated that pigs may be more content than humans because they are without reason. John Stuart Mill, a fellow utilitarian of

Bentham's, elaborated on this idea, saying, "It is better to be a human being dissatisfied than a pig satisfied; better to be Socrates dissatisfied than a fool satisfied. And if the fool, or the pig, is of a different opinion, it is because he only knows his own side of the question." The earlier utilitarian thinker David Hume stated that "the best action is the one that procures the greatest happiness for the greatest numbers." Overall, utilitarians support John Stuart Mill's view on freedom that an individual's amelioration of personal quality and self-improvement is the sole source of true freedom.[22]

The roots of utilitarianism can be found in the thoughts of Aristotle, the epitome of ancient Greek thought. He regarded people's lives, feelings, and desires according to rational principles, emphasizing that "morality is the habit of making the right choice in behavior, and this choice is a reasonable desire."[23] Therefore, he believed that the goodness of a matter lay in the realization of its unique characteristic, while the purpose or aim of each creature was to realize its own unique characteristic, distinct from those of other creatures. The supreme kindness of people was to completely and habitually perform the function that could accomplish a person, that is, the attainment of personal happiness through the realization of personal benefit. Later Western thinkers and educators, such as Helvétius, Locke, and Rousseau, all built upon and developed this thought, cementing the utilitarian style of Western culture.

In contrast, China's ancient educational thought from the very beginning objected to material gains and advocated morality. The concept of wu-wei (no deliberate action) of Laozi and Zhuangzi publicly declared the view of being against material gain. Laozi said, "Therefore the sage, in the exercise of his government, empties their minds, fills their bellies, weakens their wills, and strengthens their bones. He constantly tries to detach them from knowledge and desire, and where there are those who have knowledge, to keep them from presuming to act (on it). Then good order is universal."[24] He considered detachment from knowledge and desire to be the basic precondition for the politics of a country and the morality of a people. Due to its emphasis on the actual lives of people, Confucian educational thought advocated entering into society positively. But in terms of the view of opposing material gains, it held the same view as Daoism. For example, Confucius said, "A noble man values righteousness, while an inferior man values benefit."[25] Confucius believed that a virtuous man pursued morality and justice, while an amoral man pursued material gains. Although he did not absolutely object to material gain, he always constrained it with morality and was opposed to "sacrificing moral principles for profit." There is a famous quote from Confucius that states, "With coarse rice to eat, with water to drink, and with my bended arm for a pillow, I have still joy in the midst of these things. Wealth and honors acquired by unrighteousness are to me as a floating cloud."[26] That is to say, people's real joy lies in the moral realm; in this realm, although one is still poor and lowly, he should treat his circumstances calmly. Benevolence is the core value of Confucianism, and the character for benevolence appears as many as 105 times in *The Analects of Confucius*. *The Analects* set blood relations as the fundamental element of society and the amiableness of the father and the filial piety of the son as the core. Importance is placed on interpersonal relationships, forming an ethical and moral education system that stressed a humanistic spirit in terms of the affairs of the outside world and the pursuit of an ideal personality in terms of the internal world. Hereafter, from Mencius' view of "sacrificing one's life for justice" and the "five cardinal relationships," in which "there is kinship between father and son, righteousness between emperor and minster, distinction between husband and wife, sequence between senior and junior, and trust between friends," to the view of "keeping the nature and eliminating human desire," and that "the ancient kings set the clarification of human relations as the fundamental"[27] proposed by Neo-Confucianism in the Song and Ming Dynasties, ethical and moral education were honored as the supreme tasks in life. Therefore, in terms of its overall characteristics, China's ancient educational thought had the Confucian principal of ethics at its core. In a certain sense, it can be said that the history of China's ancient educational thought is the history of China's ethics.

As for the non-mainstream theories in the history of China's ancient educational thought that emphasized material gains, they did not neglect the function of morality and were in fact based on morality. Take Mo-tse as an example. He proposed the view "to love universally and to benefit mutually." But first, the "love" and "benefit" he proposed were not related to the individual but to "the whole world." The "benefit" was "mutual," restraining the subject in nature while negating individual material gains. Second, the "love" and "benefit" he proposed established a hierarchy and loyalty, as well as filial piety, as preconditions. He said, "If one thing deserves to be loved deeply according to ethical principles, then love it deeply; if it deserves to be loved slightly according to ethical principles, then love it slightly. That is the so-called love without distinction. Those with virtues, the emperor, the elder, and the relatives, are to be loved deeply. Love the elder deeply, as well as the younger. Love those of close relationship deeply, while those of distant relationship slightly. There are those with the closest of relationships, but no one with the slightest of relationships,"[28] and "Righteousness is the most valuable among all matters."[29] Hence, the practice of "love" and "benefit" was carried out under ethical principles in the sequence of virtuous men and the emperor, then the elder, and then one's relatives. Is this not the same as the emphasis on morality, obedience to the elder, and respect for one's predecessors in Confucian theory?

The values of emphasizing morality and disdaining material gains in China's ancient educational thought reflect the emphasis on ethical values and the debasement of the practical value of education. The relation between ethical education and practical education had always been the relation between the fundamental and the incidental. Giving up the fundamental to pursue the incidental would lead to attacks and repulsion. The reason lay in that, in China's ancient educational thought, there were only views of being taught after becoming rich but seldom the idea of becoming rich after being taught, which to a great degree restrained the active function of education for the development of the social economy.

3. Emphasizing Political Affairs and Neglecting Nature

In ancient China, there was a tradition of incorporating political ideas into educational thought. In contrast, Western educational thought stressed the adaptation of education to nature. Therefore, the emphasis on political affairs and the neglect of nature characterize the third important feature of China's ancient educational thought.

The scientific spirit of exploring nature in Western thought has a long-lasting tradition. Bertrand Russell, the British philosopher, pointed out that, "Western civilization originated from Greece and is based on Miletus' philosophy and science from 2,500 years ago. Hence, it is distinct from other great civilizations in the world. The dominant concept threading through Greek philosophy is the noun 'logos,' which, apart from other meanings, refers to speech and measurement, thus combining philosophical discussion closely with scientific exploration."[30] Therefore, the philosophy and natural science of ancient Greece were inter woven with each other and even integrated as a whole, and the philosophers of the time were mostly erudite natural scientists themselves. The gate of the "academy" established by Plato is engraved with the admonition that "No one entering this academy knows not geometry."[31]

Considered a father of modern science, Aristotle was an encyclopedia of knowledge in terms of natural science and created important works in the fields of physics, zoology, botany, astronomy, biology, and psychology. The reason that he proposed the view that education had to follow nature and had scientific opinions with regard to children's physical and psychological development in Western educational history lay in his scientific nature, which stressed the research of nature. The rise of the philosophy of science, as well as scientific education, in modern Western educational thought originated from the scientific spirit of ancient Greece.

In contrast, China's ancient educational thought was characterized by a political emphasis from the beginning. Mr. Jin Yuelin said when reviewing China's ancient philosophy, "The Confucian held the view that one's extraordinary internal wisdom could be externalized as the method to administer state affairs and bring peace and stability to the country. Therefore, every philosopher considered himself a potential politician. A person's philosophical ideal was fully realized in the practice of administering the country and doing good in society."[32] If the word "philosopher" in the above view is changed to "educational thinker" (actually, the two were interchangeable in ancient China), and "philosophical ideal" to "educational ideal," the phrasing also makes sense. In ancient China, the most general purpose of education was to "learn to be excellent and then be selected as an official."[33] The fundamental way to achieve in education was to cultivate talents with the feudal ethics needed by the ruling class. Learning while administering political affairs, individuals worked on learning in order to consciously master ethical principles and methods of ruling the people, through which they could ascend to the official class. Guided by the ideal personality, which required extraordinary wisdom and knowledge of how to administer state affairs, the simplest approach for one's internal morality and righteousness to be externalized into an ideal society was to "have a promising official career." Only in this way could one "contribute to the society."[34] Thus we can understand Confucius' intention when he preached to his disciples.

Both the views that "one does not worry about the insufficiency of positions but the insufficiency of his own competence" and that "profit may be found in learning"[35] reflect the inclination of Confucius to emphasize political affairs. In researching the content and methods of China's ancient education, one will discover the three key areas of psychology, ethics, and politics. The most typical elaboration in *The Great Learning* states the following:

> The ancients, who wished to illustrate illustrious virtue throughout the kingdom, first ruled well their own states. Wishing to rule well their states, they first regulated their families. Wishing to regulate their families, they first cultivated themselves. Wishing to cultivate themselves, they first rectified their hearts. Wishing to rectify their hearts, they first sought to be sincere in their thoughts. Wishing to be sincere in their thoughts, they first extended their knowledge to the utmost. Such extension of knowledge lay in the investigation of things. Things being investigated, knowledge became complete. Their knowledge being complete, their thoughts were sincere. Their thoughts being sincere, their hearts were then rectified. Their hearts being rectified, they themselves were cultivated. They themselves being cultivated, their families were regulated. Their families being regulated, their states were rightly governed. Their states being rightly governed, the whole kingdom was made tranquil and happy.

That is to say, the psychological efforts of the "investigation of things," "extension of knowledge," "sincerity of thoughts," and "rectification of the heart" were aimed to reach the ethical states of the "cultivated personality" and "regulated family," which then realized the political ideal of "rightly governing the state" and "tranquilizing the whole kingdom." Elaborated on and then affirmed by Zhu Xi, the ethical education process of psychology, ethics, and politics became the basic model of feudal education in later generations. Further, the imperial examination system powerfully fixed the administrative and legal aspects of this process. Education then completely became a tool for the ruler to conduct "moral governance" and to maintain "stable" order in feudal society.

The emphasis on political affairs and the neglect of nature in China's ancient educational thought had an obvious duality. In terms of its positive effect, it encouraged people to enter political life in society, equipping Chinese intellectuals with the sense of social responsibility and political mission, who never cowardly escaped but sacrificed themselves nobly when the country was in danger. In terms of its negative effect, due to the excessive emphasis on education's political function of governing and stabilizing the country, as well as edifying the people, the function of education was actually narrowed, thus limiting the development of natural science and the progress of production techniques, as well as education of natural science and production techniques. In the article "Collection of Informal Essays: Academic Independence," Chen Duxiu analyzed the reasons China's ancient science stopped developing. He said:

The essential reason for the underdevelopment of China's science lay in the fact that scholars had no awareness of the sacredness of academic independence. For example, though literature had its own value of independence, the scholars didn't acknowledge it; instead, they always dragged the *Six Classics* in and claimed that "writings are for conveying truth" and "they expound ideas representing the sages" to belittle themselves. Though the history of science had its own value of independence, the historians didn't acknowledge it; instead, they always dragged *Chun Qiu* (the *Spring and Autumn Annals*) in and emphasized the righteous cause of the title, preferring to call history the accessory of ethics. Though music had its own value of independence, the musicians didn't acknowledge it; instead, they always dragged the emperor's cause and the benevolent government in, preferring to call music the accessory of politics. Though medicine and Chinese boxing had their own value of independence, the doctors and boxing masters didn't acknowledge it; instead, they always dragged the Daoist arts in to discuss the way of repose and breathing exercises in order to "be harmonious with the heaven, the earth, the ghost, and the god," thus making "the art similar with Dao (the Way of nature)." If the scholars didn't respect the science they learned, how could science develop?

Although his idea was too radical in some ways, it revealed the exclusivity caused by the politicization of education from a unique perspective, which was also reflected in some educational thought. For example, Xuncius proposed that knowledge unrelated to politics was "of unpractical use, unnecessary to investigate, and to be discarded…while the righteousness between emperor and minister, the kinship between father and son, and the distinction between husband and wife should be studied every day unremittingly."[36] *The Book of Rites: Wang Zhi* (the *Imperial Ranking System*) even regards "serving the higher authority with skills or crafts" as activities that "should not be talked about with scholars." It also claims that "those who play evil music, wear bizarre dress, portray odd skills, or make odd implements to captivate the public are to be slain." Originating from this, later generations considered science and technology to be "odd skills and evil arts," as well as the "worst implements." Further, due to the emphasis on political affairs in ancient educational thought, scholars all believed that a "promising official career" was the only way to achieve and could not form independent personalities, thus creating a negative psychological character, which submitted to authority and sought wealth and profit.

4. Emphasizing Harmony While Neglecting Competition

Harmony was the supreme state pursued by China's ancient culture. China's ancient educational thought was characterized by the spirit of harmony, while Western educational thought emphasized the practice of competition principles. Therefore, the emphasis on harmony and neglect of competition formed the fourth important characteristic of China's ancient educational thought.

It should be noted that Western educational thought also included a number of theories that advocated harmony. For example, Pythagoras once made the proposition that "virtue is a kind of harmony."[37] Aristotle also proposed the "middle path" of moral education, which said, "Morality involves the handling of emotions and behaviors, which may be excessive or insufficient, and excess and insufficiency are improper. Due to this, only in appropriate time and with appropriate opportunity, with appropriate people or objects, can one handle matters with appropriate attitude, which is the middle path and the best path. This is the characteristic of morality."[38] But the thought emphasizing competition has existed since ancient times and became the dominant educational thought in the West. The earlier thinker of ancient Greece Heraclitus said, "For things repelling each other, when combined together, their different tones will make the most beautiful harmony; all are generated by fighting." He also held that, "Competition (war) is the father of everything and the king of everything. It makes some gods, some people, some slaves, and some free men."[39] Competition was then clearly set as the precondition for people's survival and development. Since then, from Hobbes and Malthus to Darwin, Huxley, and

Galton, among others, all have stressed the principle of competition for survival. Therefore, competition and distinction have always been qualities intentionally cultivated by Western educators.

In contrast, the harmonious state was the overall target in ancient China, in which the pursuit of the unity of truth (the harmony of nature), the good (interpersonal harmony), and beauty (harmony between heaven and people) was emphasized, dominated by interpersonal harmony in particular. Confucius originally proposed the ideal of "valuing harmony,"[40] defining harmony and stability as the principles of handling affairs and administering a country. He said, "I have heard that rulers of states and chiefs of families are not troubled lest their people should be few, but are troubled lest they should not keep balanced distribution; that they are not troubled with fears of poverty, but are troubled with fears of a want of stability among the people. For when the people have balanced distribution, there will be no poverty; when harmony prevails, there will be no scarcity of people; and when there is stability, there will be no rebellious uprisings. Therefore, according to this principle, if more remote people are not submissive, all the influences of civil culture and virtue are to be cultivated to attract them to be so; and when they have been so attracted, they must be made contented and tranquil."[41] Confucius was speaking here in terms of interpersonal relationships. In terms of personal cultivation, *The Doctrine of the Mean* says, "When there are the emotions of pleasure, anger, sorrow, and joy in one's heart, and he does not express them, it may be called the mean; if he expresses these emotions while remaining in control, it may be called harmony. The mean is the fundamental element of the world, while harmony is the general law of the world. When reaching the state of harmony and the mean, heaven and earth will be in their right places, and everything will grow and develop." The principle of harmony and the mean should be conducted to guide oneself and other people.

In the context of the harmonious principle, China's ancient educational thought emphasized the molding of a harmonious character. For example, Confucius requested students to talk and behave according to the doctrine of the mean. When evaluating the behavior of his disciples, he also applied the standard of harmony and the mean, opposing not only "excess" but also "insufficiency."[42] This standard also became the starting point for "teaching according to students' aptitudes" in ancient education. For example, Confucius' practice of "encouraging Ran You, for he always cowers, and restraining Zilu, for he always acts rashly,"[43] fulfilled the principle of harmony. Therefore, China's ancient educators advocated modesty, a combination of rigidness and flexibility and no extreme doings. Ancient educators encouraged the ideas of never being first, happiness in a contented mind, and harmonious coexistence. The biggest disadvantage brought by harmony and the mean was the repression of the competitive and progressive spirit. The prevalent idioms in society that "trees taller in the woods are to be destroyed by the wind; soil piled beyond the bank is to be flushed by the stream; behaviors prominent from others are to be reproached by the public," "the success of a cause will attract slanders; the nobility of virtue will attract defamation," "fame portends trouble for men just as fattening does for pigs," and "the bird which takes the lead will be shot," all revealed to a certain extent the negative effects brought by the idea of emphasizing harmony while neglecting the value of competition.

The value inclination of emphasizing harmony while neglecting competition also had a certain influence on the educational methods of ancient China, forming the traditions that stressed self-education and moral introspection. For example, Confucius described the ability for conscious introspection as the mark distinguishing "the noble man" from "the base man," cultivating the models of self-constraint and retrospection, like Yan Yuan who could "pass the examination of his private behaviors after class,"[44] and Zeng Shen who could "introspect several times a day."[45] Mencius regarded self-education and moral introspection as the "restoration of one's lost conscience." He said, "Ren (benevolence) is people's conscience; Yi (righteousness) is people's route. It is so sad that one should desert the route instead of following it or lose one's conscience without restoration! When losing his chickens and dogs, one knows to look for them. When losing his conscience, he knows not to restore it. The way of learning lies in nothing but the restoration of one's lost conscience."[46] He held that the purpose of learning was to foster the only route to "righteousness" and to introspect to find the lost but inherent goodness of "conscience" in order to restore natural virtue. This method of self-education and moral introspection was then developed by the Neo-Confucians in the Song and Ming Dynasties into systematic dogmas, such as the ideas of "being respectful," "maintaining the conscience and cultivating benevolence," "introspection," and "self-discipline," thus forming the characteristic of internalization in China's ancient educational thought.

5. Emphasizing the Whole While Neglecting the Individual

The value inclination of emphasizing ethics, harmony, and the mean, as well as secular political affairs, also determined the inclination toward emphasizing the whole. This is in contrast to the enduring tradition of individualism in Western educational thought. Therefore, the emphasis on the whole and neglect of the individual formed the fifth characteristic of China's ancient educational thought.

As early as the Pericles Golden Age of ancient Greece, Protagoras proposed that "humanity is the measurement of everything," indicating that the individual need not submit to the external law of the city-state, wishing to determine individual behaviors according to one's own desire and benefit. The proposition of Protagoras, in terms of ethics, meant that in social and moral life, people should take the individual desire and benefit as the origin of morality and the standard for moral behaviors.[47] This idea had far-reaching influence on the development of Western culture. At the beginning of the seventeenth century, Grotius, an expert on international law in the Dutch Republic, declared freedom and property as individual rights and elevated these rights to natural laws. This idea gradually became the social axiom in the West: to care about one's own benefit above all is natural and reasonable; the pursuit of increasing one's benefit is the best approach to increasing the benefit of the whole society. This axiom could be applied not only to the property relationship between individuals, but also to other ethical and legal relationship between individuals, the individual and the family, and the individual and the country.

These principles, which emphasized the individual's sovereignty, have been compiled into Western textbooks. For example, an individual has the right to act in his own way without intervention except when violating the law; parents are not allowed to affect the benefit of their adult children; an individual is to be responsible for his own behavior and has the right of choice; privacy is an individual right that people cannot be deprived of; an individual has personal inviolability; only in moments of national crisis is sacrifice for one's country reasonable; the government has no right to intervene in individual freedom and privacy; and every individual has the right to vote and be voted for.[48] Therefore, most Western education thinkers regarded those with strong character and ingenuity as the basic standard of the ideal talents to be cultivated. For example, John Stuart Mill claimed that, "A person whose desires and impulses are his own—are the expression of his own nature, as it has been developed and modified by his own culture—is said to have a character. One whose desires and impulses are not his own has no character, just as a steam-engine has no character."[49] The pragmatism scholar John Dewey said more directly that, "In school, the life of children becomes the target to determine all, which is the concentration of all the necessary measures to promote the growth of children."[50] The theory of the individual child as the focus of education has been approved by most Western educational workers and has become one of the theoretical cornerstones of Western education.

In contrast, ancient China regarded the maintenance of group harmony and social stability as the supreme ideal of ethical political principles. This set the benefit of the entire society as the only reference point for individual benefit, holding that the benefit of the entire group was the starting point and the end result of individual benefit, the former consisting of the latter. Overall, the individual had more obligations, than rights and must make more contributions than requests. Only within the entire society could the value of the individual be realized; the ultimate purpose of individual improvement was not for oneself, but to serve the supreme aim of group harmony and social stability. The ultimate ideals taught by *The Great Learning* were "illustrating illustrious virtue," "renovating the people," and "resting in highest excellence." Its specific requirements were that "as a sovereign, he rests in benevolence; as a minister, he rests in reverence; as a son, he rests in filial piety; as a father, he rests in kindness; in communication with his subjects, he rests in good faith." These passages reflect the values of putting family and society ahead of the individual that were dominant characteristics of ancient Chinese culture.

This characteristic that emphasized the whole over the individual was also reflected in the thought of ancient China, such as advocating "unity of heaven and man," "unity of knowledge and action," "unity of official and teacher," "unity of politics and religion," "unity of family and country," and "unity of the outside and the internal world." It emphasized the overall understanding of nature and human society, while neglecting the analysis of all the details making up the whole, as well as the analytical thinking pattern at the micro level and concrete observation and experimentation. In education activities, therefore, it also emphasized the understanding and awareness of "the general" and neglected the dissection and analysis of "the fragmented." The value inclination of emphasizing the whole while neglecting the individual had certain positive effects on educating people to pursue the benefit of the country, the consolidation of national cohesion, and students' overall and systematic thinking ability. However, to a certain degree, it also invoked paternalism, royal authoritarianism, and even despotism, repressing and restraining people's personalities and initiative. This value inclination might not only foster lofty qualities, such as being open-minded, respecting one's teachers and elders, and devoting oneself to the collective, but also cultivate negative personality traits, such as being timid and overcautious, unthinking obedience, and self-abasement and self-repression. The idea of "no foregone conclusions, no arbitrary predeterminations, no obstinacy, and no egoism,"[51] proposed by Confucius was put forth to warn that one should make no subjective assumptions, seldom express one's own opinions, make no certain predictions about things, make no affirmation of one's own views arbitrarily, not be insistent in one's own ideas, and never be opinionated, wasn't it?

In other words, "no foregone conclusion" was the starting point for losing oneself, "no arbitrary predetermination" equaled the affliction of depriving oneself, "no obstinacy" was the core of self-abandonment, and "no egoism" was the ultimate goal. Without the protection and advocacy of individual progressive awareness from society, the individual had no choice but to follow others' opinions and stoop to compromise. Therefore, coordination between the whole and the individual, as well as the unity of the individual benefit and the group benefit, is one of the tasks that should be accomplished in the present educational thought.

Of course, China's ancient educational thought had more than the five characteristics just discussed, including other notable traits such as emphasis on accumulation and neglect of discovery, as well as emphasis on following the good and the neglect of pursuing the truth. Further, the so-called emphasis and neglect are discussed in comparison with Western educational thought in terms of overall characteristics, without any bias or detailed analysis. It should be noted that there were also many ancient educational thinkers in China who promoted utility and a pragmatic learning style and who emphasized personality.

The Modern Significance of Ancient Educational Thought

When elaborating the meaning of national spirit, Hegel held that it was the basis and content of other forms of national awareness.[52] The ancient educational spirit that evolved through ancient educational thought continues to influence modern education in many ways.

Undoubtedly, today's education is the succession, extension, and sublimation of past education. Ancient educational thought has had various effects on modern times, both positive and negative. This requires us to actively assess the function of education in order to evaluate and innovate culture. Doing so will allow us to assimilate the essence and reject the dross, bringing back the glory of ancient educational thought.

When talking about human cultural heritage, Hegel pointed out that, "When we absorb it and make it ours, we attach to it some characteristics that are different from its previous one," and "the accepted heritage is then changed in this way."[53] In this sense, when we inherit and develop the heritage of China's ancient educational thought, we always make it useful to us, both consciously and unconsciously, marking it with some new characteristics to interpret the modern meaning of ancient educational thought. The so-called promotion of the excellent tradition of ancient educational thought in itself includes succession and creation, with the two aspects embodying each other; likewise, history and the present embody each other. These are the dialectics of promotion. Specifically, ancient educational thought has certain modern meaning in the following aspects.

1. The Secular Spirit

As China's ancient educational thought was characterized by the tradition of emphasizing the secular and neglecting the divine, ancient educators advocated the attitude of discussing social reality in terms of life. The Chinese do not concentrate their minds toward a "next world," but focus on present society; they do not look toward an "afterlife," but devote themselves to "this life." It is said that Western Christian culture is the "study of heaven" and that Indian Buddhist culture is the "study of ghosts," while traditional Chinese culture is the "study of people." The culture of "studying people" encourages going into society actively with an intense secular spirit. Therefore, the educational thinkers of ancient China all emphasized the education of people and the cultivation of customs and concentrated on the application of knowledge to handling state affairs and the administration and development of the country. Although the Confucians, including the so-called new Confucians of Neo-Confucianism in the Song and Ming Dynasties, stressed the cultivation of the individual spirit and the improvement of morality, their ultimate target was to externalize the internal thought into positive contributions to the whole. Only when "internal extraordinary wisdom" was externalized into "the method to administer state affairs" could the ideal of "contributing to society" be realized. With rewarding farming and battle, and focusing on legal institutions and practical effects as its features, the educational thought of Legalism was undoubtedly a more positive attitude of going into society. Even Daoism and Buddhism were marked with an obviously secular spirit. In *The Annotations and Evaluation of Laozi*, Mr. Chen Guying points out that Laozi's ideas, such as wu-wei, humility, and everlasting peace, "had not only no negative thought, but on the contrary, the ready-to-take-off spirit. On one hand, he was concerned about the chaos of society and was eager to provide a method for people to get along peacefully; on the other, he asked people to condense the depth of internal life."[54] Therefore, wu-wei was in fact for "action without exception." It can be seen in the special significance of the philosophy of Emperor Huang and Laozi functioning in every transforming period from chaos to peace in ancient China. Buddhism is the same. Buddhist scripture says that "the Buddhist doctrine is of the secular world without leaving it; leaving the secular world to look for the Bodhi is like looking for the horn of a rabbit." This passage discusses the practice of Buddhism and coming to understand the human world. The supreme state of Buddhism was to deliver all living creatures from torment, to "undertake the secular cause with the supramundane spirit,"[55] to change the human world into a dignified, pure land and to transform hell into a paradise.

The secular spirit in ancient educational thought enhanced the relationship between education and social politics, offering us a helpful reference to assess the function of education in modern society. However, we also have to prevent the excessive emphasis on the secularity of education lest we neglect its relative independence or equal influence on social politics and productivity, thus ignoring the internal law and other functions of education.

2. The Moral Spirit

Overall, the educational thinkers of ancient Greece and Rome had a "style of a wise man," who was concerned primarily about the relationship between people and nature with scientific spirit. But China's ancient educational thinkers had a "style of a virtuous man," who was more concerned about the interpersonal relationship with the moral spirit. When Confucius was talking about the relationship between knowledge education and moral education, he demonstrated this spirit. He said, "A young man should be filial at home and be respectful to elders outside his home. He should be earnest and truthful, loving all, and befriend those who have virtues. After doing so, if he has energy to spare, he can take part in the study of literature and the arts."[56] He placed the utmost emphasis on moral education and its practice. It could also be said that ancient China's moral education could replace others to be the only "knowledge." Dong Zhongshu said, "The knowledge that the sages were to talk about was not the knowledge of birds or beasts, but benevolence and righteousness; then they elaborated on this knowledge and sorted it into categories to help people understand the concepts and their attached meaning without confusion. That was what the sages valued."[57] Zhu Xi pointed out more concisely that, "Today's education does not expound the principle of the heaven, human ethics, or the sages' ideas but abruptly concentrates the mind on a blade of grass or a utensil. What on earth is this kind of knowledge?"[58] Therefore, China's ancient educators focused on the cultivation of students' moral qualities and wholesome personality, encouraging students to defy steadfastly all brute forces, to be unswerving from principles even in poverty-stricken or lowly condition, to sacrifice for justice, to repay their country with supreme loyalty, to serve their parents filially, to respect teachers and elders, to foster interpersonal relationships, and to be kind and upright men who could "bear the burden of righteousness on their shoulders as well as write excellent articles with their hand."[59]

The moral spirit in ancient educational thought enhanced the moral awareness of the people of China, forming several effective methods of moral education that can be used in the development of theory and the practice of moral education at present. However, the moral education content of the three cardinal guides and five virtues emphasized in ancient educational thought and the practice of replacing other forms of education with moral education must be abandoned.

3. The Spirit of Harmony

The Chinese nation is a tolerant and peaceful nation. Mr. Cai Yuanpei once observed that the Chinese national character "best accords with the Confucian doctrine of the mean."[60] Corresponding to this, China's ancient educational thinkers focused on cultivating students to pursue harmony and a broad mind.

The ideas of "harmony in diversity" and "taking proper measures according to different situations" advocated by Confucius, and the tenet of *The Doctrine of Mean* that "all things are to be nourished together without injuring one another; the courses of the seasons, the sun, and the moon are pursued without any collision among them" had produced an important influence in educational practice. They also formed the Chinese national tradition of focusing on harmony between people, between people and nature, between people and society, and even between countries. The Western missionary Matteo Ricci, after studying in detail the four-thousand-year history of China, observed that the Chinese "have no ambition of conquering, which is significantly different from the Europeans." This reflects the Chinese national spirit of pursuing peace and harmony, which enabled the Chinese to revere the state of absorbing the gentle and cultivated style with self-restraint, the impartial and harmonious while maintaining diversified thinking patterns, and the teacher–student relationship, in which the students respect the teacher, the teacher in return loves the students, and all exchange ideas with one an other. The spirit of harmony in ancient educational thought fostered the unique psychological state of the people of China, enabling them to view life and society from an optimistic and macro perspective and to determine their own destiny through the insight of everything in the world. If they are frustrated in life, they can find a remedy from the unity with heaven; if they encounter injustice in the outside world, they can seek balance in the internal mind. Thus, an incomparable psychological defense mechanism is established. However, at the same time, one may lack the motivation and mechanism of competition or the challenging spirit of taking initiative, and even make concessions to avoid conflict, which should be taken into consideration when promoting the spirit of harmony.

4. The Spirit of the Group

Emphasizing group education and benefit for the whole was one notable trait of China's ancient educational thought, as well as a trait closely related to moral spirit and the spirit of harmony. The supreme aim of moral education, "Ren" (benevolence), promoted by Confucius, was targeted at the level of the interpersonal relationship and the group. As for the sayings that those who are benevolent "love all"[61] and "now the benevolent man, wishing himself to be established, seeks also to establish others; wishing himself to be successful, he seeks also the success of others,"[62] was not a guide to developing an independent personality, but rather describes the ethical obligation of the individual, as a member of a group, toward the group. The interpersonal relationships in ancient China can be divided into four basic types: the other–self relation of kinship, the other–self relation of emperor to minister, the other–self relation of bosom friends, and the other–self relation of encountered strangers.[63]

These four types of relationships formed an organic unity, covering all inter-personal communication in ancient society. Further, the primary purpose of education at the time was to make people understand and master the ethical standards system that defined these relationships. In other words, the core of China's ancient educational thought was to teach people to handle various rela-tionships in order to survive and develop in their group.

The spirit of the group in ancient educational thought formed the individ-ual's sense of responsibility and obligation toward others, including the group and society, as well as the sense of affiliation that considered all people of the world as compatriots. However, due to the excessive emphasis on the spirit of the group, the individual benefit was relatively neglected, which hindered the development of individual creativity and obscured the individual in the group. Therefore, group education at present should not be the reproduction of his-torical group education, but should "integrate the individual's independent personality needed for the development of modern society into the social-istic collective education, combining personality, group character, and national character properly."[64]

5. The Human-Oriented Spirit

In ancient China, from the saying "man is the wisest of all creatures" in *Shang Shu: Tai Shi* (the *Great Speech*) to Guan Zhong's proposition that "to start obtaining the dominant position, one should consider the people first,"[65] and to the words said by Gong Zizhen in *Shi Feng* (*Ideas about the Wind*) in the Late Qing Dynasty that "only with humanity did the most ignorant heaven and earth become intelligent," the tradition of humanism has lasted for thousands of years. In the past, people felt that China's ancient educational thought had the fatal defect of "having no regard for people," which actually judged China's humanism by the standard of individual supremacy in the Western humanist tradition. In fact, Eastern humanism and Western humanism have their own characteristics. Humanism in Western educational thought is independent, self-centered, and self-fulfilling, while humanism in China's ancient educa-tional thought is collaborative, other-centered, and self-improving. China's ancient education was directed by just this kind of humanism.

The human-oriented spirit of ancient educational thought penetrated into all corners of social life, such as through its emphasis on the group over the individual and its people-first view in political life. Emperor Taizong of the Tang Dynasty believed that "water can both carry a boat and overturn it," rec-ognizing that "everything stands on its foundation; the country stands with the people as its foundation, while the people stand with clothing and food as their foundation."[66] In moral life, the human-oriented spirit also empha-sized continuous self-improvement, considered people's cultivation and development as a continuous, lifelong process, and encouraged people to follow the example of sages such as Yao and Shun to introspect and constantly strive to become stronger. However, due to its excessive emphasis on collaboration and self-improvement, ancient educational thought neglected another aspect. Therefore, in promoting the ancient human-oriented spirit, we should also consider the reasonable core of the humanistic spirit in Western educational thought, focusing not only on the cultivation of students' independence, but also on their collaborative spirit, paying attention not only to the restraint of their external behaviors, but also to their ambition for self-improvement.

In summary, research on ancient educational thought is never conducted with the intention to simply muse over past things or to judge specific aspects, but in an effort to establish significance for modern education, in order to establish a foundation for a system of modern educational theories, to form educational ideas with national characteristics, and to contribute to the guidance of educational practices.

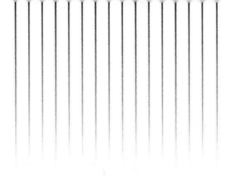

3

The Theoretical Basis of China's Ancient Educational Thought

The generation and development of any school of educational thought are based on certain theories. Any educator or school of educational thought will express a general view of education differently from the theoretical basis of the educator or school of thought, thus forming the nature and features of educational thought. The theoretical basis of China's ancient educational thought derives from three main fields: the theory of governing (a discussion of the relationships among education, politics, and the economy in society), the theory of humanity (a discussion of the dialectical relationship between education and the development of people), and the conception of talents (a discussion of the purpose and value of education). The theoretical basis of China's ancient educational thought is similar to a discussion of the modern philosophy of education with regard to its questions about the function and value of education.

Theory of Governing: Education and Social Development
What are the fundamental reasons for peace and chaos, and for the rise and fall of a country? What is the role of education? In terms of the educational theory, we must start with the so-called theory of governing. As mentioned earlier, in the germination stage of China's ancient educational thought, the social and political function of education was honored. The "instruction, protection,

and education" of the people proposed by Duke Zhou was aimed at keeping the people in their place, as well as honest and devotional. He proposed that "morality should be promoted and punishment should be carried out cautiously" and that moral education should come before punishment. This belief had a direct influence on the ancient tradition of moral governing. Confucius, in the Pre-Qin Period, further developed Duke Zhou's theory. He expounded the different functions of punishment and edification in reassuring the people that, "If you govern the people by law and control them by punishment, they will avoid crime but will have no personal sense of shame. If you govern them by means of virtue and control them with propriety, they will gain their own sense of shame and submit themselves to you."[1] He held that to govern the people by law and punishment would make them avoid crime, but with no sense of personal shame.

On the other hand, to nurture the people through edification and etiquette would make them gain a sense of shame as well as make them submissive. Accordingly, Confucius emphasized the edification of people and proposed that governing must start with teaching people, which can be seen from his words when he said, "Only when good men have instructed the people for seven years, may they take up arms,"[2] "To lead untrained people into battle is the same as throwing them away,"[3] and "To execute someone without explaining what they did wrong is cruelty."[4] Moreover, through Ran You's questions, Confucius put forth the concept of governing of being "populous, rich, and educated." The Analects of Confucius: Zilu states:

> When the Master went to Wei, Ran You drove his carriage. Confucius said, "How populous it is here!" Ran You said, "Once there are so many people, what should be done?" "Enrich them," was the reply. "And when they have been enriched, what more shall be done?" Confucius said, "Educate them."

This is the earliest expression of the relationship between education and the economy in ancient China. Confucius held that in order to govern a country well, one must first have abundant labor, that is, the country must be populous, and then production should be promoted in order to make people rich in clothing and food. Education was then conducted based on the people's abundance and wealth. From this view, it can be seen that the economy should be developed prior to the education system, and also that education and the economy affect each other.

As the "true heir" and "Second Sage" of Confucianism, Mencius inherited and developed Confucius' theory of governing. He held that it was not "the exterior and interior walls being incomplete, or the supply of offensive and defensive weapons being insufficient" that constituted the real calamity; nor was it that "arable land was not being extended or that stores and wealth were not being accumulated." Rather, it was the lack of education. "When superiors do not observe the rules of propriety, and inferiors do not learn, seditious people spring up, and the state perishes in no time,"[5] thus causing the country to be in a state of unrest. Therefore, he pointed out that "Good government does not gain hold of the people so much as good education. Good government is feared by the people, while good education is loved by them. Good government gains the people's wealth, while good education gains their hearts."[6] In terms of educational content, Mencius set the administration of state affairs and the stabilization of the society as the key priorities, that is, the "human relations" of "kinship between father and son, righteousness between emperor and minister, distinction between husband and wife, sequence between elder and younger, as well as trust between friends." Only when civilians have kinship, love, and trust between each other will they choose not to "rebel against their superiors."

Xuncius, the master of the Confucian School in the Pre-Qin Period, related education to the fate of a country more clearly. He said, "A prospering country respects teachers; respecting teachers, the law and norms can be maintained. A declining country disdains teachers; disdaining teachers, the people will indulge themselves; people indulging themselves, the laws and norms will break down."[7] He held that without respect for teachers or the development of education, people will be indulgent and break the law, thus leading to the country's decay.

Of the early Confucian works, those which had the most detailed elaboration on the relationship between education and social development are the articles "The Great Learning" and "The Records on the Subject of Learning" in the *Book of Rites*. "The Great Learning" states:

The ancients, who wished for illustrious virtue throughout the kingdom, first ruled their own states well. Wishing to rule their states well, they first regulated their families. Wishing to regulate their families, they first cultivated themselves. Wishing to cultivate themselves, they first rectified their hearts. Wishing to rectify their hearts, they first sought to be sincere in their thoughts. Wishing to be sincere in their thoughts, they first extended their knowledge to the utmost level. Such extension of knowledge lay in the investigation of things, and once things were investigated, knowledge became complete. Once their knowledge became complete, their thoughts were sincere. Once their thoughts became sincere, their hearts became rectified. Once their hearts became rectified, they themselves became cultivated. Once they themselves became cultivated, their families became regulated. Once their families became regulated, their states became rightly governed. Once their states became rightly governed, the whole kingdom was made tranquil and happy.

Since "The Great Learning" was the Confucian treatise on college education, the above paragraph reveals eight steps in college education: investigation of things, extension of knowledge, sincerity of thought, rectification of heart, cultivation of personality, regulation of family, right governance of the state, and tranquility for the whole kingdom. Education was undoubtedly the link among all of these elements. "The Records on the Subject of Learning" states:

> When a ruler is concerned that his measures should be in accordance with the law, and he seeks for the (assistance of the) good and upright, this is sufficient to secure him a considerable reputation, but not enough to move the multitudes. When he cultivates the society of the worthy and tries to embody the views of those who are remote (from the court), this is sufficient to move the multitudes, but not to transform the people. If he wishes to transform the people and to perfect their manners and customs, then he must start from education.
>
> The jade uncut will not form a vessel for use, and if men do not learn, they will not know the way (in which they should go). On this account, the ancient kings, when establishing states and governing the people, made education and schools a primary objective. As it is said in the *Charge to Yue*, "Thoughts from first to last should be fixed on learning."

The first paragraph above means that it is not enough for a ruler to have foresight, amass talents, and respect the wise. To edify his people and establish sound social customs demands the development of school education. The second paragraph means that just as jade must be cut to form a vessel for use, people become sensible only through school education. To establish a country and rule his people, a ruler must start from school education. Therefore, "The Records on the Subject of Learning" asks people to remember the famous quote from *Shangshu: Charge to Yue*: "Thoughts from first to last should be fixed on learning."

The Mohists also emphasized the relationship between education and social development. For example, Mo Di said, "With all their strength unused, they would not help one another; with all unused supplies rotting and fermenting, they would not share with one another; hiding the excellent Dao (Way) they would not show it to others. As a result of this, the hungry are not fed, the cold are not clothed, and the disturbed are not given order."[8] He held that without emphasis on education, the political system will not stabilize, and the economy will not develop. He also said, "Common people in the world now know little about righteousness. Naturally, those who teach them righteousness deserve merit."[9] The theory of "loving all and benefiting mutually" requested people to act as follows: if they had strength, they could help others; if they had wealth, they could share with others; if they had proper ways (knowledge), they could teach others.

Moreover, the Mohists noted the significance of education in promoting social productivity. In *Lu's Question, Lu Wen* recorded a story as follows: A farmer, who was also a hermit who lived alone, named Wu Lv said to Mo Di, "Righteousness is just righteousness. Why do people need all the verbosity?" Mo Di asked in return, "Suppose the world does not know how to plow. Then who has more merit, the man who teaches people to plow, or he who does not teach people to plow but simply plows for himself?" Wu Lv admitted, "He who teaches others to plow deserves more merit." This was actually the very conclusion that Mo-tse came to.

Although the Legalists advocated ruling a country by law and rejected the private education system proposed by the Confucians, they actually emphasized the significance of social education in another aspect. Specifically, they stressed the significance of legal education for the prosperity of the country and the peace of the people. The Legalist concept of "educating through law and teaching by officials" was targeted to the problems of governing society. For example, *Guanzi* said, "If the emperor can share his great kindness and benefit, he can be close to the people; if he is wise and respects etiquette, he can educate the people. He needs to regulate himself in order to lead the people, to set rules and regulations in order to keep watch on the people, and to appoint officials in the counties in order to guide the people. Then he can restrain them with orders, encourage them with awards, and deter them with punishment. In this way, the people are willing to do good deeds, and rebellious behavior will not occur anywhere."[10] These ideas were very similar to the Confucian theory of education before punishment.

The Daoists, on the surface, also negated the social function of education as a social phenomenon. Originator Laozi stated directly, "When the Great Dao ceased to be observed, benevolence and righteousness came into vogue. (Then) appeared wisdom and shrewdness, and there ensued great hypocrisy. When harmony no longer prevailed throughout the six kinships, filial sons found their manifestation; when the states and clans fell into disorder, loyal ministers appeared."[11] He held that the inevitable result of the Confucian cultivation of the qualities of wisdom, benevolence, righteousness, filial piety, and tenderheartedness was the desertion of the Great Dao, causing unrest in the family and chaos in the country. However, the Daoists who negated education, including Laozi, Zhuangzi, and those of the School of Emperor Huang and Laozi, all undertook educational activities. They were willing to offer education to all disciples who came to them seeking knowledge. Moreover, their opinions of wu-wei (no deliberate action), contentment, and pacifism were in themselves positive educational activities. It was these educational activities that nurtured Daoist educational thought.

In the Han Dynasty, Dong Zhongshu continued the Confucian tradition of "applying moral education instead of punishment" of the Pre-Qin Period, proposing that "education is the fundamental element of government, while prison is incidental."[12] He regarded education as the fundamental foundation of governing a country and reassuring its people. He held that to effectively prevent the people from "rebelling against their superiors," social edification had to be built up like a dam. He said:

The multitudes pursuing benefit is like water flowing downward; without edification as a dam to prevent flooding, the people cannot be stopped. Therefore, with edification accomplished and the evildoings stopped, the dam will stand in good condition; but if edification is deserted and the evildoings, which cannot be controlled by punishment, the dam is then destroyed.[13]

The edification of the governing of society was realized through the psychological mechanism of internalization. This means that under the influence of edification, the people would have a sense of shame and reach the state of "a harmonious kingdom, in which the people are living in peace and pleasure and are righteous, and all are at their proper status, behave with etiquette, and accord naturally with heavenly principles."[14]

Wang Chong, though he strongly rebuked the orthodox Confucianism represented by Dong Zhongshu, had similar views in emphasizing the social functions of edification. He pointed out that people educated with etiquette and righteousness "have noble ambitions and outstanding behavior, pursue no official rank or profit,"[15] and can "be honest with few desires" under any circumstances, conceiving no evil ideas. Therefore, he opposed the view of "setting punishment first in a chaotic society" and "setting etiquette as the dominant feature of a peaceful society," holding that the education of etiquette and righteousness, as well as the special effect of school education, should be stressed at all times. He said, "The supreme method does not abolish officials who administer school affairs, nor does it eliminate those administering imprisonment, but educates ordinary people with etiquette. Encouraged through school education at first and then governed by laws, people, even with Danzhu's moral character, could also be exhorted to do good deeds."[16] It can be seen that the function of school education was "to first encourage" as a preventive measure, while legal restraint was "to prevent afterward" what could have happened. Combining these two functions can enable a society to develop soundly.

In the period of the Wei and Jin Dynasties, Fu Xuan elaborated on the social function of education from the different perspectives of a country's stability and prosperity. He emphasized the social and economic foundation of education, holding that "rich people tend to be attached to their native land and value their home, and therefore respect their superiors and pursue education; poor people tend to endanger their hometown and pay little attention to their home, thus gathering to act in rebellion." If the people were rich and well educated, they would "respect scholars and value learning, and they would be righteous."[17] This belief established the foundation for the idea of governing a state and tranquilizing the kingdom. On the other hand, a prosperous and powerful country could not be separated from education. Since developing schools and cultivating talents were seen as the primary ways to vitalize a country, Fu Xuan also said that "it lies in people to vitalize a country," and "it lies in education to promote moral cultivation."[18]

In the Tang Dynasty, when developing Mencius's proposition of "gathering the talents of the world to educate them," Han Yu quoted Mencius, saying, "A noble man has three things in which he delights, and to win the world with virtues is not one of them. One of the three delightful things was gathering all the talents to educate them. These were all the best theories of the sages and wise men and should be followed today. However, who then can educate all the talents in the long term? Should it be our emperor or our prime minister? It is fortunate that society is peaceful at present, all the officials are dutiful in their positions, and the issues of wealth, food, and military are not worrying the royal court. When discussing the governing methods for a country, nothing is more important than this (education)."[19] He considered that the most important duty for a ruler was to cultivate talents, especially in times of peace, and he regarded the education of all the talents as a top priority, believing that these were the keys to managing a country.

In the Northern Song Dynasty, Wang Anshi broke the pattern of discussing education's social function on the basis of social edification followed by previous scholars. He stressed the function of school education, proposing the education-reforming claim that "the world cannot exist without government or education for just one day, and there cannot be even one day during which the world runs without schools."[20] He believed that school had to be the main core of the educational cause. In *A Request for the Reform of the Imperial Examination*, he said, "The selection of officials in ancient times was all based on school. Therefore, with unified moral principles set at the upper level, and customs then formed down among the people, the talents selected were capable of outstanding achievements. Since the loss of the grace of the former emperor, the education and cultivation of talents have had no model to follow. The scholars, though having excellent qualities, cannot be cultivated by school, teachers, or friends, which is a concern of those who discuss government. If we want to restore the ancient (talent selection) system without its defects, the worry is that there is no progressive way to do so. The best way to start is with the elimination of essays with defects in rhyme and antithesis. First, the articles that stress the "four tones," "eight ills," and parallelism should be abolished to concentrate the learners' minds on the study of classics, preparing for the establishment of schools by the government." Through replacing the imperial examination by school education, the phenomenon of "moral principles unified at the upper level and customs formed down among the people" was formed. Further, the problem that the imperial examination "at the higher level, is not great enough to rule the world, and at the lower level, will not be used in the governance of the world"[21] was solved.

Different from most Confucians, who tended to promote morality instead of punishment, the Neo-Confucians in the Song Dynasty held that neither punishment nor education could be deserted in the maintenance of feudal governance; moreover, they paid much attention to the function of vigorous law and punishment. The Cheng brothers, Cheng Hao and Cheng Yi, said, "Enlightenment education should be delivered to people for their lack of knowledge in laws. Laws should be clarified and advertised; thus, the fear of punishments can foster the awe of laws in people and make them submit to guidance and education."[22] Zhu Xi also said, "Ignorance is the ruler's tool for governing. Punishment is the assisting measurement. Morality and etiquette are the fundamental elements of governance, whereas morality is the fundamental element of etiquette. They supplement each other and any one among them cannot be biased. However, governance and punishment can only keep the people away from crime, while morality and etiquette can encourage the people to be motivated to be kind from within."[23] They held that common people were born to be ignorant, foolish, and stubborn, inclined to behave unscrupulously and commit all manner of crimes. They believed that only with rigorous law and punishment to restrain them could the commoners be subdued, thus generating no evil intentions to commit crimes. The function of punishment was to subdue people and prevent them from taking part in criminal activities; the function of edification was to promote people to behave well and "be naturally kind." In the Neo-Confucians' view, punishment was the basis of education, and only by "setting the punishment" could "education be implemented."[24]

The Cheng brothers said, "At the beginning of enlightening the ignorant people, they must be subdued by punishment, thus freeing their shackles, or restraint, of ignorance. Without freeing the shackles of ignorance, the education of kindness cannot begin. Subdued by punishment and prohibitions, though they may not understand the reason, they may be obedient out of fear and dare not indulge in their ignorant desires. Afterward, they may gradually know the good way and correct their false mind, and thus customs may be changed."[25] This means that before the people are enlightened, it is hard for them to learn through edification; only with punishment forcing them to abide by the law can they form certain habits, which lay the foundation for them to accept edification.

Therefore, "punishment" in the Neo-Confucian sense included the element of "edification." Cheng Yi and Cheng Hao once clearly pointed out this view, saying, "The methods of enlightenment include setting limitations, defining punishment, and rectifying the law in order to make the people follow it, and then edifying them gradually. Carrying out punishment suddenly at the beginning of enlightenment is equal to killing the people without instructing them. It is better to set up laws and punishment, which will be explained to the people. Therefore, later generations, when talking about punishment, will not know that it actually embodied edification in the past."[26] The Neo-Confucians in the Song Dynasty held that although punishment and edification had significant functions in maintaining social stability and preventing crime, and that to a certain degree punishment was a necessary precondition for edification, in terms of their importance, edification was more important. Zhu Xi said, "Governance and punishment keep the people from committing crimes. But without morality and etiquette, their false intentions cannot be rectified."[27] Cheng Yi also said, "Rigorous punishment can only work for a while; high ranks and generous rewards cannot shelter later generations. But when good or ill fame is settled, the reputation of honor or humility will be passed on and on. All the former virtuous emperors and ministers encouraged social morality with this saying."[28] They thought that the function of punishment was to prevent people from committing crimes, but that this was only a means of external regulation. Because of this, it could not be counted on as a fully proved measurement and had limited effect. Only through edification could people "rectify their false intentions" and move on to do good deeds with the encouragement of fame and an honorable reputation, thus forming a sound social morality and fundamentally severing people's intentions of committing crimes.

In the period of the late Ming Dynasty and early Qing Dynasty, Wang Fuzhi proposed his own theory of governing when elaborating Mencius's view that "good governance gains the people's wealth and good education gains the people's hearts." He said:

When [the people] are afraid, no one dares resist. Since the ruler has already designated their tribute of what can be spared from their possessions, he obtains their wealth. If he obtains their wealth when the people do not know goodness, how can they generate loyalty and affection? Only by loving the people can the ruler encourage the people with education, and can the people come to not place blame on the ruler but dedicate themselves with their loyalty and filial piety. This is obtaining the people's hearts. If the ruler obtains the people's hearts and unite them, will people delay the tribute?

Fear will disappear where governance cannot work, whereas love will reach the place where education has not yet been established. Obtaining wealth will lose the hearts of people. Obtaining people's hearts, which are infinite, will keep the people from leaving. Aren't the two significantly different in obtaining the people in terms of scale and duration?[29]

The above means that good governance always makes the people fear the government, while good education can make them love the government. Good governance always forces the people to pay their wealth as tribute, but good education will enable the people to offer their wealth willingly. "The effect of political governance is limited, passive, and temporary; the effect of education is far-reaching, automatic, and long-lasting."[30]

Therefore, on governing the country and stabilizing society, education has a crucial effect, which is irreplaceable by political governance. Another famous educator, Yan Yuan of the period of the late Ming Dynasty and early Qing Dynasty, summarized his political ideal into three aspects: enriching, strengthening, and stabilizing the country. He said, "You can enrich the country with seven words: land reclamation, land equalization, water conservancy development. You can strengthen the country with six words: people as soldiers, officials as generals. You can stabilize the country with nine words: selecting talents, studying great classics, promoting rituals and music."[31] He felt that agriculture was the foundation of developing the state economy, the military was the condition for a country's prosperity, and education was the fundamental element of a country's long-lasting stability. Therefore, he attached great importance to educational activities, which he believed nurtured the people: "Generally, learning is the fundamental element of talents; talents are the fundamental element of governance; governance is the fundamental element of people's lives. Without learning, there will be no talents; without talents, there will be no good governance; without good governance, there will be no stability, and people will not be able to survive. How does this influence the tradition of learning? How does this influence social morality?"[32] These statements indicate that only through education can the political talents who are courteous and sensible, the military talents who are smart and brave, and the practical talents who can administer state affairs be cultivated. Through the influence of the talents on social politics and the economy, the social ideals of enriching the country, strengthening the people, and governing and stabilizing society can be realized.

In conclusion, China's ancient educators' theories of governing were dominated by Confucianism, and their intention was to emphasize the social function of education and the significance of education for the prosperity of the state and governance, as well as social development. China's ancient educational thought had a more utilitarian awareness to serve the needs of political, economic, and social stability.

The Theory of Humanity: Education and the Development of People

Since every view of education is related to the educator's hypothesis and opinion about humanity, the theory of humanity is also an important theoretical foundation of educational thought. American educational psychologist Edward Thorndike once said that an important duty for educational researchers was to provide scientific knowledge to change human individuals, that is, to reveal the nature of human individuals before they were educated, as well as to change the nature of individuals and to develop individual differences through education.

In ancient China, it was Confucius who first discussed the question of humanity. His proposition that "by nature, men are similar; by practice, men are wide apart"[33] provided the foundation for the formation of various theories of humanity. The so-called "similar human nature" Confucius mentioned indicates his belief that people are born with similar qualities or characteristics. "Growing apart by practice" means that people grow different from one another through nurture and learning. According to their own understanding, educators in later generations derived such theories as Mencius's "theory of good human nature" and Xuncius's "theory of evil human nature" through Confucius' discussion of being "born with knowledge" and "learning to acquire knowledge."[34] Mencius's "theory of good human nature" held that people were born with four "good beginnings," including compassion, shame, modesty, and knowing the difference between right and wrong. If they were expanded and enriched, four further qualities could be developed, including benevolence, righteousness, propriety, and wisdom. The nurturing of education and the initiative of individual effort acted as the key elements of the process of developing the "good beginnings" into the four qualities. But the "good beginnings" provided just the possibility of the development of kindness; it is through education and individual effort that kindness becomes both real and necessary.

In contrast, Xuncius made the proposition that "people's nature tends to the evil side, and their kind deeds are contrived," holding that the original human nature was evil and had no "good beginnings" of compassion, shame, modesty, and knowing the difference between right and wrong. Rather, original human nature is characterized by a nature of profit orientation, fighting to obtain wealth, jealousy, hatred, cruelty, and licentiousness. Only by "changing nature" through the influence of living environment and education could evil humans become good. The views of good versus evil human nature espoused by Mencius's and Xuncius's different theories of human nature belong to the field of ethical thought.. The theoretical basis of China's ancient educational thought primarily involves the following two aspects.

1. Hypothesis About the Formation of Human Nature: The Endowment of Qi and Habitual Practice

As early as more than 2,000 years ago, the theory of Qi (natural energy), that is Yin and Yang, the Five Elements of ancient China, was developed. This theory would be elaborated on by many educational thinkers in later generations to establish their own academic theories, including the theory of the endowment of Qi in human nature. The substance of the theory of Qi endowment had three meanings: first, everything in the universe has its own nature, which originated from the movement of the Qi of heaven and earth; second, as with substances, humans also have their own nature, which is the result of nurturing by the Qi of heaven, earth, and Yin and Yang; third, due to the differences in people's Qi endowed at birth, complete or incomplete, pure or turbid, light or dark, thick or thin, many or few, human nature is then different among individuals: smart or stupid, virtuous or unworthy, noble or lowly, long- or short-living. In brief, Qi endowment refers to people's endowment of Qi at birth, which generally means it is a genetic element. The concept of Qi endowment was first discussed in *Han Feizi: Annotations of Laozi*: "Life and death are determined by Qi endowment." This text regarded Qi endowment as the origin of people's lives.

Although in the Han Dynasty, Wang Chong publicly declared war on superstition, he also wrote that, "People are born by the endowment of Qi and grow up with Qi inside. They become noble if their Qi endowment is noble or become lowly if their Qi endowment is lowly."[35] He also said, "Due to the Qi of the five virtues (benevolence, righteousness, propriety, wisdom, and trustworthiness) contained within the five human internal organs, people have these five virtues within them. If the Qi endowed in an individual is thin and few, his virtues and behaviors are inferior to those of kind people. This is similar to the taste of wine: some are strong, some are light. This difference in taste is caused not by different wine-making techniques but by different quantities of yeast. Therefore, the taste of wine is caused by the yeast; similarly, the kind or evil nature of humans is caused by the Qi. The intelligence of a person depends on the quantity of Qi endowed from heaven."[36] In this way, Wang Chong defined the genetic element of Qi endowment as the dominant element determining human nature, including social character. Of course, Wang Chong did not regard this kind of human nature as the final human nature; rather, he affirmed the significance of environment and education in the development of human nature, emphasizing the potential for variability.

The Neo-Confucians of the Song Dynasty proposed the theory of a dual human nature, which distinguished the nature of temperament from the nature of heavenly destiny. For example, the Cheng brothers held that the origin of human nature was the pure truth, which was supreme good, like water. This was the nature of heavenly destiny, which was the same for any individual, from Yao and Shun to ordinary people. The abstract nature of heavenly destiny descended to the human body through the medium of Qi; nature formed when humans took in this Qi as the so-called nature of temperament. The nature of temperament and the nature of heavenly destiny together composed the true human nature. When the abstract nature of heavenly destiny was combined with the real nature of temperament, people's individual differences in the aspects of intelligence, temperament, and character would manifest themselves. When elaborating the theory of Qi endowment of Zhang Zai and the Cheng brothers, Zhu Xi reinforced the above views, saying, "Those who are endowed with the essence of Qi will become sages or virtuous men and will obtain complete and correct truth. Those who are endowed with clear Qi will become valiant men; those with honest Qi will be mild; those with pure and lofty Qi will be noble; those with abundant Qi will be rich; those with long-lasting Qi will be long-living; those with declining, thin, and turbid Qi will be stupid, unworthy, greedy, lowly, and short-living."[37]

Further, with the theory of Qi endowment, he interpreted the four people categorized by Confucius, including those who were "born with knowledge," those who are "learning to know," those who are "learning because of confusion," and those who are "confused but unwilling to learn." He held that the four categories were caused by the Qi endowment, whether "clear and pure" or with "dross." Chen Chun, a brilliant disciple of Zhu Xi in his late years, made a complete and systematic conclusion of Qi endowment in the *Annotation of Beixi: Nature*, putting forward the basic idea of the theory of Qi endowment. First, he affirmed the significance of Qi endowment in the formation of individual differences, holding that "the differences of people lie in the difference in their endowment of Qi," and "staunch people have more Yang Qi; weak people more Yin Qi; ill-tempered people are endowed with evil Yang Qi; treacherous people are endowed with evil Yin Qi; some are sophisticated and flexible; some are stupid and stubborn, heeding no good words, just like animals; these differences are all caused by Qi endowment." Obviously, this idea exaggerated the influence of genetics on people's development. Second, he pointed out the variability of human nature.

Though the theory of Qi endowment exaggerated the decisive influence of Qi, it did not advocate the theory of destiny, which put humans in a helpless state, their worth determined by their Qi endowment, but instead affirmed the variability of human nature. Chen Chun stated that "though one may be lowly and stupid, he can become a good person." When a person could put all his effort into "learning a hundred times to acquire what others learn only once, learning a thousand times to acquire what others learn only ten times," he could correct the deficiency of his Qi endowment and develop soundly. It is because of these ideas that the scholars who advocated the theory of Qi endowment, such as Wang Chong, the Cheng brothers, Zhu Xi, and Dai Zhen, in later times, all emphasized the significance of education, as well as individual learning.

Confucius proposition that "by nature, men are similar; by practice, men are wide apart" did not gain enough attention in the long-term contention between the theories of good and evil human nature. It was the elaboration of Wang Anshi that brought out its brilliance, gradually making it mainstream in theories of human nature. He held that the similar human nature of Confucius theory referred only to the similarity of human nature at birth, which then grew wider apart due to differences in practice. Since practice acted as the key element in the formation and development of human nature, "practice must be carried out cautiously."[38] Further, through his view of "the invariability of superior wisdom and extreme stupidity," Confucius made a unique comment that superior wisdom and extreme stupidity were not inherently invariable but determined by the practice of a person: if a person does good deeds unremittingly, he will gain superior wisdom; otherwise, he will be reduced to extreme stupidity.[39]

In the Ming Dynasty, Wang Tingxiang stressed the physical element of gifts, in terms of the origin of human nature, emphasizing the social element of "habitual practice," in terms of the development of human nature. He proposed that "one's nature is formed by one's practice"[40] and affirmed that "learning can change one's temperament."[41] He held that although one's endowed nature might be different from another's, it could be altered to reach the supreme good state through creating a sound social environment, as well as through teaching and learning.[42]

Wang Fuzhi also furthered the tradition advocating the theory of habitual practice, paying attention to the combination of nature and practice, emphasizing the significance of practice in people's development. He held that "nature is the heavenly way, whereas practice is the human way."[43] Nature is not invariable from birth but "becomes accomplished day by day,"[44] changing continuously. The formative process of human nature is the process of continuous practice, as well as the constant acquisition of educational and environmental influences.

As for the variability of human nature, Yan Yuan once provided an example, saying, "Oh! Adversity starts off concealed and is fostered through habitual practice. Born with the same ears, eyes, mouth, nose, limbs, and bones as the sages, one should be called an animal! When a piece of plain silk, after being dyed, is called red or black silk, is that its natural color? However, as the wisest among all beings, humans cannot be compared to silk. After being dyed, the silk still exists but cannot be returned to its original color. But as for the human, although extremely evil, if he is still alive, he still has the chance, depending on his mind, to restore himself through his efforts."[45] This means that the natures of humans and silk are equally good but different. Silk cannot return to its original color after being dyed, but a person, although "extremely evil," can be restored to his original kind nature if he makes unremitting efforts.

In terms of the formation of human nature, though the theory of Qi endowment and the theory of habitual practice are different in their emphasis on nature versus nurture, respectively, the two theories are not mutually exclusive. Their common points lie in their admission of the variability of human nature and the significance of education in people's development. Dai Zhen, an educator in the Qing Dynasty, combined the two theories well. He said, "The nourishment of food can help maintain the blood and Qi in people's bodies. The nourished Qi and the originally endowed Qi both originate from heaven and earth. Therefore, although the nourishment is from the outside, it can be transformed into blood and Qi to benefit the inside. But if there is no endowed Qi inside, it cannot simply be nourished from the outside. It is the same with the significance of learning morality. With one's original morality, learning to understand the morality of the ancient sages is to obtain nourishment from the ancient sages' words to benefit one's own morality."[46] In Dai Zhen's view, Qi is both endowed and developed through practice. The inborn Qi endowment was considered the internal basis for human nature, which later had to be nourished by outer Qi in order to nurse the endowed Qi and benefit one's personal morality, thus enabling human nature to develop completely. It can be seen that in terms of people's development, Dai Zhen followed a theory that emphasized heredity and the environment, with an emphasis on education. This theory combined a natural element or internal base with a nurtured element or external condition.

2. Methods to Cultivate Human Nature: Internal Exploration and External Acquisition

In terms of the methods to cultivate human nature, there were two different voices among China's ancient educators: internal exploration and external acquisition. The method of internal exploration held that knowledge, intelligence, and virtue were inherent in the hearts of people. Accordingly, the method to cultivate human nature was to explore the heart. The method of external acquisition held that knowledge, intelligence, and virtue were not inborn but were acquired under the influence of the external conditions. Accordingly, the method to cultivate human nature was to be influenced by the outside world.

Mencius might be the first educational thinker who distinguished between internal exploration and external acquisition. He said, "Benevolence, righteousness, propriety, and wisdom are not acquired from the outside but are inherent."[47] He regarded the four good beginnings as seeds bred in people's hearts, which could be maintained and developed through methods of internal exploration, including "expanding and filling," "restoring the lost heart," "nurturing the inner noble spirit," and "having few desires to cultivate the heart."

In the Northern Song Dynasty, Shao Yong further developed Mencius's theory of internal exploration, proposing the concept of observing objects. He explained that although people's sensory organs, such as the ears, eyes, mouth, and nose, perceive things, the observation of objects does not need the above organs. Rather, the observation of objects requires internal "retrospection."[48] The method of retrospection is very similar to the intuitive understanding of Zen Buddhism. Shao Yong said, "The problem of learning and cultivating the heart lies in the deviation from the straight way. Detaching from greed, following the straight way, and acting with complete sincerity will get people across to every corner. The way to heaven is straight, which requires people to reach it the straight way. To attempt to reach heaven with schemes through a winding way is to subdue heaven and earth and follow human desires. Is that not more difficult?"[49] Obviously, to truly obtain knowledge and master the law of nature depends not on the social practice of external acquisition, education, or people's wisdom, but on activities of internal retrospection, such as no thought and wu-wei.

The Cheng brothers also advocated the theory of internal exploration. They held that the process of learning was in itself the process of internal exploration: "Learning is to explore internally. To explore the outside instead of the inside is not the learning of the sages…. To explore the incidental instead of the fundamental is not the learning of the sages."[50] One of the Cheng brothers' students, Xie Liangzuo, was, at the beginning, quite full of the spirit of external acquisition. He "at first learned mainly through collecting and remembering information, and, with his self-considered profound knowledge, could recite historical books without any omission." But the Cheng brothers evaluated him as "sapping his spirit by seeking pleasure."[51] They paid much attention to the cultivation of people's minds, holding that "learners need to explore not from afar but from within themselves, to understand human norms and then respect them."[52]

In the Ming Dynasty, Wang Shouren posed more directly the proposition that "there is nothing beyond the heart in the world," holding that "there are neither affairs nor reasons beyond the heart, so there should be no learning beyond the heart."[53] Therefore, the method of cultivating human nature was not through the exploration of objective knowledge from the outer world, but "recognition from one's own heart" and a process of internal exploration to "obtain conscience." He said, "The attainment of knowledge is not the expansion of one's knowledge as called by the later Confucians but the attainment of conscience from our hearts. The conscience is what Mencius described as 'the sense of right and wrong known by everyone'. This sense of right and wrong is known without thinking and without learning and is therefore called conscience. It is the heavenly nature and the original form of our heart, naturally wise and sensible. Every time we generate an idea, it is known by our conscience; whether it is good or evil can only be sensed by the conscience."[54]

If Mencius originated the theory of internal exploration in the Pre-Qin Period, Xuncius first advocated the theory of external acquisition. He held that learning through internal exploration, which required "thinking all day long," would not achieve any results, whereas learning through external acquisition could lead one to "gain knowledge in just a moment" and "make good use of objects."[55] It was believed that the latter could offer people incredible benefits. Only through hard study, good observation of objective matters, and mastering outside conditions could one succeed in his study and foster excellent qualities. Therefore, he said, "Hearing is better than not hearing, seeing is better than hearing, knowing is better than seeing, and acting is better than knowing."[56]

Chen Liang and Ye Shi, of the Utilitarianism School in the Southern Song Dynasty, also challenged the theory of internal exploration. For example, Chen Liang held that the Dao, as the objective law of things, could not be mastered through the effort of internal exploration, which "fiddles with the heart invisibly." Because "the Dao lies in the world" and cannot be detached from things, it is truly mastered only through contact with objective things and specific efforts of external acquisition, which "set principles according to objective things." Otherwise, it is "ended like dead wood and embers,"[57] benefiting neither the study of "investigating things to obtain knowledge" nor the development of people.

Ye Shi, on the other hand, proposed the "way of combining internal and external efforts," stressing the view that internal exploration and external acquisition could jointly promote people's development. He said, "The ears are acute in hearing and the eyes are clear in seeing without thinking, supplementing the inside from the outside; thinking is seen as farsighted, supplementing the outside from the inside. Therefore acute hearing acts as the philosophy, and bright sight acts as the strategy, while farsightedness acts as the wisdom. Appearance and words also come out from the inside to supplement the outside. None of the ancients became sages without the mutual supplement of the inside and the outside. Therefore, acute hearing and clear sight led among all the virtues possessed by Yao and Shun."[58] He held that both internal exploration and external acquisition were indispensable for the attainment of knowledge and morality and that both were effective methods cultivating human nature. However, if one should study the heart exclusively without the actual effort of external acquisition, as the Neo-Confucians advocated, one would not reach the state of "knowing the Dao" or of "entering into the moral realm of the sages," nor would one fully and completely develop.

Wang Tingxiang, an educator in the Ming Dynasty, also advocated the theory of external acquisition and criticized what he saw as the mistakes made by Cheng-Zhu Neo-Confucianism and Lu-Wang Mind Philosophy. He said, "The late scholars made two mistakes: one is their vain and vague lecturing; another is their effort to maintain hollowness and tranquility in order to preserve their hearts. Neither makes efforts in practicing or experiencing human affairs. In most cases, when something occurs, those who lecture in vain always lose the proper chance to take measures, because everything is changing, but lecturing cannot include all of them. And those who preserve their hearts in vain have no real use, because they are maintaining hollowness and loneliness, know little about the truth, and are unfamiliar with current trends."[59] He held that both the "vague lecturing" of Cheng-Zhu Neo-Confucianism and the "hollowness and tranquility to preserve the heart" of Lu-Wang Mind Philosophy were misguided in that they did not "make efforts in practicing or experiencing human affairs" and were lacking in the effort of external acquisition based on human practices. Therefore, these methods had little use and made no difference to matters, nor could they improve one's personality. He further pointed out that although people obtained knowledge through endowed physical intuition and sensory competence (which he called "heavenly knowledge"), people's cognitive abilities could not be developed without contact with the outside world and participating in social activities (the "knowledge of humanity"). Therefore, people should obtain true knowledge and develop through learning, thinking, making mistakes, and disambiguation.[60]

As with the theory of Qi endowment and the theory of habitual practice, the theories of internal exploration and external acquisition are not incompatible. In fact, the theory of internal exploration does not absolutely negate the need for external acquisition or human contact with objective things. Rather, it regarded limited external acquisition as the means to explore internally. Nor did the theory of external acquisition absolutely negate the need for introversive exploration. Rather, it placed more emphasis on the attainment of experience and knowledge to develop morality and personality through practice.

These differences in educational thought, when manifested in educational practices, represented the differences in educational styles and methods. For example, in moral education, the theory of internal exploration usually placed more emphasis on preserving the heart to cultivate human nature, taking precautions, and self-introspection and self-dispute, whereas the theory of external acquisition placed more emphasis on the influence of environment, observation by friends, and guidance from teachers.

The Development of Talents: The Purpose and Value of Education

The development of talents is the basic starting point for the theory of the purpose and value of education. In educational theories, the purpose of education is to cultivate the educated according to a certain quality demanded by society, regulating the standard of quality of particular talents. Determining the value of education evaluates whether educational activities can realize the purpose of education in order to cultivate certain talents needed by society, which, in other words, defines the social value of talents. The purpose and value of education are the starting point and end result of educational activities, in which they have the significance of macro-management and guidance. Of course, the purpose of education is not subjectively designed by educational thinkers but is a reflection of social politics and the economy; its successful realization is restrained not only by social politics and the economy, but also by the objective conditions of the educators and the educated.

The educational purpose of Confucius was to cultivate three kinds of talents, among whom the first was the virtuous man or sage. This is the supreme state of talents, as well as an ideal state seldom existing in real life. Therefore, he said, "I cannot meet the sages! It will be good if I can meet a virtuous man,"[61] and "The sage and the virtuous man, how dare I rank myself with them? It may simply be said of me that I strive to become such a person without satiety and teach others without weariness."[62]

The second talent to be cultivated was the noble, or complete, man, which was a higher state for a talent. It referred to a well-rounded person with noble virtues and was a talent typically achieved by high-ranking rulers. Confucius set many standards for this talent, such as "the cultivation of oneself in reverential carefulness," "the cultivation of oneself to give rest to others," and "the cultivation of oneself to give rest to all people."[63] Other standards included "to seek the truth instead of food," "to have anxiety lest one should not find truth, but not lest poverty should come upon one,"[64] "to seek no gratification of appetite from food or the appliances of ease in one's dwelling place," "to be earnest in one's actions and careful in one's speech," and "to frequent the company of men of principle so that one may be rectified."[65]

The third talent to be cultivated was the scholar, which was a sound state for a talent. This talent was reserved mainly for the assistant talents to the ruler, who could manage all levels of political, diplomatic, military and cultural activities, as well as assist in the management of financial affairs and rites. Seen from the educational practice of Confucius, the scholar was the most realistic talent to be cultivated. To cultivate these talents, he established four subjects, including virtue, language, literature, and politics, educating disciples through poems, books, rites, music, literature, behavior, loyalty, and trust. In this way, the educational purpose of Confucius was realized.

Sima Qian recorded the general situation of Confucius disciples after his death: "After the death of Confucius, his 70 disciples were scattered in various states, with those superior ranked as masters or ministers, those inferior ranked as teachers or Dafu (a senior official in feudal China), and others secluded. Thus, Zilu lived in Wei State, Zizhang in Chen State, Tantai Ziyu in Chu State, Zixia in Xihe, and Zigong in Qi State. And those, such as Tian Zifang, Duan Ganmu, Wu Qi, and Qin Huali, who were the disciples of Zixia and his peers, then became the teachers of the kings."[66] Apart from some who lived as hermits, most disciples of Confucius continued to practice his instructions of "learning to be excellent and then being selected as officials."[67]

If Confucius educational ideal was to cultivate intellectuals to be engaged in politics, Mo-tse's educational purpose was then to cultivate the "universal man," who had the abilities "to love universally" and "to benefit mutually." With agriculture and the handicraft industry as the main arenas for education, Mohist education defined practical knowledge and techniques as the main subjects of the educational content, expecting to cultivate students into "universal men" who could "take up their capable works" and seek social welfare while "sharing and cooperating." The opposite of "universal men" was "differential men," who were selfish, providing no food when their friends were starving and no clothes when their friends were cold. They were the most undesirable type in the talent conception of Mo-tse, who tried to "turn differential men into universal men."[68] Of course, this was just wishful thinking on the part of Mo-tse, a fantasy in the social climate of the time.

The educational purpose of Mencius was to foster the moral talent: the "great man." The main quality of the great man was a strong will that would mean that "neither riches nor honors can corrupt him; neither poverty nor lowly condition can make him swerve from principle; neither threat nor force can bend him."[69] The great man should be equipped with the noble spirit of sacrificing for righteousness and dying to achieve virtue. To cultivate great men, Mencius focused on the educational function of the environment, advocating tempering willpower with the method of "exercising one's mind with suffering, his sinews and bones with toil, and exposing his body to hunger," as well as the method of restoring one's lost heart, refining one's study and exercise. Thus, the spirit of the great man who has high consciousness and strong will would be fostered.

The ideal personality for the Daoist was also the "sage" (also referred to as the true man, the holy man, or the perfect man), who was not the secular and moral sage advocated by the Confucians but the natural sage, who stood aloof from worldly success and had few desires and a free spirit. The *Zhuangzi* states: "But suppose one who mounts on the ether of heaven and earth in its normal operation, and drives along the six elemental Qis (energies) of the changing seasons, thus enjoying himself in the illimitable—what was he to wait for? Therefore it is said that the perfect man cares for no self; the holy man, no merit; the sage, no fame."[70] That is to say, although the sage was in the secular world, his spirit could stand aloof from it, at leisure and unrestrained, reaching the natural and unrestrained state, which was absolutely free. Therefore, in terms of educational content, Mencius advocated starting no disputes, fostering contentment, and valuing mildness, no self, no merit, no fame, and no emotion. In terms of educational method, he created the natural educational environment in order to cultivate the natural sage, with the goal of eliminating authority and opinionated views, clearing the mind, referring to the far-reaching Dao, following nature, hollowing the heart, and forgetting oneself to experience the universe.

Starting from the educational view of "being educated by the law and taught by officials," the Legalists focused on cultivating talents who could promote legal governance, that is, strategic men, with great insight and reasonable understanding; judicial men, with an unswerving moral center and the courage to fight; and upright men, with righteous behaviors and upstanding personalities. These talents could restrain their private desires, judge impartially, consider the interests of the whole, and seek truth from facts. They "do not encumber their mood by wisdom or themselves with private profit, depend on the law and strategies to handle the chaos, depend on reward and punishment to judge the right and wrong, depend on scales to weigh objects, do not violate natural principles, or damage human nature. They are not fault-finding and do not pry; they do not cite things outside the law or apply the law arbitrarily; they are not concerned with things outside the law or hamper those inside it; they stick to settled laws and regulations and depend on objective nature. The occurrence of adversity and fortune depends on natural law instead of personal interest or hatred; the honor and humility of responsibility depend on one's own abilities, not others."[71] To cultivate these qualities, the Legalists focused on enriching the content of legal education, proposing several specific principles and methods in terms of learning and self-cultivation.

In the Eastern Han Dynasty, Wang Chong categorized talents into four levels: the Confucian scholars, the learned scholars, the literati, and the great scholars. He said, "Those who can lecture on a classic book can be called Confucian scholars; those who read extensively can be called learned scholars; those who can edit books and submit reports can be called literati; and those who have refined thinking and can write compact chapters can be called great scholars. Therefore, the Confucian scholars were superior to ordinary people, the learned scholars to the Confucian scholars, the literati to the learned scholars, and the great scholars to the literati."[72] Wang Chong was not content with the level of the Confucian scholar. He thought that these scholars knew only how to give lessons about sentences and phrases day and night, how to study argumentative philosophy, and how to explain the *Five Classics* (the *Book of Songs*, the *Book of History*, the *Book of Changes*, the *Book of Rites*, and the *Spring and Autumn Annals*). He felt they did not have an understanding of history and were therefore "blind." Moreover, he felt they knew little outside of the *Five Classics*, which were out of accord with the times. Therefore, among Wang Chong's training targets, the Confucian scholar was not the ideal personality.

Wang Chong's standards for talents were the three levels higher than the Confucian scholars: the learned scholars, the literati, and the great scholars. The learned scholars, who were refined and elegant, had read between one thousand and ten thousand books and were able to revise articles and punctuation in unpunctuated ancient writing, teaching others knowledge.[73] The literati and great scholars expressed their opinions and thought over their writings before submitting their reports to the ruler or establishing theories in serial chapters.[74] They were noted for not repeating others' words like a parrot but for their original creations, and not for rigid adherence to books but for their combination of knowledge and practice to solve various problems in social and political life. To cultivate these three kinds of talents, he advocated the principles of diligent study, thorough research into problems, practical exercise, critical verification, and application of knowledge to social affairs. In the educational field, Wang Chong also tried to break the ancient pattern of the exclusiveness of the study of the *Five Classics* in class during the Han Dynasty, as well as the focus on a single academic field. These actions were fairly significant for the cultivation of the great scholars, who were erudite in both ancient and present knowledge, as well as all schools of thought.

In the period of the Dynasties of Wei and Jin, Yan Zhitui thought deeply about the targets for education at that time. Through revealing the situation of the scholar-officials, who felt shame in engaging in agricultural and commercial business or developing skills, but who failed at shooting through a piece of thin wood and who were able to write little except their own names, and who were regularly full of food and wine,[75] he pointed out the crisis of education. He held that education should not cultivate those who could speak only hollowly or study just sentences and phrases, but those who could be useful talents for the country. His view of talent and systematic cultivation were developed as follows.

The value of a noble man in society lies in his benefit to others. Noble men never spoke loudly or hollowly with musical instruments and books around them to waste the wealth of their emperor. The useful talents for the country were no more than six types: first, the ministers of the court, who, learned and virtuous, had mastery of political laws and regulations and could handle state affairs; second, the civilians and historian officials, who could write articles to describe the previous governance of chaos and reforms to remind their contemporaries of past experiences; third, the military officers, who were strategic and decisive, strong and capable, and acquainted with war affairs; fourth, the officials in charge of vassal states, who were familiar with local customs, free from corruption, and able to protect the people; fifth, the envoys, who could be flexible according to situations, choose the best solution, and always live up to the diplomatic mission entrusted to them by the emperor; sixth, the architectural officials, who could efficiently save costs and design effective plans. These talents could be cultivated in those who studied diligently and remained virtuous. Since people differ from each other in their aptitude, no one was to be forced to perfect these six types of affairs. However, everyone was to know the fundamental significance of these positions and make a conscientious effort to achieve the standards of these positions.[76]

Yan Zhitui categorized the useful talents for the country into types: political talents, cultural and academic talents, military talents, domestic and diplomatic talents, and technical and management talents, who were engaged in architectural and manufacturing affairs. Also, he held that education was not expected to cultivate all-around talents, who would be "capable in all six types of affairs," but should foster the specialized talents of those who were proficient in a particular field.

Since the Tang and Song Dynasties, the talent ideals of China's ancient educators took two different paths: one emphasized the benevolence, righteousness, and morality represented by Han Yu and Zhu Xi; the other emphasized the practical application in state affairs represented by Wang Anshi and Yan Yuan. In the Tang Dynasty, under the circumstances of declining national power and the inundation of Buddhism and Daoism, Han Yu set the defense of the Dao (the traditional moral principles) as his task and proposed the educational purpose of "learning for the Dao" and "restoring the education of previous emperors." The "education of previous emperors" was an educational system with benevolence, righteousness, and morality at its core: "What was the educational concept of previous emperors? Fraternity is benevolence, while proper action is righteousness, and behaviors following benevolence and righteousness can be called the Dao. Equipped in oneself without dependence on the outside, it can be called De (morality). Books that discuss benevolence, righteousness, and morality (including the Dao) are the *Book of Poetry*, *Shangshu*, the *Book of Changes*, and the *Spring and Autumn Annals*; the methods to reflect these qualities are rites, music, penal laws, and political orders; people educated with these qualities are engaged in official, agricultural, industrial, and commercial affairs; their ethical superior–inferior relationships include emperor–minister, father–son, teacher–friend, guest–host, elder brother–younger brother, and husband–wife; their clothes include linen, cotton, silk, and pongee; their dwellings include palaces and houses; their food includes grains, fruit, vegetables, and meat. As theories, these qualities are easy to understand, and as education, easy to be practiced. Therefore, to educate ourselves with them could obtain harmony and blessing; to treat others with them could achieve fraternity and justice; to rectify the internal mind could result in tranquility and calm; to administer the world with them would be suitable for every corner."[77] It can be seen that "the education of previous emperors" had rich connotations, including the Confucian classics and the ethical norms advocated by Confucianism, as well as the political policies, material civilizations, and lifestyles in feudal society. Talents cultivated by this kind of education not only study the books of ancient sages and abide by the law of previous emperors, but also master human relations, handle their life steadfastly, and deal with affairs soundly.

Zhu Xi further developed Han Yu's idea of "the fundamental significance of the clarification of human relations in the education of previous emperors." Based on the social situation of "declining customs and talents," when criticizing the imperial examination education, which "attends to the incidentals, neglects the essentials, and avoids righteousness to pursue profit," he proposed the educational purpose of "investigating things, extending knowledge, having sincerity of thought, rectifying one's heart, and cultivating one's personality to further regulate the family, rightly govern the state, and rule the whole world."[78] In the *School Regulations of Bailudong Academy*, he even set "kinship between father and son, righteousness between emperor and minister, distinction between husband and wife, sequence between senior and junior, and trust between friends" as the core content of education, with the goal of cultivating talents who had the above virtues. Zhu Xi's educational view was that the purpose of education was to cultivate the "pure Confucian."

As an important advocate who emphasized the practice of state affairs, Wang Anshi pointed out that the biggest problem of school education at the time was the inability to cultivate the practical talents needed by the country. Therefore, "although one has been learning in school for a long time, until he is old, making all efforts to follow the teacher's instruction, when he is engaged in political affairs, he does not know how to handle them." It was not the "cultivation of talents" but rather the "hampering and destroying"[79] of talents. With the goal of correcting this, Wang Anshi conducted reforms in the standards of talent selection. He held that correcting the method of talent selection was "an urgent affair for society," because talent selection could orientate the "cultivation of talents by education." He said, "The so-called scholar-officials are studying not only literature, but are also learning about past and present events, rites, astronomy, worldly affairs, and changes occurring in politics and education.

Thus, they can deal with government affairs with thoroughness and justice, and refer to ancient and modern precedents in the discussion of key issues. The so-called learners study not only the punctuation of sentences, but also rites, institutions, and regulations, the authority of the emperor and the minister, and the trends in political affairs. Thus, when they apply their knowledge in their work, they can improve the governance of state affairs and make judgments following the methods of the classics when discussing."[80] The change to talent selection standards would lead to a change in talent cultivation, which would lead to a change in the content and method of education. The education promotion movement directed by Wang Anshi himself, which had its greatest impact from the Han Dynasty to the Tang Dynasty, had several beneficial effects.

Chen Liang and Ye Di, of the Utilitarian School in the Southern Song Dynasty, argued with Zhu Xi on the issue of how to cultivate talents. Zhu Xi once advised Chen Liang to "restrain himself with the Pure Confucian standard," which was despised by Chen Liang, who held that the purpose of education was to teach people "how to be a person," not "how to be a Confucian." He pointed out that the so-called "Pure Confucian" idealized by the Neo-Confucians was only the moralistic scholar who "studies the details of classics, analyzes the differences between the past and the present, bothers about his mind and etiquette in every detail, and considers the accumulation of merit and self-cultivation as decent deeds, in order to be regarded by others as reaching the supreme state."[81] Although they could lecture on the classics and life, they did not know how to make a country prosperous or how to strengthen its military power. Further, they did not know how to promote the benefit of the country or how to eliminate malpractice, and were thus useless to the cause of social welfare and people's benefit. Instead, he advocated cultivating talents who were equipped with wisdom, bravery, and versatility. These talents, as the "heroes of the time," with morality and talent, as well as literacy and military competency, could exploit the learnings of the past and present for great benefit. Ye Di regarded this kind of "complete man" as the real "scholar" and pointed out the differences between the "complete man" and the "scholar" of the Neo-Confucians. The latter was deemed to "sit and talk about the sages besides day-long lecturing, composing, reciting, and studying; their discussion talks emptily about heaven, people, and life, holding that the Way of Yao, Shun, Duke Zhou, and Confucius ends there; they make sculptures and paintings that affront the principles of previous kings."[82] However, the real "scholar" had genuine talent, was always righteous, knew the principles, and excelled in both morality and the arts. In educational methods, they opposed sitting still to read, the cultivation of the heart, and hollow talk about morality, instead advocating the active practice of their knowledge, exploring the outside, and making definite goals, publicly encouraging students to save the world and strive for merit.

In the period of the late Ming and early Qing Dynasties, Yan Yuan proposed the concept of talents to cultivate "scholars with genuine competence
and virtue," with "practice in state affairs as the ultimate goal." He held that
if school education could not provide useful talents for the country, "none of
the schools would produce scholars with competence and virtue, and thus the
court would be filled with commonplace officials"; otherwise, if "scholars in all
schools are encouraged to develop genuine competence and virtue, then the
officials in the court will all be suitable for the role of ministers."[83] The scholars
with genuine competence and virtue were usually specialized in their professions, having their own special talents. According to Yan Yuan, there was
no omniscient or omnipotent person in the world, not even among the sages
throughout history. He said, "For the six arts, if one can study and discuss one
or two of them in depth, focusing on the practice needed to carry it out, he will
become a sage like Yu, who devoted his life to the control of water, Qi, who
devoted his life to teaching farm work, Gao, who devoted his life to prison management, and Qi, who devoted his life to education. Further, he will become a
worthy man, like Zhong, who specialized in the management of taxes, Ran,
who specialized in enriching the people, and Gongxi, who specialized in ritual
music."[84] Therefore, "accomplishing study in one field will be useful and will
allow one to rank himself among the sages and worthy men."[85] In this way, Yan
Yuan most thoroughly developed the view of Yan Zhitui to cultivate specialized
talents, completely negating the concept of educating sages and worthy men to
become wise and competent in all areas, as advocated in Confucian tradition.
The educational thought that a single professional skill or specialty could make
one a sage or worthy man, and that all professions could be mastered in this
way, enjoyed epoch-making historical significance. To cultivate these kinds of
talents, he advocated practical education, which combined learning and application, rather than useless "literature-only" education; at the same time, he proposed a practical teaching method.

It should be pointed out that neither the talent view that emphasized
benevolence, righteousness, and morality nor the talent view that emphasized
practical application in state affairs negated its counterpart definitely. In their
educational thought and practice, these views influenced and contained elements of each other from time to time. For example, when Zhu Xi talked about
the mind (the heart), he also advocated practical education. He said, "Talking
about the cultivation of one's own education and the regulation of that of
others, there are various matters to be considered, including astronomy, geography, rites, music, regulations, the military, punishment, and the law, which
are definitely useful, but which involve no subjective elements. The reason the
ancients let one's heart wander among the six arts when teaching them lies in
this. Compared with pondering words to distinguish superior from inferior

writings, studying these matters is far different."[86] In terms of the breadth of the domain and the abundance of the content, the "useful causes" were not much different from the educational content proposed by the practical talent view. But the Neo-Confucian education advocated by Zhu Xi was based on benevolence, righteousness, and morality.

At the same time, when Wang Anshi advocated practical application in state affairs, he did not reject the concepts of benevolence, righteousness, and morality. He wrote, "The good teacher teaches righteousness and loyalty so that the emperor can have righteousness and the ministers loyalty; when he teaches filial piety and amiability, all fathers can be amiable and children filial; when he teaches fraternity of brothers, all brothers can behave fraternally; when he teaches etiquette for husbands and wives, all couples can demonstrate etiquette with each other. The proper behaviors of the emperor, ministers, fathers, children, brothers, husbands, and wives are what is to be educated."[87] Here, the righteousness and loyalty between emperor and ministers, the filial piety and amiability between father and children, the fraternity between brothers, and the etiquette between husband and wife were not contradictory with the education of benevolence, righteousness, and morality advocated by the Neo-Confucians. However, the educational thought of Wang Anshi was based on practical application in state affairs.

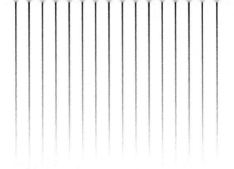

4

The Conception of Moral Education in Ancient China

Moral education is an important part of education as a whole. Its main function is to transmit certain political views, philosophical thoughts, and ethical norms to younger generations and to imbue them with certain moral qualities. In the history of educational thought, moral education has been the focus for educators. For example, Herbart, one of the founders of modern pedagogy, said, "The only and entire work of education can be summarized in this conception: morality. Morality is universally acknowledged as the supreme purpose of humanity and therefore the supreme purpose of education."[1] Even contemporary educators hold that for the harmonious development of people, "such as the improvement of morality, thinking, citizenry, intelligence, creativity, labor, aesthetics, emotion, and the physical body, the critical and dominant element is morality."[2]

Moreover, the issue of moral education was the theme of education in ancient China. As early as the Western Zhou Dynasty, the ruler emphasized moral education. Many inscriptions on copper vessels from the Western Zhou Dynasty bear the word "De" (morality or virtue).[3] For example, in the 197-character inscription on Shi Ding (an ancient tripod), which was made in the later period of the Western Zhou Dynasty, "De" appears six times, and there is a description of King Gong wishing to aid the governance of the Kingdom of Zhou through the use of "De."[4]

In the Pre-Qin Period, Confucius not only advocated "teaching the people through morality," but also created the subject of morality in school and began conducting moral education. He said, "A young man should serve his parents at home and be respectful to elders outside his home. He should be earnest and truthful, loving all, but become intimate with his innate good-heartedness. After doing this, if he has energy to spare, he can study literature and the arts."[5] He regarded the cultivation of morality as the most important task for students. It can be said that the history of China's ancient educational thought is the history of moral education. No wonder it was said that, "For China's traditional feudal education, the transmission of knowledge to the educated was just the byproduct. The real purpose of education was to edify the educated with the principles and virtues of the Confucian ethical code and to cultivate them into moral talents who could maintain the feudal society. Confucian ethical education led to the creation of the "ideal personality" for traditional education, a moral personality instead of an intelligent personality.[6] This chapter will analyze and comment on the views of moral education in ancient China from three aspects, including the function of moral education, the process of education, and the principles and methods of moral education.

The Function of Moral Education

As mentioned above, the primary feature of China's ancient education was its emphasis on ethical and moral education. The reason for this was related to the views of past politicians and educators on the function of moral education.

1. Moral Education Edified the People and Stabilized the Country

In the Pre-Qin Period, Confucius directed much attention to the function of moral education, advocating moral education for all people in society: "If you govern the people legalistically and control them by punishment, they will avoid crime, but have no personal sense of shame. If you govern them by means of virtue and control them with propriety, they will gain their own sense of shame and thus correct themselves."[7] This means that if the ruler governs the people through law and punishment, they will avoid crime but will have no sense of shame, but if he instructs and edifies them with morality, they will gain a sense of shame and become submissive, restraining their behaviors and following the ethical norms designed by the ruling class. Thus, moral education is irreplaceable by laws and punishment.

Mencius clearly defined the ultimate purpose of school education as the "clarification of human relations": "Establish Xiang, Xu, Xue, and Xiao, all educational institutions, for the instruction of the people. The name Xiang indicates nourishing as its object, Xiao indicates teaching, and Xu indicates archery.

By the Xia Dynasty, the name Xiao was used; by the Yin, that of Xu; and by the Zhou, that of Xiang. As to the Xue, they belonged to the three dynasties and were called by that name. The purpose of them all is to illustrate human relations. When those are thus illustrated by superiors, goodwill will prevail among the inferior people."[8] This means that the schooling of the juniors of the ruling class can help the superiors clarify human relations and can help inferior people develop goodwill toward each other without any "rebellious" behavior.

The classic Confucian work *The Great Learning* describes the main ideas of the Confucian views of moral education, proposing school education guidelines that would go on to influence later generations for thousands of years: "What *The Great Learning* teaches is to demonstrate illustrious virtue, to improve the people, and to rest in the highest excellence." This means that the ultimate task of great learning is to bring out people's inherent good nature, to love people, and to perfect them. In the Han Dynasty, due to the implementation of a policy of exclusively Confucian education, the thought of Dong Zhongshu was paid great attention to, and "teaching the people with morality" became the basic national policy of the Han Dynasty:

> The multitudes pursuing benefit is like water flowing downward; without edification as a dam to prevent flooding, the people cannot be stopped. Therefore, with edification accomplished and the evildoings stopped, the dam will stand in good condition; but if edification is deserted and the evildoings, which cannot be controlled by punishment, appear, the dam is then destroyed. The ancient kings believed this and therefore they all viewed edification as the most important issue when sitting toward the south to rule.[9]

These words emphasize the function of moral education in ancient China. Although Wang Chong disagreed with several basic views of Dong Zhongshu, he also put primary emphasis on moral education. He said, "To learn is to change one's temper and nature in order to perfect his talent and morality."[10] This means that the learner's fundamental task is to change and control his temper in order to perfect his talent and morality.

The Great Learning proposed education guidelines and the ideal approach to the cultivation of personality: regulating the family, rightly governing the state, and tranquilizing the whole kingdom. This approach was dominant in the Song and Ming Dynasties. In *The School Regulations of Bailudong Academy*, Zhu Xi, an educator from the Song Dynasty, viewed the "kinship between father and son, righteousness between emperor and minister, distinction between husband and wife, sequence between senior and junior, and trust between friends" as the essential content of education, stating that "it is enough for the learner to learn this." He also said,

"I used to observe the motivation of the ancient sages to teach. They all aimed to elaborate the principles to the students in order to cultivate their personalities and teach them to take others into account, instead of making them recite and write verses or pursue fame and seek profit." In Zhu Xi's view, the purpose of education was not to make people recite verses or to seek fame or profit, but to enhance people's good virtues in order to contribute to the great cause of society. In the Ming Dynasty, Wang Yangming also criticized the method of moral education that advocated reciting of verses:

> The ancients taught people human relations; later generations formed the habit of reciting verses while deserting ancient teaching principles. At present, when teaching children, the education of filial piety, fraternal duty, loyalty, trustworthiness, propriety, and a sense of shame should be the exclusive focus; whereas the method of fostering their self-restraint should be through promoting their interest in poetry, regulating their manners with etiquette, and enlightening their self-consciousness through reading.[11]

Wang Yangming advocated moral education as the exclusive focus of education and described the proper method: enlightening students' consciousness by guiding their feelings, promoting their interests, and regulating their manners.

Wang Fuzhi viewed the "demonstration of illustrious virtues" as the purpose of school education, holding that the true meaning of education was to "cultivate a person himself and govern the people in order to achieve the great virtue and cause."[12] He also said, "There is meaning in obtaining virtues. A person is called human for the virtues he obtains. If one has illustrious virtues, he knows it is possible to gain a virtue and thus gains it. If outstanding virtue is demonstrated from the limbs and reflected in one's cause, he is to cultivate himself to regulate the family, administer the state, and rule the whole kingdom."[13] Therefore, the purpose of moral education on earth was not primarily to improve an individual, but to improve society through individual improvement in order to achieve the prosperity and stability of the country.

2. Moral Education Fostered the Ideal Personality of Students

China's ancient educators designed a series of ideal personality models for students, in which the core content was steadfast moral belief. For example, Mencius's ideal personality was the spirit of the "great man":

> Dwelling in the wide house of the world, standing in the correct position of the world, and walking along the great path of the world, when he obtains his desire for governance, he practices his principles for the good of the people;

and when that desire is disappointed, he practices them alone. He is above the power of riches and honors to become dissipated, and of the power and force to bend, and of the power of poverty and mean conditions to make him swerve from his principles: these characteristics constitute the great man.[14]

To cultivate the spirit of the "great man," to remain unswerving in the face of poverty or mean conditions and unyielding in the face of power and force, he requested his students to enhance their self-education, endeavoring to preserve and promote the good nature endowed within them by heaven. Therefore, he said, "A great man does not lose his original heart."[15]

The ideal personality as described by Xuncius was the "complete man" with moral virtues. He said:

A noble man knows that incomplete and imperfect learning cannot be called good learning. Therefore, he reads plenty of books to achieve mastery; he speculates to deepen his comprehension; he follows the good examples of his teachers and friends; he cultivates himself by eliminating defects. If the eyes are used wrongly, he does not see; if the ears are used wrongly, he does not listen; if the mouth is used wrongly, he does not speak; if the heart is used wrongly, he does not think. The ideal state was considered to be an addiction to learning, which was viewed as being like the eyes favoring various colors, the ears favoring various sounds, the mouth favoring various flavors, and the heart desiring possession of the world. If one can reach this state, he will not have evil ideas in the face of power and private desires, nor will he yield in the face of overwhelming strength, nor will anything change his mind. This is called the possession of virtue and integrity. With virtue and integrity, one can persevere and then be flexible. With perseverance and flexibility, he can be the mature and complete man.[16]

Obviously, the basic requirements for being a "complete man" were very similar to those of the "great man" proposed by Mencius: requesting that people should have unswerving virtues and integrity, should not yield in the face of threat or the temptation of power, or be changed by overwhelming strength, all of which should be adhered to for life. However, the development of this ideal was different from Mencius's view. Xuncius felt that it could not be formed just by subjective introspective exploration, but through "reading, speculation, and cultivation," which were learning, thinking, and behavioral training in the modern sense.

The ideal personality for Zhang Zai of the Song Dynasty was the "benevolent man." He held that the purpose of education was to cultivate people into real men, that is, "benevolent men." He said, "The learner has to develop his human personality. Those who are benevolent are human. One should know the reason a person is human and then he can learn how to be human."[17] That is to say, humanity is not defined by the biology of being human, but rather by being a social human. Only with perfect morality and the ideal personality (benevolence) can one be called a social human. The cultivation of this kind of human and the formation of this kind of personality can be realized through learning and education. As for the "noble man," the "virtuous man," the "sage," and the "scholar" proposed by other educators, most also possessed a similar ideal personality defined by persevering virtue. This indicates that China's ancient educators paid much attention to education, especially in terms of the significance of moral education in cultivating students' ideal personalities.

3. Moral Education Contributed to the Development of Students' Intelligence

China's ancient educators conducted a great deal of research on the relationship between the development of morality and intelligence, discovering that the former could greatly promote the latter. There were even educators who believed that morality was of equal importance to intelligence, holding that with good morality, the development of good intelligence would follow, which emphasized the significance of moral education.

Shangshu, the earliest known work of ancient China, discussed the relationship between morality and intelligence. It said, "The wise, without thinking, become foolish, and the foolish, by thinking, become wise."[18] This means that although one is reasonable and wise, without concern for benevolence or morality, he will become an unscrupulous man; although one is unscrupulous, with concern for benevolence and morality, he will become a reasonable and wise man. Moreover, Confucius pointed out that if a man was of low morality, his intelligence would not become developed, and he might even lose what has been gained. Therefore, he said, "When a man's knowledge is sufficient to attain, but his virtue is not sufficient to enable him to hold, whatever he may have gained, he will lose."[19] He also said, "If a scholar is not grave, he will not call forth any veneration, and his learning will not be solid."[20] No wonder Confucius placed primary importance on morality when evaluating his students:"Though a man have abilities as admirable as those of the Duke of Zhou, yet if he should be proud and niggardly, his other things are really not worth being looked at."[21]

The emphasis on morality was more obvious in the Song Dynasty. For example, although the historian Sima Guang emphasized "benevolence and wisdom," he held that "morality is the integration of talents, and talent is the resource of morality." However, in *Zi Zhi Tong Jian* (*History as a Mirror*), he divided people into four types: the sages, who had talent and principles; the virtuous men, who had morality but no talent; the fools, who had neither talent nor morality; and the base men, who had no morality but did have some talent. He also prioritized virtuous men who had morality but no talent over base men who had no morality but did have talent.

Zhang Zai, another educator in the Song Dynasty, emphasized the positive influence of moral development on intelligence. He wrote:

> Without a lofty ambition and the concentration of the mind, one will achieve nothing in learning. If he idles in the process of progress, he will of course not reach his destination. If he is not a noble man with good virtues, he will have to work diligently and not relax until he can do whatever he wants within the norms. Those with little morality will ultimately fail in learning.[22]

Zhang Zai thought that only those with perfect morality could set lofty ambitions. Those with a keen interest in learning and a highly concentrated mind could develop a persevering willpower and achievements in learning and develop their intelligence. This idea in fact revealed the chain development of morality, the non-intelligent element and the intelligent element.

In ancient China, there were also several educators who described the interactive relationship between morality and intelligence, emphasizing both the significance of moral education and the influence of intelligence on moral development. For example, in the Western Han Dynasty, Dong Zhongshu said, "Benevolent but without wit, one will have love but make no distinctions; wise but without benevolence, one will have awareness but conduct no actions. Therefore, the benevolent love people in the same way and the wise eliminate evildoings."[23] If one's morality contains benevolence but no wit, he will feel universal love but make no distinction; if his morality contains wit but no benevolence, he will not apply his wit to good deeds to make a difference. In the period of the Three Kingdoms, Liu Shao further analyzed the internal relationship between morality and intelligence. He wrote:

> Benevolence is the basis of morality; righteousness is the character of morality; etiquette is the literary grace of morality; trustworthiness is the pillar of morality; wisdom is the integration of morality. Wisdom originates from intelligence, or brightness; for people, intelligence, or brightness, is like the sun in the day and candlelight at night. The more intense the brightness, the more distant it illuminates; and the more distant, the more difficult to illuminate.[24]

In Liu Shao's view, benevolence is the fundamental element of morality; righteousness is the character of morality; etiquette is the literary grace of morality; trustworthiness is the pillar of morality; and wisdom is the integration of morality. Further, wisdom comes from intelligence, which, for humans, is like the sun being needed during the day and the candlelight being needed at night. Obviously, Liu Shao clarified the significance of the development of intelligence in moral development.

In the period of the late Ming and early Qing Dynasties, the educator Zhang Lvxiang also had some brilliant ideas with regard to the relationship between intelligence and morality. He said, "For the learner, his moral character should be observed in the first place. If his moral character is shallow, he will not achieve a great result."[25]

Zhang Lvxiang also said, "Morality is the fundamental reason for one's cause, and his cause is the presentation of his morality. To refine his morality is to improve his cause, and to improve his cause is to improve his morality. Each promotes the other's development mutually, and both are, in fact, based on the same kind of effort."[26] On the one hand, he pointed out that moral character was the priority; if one's moral character was profound, he would have a well-developed intelligence and achieve greater results. On the other hand, he pointed out that one's "morality" and "cause" were supplementary and could promote each other mutually, which meant that development of one's "morality" could promote the development of one's "cause" in order to drive the development of one's intelligence. One's "cause" could also promote one's "morality" in order to benefit people's moral development. In the Qing Dynasty, Dai Zhen also pointed out that, "Morality originates from learning and then progresses into sage wisdom."[27] He held that once a person had cultivated his morality well, he could then step into the state of sage wisdom by the means of learning.

The Process of Moral Education

From the viewpoint of modern educational theories, the process of moral education can be regarded as the process in which educators influence the knowledge, emotion, motivation, and actions of people to promote the development of their morality. In ancient China, Lu Jiuyuan of the Song Dynasty made a relatively complete and systematic elaboration on the process of moral education. In explaining and developing the meaning of moral education in the *Book of Changes*, he said:

> Lv (manner) shows us the foundation of virtue; Qian (modesty), its handle; Fu (restoration), its root; Heng (perseverance), its solidity; Sun (decrease), its cultivation; Yi (correction), its abundance; Kun (difficulty), its exercise of discrimination; Jing (well), its field; and Xun (compliance), its principle."... The nine diagrams [at the beginning of the *Book of Changes*] are the essential

components for the cultivation of a noble man, which are arranged in the above sequence [in the *Book of* Changes], and are all indispensible.[28]

This process involves moral feelings (for example, "Sun," to eliminate desires that obstruct moral development; "Qian," to possess without claiming credit or pride; and "Jing," to benefit other people and things selflessly), moral willingness (for example, "Heng," to persevere in doing something, and "Kun," to practice in difficult situations), and moral behaviors (for example, "Lv," the training of moral behaviors, and "Yi," to correct mistakes and improve).[29] Lu's explanation of the process of moral education could be called a miracle in the history of China's educational thought and even in the world's educational history. Although other educators in ancient China did not make as systematic or complete elaborations as Lu Jiuyuan, there were plenty of fragmentary views. In the following section, these views will be reviewed from modern perspectives in order to define their essence.

1. The Recognition Stages of Morality

The recognition of morality is the awareness, evaluation, and judgment people make about the right and wrong, good and evil, beautiful and ugly of social phenomena. The formation and development of students are generally based on their moral recognition. Only when a person knows how to act and the reason to act a certain way can he act self-consciously. Only when one knows the distinction between right and wrong, good and evil, beautiful and ugly, as well as honor and disgrace, can he define his own behavioral principles. The formative process of moral recognition mainly contains the revelation and lecturing of moral concepts to students, in order to clarify certain moral standards and norms, encourage them to analyze moral phenomena, and develop their evaluation ability, as well as effectively develop social awareness into the students' individual awareness.

China's ancient educators paid much attention to the recognition stages of morality. For example, Confucius held that with wisdom, one could have unswerving moral belief, which corresponded to the saying that "the wise are free from perplexities."[30] He also held that wisdom was the precondition for people's moral behaviors: "There may be those who act without knowing why. I do not do so."[31] Xuncius pointed out that only by "recognizing the Way" through reason could one improve his moral self-consciousness; only by "having a clear awareness" could one "conduct no wrong deeds." He also said, "Generally, people always follow what they approve of and desert what they disapprove of. There's no one who does not follow the right Way when he knows it is the best thing in the world."[32] Therefore, "the mind should know the Way; knowing not the Way, the mind will not approve of the Way but the wrong ways."[33] Zhu Xi further developed this idea, holding that the possession of clear moral knowledge was a guarantee for the conduct of reasonable actions: "If one knows moral principles clearly, he will naturally act filially when attending to his parents, behave intimately when interacting with his brothers, and be trustworthy when interacting with his friends."[34] At the same time, he also held that the mastery of moral knowledge set down principles for one's own thought and behaviors, needing no restraint from others: "If one knows the reasons and regulates himself rigorously, why should he wait for others to set the regulations and restraint before following them?"[35]

China's ancient educators realized the significance of mastering moral concepts in forming moral awareness. For example, Confucius once proposed a complete series of moral concepts and encouraged his students to grasp them. Among the moral concepts of Confucius, propriety and benevolence were considered the most important. In *The Analects of Confucius*, there are 74 entries which include the character "Li" (propriety) and 105 entries which include "Ren" (benevolence). When evaluating his students' school work and morality, "Li" and "Ren" were often referred to.

Mencius proposed a more specific moral concept. He put forward three groups of terms: first, "benevolence, righteousness, propriety, and intelligence"; second, "filial piety, fraternity, loyalty, and trustworthiness"; third, "kinship between father and son, righteousness between emperor and minister, distinction between husband and wife, sequence between senior and junior, and trust between friends." These three groups of terms laid the foundation for the moral concept of the three cardinal principles and five virtues, which was dominant after the period of the Qin and Han Dynasties.

To help students grasp moral concepts, China's ancient educators also focused on revealing their own connotations of moral concepts. For example, Confucius repeatedly elaborated on the concepts of "Ren" and "Li" to his students. To impress the students more and provide vivid explanations, ancient educators also made sure to illustrate examples from daily life. For example, Mencius once expounded on the concept that people all have fear and compassion (benevolence) through the example of a child falling into a well.[36] He explained the two moral concepts of benevolence and righteousness through the example that even all children have the awareness to love their parents and to respect their elder brothers when they grow older.[37]

When explaining the moral concept of loyalty, Zhu Xi not only stated that "loyalty is the name for honesty without cheating,"[38] but also said that, "When talking with people, one should state honestly what he really means. If he is treated like this while he himself does not speak his intention, then he is disloyal."[39] He also said that when working with others, "one should directly state that his work is proper; if it is improper, he should directly express that it should not be conducted, instead of acting ambiguously, saying that it may either be conducted or not; this is called disloyalty."[40] Examples as vivid as these were easier to understand and memorize than abstract and dull articles, and it thus became more feasible to carry out the moral concepts they described.

China's ancient educators also paid attention to the evaluation of students' moral qualities in educational practices, which were regarded as the means to foster the students' moral awareness. For example, Confucius often evaluated his students' moral qualities, and one method he used was to express his views directly to his students. For example, Zigong once said to Confucius that he could live up to the saying, "Do not do to others what you do not want others to do to you," to which Confucius responded that he could not manage it. The second method he used was to evaluate a student in the presence of other students. For example, Zaiwo once complained to Confucius that a three-year mourning period was too long and that one year was enough. Confucius, on one hand, criticized to Zaiwo's face that "a noble man, during the whole period of mourning, does not enjoy pleasant food which he may eat, nor derive pleasure from music which he may hear. He also does not feel at ease if he is comfortably lodged. Therefore, he does not do what you propose. But now you feel at ease and may do it."[41]

Confucius also blamed Zaiwo in other students' presence for "having no benevolence," stating, "Yu is in want of benevolence! It is not until a child is three years old that he is allowed to leave the arms of his parents. And the three years' mourning is universally observed throughout the kingdom. Did Yu enjoy the three years' love of his parents?"[42]

To take another example, Zigong asked, "Who was more virtuous, Shi or Shang?" Confucius said, "Shi was excessive and Shang was insufficient." Zigong then asked, "So is Shi more excellent?" Confucius answered, "Excessiveness is equal to insufficiency."[43]

The third method Confucius used was to evaluate his students in the presence of others. For example, when Duke Ai of Lu asked, "Which of the disciples loves to learn?" Confucius appraised the learning attitude and spirit of Yan Yuan, saying, "There was Yan Hui who loved to learn. He did not transfer his anger; he did not repeat a fault. Unfortunately, his appointed time was short and he died, and now there is not such another. I have not yet heard of anyone who loves to learn as he did."[44]

The fourth method Confucius used was to reevaluate others' evaluations of his disciples when they did not accord with the facts. For example, Confucius sighed, "I have not seen a firm and unbending man." Someone present replied, "Shen Cheng (Gang) is firm and unbending." Considering that the evaluation of Shen Cheng did not accord with the facts, Confucius corrected the speaker, saying, "Cheng is under the influence of his passions; how can he be pronounced firm and unbending?"[45]

Yan Yuan, an educator in the late Ming and early Qing Dynasties, also evaluated his students' moral qualities frequently. For example, a student once "intended to gather some firewood to make a fire in winter. Someone else put some firewood near his room, which he wanted to take in the beginning. Considering that this would not be lawful, he decided to take his firewood from another place." When Yan Yuan heard of the "good deed" of this disciple, he went to the school the next day and praised him in the presence of other students, saying that "with this regard, one can become a sage."[46] He then went on to ask his other students to develop this same spirit of selflessness.

China's ancient educators also guided their students to conduct self-evaluation, combining this with the evaluation of the teacher. For example, when Confucius guided his disciples to conduct self-evaluation, he proposed two points. First, when the disciple's self-evaluation accorded with the facts, he affirmed it. When Zigong considered that he was not as intelligent as Yan Yuan, Confucius affirmed that, "You are not equal to him. I grant you, you are not equal to him."[47] Second, when the disciple's self-evaluation did not accord with the facts, he corrected it. Once Zigong said to Confucius, "What I do not wish others to do to me, I also wish not to do to others."

Thinking that this was exaggerated and inaccurate, Confucius corrected him, saying, "Ci, you have not attained that."[48] This act of affirmation or correction was important for the promotion of the students' ability to make their own moral evaluations and form the correct moral awareness.

2. The Stage of Moral Emotions

Moral emotions are the emotional experience of gladness and anger, sorrow and delight, love and hate, expressed by people in response to true or false, beautiful or ugly, good or evil social phenomena. Moral emotions have a significant effect on people's moral behaviors, just as Sukhomlynsky described, saying, "Emotion, this is the flesh heart of the moral faith, principle, and spiritual power; without emotion, morality will become the boring language which can cultivate only hypocrites." If a student delights in certain moral issues, he can easily accept moral knowledge and quickly incorporate it into his behavior; otherwise, if he expresses an indifferent attitude, he will just keep the words on his lips. Moreover, the process of developing moral emotions is a process of emotional appeal to students, and it requires teachers to affect the students through specific moral images and to stimulate their moral emotions through various artistic forms on the basis of improving their moral awareness, helping them to foster a noble moral sentiment.

China's ancient educators also focused on the significance of the stage of moral emotions in cultivating students' moral qualities. They realized that all moral qualities included two elements: awareness and emotions. With just awareness but no involvement of emotion, no true moral quality could be formed. For example, Confucius proposed the concept of "Ren" (benevolence), requiring his students to understand the importance of "loving others" and "restoring propriety through self-discipline" on one hand, and to embrace the emotions of "loving others" and "restoring propriety through self-discipline" on the other. Obviously, loving others required the students to have sympathy, while restoring propriety through self-discipline required them to restrain certain undesirable emotions. Only when equipped with the proper emotions in these two aspects could one become a truly virtuous man.

When discussing the moral function of emotions, Zhu Xi proposed to distinguish between positive and negative emotions. For example, for the same emotion of anger, "anger for personal trivialities" was evil, while "anger for righteousness" was kind; sentimental anger "should not exist," while compassionate anger "should not be absent."[49] Only the evil emotion and the emotion that could not be contained or restrained could affect the justice of people's hearts; but the kind emotion and the emotion that could be contained and restrained should not be eliminated. He said:

> With pleasure, anger, sorrow, and joy in the heart, justice cannot be attained. It does not mean that these sentiments cannot exist, for they are indispensible emotions. However, when expressing them with containment and restraint, it will be right; without containment or restraint, impartiality will exist and injustice cannot be attainted.[50]

He went on to say that the eight tones of song and dance can cultivate people's temperament, cleaning the evil stains and melting the dross. Therefore, for a scholar who masters the principle of righteousness and benevolence and naturally complies with morality, he will in the end accomplish his learning through this aspect.[51]

Since the kind emotions could improve people's psychological qualities and make them adherent to feudal ethics, Zhu Xi naturally promoted them. In the Qing Dynasty, Dai Zhen further elaborated on the meaning of moral emotions, saying, "Reason will be lost without good emotion; reason cannot be right if emotion is wrong."[52] He held that only with positive moral emotions could one attain certain moral knowledge; only with "the right emotion" could "the right reason" be attained.

China's ancient educators cultivated students' moral emotions by means of music and poetry. For example, Confucius advocated that one should "start from the *Book of Poetry*, be established in propriety, and accomplish himself through music."[53] This means that people's moral emotions are to be stimulated through poetry and people are to become cultivated through music.

Confucius not only reorganized the *Book of Poetry* and described the moral educational function of poetry,[54] but also affirmed the significant power of music.[55]

Even when there was a lack of food and his disciples were falling ill when traveling around the states, he still "kept playing the music." Later educators continued to develop this idea. For example, Zhu Xi and Wang Yangming both pointed out that poetry education had the function of soothing students' moods, cultivating their emotions and morality, and keeping them from evil and despicable thoughts and emotions.[56] In the Qing Dynasty, Wang Fuzhi made the most detailed elaboration on this idea and thoroughly analyzed the significance of poetry in promoting the moral emotions of young students. He wrote:

> There are those who are heroic but not virtuous, but there is no one who is virtuous without having heroic quality. Those who can "Xing" are heroic. "Xing" is the Qi (natural energy) born in nature. Sluggish and submissive, agreeing to the agreement and disagreeing to the disagreement of the world, laboring all day and being contained in the affairs of official positions, fields, houses, wife, and children, counting rice and firewood, one's aspiration will be reduced day by day. He knows not the height of the sky when looking up and knows not the thickness of the earth when looking down. Living in dreams even when awake, blind even when he can see with eyes, and dull in the heart even when he labors diligently, he can never "Xing." The sages then clean his stained heart and shake away his lifelessness with poetry, including him in the heroic ranks and expecting him to become a virtuous sage. This is a great measure to save humanity in the chaotic world.[57]

In the view of Wang Fuzhi, heroic people were those who could "Xing" or those with righteousness or moral emotions. On the contrary, those without righteousness or moral emotions, who were sluggish, dispirited, and contained by the affairs of food, official positions, fields, houses, and wife and children, could not help being trapped in the vulgar flow after years of a befuddled life. The value of studying the *Book of Poetry* was to clean young learners' stained hearts, wipe away their lifelessness, and encourage their moral emotions, helping them to determine to become a hero and then a virtuous sage.[58]

As for the function of music in cultivating emotions and transforming customs, the *Record of Music* gave the clearest explanation:

> When evil sound touches people, bad customs come; after the formation of a bad custom, lewd music will prevail. When righteous sound touches people, harmonious customs will come; after the formation of a harmonious custom, harmonious and noble music will prevail.

Wang Fuzhi also paid much attention to the "cultivation of morality through music," interpreting three values of music: first, religious value, which was enough to "learn from the gods" and promote the original energy of heaven and earth; second, social value, which was enough to "transform the customs"; third, moral value, which was enough to "cultivate the harmony of people's hearts"[59] in order to foster moral sentiment. Wang Fuzhi emphasized the latter two most because he held that, "with learning, one can gradually get across the reason and move on to be good through changing his temperament, which is the grounds for the establishment of the education of music."[60]

To enhance the persuasive effect of moral education, China's ancient educators also affected and educated students with specific moral images in order to arouse their sympathy and stimulate their moral emotions. For example, Confucius often introduced historical and contemporary figures who had made a difference, such as Yao, Shun, Yu, Tang, Wen, Wu, Duke Zhou, Boyi, Shuqi, Weizi, Jizi, Bigan, Duke Huan of Qi, Duke Wen of Jin, Guan Zhong, Zichan, Yan Pingzhong, Zang Wenzhong, Zang Wuzhong, Liu Xiahui, Duke Jing of Qi, and Duke Ling of Wei, describing the educational contributions of these figures. He also set specific examples, such as Yan Yuan, among his disciples to make the concepts pertinent to them.

3. The Stage of Moral Will

Moral will refers to the effort people make to overcome difficulties self-consciously in the process of fulfilling their moral obligations. Moral will is also an indispensible part of the process of moral education, which can help people to eliminate interference and obstacles from all aspects, keeping moral behaviors determined by certain moral motivation to the end and performing bravely, firmly, and indomitably in their moral actions. On the contrary, without a firm moral will, one will act cowardly, give up halfway or even yield to the evil power, and give up his original intentions, betraying righteousness. The process of cultivating moral will is the process of requiring students to persevere. It lies mainly in the cultivation of students' spirits and habits to be consistent and persistent through tough tempering based on the improvement of their moral awareness and moral emotions.

China's ancient educators had numerous discussions about the stage of moral will, paying much attention to its significance. For example, Confucius required students to set up "far-reaching" and "noble" ambitions, which, in his own words, required them to "set their aspirations on the Way." Only when a person set his aspirations on the Way could he "hold to virtue, rely on benevolence, and relax in the study of the arts."[61] "Setting aspirations on the Way" was actually the moral motivation in the moral will. Only with a pure motivation and a noble ambition could one act in the right direction and detach himself from material comforts.

Mencius gave a detailed description of moral will, putting it in a special place in the process of moral education: "Aspiration is the integration of one's Qi; Qi is filled within one's body. Aspiration is superior, whereas Qi is inferior. Therefore, it is said to 'maintain your aspiration while not breaking any Qi.'"[62] He held that only with a sturdy moral will could one hold his Qi and reach the state of "a great man," that "neither riches nor honors can corrupt him; neither poverty nor lowly condition can make him swerve from principle; neither threats nor force can bend him." Zhang Zai regarded "first setting the scholar's aspiration" as the "great ethical principle of education" and the setting of ambition as the basis of one's cause and morality. "A great aspiration indicates the great talent and cause; therefore, it is said that 'it can be great' and 'it can be rich.' With a long-lasting aspiration, one's Qi and morality can be long-lasting; therefore it is said that 'it can last long' and 'it progresses constantly.'"[63] Lu Jiuyuan regarded first deter-mining one's aspiration as the precondition for moral education:

> Small virtue is like the flowing stream, while great virtue can edify people, who are equipped by the sages. With the nine virtues in *Gao Yao Mo* (the *Counsels of Gao Yao*) and by practicing the six virtues strictly, one can establish a state; performing three virtues every day, one can establish a family. Since virtue lies within people, we cannot request it to be perfect or the people to definitely have three virtues; with just one virtue, one can be called virtuous. For the one virtue, its perfection is not required. If there is a bit of kindness similar to a kind of virtue in one's character, one can also be called virtuous. If the virtue can be maintained without error, it can be accumulated, improved on, and prosper from day to day. If it cannot be maintained, it will be lost gradually; and then how can it be expected to accumulate, be improved on, and prosper from day to day? When a scholar sets his aspiration on the Way, how can he act without any virtue? Therefore, the master taught us to "hold to virtue."[64]

This means that if a person "sets his aspiration on the Way" with gradually accumulated sturdy moral will, the foundation of his virtue can be consoli-dated, expanded, and refined to a state of "perfect virtue." Wang Fuzhi regarded virtue as the essential characteristic distinguishing humans from animals, saying, "The reason people are different from animals lies in their aspiration. Without the maintenance of their aspiration and the expansion of tolerance, how do they differentiate themselves from animals?"[65] He also regarded moral will as an important mark to evaluate students' "moral work": "With a sturdy aspiration, one's Qi will follow his aspiration, unremitting and progressing every day. This generally means that the moral work of scholars should be eval-uated by the greatness and duration of their aspirations."[66]

China's ancient educators not only emphasized the function of moral will but also proposed a series of feasible measures to cultivate moral will. The first method was to toughen one's will in difficult situations. Ancient educators held that people who lived in a cozy environment had no worries and therefore made no achievements. Mencius once made examples of some talents who had great achievements in ancient times, such as Shun, Fu Yue, Jiao Ge, Guan Yiwu, Sun Shuao, and Baili Xi, holding that they were all tempered by predicaments. He said:

> Therefore, when heaven endows a great task to someone, it will exercise his mind with suffering, his sinews and bones with toil, expose his body to hunger, make him destitute, and overturn his actions. By these actions, his heart will be alerted and his temperament will be determined, adding to him talents he did not have before.[67]

Although in these words Mencius regarded people's capacity for taking on the burden of a great cause as the arrangement of heaven, with mysterious idealism as its precondition, he focused on creating an environment that could exercise one's heart and temper his character in order to toughen his will, thus being reasonable to some extent. This was regarded by later virtuous people not only as a motto to encourage them but also as principles on which to educate their students. Moreover, this idea was precipitated in the national psychology, making it the spiritual driver for later Chinese generations to be persevering and indomitable.

The second method to cultivate moral will was to cultivate the ability to resist temptation. China's ancient educators emphasized the ability to resist temptation and insisted on faith as the important standard to evaluate one's willpower, especially in cultivating students' moral will. Mencius made the most typical description of "sacrificing for righteousness":

> I like fish, and I also like bear's paws. If I cannot have the two together, I will let the fish go, and take the bear's paws. So, I like life, and I also like righteousness. If I cannot keep the two together, I will let life go, and choose righteousness. I like life indeed, but there is something I like more than life, and therefore, I will not seek to possess it by any improper ways. I dislike death indeed, but there is something I dislike more than death, and therefore there are occasions when I will not avoid danger.[68]

Mencius held that to realize one's moral ideal, one had to use the power of will and overcome base desires with superior ones. To resist temptation, one might even have to sacrifice his own life. Han Fei, the epitome of the Legalist philosophy, also described this concept: "With few desires, one is able to make choices; with simplicity and peace, one can predict his fortune. But at present, he is touched by precious playthings and tempted by the outside; Laozi called following temptation 'Ba' (being abstracted). As for the sages, it is different. He sticks firmly to the standard of choice-making and never being tempted by what he likes. Detaching from temptations is called 'Bu Ba' (being nonabstracted). With a concentrated temperament, though there are temptations, the sages will not be abstracted spiritually. Spiritual nonabstractedness is called 'Bu Tuo' (not being detached)."[69] "Ba" and "Bu Tuo" were meant to prevent people from being tempted by the outside and desiring things. In terms of many issues, the Legalists had different views from the Confucians, but they were very similar in their emphasis on resisting temptation.

This thought was pushed to the extreme in the time of the Neo-Confucians in the Song and Ming Dynasties, who proposed the moral sermons of "keeping to nature and eliminating human desire."[70] In the Qing Dynasty, Wang Fuzhi argued against the proposition of the Neo-Confucians, proposing the view that "reasonable desires are natural." His view on the cultivation of moral will was more similar to Confucius' thought. For example, he said, "At first, when one sets his aspiration, he should avoid being self-abased but follow the Way. Then he should stick to his aspiration, instead of breaking it, but follow the Way. In the end, when he accomplishes his aspiration, he should not be conceited or break from the Way."[71] Here, "sticking to one's aspiration" requires people to have a faithful moral will, neither disturbed by internal desires nor swayed by external matters.

The third method of cultivating moral will was to cultivate unremitting perseverance, to which ancient educators also paid much attention; they even praised it as the supreme state of moral cultivation. For example, Confucius said, "I do not expect to see a good man; were I to see a man possessed of perseverance, that would satisfy me."[72] Confucius also said, "The noble man does not, even for the space of a single meal, act contrary to virtue. In moments of haste, he cleaves to it. In seasons of destitution, he cleaves to it."[73] He requested that people not ignore virtue, even during the time of a meal. In moments of haste and destitution, virtue was to be maintained in order to be "a persevering man."

Wang Fuzhi had a more creative view about moral perseverance, holding that perseverance could not only maintain the already wrought moral quality but also renew his morality. He said:

> The water flows continuously regardless of the time of day; the wave billows consistently; as the water in the later wave is not the same water as in the earlier wave, perseverance lies in everyday renewal. The constancy of morality lies in not just one virtue; the matter of education lies in not just one lesson.

Based on the fundamental and flowing out unceasingly, morality will prosper and education will be furthered gradually, which is the benefit the noble man attains from difficulties.[74]

Just like the constancy of the fountain, with the later water being not the earlier water, and the water being renewed day after day, a person who cultivates his morality perseveringly, with his present virtue being not the past one, and his morality renewed and made prosperous day after day, will develop constantly.

4. The Stage of Moral Behaviors

Moral behaviors are the behaviors conducted by people according to certain moral norms. Moral behaviors are the end result of moral education; the final aim of forming moral awareness, developing moral emotions, and cultivating moral will is to practice moral behaviors. The important mark of a person's moral quality lies not in his words but in his behaviors, whether conforming to the requirement of society. Therefore, the fundamental task in the process of moral education is to transform moral awareness, moral emotions, and moral will into moral behaviors. The process of cultivating moral behaviors is the process of guiding students with actions. This means that through the instruction of enlightenment education, students are required to match their words to their deeds; through organizing and guiding students to participate in practices, their behaviors are restricted and trained strictly, helping them to master the method of moral behaviors and form sound moral habits gradually.

The stress on practice was a strong tradition in China's ancient academic thought. Reflected in the process of moral education, it is the special attention paid to moral practice, the training of moral behaviors, and the formation of moral habits. Ancient Chinese educators generated plenty of insights on this matter. For example, Confucius said, "To practice with vigor is to be near to benevolence." He also said, "In letters I am perhaps equal to other men, but the character of the noble man, carrying out in his conduct what he professes, is what I have not yet attained."[75] This means that as for the knowledge found in books, Confucius had learned as much as others, but he had not yet attained the status of a noble man in practice. He stressed the actual conduct of performing morality.

The Mohists also focused on moral practice, proposing to "observe both a person's intention and consequences."[76] They thought that when evaluating a person's moral quality, people should observe both his moral motivation and his behaviors. The Neo-Confucians in the Song Dynasty proposed the view of putting knowledge before action and weighing action more than knowledge, which, to a certain extent, reflected their stress on moral practice.[77]

In the Qing Dynasty, Wang Fuzhi further put forward the view of combining practice with knowledge, holding that only through actual moral behaviors could moral knowledge be obtained. He said, "Generally speaking, what can be called virtue? It is what is obtained in behaviors. What can be called kindness? Getting along well with others is kindness. Without behavior, how can one obtain virtue? Without getting along, how can one be properly virtuous?"[78]

In terms of the specific measures and methods of cultivating students' moral behaviors, China's ancient educators proposed three valuable opinions. First, students were required to be consistent in their words and deeds, as well as in their internal and external sides. For example, Confucius asked his students to honor their promises, saying, "I do not know how a man without truthfulness is to get on."[79] He praised Zi Lu for his trustworthiness, saying that Zi Lu "never slept over a promise."[80] He also advocated doing more deeds than one's words, to be cautious in speech and action, and to put action before words. He said, "The noble man wishes to be slow in his speech and earnest in his conduct,"[81] "to be earnest in what he is doing, and careful in his speech,"[82] and "to act before he speaks and then speak according to his actions."[83]

He objected to boasting, saying, "The noble man is modest in his speech but exceeds in his actions."[84] He objected to hollow talk, saying that "he who speaks without modesty will find it difficult to make his words good."[85] He objected more to cheating, saying, "I hate those who, with their sharp mouths, overthrow kingdoms and families."[86] He also objected to believing and transmitting rumors, saying, "To tell, as we go along, what we have heard on the way is to cast away our virtue."[87] He objected to the inconsistency in people's internal and external sides, hating most the "double-dealers," who "assume the appearance of virtue but betray it in their actions." He regarded those who had "fine words and an insinuating countenance" as those with few virtues. Influenced by Confucius, his disciples also paid much attention to the consistency of their words and deeds, as well as their internal and external sides. For example, "When Zi Lu heard anything, if he had not yet succeeded in carrying it into practice, he was only afraid lest he should hear something else,"[88] which was strong proof. The author of the *Doctrine of the Mean* also required his students to respect their words and deeds at the same time.

Earnest in practicing ordinary virtues, and careful in speaking about them, if, in his practice, he has anything defective, the noble man dares not but exert himself; and if, in his words, he has any excess, he dares not allow himself such license. Thus, his words have respect for his actions, and his actions have respect for his words. Is it not an entire sincerity which marks the noble man?

This means that one should practice ordinary virtues and be careful in his daily talk; if there is an insufficiency in his moral behaviors, he dare not but exert himself; if any of his words have not been put into practice, he dare not boast; his words should respect his actions, and his actions should respect his words. How can a noble man not be honest in order to be consistent in his words and deeds? When evaluating students' moral qualities, China's ancient educators also observed both their words and their deeds, with an emphasis on deeds. For example, Confucius advocated "hearing their words and looking at their conduct."[89]

The second method of cultivating students' moral behaviors involved asking students to acknowledge their weaknesses and mistakes correctly. For example, Confucius held that it was impossible for a person to make no mistakes, because "human beings are not like the sages who make no mistakes." The problem lay in people's unwillingness to correct their mistakes. If they were willing to correct their mistakes, it accorded to the saying that "knowing one's mistake and correcting it is the best kindness." If people were not willing to correct their mistakes, it accorded to the saying that "making mistakes while correcting nothing is wrong."[90] Therefore, Confucius asked his students to be brave in correcting their mistakes: "If you have made a mistake, do not be afraid to correct it."[91] He spoke highly of Zi Lu's attitude towards mistakes, praising Zi Lu as he "becomes glad when knowing his mistakes." He held that the noble man always corrects himself when knowing his mistakes, whereas base men only cover up their errors. Therefore, his student Zigong said, "The faults of the noble man are like the eclipses of the sun and moon. He has his faults, and all men see them; he changes again, and all men look up to him."[92] This means that people's mistakes exist objectively like the eclipses of the sun and moon, which are obvious enough for everyone to see. The act of a person correcting his mistakes self-consciously is like the sun or moon regaining its glory. This showed that Confucius was rather successful in teaching his students to be brave in correcting themselves.

In the Ming Dynasty, Wang Shouren created a course timetable in the school principles, setting the "examination of virtue" as the first lesson of every day. He wrote, "Every day in the morning, after the students greet the teacher, the teacher asks the students questions in the following order: Have you remitted your love and respect to your parents and decreased your sincerity at home? Have you ignored your obligations to serve your parents, such as to warm the bed in the winter, to cool the room in the summer, to bid them good night, and to greet them in the morning? Have you dissipated instead of restrained yourself to exert your propriety when you meet others on the street? Have you deceived or behaved imprudently in your words, deeds, or intentions, instead of remaining loyal, faithful, or respectful? All you young children should answer these questions honestly, correct mistakes if you have made any, and guard against them if you have not. The teacher then instructs on certain problems, after which the students go back to their seats to start their learning."[93] According to this procedure, when the students went to the school, they first bowed in greeting, and then the teacher asked all the students to rethink their deeds of the past day: all behaviors and intentions at home, in the school, and on the street. If they had made any mistakes, they had to admit them and express their determination to correct themselves. In the end, the teachers encouraged or criticized the students according to particular problems.

In the third method of cultivating moral behaviors, students were asked to form sound moral habits through behavioral training. Confucius made some contributions in this regard. For example, when Fan Chi asked about the exalted virtue, Confucius answered, "If doing what is to be done is made the first business and success a secondary consideration, is this not the way to exalt virtue?"[94] This means that to practice as the primary motivation, and to have achievements as the secondary motivation, is the method to develop a virtue. Therefore, he often encouraged his students to conduct moral practices in order to train and cultivate their moral qualities. He said, "Is virtue a thing remote? I wish to be virtuous, and virtue is at hand,"[95] and "Is the practice of perfect virtue from a man himself, or is it from others?"[96]

Zhu Xi also paid great attention to the training of moral behaviors. He specifically composed the book *Instructions for the Enlightenment of Children* as a set of teaching materials for the training of children's moral behaviors. *Instructions for the Enlightenment of Children* gave detailed regulations on the moral norms that should be followed by children, which could be divided into the following categories: apparel, words and manners, cleaning, reading and writing, and miscellaneous matters. For example, the "words and manners" section declared that, "As juniors, you have to be humble and tolerant, speaking kindly and slowly and making no noise or frivolous movements. If your father or elder brother lectures you, you have to listen obediently without any improper comments." The "miscellaneous matters" section declared that, "When serving beside seniors, you should stand at attention submissively. If asked any questions, you should answer honestly. Do not speak improperly."

The content of these moral behaviors embodied feudal ethical norms, and through these regulations, children were restrained in their words and deeds and cultivated to form the ideal well-behaved feudal moral habit. Through this training, students could enter the state in which "their habit grows with their intelligence, and their learning develops with their mind without any conflict."[97] Further, "they have sturdy personal integrity and practice self-restraint."[98]

Wang Yangming also had similar opinions. He said:

> There should be no one who never practices what he has learned. For
> example, when learning filial piety, one should support and serve his parents

to practice his filial duty, and thus he can be said to be learning it. Can one be learning filial piety with just hollow talk?[99]

In the view of Wang Yangming, to form students' moral qualities, the teacher could not simply discuss a few moral concepts but must conduct them through specific moral practices. For example, the virtue of filial piety should be rooted in one's psychological structure of virtue through "supporting and serving his parents as well as practicing his filial duty" in person.

Throughout the discussions of China's ancient educators on the process of moral education, it can be seen that although ancient educators made certain elaborations about moral awareness and moral emotions, they primarily focused on moral will and moral behaviors. In ancient China, great importance was attached to the moral personality with strong willpower, which is reflected in the principles and methods of ancient moral education.

The Principles and Methods of Moral Education

The principles of moral education are the basic requirements which should be followed by educators to conduct moral education and the basic codes which should be followed when handling some basic conflicts and relationships in the process of moral education. The methods of moral education are the ways to accomplish the tasks of moral education. The principles and methods of moral education are formed through practice during the process of moral education and are the summary of the practice and experience of moral education, which, in return, guide the practice. In long-term educational practices, China's ancient educators established some effective principles and methods of moral education, which became an important part of China's treasury of educational thinking. Through applying these principles and methods, a great many upright people with noble virtues who loved their country and were concerned about its people were cultivated.

Ancient China's principles and methods of moral education can be roughly divided into four aspects and nine codes as follows.

1. The Principles and Methods of Moral Education—External Influence

Moral education cannot be conducted in a vacuum, but instead is influenced by the social environment at all times. Professor Lu Jie said, "There are many influences that can work on people's morality, and they penetrate into every corner and every relationship in social life."[100] Among these influences, there are positive as well as negative influences. Therefore, the way to choose and control these influences is an important matter, which should be considered in terms of the principles and methods of moral education.

1) The Environmental Influence

China's ancient educators believed that the influence of environment on students in the process of moral education should be paid attention to and that a sound environment of moral education should be provided. For example, the Mohists started from the theory of "plain silk" human nature, which "changes blue when dyed in blue and changes yellow when dyed in yellow," warning people to be cautious about the color to be dyed. Mo-tse's *Suo Ran* (the *Color Dyed*) states:

> Watching a dyer of silk at work, Mo-tse sighed, "What is dyed in blue becomes blue, what is dyed in yellow becomes yellow. When the silk is put in a different dye, its color becomes different. Having been dipped in five times, it changes color five times. Therefore, dyeing should be done with great care.

This means that man is to his environment as silk is to dye; when put into a different dye, or environment, its color, or his behavior, will become different. Through the metaphor that "growing among the hemp, the fleabane will become straight without support; in the alunite, the white sand will become black," Xuncius made the conclusion that "a noble man must choose his dwelling place and be close to virtuous men when traveling in order to be upright and avoid evil things."[101] Xuncius required his students to choose a good place to dwell and to associate with virtuous and learned men when traveling. Xuncius regarded the environmental influence on individuals as "Zhu Cuo" (injecting) or "Jian" (steeping), and the individual's continual acceptance of the environmental influence as "Ji Mi" or "Ji" (both of which mean accumulating). He witnessed the great significance of the environment in forming students' morality: "They can be like Yao and Yu, or Jie and Zhi; they can be craftsmen, farmers, or businessmen; it all depends on their accumulation of environmental and customary influences."[102] He also cultivated his students' ability to defend against negative environmental influences: "Rotten meat breeds maggots and dead fish nurture worms. If one remits and slacks off, he will encounter misfortune. Things that are too rigid will break, and things that are too soft will constrain themselves."[103] With an enhanced power to resist negative influences, negative influences will have no way to swoop in. Xuncius's explanation of the dialectical relationship between the objective environment and the subjective effort in moral education is quite insightful.

Wang Tingxing, an educator in the Ming Dynasty, divided the environment into two levels: the macro-environment of social customs and the micro-environment of community associations. He also described the influence of these two environments on people's moral qualities:

The character of the common people is formed from their habits, and the sages guide them by education and rule them by law; therefore the country's customs from ancient times until now have long regarded kindness as the destination and evil as forbidden.[104] The forbidden activity in the palace is to play with women; misconduct in spare time is to flirt with eunuchs. Have these people been educated by the principles of benevolence, filial piety, propriety, and righteousness? Since they have formed their character from their habits, they will be extravagant and dissipated or obscene and indolent.[105]

Wang Tingxiang held that if the social environment was sound, people would become kind, but if the social environment was negative, people would become evil. Those rakes who were associating in the forbidden palace to play with women and flirt with them idly would definitely form a bad character: "extravagant and dissipated," as well as "obscene and indolent."

Through the famous story of ancient China of Mencius's mother changing residence three times, it can be seen that the ancients placed much stress on the influence of the environment on children:

Meng Ke (Mencius) and his mother once lived close to the tombs. At that time Mencius was young and liked to make games out of the funeral rituals and build mounds. [Seeing this,] Mencius's mother said, "This is not the place to live." Then she left there and moved to a place which was close to the market. Mencius then made games out of peddling. [Seeing this,] Mencius's mother said, "This is not the place to live." Then she left there and moved to a place near the school. Mencius then made games out of sacrificial vessels, bowing, acting modestly, and learning propriety. [Seeing this,] Mencius's mother said, "This is the very place to live." Then she settled down there.[106]

That Mencius's mother emphasized the educational environment of her son is still a positive influence today.

2) The Observation of Friends

China's ancient educators not only stressed the importance of environmental influence, but also stressed the choice of friends in the process of moral education. Through communication with his friends, one can improve his learning and cultivate his morality. Confucius said, "When I walk along with two others, they may serve me as my teachers. I will select their good qualities and follow them, their bad qualities and avoid them."[107] He proposed to take one's friends as a mirror to reflect one's own behaviors in order to learn the good qualities of his friends and avoid their bad qualities, thus reaching the goal of "improving one's benevolence through friends."[108] Confucius was good at guiding his students to choose friends wisely in the process of moral education. He said:

> There are three friendships which are advantageous, and three which are injurious. Friendship with the upright, friendship with the sincere, and friendship with the well-informed: these are advantageous. Friendship with the man of specious airs, friendship with the insinuatingly soft, and friendship with the glib-tongued: these are injurious.[109]

Confucius asked his students to make friends with upright, sincere, and well-informed men, instead of insinuating, double-faced, and glib-tongued men. Confucius also said to his students, "There are three things men delight in, which are advantageous....To find delight in the discriminating study of ceremonies and music, to find delight in speaking of the goodness of others, to find delight in having many worthy friends: these are advantageous."[110] This means that there are three kinds of pleasure in life: the first is the study of ceremonies and righteousness, the second is the speaking of others' goodness, and the third is the acquaintance of many virtuous friends. No wonder the beginning words in *The Analects of Confucius* are, "Is it not delightful to have friends coming from afar?"[111] *The Records on the Subject of Education* systematically described the principles and methods of moral education in terms of the observation of friends, clearly proposing that "to observe and improve one another is called the good influence of examples," and including the observation of friends in order to learn from each other as one of the four elements in a successful education, which was discussed in Chapter One of this book.

In the Eastern Jin Dynasty, Su Jun divided friends into four categories in *Ji Ming Ou Ji (Manuscript Notes)*: "Those who can encourage you in moral principles and remind you of your mistakes are respectable friends; those who can share everything with you and can be relied on in life-related moments are close friends; those who speak sweet words and spend time with you are intimate friends; those who compete with you when seeing profit while trapping you when seeing trouble are injurious friends." Naturally, "respectable friends," who can mutually encourage moral principles and persuade and help each other when there are mistakes, and "close friends," who can share sorrows and happiness and be trusted throughout life, are the most helpful in the aspect of morality.

In the Song Dynasty, the educator Zhang Zai also witnessed the significance of friends in learning and cultivation. He said, "If one cannot concentrate on his learning, he has no other measure but to exchange his views with his friends on studying."[112] The learning he mentioned did not only refer to the learning of knowledge, but also included the learning of morality. In the

Ming Dynasty, Wang Yangming set "kind blame" as an important element in the observation of one's friends:

> Kind blame is the way of friends. But one should advise and kindly guide his friend to make him know the principles of loyalty and love, as well as the reasons for his errors, thus making him accept what he has heard and correct his mistakes, leaving him touched but not angered. Therefore, this is called "kind blame." If one should first straightforwardly expose his friend's mistake and bitterly rebuke him, leaving him no face, his shame and resentment will be stimulated, under which circumstance he will not succumb to the blame even if he would like to. It is the stimulation of shame and resentment that will make him refrain from recognizing and correcting his mistake.[113]

Wang Yangming thought mutual "kind blame" between friends was quite beneficial and could not be replaced by that shared with teachers or elders. Since there were profound sentiments and trust between friends, they could accept the advice of their friends with joy and not resistance. If one's mistakes were "exposed straightforwardly and rebuked bitterly," he would have no face, and therefore there would be no sound educational effect.

Wang Fuzhi also held that the observation of friends had important meaning for the cultivation of virtue. He said:

> Only the virtuous can like or dislike others in the right way. If one's virtue is not mature when handling affairs, his judgment of liking or disliking must be biased, and there must be something (or someone) to rely on in order to conduct his actions according to his likes and dislikes. Getting along with the noble man, he will like what the noble man likes and dislike what the noble man dislikes. Getting along with the base man, he will like what the base man likes and dislike what the base man dislikes. What's worse, when getting along with the despicable men, he will also follow their likes and dislikes. Therefore those who make friends with the kind, including those from the counties, the states, the kingdom, and even the ancients, are "cultivating their virtue through making friends," which will guide the emotions of like and dislike and enhance the ability to like the kind and dislike the evil."[114]

Wang Fuzhi held that people's virtue and behaviors were influenced to a great extent by those with whom they associate. By getting along with and making friends with noble men, one will assimilate noble men's likes and dislikes, as well as their excellent characters and behaviors. By getting along with base or despicable men and making friends with them, one will assimilate their likes and dislikes and develop bad characters and behaviors. Therefore, he advocated that his students should try to "cultivate their virtue through making friends" and develop themselves through the influence and help of their friends.

However, Wang Fuzhi didn't agree with Confucius' view of "not making friends with those who are inferior to you," but held that one could not only make friends with the virtuous but also with those who were not virtuous. When making friends with a virtuous person, one should not only respect and praise him psychologically or verbally, but also aspire to attain his virtue and knowledge in order to keep pace with him. When making friends with a less virtuous person, one should not only express his dislike of his friend's bad character, but also rethink himself as to whether he also has the same weaknesses in order to develop himself through helping his friend.[115] This means that the observation of friends could not only have a direct effect of "emulating better ones," but also have the reverse effect of "self-retrospection."

2. Principles and Methods of Moral Education—Subjective Effort

Subjective effort means that during the process of moral education, the enthusiasm of the educated to conduct self-education should be aroused to develop their subjective initiative. In the process of moral education, if the educated are passive and negative and merely the object to "be educated," there will be no good effect of moral education. Only when students' consciousness of self-education is aroused and their subjective initiative developed can the educational work achieve twice the effect. When describing the significance of subjective effort, Soviet educator Sukhomlynsky stated, "According to my deep belief, education that arouses people to conduct self-education is a kind of true education. To teach people to conduct self-education is much harder than organizing Sunday entertainment."[116]

China's ancient educators placed much stress on the significance of subjective effort in cultivating moral qualities. For example, Confucius said, "Is the practice of perfect virtue from a man himself, or is it from others?"[117] "Is virtue a thing remote? I wish to be virtuous, and virtue is at hand."[118] Confucius thought that virtue could be formed through personal effort. Mencius also emphasized "seeking the reason in oneself." He said:

> The noble man makes his advances in what he is learning with deep earnestness and by the proper course, wishing to get hold of it in himself. Having got hold of it in himself, he abides in it calmly and firmly. Abiding in it calmly and firmly, he reposes a deep reliance on it. Reposing a deep reliance on it, he seizes it on the left and right, meeting everywhere with it as a fountain from which things flow. It is on this account that the superior man wishes to get hold of what he is learning in himself.[119]

Mencius held that if a person could maintain his kind nature, endowed by heaven, and further his own cultivation, he would not lose his endowed excellent virtue. In the poem "Bi You Ling" ("There Must Be a Neighborhood"), Zhu Xi also vividly described the meaning of subjective effort:

> People are similar to each other in terms of their morality, and they store similar virtues within themselves if they have any. One need not shut himself in and sigh for his loneliness, but should set his sincerity to making efforts in learning.

As for the principles and methods of subjective effort, China's ancient educators proposed two terms: self-introspection and self-accusation. They also described the concepts of inspection and self-supervision, which will be introduced in the following content.

1) Self-Introspection and Self-Accusation

China's ancient educators requested their students to perform self-introspection when seeing others' moral behaviors and to examine their own mistakes to perform self-criticism. For example, Confucius asked his students to "think of equaling them when seeing men of worth, and turn inwards and examine themselves when seeing men of contrary character."[120] When seeing sound moral behaviors, one can perform self-introspection to set others as his example; when seeing bad moral behaviors, he can avoid similar mistakes through self-examination. Confucius' students made excellent cultivation of this aspect. For example, Zeng Can said, "I daily examine myself on three points: whether, in transacting business for others, I may have been not faithful; whether, in communicating with friends, I may have been not sincere; and whether I may not have mastered and practiced the instructions of my teacher."[121] If one can restrain himself by certain moral norms and perform self-examination when seeing others' moral behaviors, his cultivation of morality will be benefited. Zhu Xi wrote a poem to praise Zeng Can, who made great effort in self-introspection: "Zengzi always worried about three mistakes and said that he examined himself every day. How can later learners know the meaning of their teachers' instructions without the effort of self-introspection?"[122]

Confucius also requested his students to treat their mistakes correctly, proposing the method of moral education of "self-accusation," saying, "I have not yet seen one who could perceive his faults and inwardly accuse himself."[123] He always taught his students that "when having faults, do not fear correcting them,"[124] holding that "to have faults and not correct them is called having faults,"[125] but "to correct faults is called not having faults."[126] This means that people cannot avoid making mistakes or deviating from moral principles in behaviors, but this is not to be blamed. However, if a person always makes the same mistake or repeats the same deviation, he then cannot be forgiven. Therefore, Confucius asked his students to perform self-accusation and seriously face their mistakes, trying not to "repeat their faults."

Mencius also encouraged his students to correct their mistakes and improve themselves, proposing not to blame those who performed self-accusation and attempted to renew themselves.

He said, "The faults of the noble man are like the eclipses of the sun and moon. When he has faults, all men see them; when he changes again, all men look up to him."[127]

2) Inspection and Self-Supervision

China's ancient educators asked their students to remain alert and prevent those thoughts and behaviors that did not conform to ethical norms, continuously performing self-supervision and self-encouragement. Zhu Xi gave quite a detailed description of the method of inspection:

> To inspect at the moment of germination is to be cautious when the intention starts to grow. To inspect after the occurrence is to be careful about one's words and behaviors after they have been said and acted. When the intention starts to grow, one should of course be cautious; when the words and behaviors have been said and acted, one should also be careful.[128]

Zhu Xi also gave examples to elaborate on the concept of inspection:

> When one utters words or performs behaviors, one should remember to have self-control and be cautious at all times. For example, the water flows unremittingly and fluctuates when elevated. Likewise, one should always be fearful and cautious and be even more cautious when necessary. What's more, when riding a horse, one should keep pulling from time to time and strain harder when coming to rugged paths.[129]

This means that inspection is an omnipresent, long-term method of moral cultivation, focusing on daily "self-control"; and before the occurrence of words and behaviors that do not conform to ethical norms, one should raise his prevention awareness and stifle them before they emerge.

Han Fei described the method of self-supervision. He said:

> The ancients could not see themselves with their own eyes, and therefore, they used mirrors to see their faces; their wisdom was not enough to know themselves, and therefore, they rectified themselves with the Dao. Therefore,

the mirror should not be blamed for its reflected flaws, and the Dao should not be blamed for its reflected faults. Without the mirror, the eye could not see how to trim the facial hair; without the Dao, people could not know how to solve problems. Since Ximen Bao was short-tempered, he always brought cooked cowhide with him to remind him to act slowly; since Dong An was tardy, he always brought a tightened string with him to remind him to act quickly. Therefore, to supplement a deficiency with excess and to replenish shortcomings with strengths is called wise.[130]

In the view of Han Fei, to raise one's individual moral level and rectify one's shortcomings needed constant inspection and self-supervision. For example, Ximen Bao, the leader of Ye County in the reign of Duke Wen of Wei during the Warring States Period, always brought a soft cowhide belt with him to remind him to act slowly because he was always short-tempered and reacted rashly when handling affairs; what's more, Dong Anyu, the minister of Zhao Jianzi in the final phase of the Spring and Autumn Period, always brought a bowstring with him to remind him of progressing through every day without tardiness because he was slow and tardy in handling affairs.

3. Principles and Methods of Moral Education—Educational Opportunity

Moral education is a subject of science and also a subject of art. In the work of moral education, to master the best education opportunity is significant for achieving a sound education effect. This "opportunity" can be grasped in two aspects.

1) The Education of Children to Form Sound Habits

From the perspective of a person's development, the best time for moral education is childhood. Therefore, China's ancient educators advocated that moral education should be conducted from childhood in order to help children form sound moral habits. Confucius proposed that "habits formed in childhood are like the endowed nature and are conducted naturally," which makes a lasting influence on later generations' moral education.

In the Period of the Southern and Northern Dynasties, Yan Zhitui recalled the moral education he received in childhood in the *Admonitions for the Yan Clan*:

The educational tradition of my family has always been strict. In my childhood, I was educated from time to time. Following my two elder brothers, I served my parents every day. I followed regulations in all behaviors with calm encumbrance and words; when walking, I behaved as carefully and respectfully as when presenting my respect to my parents. The elders always taught me excellent lessons, cared about my interests, and encouraged me to enhance my advantages and avoid my disadvantages. All of these teachings were sincere and keen.

In this way, Yan Zhitui emphasized the significance of moral education in childhood.

During youth, one's character has not yet been cemented. When affected by his intimates through words and behaviors, although he is not intentionally learning, he will be influenced unconsciously by and will naturally simulate others, let alone the moral conducts and skills of others, which are obviously easier to learn.[131]

Yan Zhitui held that people's psychology is not stable in their childhood and is open to influence by both positive and negative aspects unconsciously, which will lead to the development of certain moral characters. In the Song Dynasty, Zhu Xi not only emphasized the significance of moral education for children, but also edited the book *Children's Education* in order to be a set of teaching materials for the moral education of children. When describing the aim of the book, he said:

Children's education in ancient times taught people how to clean, react, behave properly, love one's parents, respect elders, respect teachers, and make friends, all of which were the basis for the cultivation of character, the regulation of the family, the governance of the state, and the tranquility of the kingdom. To be educated on these topics in childhood was to make people's habits develop with their intelligence and their learning develop with their mind without any conflict. However, all records cannot be seen at present, and most records come from biographies. When reading books, people always regard the difference between past and present books as impossible to learn, but this is because they do not know that there is no difference between the past and the present, and it is therefore not impossible to learn. Now I have specially collected texts to edit this book and teach children and offer them materials in learning, wishing to be beneficial for the development of their moral decency.[132]

In the joint period of the Ming and Qing Dynasties, Wang Fuzhi also advocated for the education for children and proposed the view that "children's education forms sound habits." In terms of early education, he said:

The Book of Changes says that to conduct children's education to form sound habits is a virtuous merit. To form habits during childhood is the basis for a child to become a sage in the future. If a person is unfortunately not educated and loses himself to bad habits, hearing inhumane words, seeing inhumane things, and spending time in narrow alleys or small villages day after day, he has to be cleaned from the inside out if he is determined to save himself after becoming an adult; otherwise it is impossible.[133]

Wang Fuzhi held that only when sound moral habits have been accumulated and the right moral qualities have been formed during childhood could one establish a sound basis for his whole life. If one lacked correct education and guidance during childhood, he would form bad moral habits and a bad character, which were hard to rectify even with great effort.

As for the specific methods of children's education to form sound habits, China's ancient educators proposed several valuable views, such as trainings focusing on behavioral habits, positive guidance, and the improvement of family education, which will be discussed in detail in Chapter 10, "Ancient China's Elementary Education."

2) Restraint Before Occurrence

In terms of the process of the formation of a person's moral character, the best opportunity for moral education is to prevent the development of bad moral character before it begins, that is, to "restrain before occurrence." Therefore, China's ancient educators emphasized using moral education to prevent accidents before they happened. When commenting on the idea of restraint before occurrence in *The Records on the Subject of Learning*, Mr. Fu Rengan said:

Education is to cultivate good qualities in the positive aspects and eliminate bad qualities in the negative aspects. To cultivate students' good qualities, the bad qualities need to be eliminated or prevented from developing, as destruction should always come before establishment. However, eliminating bad qualities that exist is much more difficult than preventing them from developing in the first place.

Therefore, to cultivate good qualities and eliminate bad qualities requires using the method of prevention. Bad qualities are the same as harmful diseases, which are difficult to treat after they have developed and are easier to prevent before they develop. Taking the bad quality of lying as an example, if lying is prevented through moral education and good examples before a child develops a habit of lying, the child will not become "infected" with this bad habit. If the child is not instructed in daily life, once he has developed a bad habit, it will be difficult to eliminate.[134] Therefore, *The Records on the Subject of Learning* stated that "restraint after occurrence causes resistance with conflict" as one of the six reasons for the failure of education. Comenius, the great Czech educator, said, "Virtues should be taught before evil things occupy the mind."[135] The explanation of restraint before occurrence in *The Records on the Subject of Learning* is in agreement with these words.

The Mohists also paid attention to the preventive function of moral education. For example, Mo-tse requested his students to "not listen to treacherous words, utter any threatening sounds, or entertain any ideas of injuring somebody,"[136] and to prevent the development of bad character. In the Tang Dynasty, Kong Yingda proposed, "For all the faults which are detested by people, are they severe faults made observably? They are all caused by trifles, which will become severe faults without prevention."[137] This means that preventive measures not only prevent "severe faults," but also notice trifles, which can truly guard against the gradual development of malpractice.

The method of "maintaining respect" mentioned by Zhu Xi also paid attention to the preventive principle and method of moral education. For example, in *Jing Zhai Zhen* (*Maxims Written in Jing Zhai*), he said:

Keep the mouth shut as that of a jar, and prevent personal desires as one would guard the city wall. Be cautious and never be casual. Do not think of the west when heading to the east or think of the north when heading to the south. When dealing with an affair, concentrate the mind on it without distraction. Do not reduce complex characters into simplified ones. Be perfect and concentrated with regard to the changes of everything in the world. Concentrating the mind on an affair is the so-called maintenance of respect. Do not have contradiction between active and static actions, and coordinate the inside and the outside. In just a moment, there are various personal desires, which are hot without fire and frigid without ice. With only a small difference, heaven and earth may change their positions. Without the three cardinal guidelines, the nine principles are abolished.

Zhu Xi asked people not only to prevent malpractice, but also to prevent evil intentions. Therefore, one should always keep nature in mind and eliminate human desires. One should have no improper intentions inside and conduct no improper behaviors outside.

Wang Fuzhi then described the principle of restraint before occurrence through the example of children's education, proposing the "teaching of prevention":

As for the child's enlightenment, the children of birds and beasts are the earliest to gain intelligence, but they gradually become stupid as they grow up. Only human children, in childhood, are ignorant in knowledge and principles and then try to restrain themselves to avoid indulgence. The pattern of the Six-Five diagram has the Yin in the lower position, which is restrained by the Yang in the upper position. The image of this diagram indicates the reason human beings are different from animals.... Since the diagram of Meng (ignorance) indicates that there are unknown dangers ahead, people keep themselves away from evil things and restrain themselves from partiality. This is the teaching of prevention."[138]

Wang Fuzhi held that people's psychology was different in nature from that of animals. Newborn animals showed their "intelligence" very early on, and their instincts kept them alive and allowed them to negotiate with the environment. However, the "intelligence" of animals and their instincts could not be further developed, and therefore, they grew to be "stupid." People were different. In childhood, humans were ignorant and could not live on their own or cope with the environment. However, people's psychological ability developed with age, which was not true of animals. Because humans experienced a longer childhood, they had a stronger ability to learn, and therefore should be "restrained from evil things and partiality," instead being guided correctly. It can be seen that the concepts of restraint from occurrence and the teaching of prevention were important principles in ancient China's moral education, especially for children.

4. Principles and Methods of Moral Education—Teacher's Instruction

In the work of moral education, although the influence of the social environment, the subjective effort of the educated, and the opportunity of moral education are important, the effect of the teacher's instruction should not be neglected. This is because teachers are the executors who choose and control the environment and the engineers who foster the development of the souls of the students. In complete educational activities, the relationship between education and self-education is always the unity of opposites.

1) Differentiated Teaching: Teaching According to Aptitude

China's ancient educators advocated following the principle of "differentiated teaching" during moral education and taking different teaching approaches according to different educational targets. For example, during his long-term practice of moral education, Confucius excelled at applying the principles and methods of differentiated teaching in the following situations.

First, for the same question asked by his students, he could answer with a unified direction while focusing on different points according to specific targets. For example, when Yan Yuan asked about the moral concept of "Ren" (perfect virtue), Confucius answered that "to subdue oneself and return to propriety is perfect virtue."[139] When Zhong Gong asked about "Ren," Confucius said, "It is, when you go abroad, to respond to everyone as if you were receiving a great guest, to employ people as if you were assisting at a great sacrifice, not to do to others what you do not want others to do to yourself, and to have no complaint when serving the state and none when serving the family."[140] And when Fan Chi asked about "Ren," Confucius explained with the words "loving others."[141] For other questions, including questions about propriety, filial piety, government, knowledge, the scholar, and the noble man," Confucius treated them with the same method according to the different moral levels of his students.

Second, for the same question asked by his students, Confucius could answer with different and even opposite meanings according to which student asked the question. For example, when Ran Qiu asked "whether one should immediately carry into practice what he has heard," Confucius answered, "You should carry it into practice." But when Zilu asked, Confucius answered, "There are your father and elder brothers to be consulted; why should you act on the principle of immediately carrying into practice what you hear?" On the surface, these answers contradicted each other, and even Confucius' student Gongxi Hua, who attended both questions, was confused. However, the two different answers reflected exactly the excellent educational wisdom and art of Confucius. He explained, "Qiu is retiring and slow; therefore I urged him forward. You has more than his own share of energy; therefore I kept him back."[142]

Third, responding to some questions proposed by a particular student, Confucius could guide and help the student according to his actual case. For example, Zilu was aggressive and inclined to act rashly. Therefore, when he asked "whether the noble man esteems gallantry," Confucius answered, "The noble man holds righteousness as the priority. A man in a noble situation, having gallantry without righteousness, will be guilty of insubordination; a base man, having gallantry without righteousness, will commit robbery."[143]

Mencius, who was called the "Second Sage," also noticed the individual differences of his students and divided his disciples into several categories:

> There are five ways in which the noble man conducts his teaching. There are some on whom his influence descends like seasonable rain. There are some whose virtue he perfects, and some of whose talents he assists in the development. There are some whose inquiries he answers. There are some who can touch others and include them as his private disciples. These five ways are the methods in which the noble man conducts his teaching."[144]

This means that some can influence others like seasonable rain, some can perfect their virtues, some can cultivate their talents, some are good at solving problems, and some can make examples from which later generations can learn.

Xuncius also advocated moral education that could differentiate students' individual characteristics. He said:

The methods of soothing the vital energy and nourishing the heart are as follows: for those who are energetic and rigid, soften them through calmness; for those whose ideas are deeply reserved, improve them with frankness and kindness; for those who are gallant and brutal, tame them with principles; for those who are rash, restrain them with gradualness; for the narrow-minded, stretch them with magnanimity; for those who are base and greedy, improve them by lofty ambition; for the mediocre and undisciplined, regulate them with good teachers and helpful friends; for the flighty and self-abandoned, alert them through the prediction of adversity; for the honest and overcautious, coordinate them through etiquette and music and develop them through thinking.[145]

This means that for those who are energetic and rigid, they should be softened through calmness; for those whose ideas are deeply reserved, they should be improved with frankness and kindness; for those who are gallant and brutal, they should be tamed with principles; for those who are rash, they should be restrained with gradualness; for the narrow-minded, they should be stretched with magnanimity; for those who are base and greedy, they should be improved by lofty ambition; for the mediocre and undisciplined, they should be regulated with good teachers and helpful friends; for the flighty and self-abandoned, they should be alerted through the prediction of adversity; for the honest and overcautious, they should be coordinated through etiquette and music and further developed through thinking. It can be seen that Xuncius paid much attention to fostering his students' sound moral qualities through targeted remedial measures according to their individual characteristics.

In the Song Dynasty, educators agreed on the theoretical aspect and formally proposed the principles and method of differentiated teaching. Zhang Zai said, "Teaching that does not develop all of a student's talents, pay attention to tranquility, or foster the character trait of honesty is incorrect. The most difficult matter of teaching is to develop all the talents of a student in order not to mislead him and to observe his potential achievement in order to guide him."[146]

He also said, "Knowing the difficulty of learning is knowing virtue; knowing good and evil is knowing humanity. Knowing both humanity and virtue, one could teach others to be virtuous, which is the reason Zhongni provides different answers to the same question."[147] He held that the first element of moral education was to learn the current moral character of the student, in order to teach him to "become virtuous" and "develop all of his talents," instead of "misleading" him. Zhang Shi once said, "Although the sages' doctrines are similar, their teaching methods always change according to the students' different aptitudes."[148] Zhu Xi further proposed, "The sage teaches according to his students' differences. If a student's potential is low, he will teach him to make small achievements; if a student's potential is promising, he will teach him to make great achievements; he does not give up on any student."[149]

In the Ming Dynasty, Wang Yangming was also good at applying the principle and method of differentiated teaching in the practice of moral education. For example, in *The Practice of Instructions*, such an affair was recorded:

> When the master taught his students, he always touched them with just several words. One day, after Wang Ruzhi returned from the outside, the master asked, "What did you see outside?" He answered, "I saw that people on the street were all sages." The master said, "When you saw the people as sages, they regarded you as one." On another day, after Dong Luoshi returned from the outside, he greeted the master and said, "I saw something strange today!" The master said, "What strange thing?" He answered, "I saw that people on the street were all sages!" The master said, "This is normal. Why do you wonder at it?" Because Ruzhi was hard-edged and Luoshi was doubtful about his discovery, the master answered the same question differently and reversed the students' understanding in order to encourage them.

The word "hard-edged" meant that Wang Ruzhi was an arrogant man; therefore Wang Yangming called him a sage to shame and restrain him. Dong Luoshi was an honest man who was not brave enough; therefore Wang Yangming said that being a sage was normal in order to reward and encourage him. It can be seen that Wang was good at differentiated teaching. Just as he said, "When the sage taught, he did not treat all the students in the same way and restrain them. If a student was arrogant, the sage then accomplished him by arrogance; if a student was honest, the sage then accomplished him by honesty. How can people's talents all be the same?"[150] This was also the conclusion of his own practice of moral education to a certain extent.

Wang Fuzhi also had unique ideas about differentiated teaching. He said, "The methods of teaching included accomplishing one by agreeing with him, correcting him by reversing his intention, guiding him in order to make him obedient and interested in the right Way, or making it difficult for him to stimulate his ambition. So there are many methods."[151] This means that, according to the particular cases of the students, the teacher can agree with their intention, correct their bias, arouse their interest, or stimulate their ambition. Wang Fuzhi also asked the teacher to develop the merits and overcome the defects of his students according to the development of their moral characters. "Teaching is an inexhaustible matter. The teacher should know the students' merits in their moral characters to correctly guide them and know their defects to change them."[152] Therefore, the principle of differentiated teaching was to enhance the strengths and supplement the shortcomings and defects of one's students in order to help them develop soundly.

2) Example Setting

China's ancient educators advocated that during moral education, the educators should pass on knowledge through both words and deeds, setting an example to the educated through one's own actions. Confucius said, "When the leader's personal conduct is correct, his government is effective without the issuing of orders. If his personal conduct is not correct, he may issue orders, but they will not be followed."[153] "If a minister makes his own conduct correct, what difficulty will he have in assisting in government? If he cannot rectify himself, what has he to do with rectifying others?"[154] Confucius not only advocated setting an example through one's own actions but also practiced this in principle. For example, he asked his students to be fond of and have delight in learning and asked himself to "be fond of ancient knowledge and endeavor to pursue it." He asked his students to think of righteousness when seeing profit, and he himself was a person who "regarded unrighteous wealth and nobility as a floating cloud." Plenty of examples like these were recorded in *The Analects of Confucius*.

In the practice of moral education, Confucius focused on guiding through lecture and action, combining "verbal teaching" with "nonverbal teaching." He said, "When a man may be spoken to, not to speak to him is to err in reference to the man. When a man may not be spoken to, to speak to him is to err in reference to our words. The wise err neither in regard to the man nor to his words."[155] He believed in the great power of nonverbal teaching. Once, he said to his students that, in the work following moral education, "I would prefer not speaking." Hearing this, Zigong immediately said, "If you do not speak, what shall we, your disciples, have to record?" Confucius then explained, "Does heaven speak? The four seasons pursue their courses, and all things are continually being produced, but does heaven say anything?"[156] The purpose of nonverbal teaching was to educate students through implication and example in order to influence them unconsciously. It can be seen that Confucius emphasized the significance of teaching by example in moral education. Mo Di also emphasized the principle and method of example setting. His political proposition of "identifying oneself with the superior" requested the borough warden, the township leader, and even the feudal lord to cultivate their own characters first.[157] It was the same for his educational practice. For example, it was recorded that Mo-tse "was sad when hearing [grievous news] and hurried for ten days and ten nights from Lu to get Ying, and did not rest even when his feet were severely callused, instead tearing his clothes to wrap around his feet."[158] This reflected his tenacious spirit to bear hardships. For the sake of his example setting, most of his students had the gallantry of "not returning even when going through extremely dangerous areas."[159]

Mo Di said, "Doctrines that can be translated into conduct may be taught frequently. Doctrines that cannot be translated into conduct may not be taught frequently. To talk frequently about what cannot be carried out is merely to wear out one's mouth."[160] This means that if a person's words can be carried out in his actions, people will look up to his virtue; if not, people will not look up to him. To look up to one whose words cannot be carried out in action means his words are all nonsense. Therefore, he held that the teacher had to "act in person"[161] to set a good example for his students.

When describing the principle of example setting, Mencius said, "If a man himself does not walk along the right path, it will not be walked even by his wife and children. If he orders men according to what is not the right way, he will not be able receive the obedience of even his wife and children."[162] If a man does not act in the right way, his wife and children will not act in the right way, either, let alone others. If one orders others in the wrong way, he cannot even order his wife and children, let alone others. Only when the educator is strict with himself can he regulate others.

In the Southern Song Dynasty, the educator Yuan Cai also discussed this topic. He said, "When a person's talent is respected by others, he can teach others the way of cultivation. When his character traits and actions are valued by others, he can teach others the way to form virtues."[163] In other words, without a high professional level and a sound moral character, one cannot take on the task of educating others.

3) Praise and Criticism

China's ancient educators advocated the method of combining praise and criticism in the process of moral education to teach students, developing their likelihood of doing good deeds and reducing their likelihood of doing evil deeds, as well as correcting their faults and helping them improve. Confucius was good at praising and criticizing students according to the cultivation of their moral character. Taking Yan Yuan and Zilu as examples, since Yan Yuan had a good self-awareness, Confucius always praised him. In the record of *The Analects of Confucius*, Yan Yuan (Hui) had been praised many times. For example, Confucius said, "Hui loves to learn," "Hui is not stupid," "Hui is virtuous," "Such was Hui that for three months there would be nothing in his mind contrary to perfect virtue," "Never flagging when I set forth anything to him, ah, that is Hui," and "I saw his constant advance. I never saw him stop in his progress." There was only one time when Confucius criticized Yan Yuan: "Hui gives me no assistance. There is nothing that I say in which he does not delight."[164] However, this was just a criticism in which Confucius actually praised Yan Yuan. And since Zilu was "rigid" and arrogant, inclined to act rashly, Confucius always criticized him.

Confucius paid attention to the facts and praised good behaviors while criticizing bad ones; sometimes he praised before criticizing, and sometimes he used the reverse method. Confucius praised Zilu (You), saying, "Dressed in a tattered robe quilted with hemp, yet standing by the side of men dressed in furs, and not ashamed, it is You who is equal to this!" He then quoted words from the *Book of Poetry*, saying, "He envies none, he covets nothing, how can he be not excellent?" Zilu felt self-satisfied after hearing this and kept repeating these words. Confucius then criticized him, saying, "Those things are by no means sufficient to constitute perfect excellence!"[165] Zilu played the lute in the style of the Period of King Zhou in the Yin Dynasty, which was considered decadent music. Confucius criticized him harshly, saying, "What has the lute of You to do in my door?" Hearing this, other students thought that the master was expelling Zilu and therefore began "not to respect Zilu." Seeing this, Confucius thought it was improper and corrected himself, saying, "You has ascended to the hall, though he has not yet passed into the inner apartments."[166]

In *The Analects of Confucius*, there are 23 records of Confucius' praise and criticism of his students, including 17 items of praise and 6 items of criticism. His positive educational method, with much more praise than criticism, was quite meaningful for cultivating students' self-respect and self-confidence in their moral conduct.[167]

Reward and punishment are important forms of praise and criticism. China's ancient educators had little to say on the subject of reward, but much to say on the subject of punishment, including physical punishment, which was related to the prevalent physical punishment in ancient China's feudal society. Zhang Zai once said the following words, which are interesting to contemplate:

Don't consider children as not having a good memory; they do not forget what they have gone through. Therefore, those who are good at cultivating their children when they are young nurture them to make them gentle. When their children grow up with a good character, they teach them frequently the examples of good and evil things. It is like when you do not want the dog to enter the central room, you rush at it once it enters the room; if you rush at it and feed it at the same time, it does not know how to behave and therefore does not obey your order even if you rush at it every day to keep it from the room.[168]

This paragraph aimed to explain that children should be shown "the examples of good and evil things frequently" when being educated in order to set a correct behavioral standard and develop it as their habit. But it also describes the relationship between reward and punishment. In the view of Zhang Zai, if one did not want the dog to enter the central room, he rushed at it once it entered the room; if he rushed at it and fed it at the same time, it would not know how to behave and therefore would not obey the order even if it was being rushed at every day. From this, it can be seen that the reward of food is more powerful than the punishment of being rushed at. In terms of this point, American educational psychologists concluded with the theory that "When the stimulation and reaction in the nervous system combine together with satisfaction, the combination is enhanced and the annoyance can seldom or not lead to reducing or eliminating the combination."[169] This indicates that in moral education, praise and criticism, as well as reward and punishment, should be prescribed according to certain standards in order not to cause students' psychological confusion. At the same time, praise and reward should be dominant, while criticism and punishment should be supplementary.

Wang Yangming had a unique view on education. He detested the physical punishment prevalent during his time and denounced it powerfully. In *General Ideas of Children's Education After Reading the Work of Liu Bosong and Others*, he wrote passionately:

Generally, children like having fun and fear restraint. It is like when the grass and trees start to germinate; they flourish in comfortable conditions and wither if thwarted. At present, when teaching children, the best method is to encourage and delight them, which will lead to their unremitting and self-motivated progress. They are then like the plants showered by the seasonable rain and grow by themselves, naturally progressing as time goes by. If damaged by ice or frost, they will become lifeless and wither gradually.

As for the education of children in later times, they are urged to learn words and sentences in books and regulate their behavior without being guided by propriety. They are expected to be smart without the cultivation of their kindness. They are lashed and roped as prisoners. They regard school as a prison, resisting entering; they regard teachers as enemies, resisting seeing them. Disguising themselves in order to have fun and concealing themselves in order to indulge in recreation, they become shallow and obstreperous, reducing themselves to become indecent day by day. How can they be expected to be kind when being driven to be evil?

In his view, children's minds were always open to all good things, and educators should kindly guide them, "instructing them by etiquette" and "cultivating them by kindness" positively, which would achieve sound effects. If teachers just negatively urged them or punished them physically, the students would "become lifeless and wither gradually" like the frosted grass and trees, thus regarding the school as a prison and teachers as enemies. They would then become fearful and resentful, leading to the development of bad moral character.

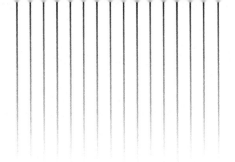

5

The Teaching Theories of Ancient China

Teaching is the most fundamental way to implement education for well-rounded development. According to modern teaching theories, teaching is an educational activity in which teachers, with certain educational aims and based on the law of students' physical and mental development, guide students to learn the basic knowledge of science and culture and grasp the corresponding basic skills in a planned and organized way, meanwhile developing students' intelligence and creativity, improving their fitness, cultivating their aesthetic abilities, and shaping their morality.

In the field of modern pedagogic theory and practice, teaching issues are at the forefront. In terms of contemporary foreign teaching schools, there are more than ten, including those advocating nondirective teaching, discovery teaching, suggestive teaching, programmed instruction, mastery learning, example teaching, teaching through investigative methods and seminars, peer coaching, open teaching, and the optimization of teaching. Most of them are based on a certain theory and have their own unique models for teaching processes, principles, and methods.

In ancient China, teaching and learning were separate in meaning but were sometimes used as one word. For example, it was said in *The Records on the Subject of Learning* that, "Jade uncut will not form a vessel for use, and if men do not learn, they will not know the Way. In this account, the ancient kings, when establishing states and governing the people, made teaching and learning a primary focus." However, teaching and learning here mean the same as education in the general sense but not in the modern sense. China's teaching theories in ancient times were the quintessence of China's educational thoughts and of great practical significance. Just as Professor Mao Lirui said when he commented on Confucian teaching theory, "Confucian 'teaching theory' is brilliant and takes precedence in the world's educational history. We should not only critically inherit this legacy, but we should also study it further, demonstrating and developing it with the findings of contemporary educational psychology in a scientific experimental way. "[1] Therefore, this chapter will analyze the teaching theories and thoughts of ancient China in a systematic way and will classify them into four aspects: the significance of teaching, the contents of teaching, the process of teaching, and the principles and methods of teaching. This chapter takes a special interest in the quintessence of China's teaching theories and thoughts in ancient times with the wish to carry them forward.

The Significance of Teaching

Most educators in ancient China had a good awareness of the significance and necessity of teaching. For example, *The Analects of Confucius* say from the very beginning, "Is it not a pleasure to study and practice what you have learned?" This statement regards learning as a pleasure in life. As said in *The Records on the Subject of Learning*, "Jade uncut will not form a vessel for use, and if men do not learn, they will not know the Way," which indicates that jade needs to be chiseled and carved to become an exquisite and useful object. Similarly, man needs to learn and practice hard to know the Way of things. This saying is concise and comprehensive in summarizing the significance of teaching.

In the history of China's educational thought, Laozi might be the only one who explicitly denied the significance of teaching by saying, "When we renounce learning we have no troubles," and "We should renounce the wise and their wisdom, the saints and their holiness."[2] He said:

> He who devotes himself to learning [seeks] from day to day to increase [his knowledge]; he who devotes himself to the Dao [seeks] from day to day to diminish [his doing]. He diminishes it and again diminishes it, until he arrives at doing nothing [on purpose]. Having arrived at this point of non-action, there is nothing which he does not do.[3]

In the eyes of Laozi, learning and knowing the Dao were in conflict. Knowledge, like lust, was considered to stand in the way of people's mastering the Dao. Therefore, only by renouncing learning and wisdom and arriving at the point of nonaction could one realize the supreme Dao. This theory of Laozi suffered opposition and refutation from the Mohist School at that time. As is written in *Mo-tse: Explanations II*:

> In the case of learning, consider taking someone who does not know that "learning is without benefit" and then teach him this. This causes him to know that "learning is without benefit" and is, in fact, teaching him. To take learning to be of no benefit yet to teach is contradictory.

This means that at first the learner does not know that "learning is of no benefit," but by telling him so, you are actually teaching him. Since you say "learning is of no benefit," then you should abolish your teaching. If you say learning is of no benefit on one hand, and teach others on the other, is this not extraordinarily absurd? Mo-tse confuted Laozi's theory that learning is without benefit with Laozi's own arguments. Moreover, he put more emphasis on "Li" (standing), expounding on the significance of teaching from the positive side. He said:

> Leading (Chang, teaching) and following (Xue, learning) are linked. The explanation lies in the merit.[4] Leading but not following: this is not to learn. If you do not learn when your knowledge is slight, your merit must be diminished. Following but not leading: this is not to teach. If you do not teach when your knowledge is great, your merit comes to an end.[5]

The first quotation above explains that both teaching and learning have merits. The second explains that one is not learning if he leads without following others in singing and that being poor in knowledge and not learning will diminish his merit. Similarly, one is not teaching if one merely follows others without leading the singing and that being knowledgeable but not teaching will lead his merit to end. So the Mohist School revealed the importance of teaching on the premise of recognition that both teaching and learning are of great use.

Chinese educators in ancient times described the significance of teaching from the following perspectives.

1. Teaching Helps Learners to Acquire and Enhance Knowledge and Skills

Although there was a dispute between the theories of "being born to know" and "learning to know" in ancient China, neither theory denied the role of teaching in the acquisition of knowledge and skills.[6] Therefore, educators in ancient China had a tradition of thinking highly of teaching. Just as the ancient Chinese philosopher Xuncius said, "Truly, if you do not climb a high mountain, you will be unaware of the height of the sky. If you do not look down into a deep gorge, you will be unaware of the thickness of the earth. If you have not heard the words inherited from the ancient kings, you will be unaware of the greatness of learning and inquiry."[7] Xuncius believed that only through the observation and experience of objective things and learning from predecessors could teaching be rewarding. *The Records on the Subject of Learning* also points out the importance of teaching to one's acquisition of knowledge, especially the objective law, or the Dao (the "Way"):

> However fine the viands be, if one does not eat, he does not know their taste; however perfect the course may be, if one does not learn it, he does not know its goodness.

Wang Anshi of the Northern Song Dynasty illustrated this issue from the opposite side. In *Pity Zhongyong*, he narrated a thought-provoking story about a has-been prodigy called Fang Zhongyong in Jinxi County. It was said that at age five, Zhongyong could "improvise verses on objects randomly picked, and his verses all showed literary talent and ingenuity in diction," which made him a legend around the county. Therefore, people in the county "started to entertain his father with dinners or simply to pay for Zhongyong's poems." Seeing profit in this, his father "took him around the county visiting people every day, ignoring his studies and schooling." As a result, Zhongyong was "reduced to an ordinary person." Thus, Wang Anshi remarked:

> Zhongyong's talent was innate. Although he enjoyed a natural gift far above most other talented people, he faded into an ordinary person because he did not receive enough education. If such a born talent can wilt into ordinariness without education, then what about those ordinary people who do not have innate talent or receive education?[8]

Wang Anshi held the view that however talented a person was, if he received no education to further acquire knowledge and increase his intelligence, then his talent would vanish day by day and he would become an ordinary person one day; as for ordinary people, it was more vital that they become educated.

Wang Fuzhi during the Ming and Qing Dynasties gave the most detailed explanation of this issue. He believed that teaching was an important way to acquire and enhance knowledge and skills. In his eyes, teaching was a process of going from ignorance to knowledge and from inability to ability. Learning was a process of going over acquired knowledge again and again, practicing mastered skills, and strengthening what has been learned. Meanwhile, he advocated that "when ignorant people desire knowledge and incompetent people desire skills, they will start to learn. Then they will acquire knowledge and skills. Those who review learned knowledge now and then will progress every day; those who practice skills frequently will become masterly day by day."[9] He thought that only through repeated study would knowledge build up every day; only through practice would skills gradually become perfect. Wang Fuzhi disapproved of sayings that denied the significance of teaching. Further, he made a comparison between a human's cognitive processes and an animal's instinctive activities.

> The being who has ears to hear, eyes to see, and mind to know is man. Ears must hear all kinds of voices to know voices, eyes must see all kinds of things to know colors and shapes, and mind must develop ideas by thought. Is there anybody who knows voices all of a sudden, identifies things only by an accidental glimpse, and understands the world without a bit of thinking? If so, then all people are no different from animals. Therefore, that baby animals cling to their mothers cannot be regarded as filial piety because it is merely out of nature and has nothing to do with virtue. It has been said that today we humans know things by nature and have innate abilities and skills with no need to learn. That is to say that baby animals are much more able and virtuous than savages and that savages are worthier than noble men.[10]

He held that if we admitted that there were people in the world who gained knowledge and skills without learning, then we must acknowledge that baby animals are wiser than ordinary people and that ordinary people are wiser than noble men who are virtuous and erudite.

In addition, Wang Fuzhi used shooting an arrow as an example to illustrate the role of teaching in shaping people's skills and techniques. He said:

> An archer has a technique of using strength to shoot an arrow, which can be obtained by learning and practice, depending little on natural gift. And compared with strength, techniques are especially more inclined to be gained by learning rather than nature. But it is not so easy and takes much effort to learn. Thus, those who are indolent attribute their failure to aptitude.[11]

This is to say, archery needs strength on one hand and skills on the other hand. Both can be attained through repeated practice, but the acquisition of skills needs more learning and practice.

2. Teaching Helps Learners to Develop Their Intelligence and Talents

Very early on, Confucius noticed the relationship between the mental development of humans and learning, as seen from his words "To be fond of learning is to be near to knowledge,"[12] which also pointed out teaching's role in the development of one's abilities. It is written in *The Family Sayings of Confucius: Zilu's First Meeting with Confucius*:

> The first time Zilu met the Master, the Master asked, "What do you like?" Zilu replied, "I like long swords." The master said, "I am not asking you about that.

I mean that you are talented and if you study hard, no one will emulate you."...
Zilu said, "In the Southern Mountain, there are bamboos that are straight by
nature with no need to straighten. If you cut them down and make them into
arrow shafts, they can shoot through rhinoceros hide. In light of this, is there
still any need to learn?" The Master said, "When the end of an arrow has been
created, feathers still have to be fixed on it; when the arrowhead has been
forged, it still needs sharpening. Thus the finished arrow can shoot even
farther, can it not?" Again Zilu expressed his gratitude to the Master, "Thank
you for your enlightenment with my greatest respect."

Zilu argued that bamboos in the South Mountain were born straight with
no need to be straightened and that shafts made out of them could "shoot
through rhinoceros hide" by nature. However, Confucius said that if we process
these bamboo arrow shafts by "fixing feathers on the end of them and sharpening well-wrought arrowheads," then the finished arrows will be sharper and
keener. This is also true of man's abilities and talents, which may exist innately
but which need learning and practice to be improved.

Wang Chong in the Han Dynasty also agreed that teaching is important
to develop learners' intelligence and talents by saying, "Things perceivable can
be perceived through thinking, and those that cannot be understood only by
thinking must draw upon learning and inquiry to be comprehended. There has
never been such a thing as knowing without learning and inquiry in human
history....So even wise and talented people need to learn and inquire to gain
knowledge and achievements."[13] Additionally, the Cheng brothers, Cheng Yi
and Cheng Hao, educators in the Song Dynasty, had said the following words
worth consideration:

Every being is born with talents, for instance, birds make their nests with great
ingenuity, which is due to the nature of birds and is not learned. Newborn
babies need to learn everything except suckling.[14]

"Talents" here refers to the natural instincts of humans, which are considered to be rare. Only suckling is seen as an inborn human instinct, with
all other skills and abilities being obtained by learning. Further, Chinese educators in ancient times depicted teaching's role in cultivating learners' talents.
In ancient China, talent (Cai, timber) had two meanings: one signifies what
we call qualities today, which lay the foundation for one's development of
mind (intelligence) and abilities (talents), and the other refers to capabilities or
capable persons in the modern sense.

Educators in ancient times were greatly in favor of the idea that teaching
is significant in the development of one's talents and abilities. For instance,
during the Three Kingdom Period, Liu Shao said, "One's becoming a useful
person lies in learning,"[15] and Zhu Geliang said, "One has to learn to acquire

and enrich his knowledge and talents."[16] In addition, Hu Yuan of the Northern Song Dynasty wrote in *The Note of Learning in Songzi County*, "A talent pool is the key to governing a kingdom well. And it is education and cultivation that produce talents. Schools are the very place to conduct education and cultivation." This explicitly points out the importance of school education and has been seconded by scholars ever since. For instance, Yan Yuan, an educator in the Qing Dynasty, said, "Learning is the key to producing talents, talents are the key to government, and government is the key to the masses' well-being. Thus, there is no talent without learning, no satisfying government without talents, and no well-being of the masses and social peace without good government."[17]

Wang Fuzhi made a relatively full elaboration on teaching's role in developing learners' intelligence and talents. He said:

> In terms of human nature, man has an innate potential to learn things and develop skills. Although this potential is inherent in everyone, education and practice are needed to activate and fully realize this potential.[18] One should set goals first and then learn and think to realize these goals. Thus one's talents and intelligence will increase every day. Finally, one will become wealthy in knowledge.[19] Man's heart is active day and night. Although man has many lusts stirring in his heart, still it is his heart and no other that he relies on to know the principles of nature. If man does not make full use of his heart but leaves it inactive and quiet day and night...talents grow every day and thought never exhausts by frequent use.[20]

Wang Fuzhi believed that although people had "an innate ability to learn things and develop skills," without education, learning, or practice after birth, or without the step of "receiving education to practice," they could not make the best and fullest use of their abilities.

So only by learning and practice can man's intellect be developed, will one's talents "build up every day," and will one's thought never wither and drain. If one just stuffs himself with food all day and stays sedentary without contact with the outside world, receiving no education and never learning, his natural abilities will wither. Similarly, it was said:

> Duke Zhou conquered Yi (backward foreign ethnic groups in different places) and drove beasts away, and Confucius compiled the *Chun Qiu* (*Spring and Autumn Annals*). Both undertook what they were doing by working hard every day. Yet they became confused in their mind, language, and behavior, whereas the wits of those who only eat all day will accumulate and never exhaust if they are forced to study principles and deal with all kinds of affairs. Then, domestic pigs are wiser and abler than human beings, while stones and insects are cleverer and more capable than domestic pigs.[21]

3. Teaching Helps the Cultivation of Morality and the Development and Improvement of Human Nature

Generally speaking, Chinese educators in ancient times all approved of teaching's function in cultivating learners' morality, and this was even regarded as teaching's foremost and only function, as was mentioned in Chapter Four. Here, we will analyze some of these educators' arguments. Confucius once said:

> There is the love of being benevolent without the love of learning—the beclouding here leads to a foolish simplicity. There is the love of knowing without the love of learning—the beclouding here leads to the dissipation of the mind. There is the love of being sincere without the love of learning—the beclouding here leads to an injurious disregard of consequences. There is the love of straightforwardness without the love of learning—the beclouding here leads to rudeness. There is the love of boldness without the love of learning—the beclouding here leads to insubordination. There is the love of firmness without the love of learning—the beclouding here leads to extravagant conduct.[22]

Benevolence, knowledge, sincerity, straightforwardness, boldness, and firmness were the moral goals pursued by ancient people with high ideals. Nonetheless, the formation of these moral qualities cannot be attained without learning. Without learning, man will definitely become "simple" (being fooled by others), develop a "dissipated mind" (squandering intellect without the foundation of wisdom), become "injured" (being harmed and hurt), grow "rude" (being biting and harsh), become "insubordinate" (being disobedient and rebellious), and "conduct oneself extravagantly" (being daring and rash).

Later educators inherited this Confucian theory. For instance, Xuncius said, "Wood that has been marked with the carpenter's ink marker will be straight, and metal that has been put to the whetstone will be sharp. By broadening his learning and examining himself each day, the gentleman keeps his awareness sharp and his actions mistake-free."[23] And Liu Xiang of the Han Dynasty pointed out in a more explicit way that "By staying close to the wise and virtuous and learning and enquiring, one's moral virtues will grow."[24]

Theories on human nature in ancient China flourished and blossomed like a hundred flowers in bloom, including the well-known Confucian theory that human nature develops by learning, Mencius's doctrine that man is good and kind by nature, Xuncius's philosophy that man is born evil, Gaozi's belief that human nature is neither good nor evil, Dong Zhongshu's thought that human nature can be rated at three levels, and Wang Fuzhi's belief that human nature is formed day by day, among others. Nonetheless, no matter what kind of theory is being discussed, they all agreed that teaching plays a significant role in developing and improving human nature. Take Confucius' theory, for example. Since

Confucius made the statement that "man is born identical but learning makes a difference," educators in later history all made their own interpretations of this thesis. Wang Fuzhi said, when interpreting this thesis, "We humans are similar to each other in nature. And if we enrich ourselves by studying, some will gain wisdom, and some will form a morality of benevolence, resulting in differences in disposition."[25] This means that from the perspective of human gifts and innate human nature, all humans are born equal, but study and learning create differences in human nature, for learning is an important way to develop and improve human nature.

Next, let's look at Mencius's doctrine and Xuncius's philosophy. Mencius, the representative of those who held that man is born good and kind, believed that man is born with "seeds of goodness" in nature, but that on their own, these "seeds" only stay in the embryonic stage. Whether they grow into goodness or not depends on whether one receives good education and studies hard. Mencius said, "If it receives its proper nourishment, there is nothing that will not grow. If it loses its proper nourishment, there is nothing that will not decay."[26] This means that if one "receives proper nourishment," namely, being in a good environment for education and learning, his "seeds of goodness" will flourish and develop into a good nature of benevolence, righteousness, politeness, etiquette, and wisdom. Otherwise, if one "loses proper nourishment," his "seeds of goodness" will decay, and he will step onto the road to being evil.

However, Xuncius, an advocate of the philosophy that man is born evil, believed that man was born a piece of bad material but could become good and even become a saint through cultivation and study. He said:

> A man in the street, one of the Hundred Clans, who accumulates goodness and achieves it completely, is called a sage. Having sought it, he will gain; having acted for it, he will be perfected; having accumulated it, he will be ennobled; having achieved it, he will become a sage. Thus, becoming a sage is the result of what a man has accumulated.[27]

This is to say that one's moral qualities must be cultivated and that there is no born "sage" at all; the so-called sublime "sage" is just an ordinary man who has received education and studied hard, whose height and sublimity everyone can achieve.

The Content of Teaching

Teaching content may refer to the curriculum of a school in a certain learning phase, such as elementary school, or it may mean the curriculum of a certain subject, such as Chinese, which is the mediator between teacher and student and an important method to achieve educational goals. Now, the content of teaching has become a specialized science: curriculum theory, including the theory of the subject-centered curriculum, the curriculum theory of structuralism, and the theory of activity-centered curriculum. This has become an increasingly popular field in the study of teaching theories.

Education in China's primitive society was not separated from social production and life, so the content of education was primarily the imparting of skills and experience related to production and daily life. In the end of clan society, schools started to come into being, and schooling content was mainly the teaching of music and filial piety. During the Xia, Shang, and Western Zhou Dynasties, educational content was gradually unified and specified day by day, forming the so-called cultivation of the "Six Arts," including the arts of rites, music, archery, charioteering, calligraphy, and mathematics.

With the characteristics of attaching equal weight to the learning of literature and the acquisition of martial arts, the cultivation of the Six Arts and pursuing the development of knowledge and talents lasted for a long time in the history of China's education and had far-reaching influence. In the Spring and Autumn Period, Confucius compiled six books, called the "Six Classics" by later generations. These not only were the first relatively complete textbooks in Chinese history, but also became the fundamental textbooks of China's feudal society. With the execution of the cultural and educational policy of "rejecting other schools of thought and respecting only Confucianism" in the Han Dynasty, Confucian classics gradually became important textbooks. Further, various specialized schools grew into maturity, all with their own teaching materials. The following section will discuss the Six Arts, the Six Classics, and textbooks on science and technology, and will have an exclusive discussion about books on elementary teaching.

1. The Teaching Contents of the Six Arts

The Six Arts are the earliest systematic collection of teachings in ancient China. *The Rites of Zhou: Offices of Spring* says, "The Bao family contends that students in the national school should learn knowledge and skills. So students of the national school are taught Six Arts, including Wu Li (five rites), Liu Yue (six kinds of music and dance), Wu She (five techniques of archery), Wu Yu (five skills of driving), Liu Shu (six origins of Chinese characters), and Jiu Shu (nine categories of mathematics)."

The Teaching of Li

The earliest teaching of Li (rites) was divided into two types: rules of propriety on national occasions taught by the national school and those on township occasions taught in local schools, the former consisting of five elements, including rituals of sacrificial ceremonies, funerals, military ceremonies, greetings and meetings between rulers and ministers, and festival occasions, and the latter consisting of six elements, including the rituals of a male coming of age, weddings, funerals, sacrificial ceremonies, formal dinners, and greetings and meetings. The schooling of Li undertakes the teaching of politics and the patriarchal clan system, ethical and moral education, and the cultivation of patriotism, behavior, and habits.[28] *The Book of Rites: Qu Li* recorded the educational function of "Li" (the rules of propriety):

> Duty, virtue, benevolence, and righteousness cannot be fully carried out without the rules of propriety; nor are training and oral lessons for the rectification of manners complete; nor can the clearing up of quarrels and discriminating in disputes be accomplished; nor can [the duties between] ruler and minister, superior and subordinate, father and son, or elder brother and younger brother, be determined; nor can students for office and [other] learners, in serving their masters, have an attachment to them; nor can majesty and dignity be shown in assigning different places at court, in the government of the armies, and in discharging the duties of office so as to secure the operation of the law; nor can there be [proper] sincerity and gravity in presenting offerings to spiritual beings on occasions of supplication, thanksgiving, and various sacrifices. Therefore, the superior man is respectful and reverent, assiduous in his duties and not going beyond them, retiring and yielding, thus illustrating [the principle of] propriety.

The Teaching of Yue

Yue (music) was one of the main courses taught by the national school, including teachings of virtues drawn from music, of musical languages, and of musical dance. Teaching virtues drawn from music refers to music's function of moral education: "There is an interaction between the voices and airs [of the people] and the character of their government."[29] It was said that "Music is the intercommunication of people in their relations and differences."[30] Musical languages involve Xing, Dao, Feng, Song, Yan, and Yu.[31] Xing is saying words in a figurative way; Dao means "using the past [ancient things] to satirize the present"; Feng is recitation; Song refers to chanting; Yan and Yu refer to composing literary works and teaching, respectively. Musical dance includes Yunmen, Daxian, Dashao, Daxia, Dahuo, and Dawu, namely the so-called Liu Yue (six kinds of music and dance). Therefore, it can be seen that the education of Yue actually involved the teaching of music, poetry, dance, drama, and the simple composition of literary works.

The Teaching of She and Yu

The teaching of She (archery) was the training in shooting skills. There were five techniques of shooting an arrow or "Wu She," namely, Baishi (penetrating through the target with the arrowhead seen), Canlian (shooting arrows in succession), Yanzhu (shooting arrows in a linear course), Rangchi (in which the elbow is so even and stable that a cup of water can be put on it and the arm is straight like an arrow when shooting), and Jingyi (in which four arrows hit the target forming the shape of Jing; 井).

The teaching of Yu (charioteering) was the training in driving a chariot. There are also many techniques of driving a chariot, or "Wu Yu": Ming He Luan (ringing the bells "He" and "Luan" after the chariot gets started), Zhu Shui Qu (being able to drive flexibly with the flow of water, keeping the chariot from falling into the water), Guo Jun Biao (being adept at driving through the outer gate of a government office or a battalion in ancient times without bumping into any obstacle or being an obstacle to others), Wu Jiao Qu (turning with propriety at road junctions when driving, like dancing to a beat), and Zhu Qin Zuo (driving to round up fowls and beasts to help in hunting).

The Teachings of Shu

The teaching of Shu (calligraphy) was the teaching of reading and writing. There were six ways to teach students to read a Chinese character, or "Liushu": Xiangxing, Zhishi, Huiyi, Xingsheng, Zhuanzhu, and Jiajie. Xu Shen of the Han Dynasty pointed out in his book *Shuo Wen Jie Zi* (*Origins of Chinese Characters*), "*The Rites of Zhou* prescribe that disciples of aristocrats begin studying at elementary school at age eight and that educational officers will first teach them six ways of constructing Chinese characters. The first way is Zhishi, which means characters constructed in this way can be recognized when seen and understood with inspection, such as "Shang" (up) and "Xia" (down). The second is Xiangxing, meaning characters are constructed by drawing pictures of things they refer to, with the streaks following the natural lines of these things, like "Ri" (the sun) and "Yue" (the moon). The third is Xingsheng, which denotes characters formed by choosing a phonogram corresponding to the nature of the things they refer to and an ideogram according to the meaning they are intended to express, such as "Jiang" (big rivers) and "He" (rivers). The fourth is Huiyi, which signifies characters constructed by combining graphemes associated with things and which can be understood by thinking over the meaning of these graphemes, like "Wu" (martial arts) and "Xin" (trust). The fifth is Zhuanzhu, which means that characters derived in this way have the same radical and can explain each other, for they have the same meaning, for example, "Kao" (exam) and "Lao' (old). The sixth is Jiajie, which means that according to the pronunciation of things, characters are borrowed to refer to things that have no original character meant for them, such as "Ling" (order) and "Chang" (long). Jiajie not only analyzed the construction of Chinese characters in ancient times, but also offered a rationale for the methods of teaching students to read in the Western Zhou Dynasty, which is said to be the time when China's earliest reading primer, the *Chapters of Shizhou* (an early dictionary of Chinese characters), was written.

The Teaching of Shu

The teaching of Shu (mathematics) was the teaching of numbers, which involved the teaching of nine categories, or "Jiushu": Fangtian (field measurement), Sumi (millet and rice), Chafen (distribution by proportion), Shaoguang (short width), Shanggong (construction consultations), Junshu (fair levies), Yingbuzu (excess and deficit), Fangcheng (rectangular arrays), and Gougu (right-angled triangles). According to the surveys of some mathematicians and educators, although some parts of Jiushu were born in the Han Dynasty, it cannot be denied that the method of counting with the aid of a counting rod and arithmetic operations had already emerged in the Western Zhou Dynasty. Further, the teaching of mathematics at that time may also have involved the teaching of natural science, technology, and religious knowledge. For instance, Lv Simian said that there were six aspects of mathematics, namely, "astronomy, the almanac, the Five Elements, divination with the help of the yarrow and tortoise shell, divination in other ways, and the law of objects' forms and shapes."[32]

As mentioned earlier, education in the Six Arts involved the characteristics of paying equal attention to the learning of literature and the acquisition of martial arts and pursuing the development of knowledge and talents. The Six Arts covered many areas of education, including what we today call moral education, knowledge education, physical education, aesthetic education, and military education. Although education in the Six Arts was dominated by teachings on Confucian classics and was even abolished in the official school since the Han Dynasty, the contents of the Six Arts have never ceased to be taught.

2. The Teaching Contents of the Six Classics

In the late Spring and Autumn Period, during which Confucius lived, the practice of "studying government authorities" was broken, and the teaching of the Six Arts, emphasizing the cultivation of skills and military training, could not adapt to the objective needs of education at that time.

So Confucius compiled six books, which would come to be known as the Six Classics. These included *Shi* (the *Book of Poetry*), *Shu* (the *Book of Documents*), *Li* (the *Book of Rites*), *Yue* (the *Book of Music*), *Yi* (the *Book of Changes*), and *Chun Qiu* (the *Spring and Autumn Annals*), which became the fundamental textbooks for his teachings. As the concept of six books being more theoretical than Six Arts adapted to the needs of a newly rising class of scholars, these books were of certain educational meaning and value.[33] These six books, the first relatively systematic and complete set of textbooks in Chinese history, were respected as "classics"[34] during the Warring States Period and thus became known as the Six Classics. Due to the loss of the *Book of Music*, the remaining "five classics" and the later "four books" became the orthodox teaching books of ancient China.

The Book of Poetry

Shi is the extant *Book of Poetry*. *The Historical Records: House of Confucius* states, "The original *Shi* recorded more than three thousand poems. Then Confucius removed the duplicate poems and reserved those that could be applied to the cultivation of etiquette and righteousness." Thus, he compiled the extant *Book of Poetry*, which included 305 poems and is the oldest collection of poems in China. *Shi* contains three sections: "Feng" (ballads and local music), "Ya" (court music), and "Song" (music used in the temples of the king of Zhou and his vassals), all of which can be played on string instruments and sung. Confucius used three words to summarize the meaning of *Shi*: "Si Wu Xie" (no depraved thoughts),[35] which signifies that this book "can be used for the cultivation of etiquette and righteousness." Further, he expounded on *Shi*'s educational functions with regard to politics, diplomacy, self-cultivation, and art.[36]

The Book of Documents

The *Book of Documents* (*Shu*) is the extant *Shujing* (the *Classic of History*), also known as *Shangshu*, which has an "Old Text" (Gu Wen, ancient script) version and a "New Text" (Jin Wen, modern script) version. It is generally believed that the "Old Text" version is fabrications, but the authenticity of some articles in the "New Text" version is also in question. However, that Confucius compiled *Shu* and made it a teaching book is a historical fact that cannot be denied.[37]

Shangshu is documentation of history dating from late primitive society to the Xia, Shang, and Zhou Dynasties before the Spring and Autumn Period. So it is "a history book of early historical times,"[38] as well as the first teaching book of history in China. Confucius aimed to carry forward the government of King Wen and King Wu (who lived in the Zhou Dynasty before the Spring and Autumn Period), explaining the basis of ruling a nation and drawing political lessons from history by compiling and teaching *Shu*.[39]

The Book of Rites

The *Book of Rites* (*Li*) is the extant *Lijing* (the *Classic of Rites*), also called *Yili* (the *Book of Etiquette and Ceremonial*) or *Shili* (the *Book of Scholars' Etiquette*). Consisting of 17 articles, *Li*, compiled by Confucius, is a teaching book dealing with the cultivation of etiquette and manners for many kinds of rituals and ceremonies, such as the rituals of a male coming of age, weddings, funerals, and sacrificial ceremonies. Confucius paid great attention to the education of rites and propriety. He thought that "if one does not learn the rules of propriety, one's character cannot be established."[40] In addition, he taught his disciples to "look not at what is contrary to propriety; listen not to what is contrary to propriety; speak not what is contrary to propriety; make no movement that is contrary to propriety." Therefore, these doctrines are also known as the "Teachings of Rites and Propriety."

The Book of Music

The *Book of Music* (*Yue*) is said to be a book on music compiled by Confucius and thus is also called *Yuejing* (the *Classic of Music*). But it has been long lost. Although it is greatly contested in academia as to whether the book *Yuejing* in fact existed, it is agreed that Confucius put great emphasis on music. He had been a trumpeter when young and later studied music under Shixiangzi, and was thus proficient in all kinds of music, both highbrow and lowbrow. He said, "It is by the *Book of Poetry* that the mind is aroused. It is by the rules of propriety that the character is established. It is from music that the end again starts."[41] This means that poems can cheer one up, rules of propriety can keep one's behavior within appropriate bounds, and music can perfect one's morality. He also said, "If a man be without the virtues proper to humanity, what has he to do with the rites of propriety? If a man be without the virtues proper to humanity, what has he to do with music?"[42] He held that a man without virtues would not have the ability to appreciate etiquette and music. Therefore, *Yue* was an important component of Confucius's aesthetic and moral education. And the teaching of music was a significant part of Confucius's educational system.

The Book of Changes

The *Book of Changes* (*Yi*) is the extant *Yijing* (*Classic of Changes*), also known as *Zhouyi*. Nonetheless, *Yi* in Confucian times was not yet finalized and may be inconsistent with modern *Yijing* in many places. *Yi* is a book about divination, but through the reorganization and notation of King Wen during the Shang and Zhou Dynasties, and the research and teachings of Confucius, it has become a book on "the relationship between heaven and humanity" studied in academia.

Confucius attached great weight to *Yi*, as well. He not only stated that *Yi* "teaches one to be pure and still, refined and subtle," but also educated the expert Shangqu on *Yi*, as is said in *The Historical Records: Biographies of the Disciples of Zhongni*: "Confucius bequeathed *Yi* to Shangqu." Shangqu then bequeathed *Yi* to Zihong of Chu State. In his later years, Confucius liked to read *Yi* even more, leaving the anecdote that "the thongs broke three times." Moreover, he said, "If some years were added to my life, I would begin to study *Yi* at 50, and then I might come to be without great faults."[43] It can be said to some extent that *Yi* was Confucius's teaching book of philosophy at that time.

The Spring and Autumn Annals

The *Spring and Autumn Annals* (*Chun Qiu*) are also called *Chun Qiu Jing* (the *Classic of the Spring and Autumn Annals*). As the first annals extant in China, they recorded the situation of politics, military affairs, the economy, astronomy, geography, and calamities in the Lu State, dating from the first year of Duke Yin of Lu to the fourteenth year of Duke Ai of Lu. If we say that *Shangshu* is Confucius' teaching book of ancient history, then *Chun Qiu* can be regarded as his teaching book of contemporary history and current affairs. Though *Chun Qiu* was not included in the list of official textbooks for violating taboos at that time, it is still a fact that disciples of Confucius "were taught *Chun Qiu*."[44]

We should not just stay at the level of talking about the Six Classics in terms of the existence of six books, It is true that Confucius' teachings of the Six Classics have made great contributions to preserving the Chinese culture of ancient times, but, in fact, because of Confucius gaining supreme status in the Han Dynasty, the historical fact of his teaching the Six Classics has a deeper meaning. The Six Classics per se created a culture, as well, shaping the hearts and souls of the people of China. Just as Guo Jiaqi said, "China is a country of propriety and courtesy, and the Chinese people obey rules and behave with propriety, which are the influence of *Li*; the Chinese people are optimistic or romantic, loving *Shi* and *Yue*; the character of the Chinese people is many-sided and multi-level, concerned with politics (*Shu*) and very fond of history (*Chun Qiu*) and pursuing truth and philosophy (*Yi Jing*)."[45] Nonetheless, Mr. Guo did not mention the negative effects of the Six Classics, for example, their over emphasis on the "rule of propriety," which can form the red tape of hierarchical society, and being too optimistic, which leads one to lack a sense of crisis. Further, the neglect and omission of natural science in the Confucian Six Classics had a direct influence on the phenomenon of later generations' making light of nature and skills.

3. The Teaching Content of Science and Technology

Although education in science and technology was not dominant in China's ancient educational system, it was still an indispensible part. Therefore, it is of great benefit to a full understanding of the characteristics of China's educational thoughts to study the education in science and technology in ancient China and to comprehend its teaching content.

Ancient China created a splendid civilization of science and technology. Joseph Needham, also known as Li Yuese, a British expert on the history of science and technology, remarked that the Chinese people "succeeded in forestalling in many important matters the scientific and technical discoveries of *dramatis personae* of the celebrated 'Greek miracle,' in keeping pace with the Arabs (who had all the treasures of the ancient Western world at their disposal), and in maintaining, between the third and thirteenth centuries, a level of scientific knowledge unapproached in the West."[46] Thus, what can we know about the education in science and technology in such a brilliant civilization?

In China's ancient educational system before the Western Zhou Dynasty, education was closely related to politics and taught by teachers who were also officials. During the Spring and Autumn Period, there appeared private schools and the content of teaching was changed to the Six Classics from the Six Arts. However, education was still very much politically oriented, and thus people avoided mentioning scientific and technological teachings.[47] Even though knowledge about nature was taught, the teaching of nature focused on "its meaning and value in a political and moral sense."[48] For instance, "the eclipses of the sun and moon"[49] and "compared to the north polar star, which keeps its place and all the stars turn toward it"[50] in Confucian sayings were not discussing astronomical phenomena but used in a metaphoric way to signify "the faults of the noble man" and the stability of government by means of virtues, which is the so-called "drawing an analogy between things observed and the virtues of man." Therefore, in such circumstances, it was difficult for the teaching of science and technology (especially parts unrelated to political or social life) to enter the palace of education (especially official education).

In ancient China, nongovernmental organizations were the main body to carry out the education in science and technology. A statistical analysis worth ruminating states that:

> From the Yellow Emperor Period to the early Qing Dynasty, there were about 243 people who made achievements in astronomy, the calendar, and arithmetic in China, among whom there were around 150 from the Western Han Dynasty to the mid-Ming, with only two being students from the official schools of the "Office of Astronomy" and the "Office of Astrology and the Calendar," these two being an official of astronomy and a worker in the Office of Astronomy. The rest were civilians.[51]

Take Mo-tse, the originator of scientific and technological education in China, for example. He was born humble and rose to be a scholar from a small handicraftsman. He had held an official position as high as "a minister in the State of Song" and was an official in the handicraft industry, his private school had taught knowledge on geometry, optics, mechanics, and machine manufacturing. His doctrine of "universal love" was "Xian Xue" (practical knowledge), which was famous for a time, yet the venerable historian Si Maqian did not write a biography of him, but simply added a short 24-character piece about him toward the end of *Biographies of Mencius and Xuncius*. So Mo-tse was merely a nongovernmental educator of science and technology. There were mainly three forms of the nongovernmental education of science and technology in ancient China, namely, running in the family (the so-called fathers' impartation to sons), running between master and apprentice (an artisan with unique skills who had no children to inherit his business took on apprentices to individually impart his skills), and running between teacher and student (in the model of one teacher with many students, which amounts to nongovernmental schools).

The format of these three forms involved a master training apprentices. The education in science and technology in this form was demanding not only in choosing an apprentice, which was conducted very carefully with the rule "If it is not this kind of person, do not teach him; if it is not this kind of truth, do not confer it,"[52] but also in imparting knowledge, meaning that both teachers and learners were serious. In addition, it was a kind of knowledge transmission from generation to generation so that skills always grew more refined and consummate, which was also the secret of the marvelous crafts of master craftsmen in Chinese history. However, the number of those who taught was too small, which not only limited the spread and popularity of scientific knowledge and skills and led much excellent and peerless scientific knowledge and skills to perish for various reasons (for example, having no heir to succeed one or the master dying suddenly), but also restricted the scientific and technological development of ancient China.

The official education in science and technology in ancient China developed at a slow rate until the Tang Dynasty. Before this, feudal offices still adopted the hereditary system of "Chou Guan" (hereditary professional officials), with sons succeeding fathers' crafts, which was the same model followed by the imparting of folk skills and was most popular among "Chou Guan" like official astronomers, experts on the calendar, arithmeticians, doctors, and pharmacists. Rulers in history were satisfied with this kind of reproduction, operated on a low level and by a small number of scientific and technological personnel. During the Han Dynasty, teachings of science and technology had no place in the large-scale Tai Xue (the Imperial School, the highest rank of educational establishment in ancient China between the Han Dynasty and the Sui Dynasty) or in local schools, like Jun Guo Xue (schools run by vassal states), Xiao, Xiang, and Xu. Emperor Ling of Han established a special school called "Hong Du Men Xue" to study and teach epistolary art, composition of Ci Fu (a literary form), handwriting, and painting, but had not the slightest idea of setting up a school teaching science and technology.

The embryonic form of specialized schools in ancient China appeared around AD 443, when a medical school was established in the Southern Dynasty. In the Sui Dynasty, Guo Zi Jian (the National School) had a subsidiary school, Suan Xue (an official school teaching arithmetic), and Tai Chang Si (a feudal office in charge of ancestral temples of the ruling house and sacrificial practices), had Tai Yi Shu (an office of imperial physicians), which, however, had little influence due to their short duration and small scale. Therefore, it is universally acknowledged that the Tang Dynasty was the period laying the foundation for China's pedagogy in science and technology.

During the Tang Period, besides Guo Zi Xue, Tai Xue, and Si Men Xue, there were specialized schools for the study of laws and decrees, calligraphy, arithmetic, and medicine. These kinds of specialized schools of science and technology not only had a specific system of leadership and government, such as the medical school of the Tang Dynasty being attached to Tai Yi Shu and having special instructors who were physicians, but also involved subject setting and teaching plans. For example, there were four departments in the medical school: medicine, acupuncture, massage, and Zhou Jin (exorcism). The department of medicine had five specialties: Ti Liao (internal medicine, whose length of learning was seven years), Chuang Zhong (surgery for ulcers and sores, five years), Shao Xiao (pediatrics, five years), Er Mu Kou Chi (oto-laryngology, two years), and Jiao Fa (external treatments like cupping therapy, two years). The medical school was therefore the earliest specialized college of science and technology in the world.[53] Its textbooks, *A Revised Book of Materia Medica* (also known as the *Book of Materia Medica of the Tang Dynasty*) and *Huang Di Nei Jing*, were revised by the imperial government and were therefore also the earliest teaching books of science and technology authorized by the government in the world.[54] Moreover, during the Tang Period, there were two Tian Wen (astronomy) Boshis (official posts in ancient China) who taught 90 Tian Wen Guan Shengs (students of astronomy) and 50 Tian Wen Shengs (students of astronomy), and there was one Li (calendar) Boshi who taught 55 Li Shengs (students of the calendar) in Si Tian Tai (the Office of Astronomy and the Calendar), which was similar to in-service education.

It should be pointed out that the Tang Dynasty was the time laying the foundation for the education in science and technology in ancient China, as well as a period of great prosperity for science and technology. After the Tang Dynasty, the scale, system, and content of scientific and technological education saw no significant breakthroughs without being included in the teaching content of ordinary school education, and many thoughts and achievements in science and technology often remained unheeded, with no one to care,[55] which surely exerted a negative influence on the social development of ancient China and, to a certain extent, was also an innate defect of traditional science and education in ancient China.

The Process of Teaching

The process of teaching is the interaction between teacher and student, the learning process of students from the instruction of teachers, and the cognitive process of students' acquiring knowledge and skills. As students are the cognitive subjects in the teaching process, modern teaching theories generally regard the process of teaching as part of human cognitive processes. Since German educator Johann Friedrich Herbart put forward the theory of teaching's four stages—teaching new knowledge, guiding students to make associations between new and old knowledge, guiding students to sum up what they have learned, and helping them to apply what they have learned to daily living—research on the teaching process has increased with each passing day. Further, the classification of steps in the teaching process has changed over time, and the study of the teaching process has been a core issue of teaching theories.

A theory on the process of teaching usually contains three aspects, namely, the essence of teaching, the steps of the teaching process, and the relationship between various elements in the teaching process. Educators in ancient China researched these three aspects and discussed the teaching process in great detail. Thus, we will now discuss their research on the steps of the teaching process.

Concerning ancient educators' theories on the teaching process in China, Professor Zhou Dechang and Professor Yan Guocai both have done in-depth research.[56] For instance, Professor Zhou Dechang promoted the formula of "Study extensively, reflect carefully, practice earnestly." Professor Yan Guocai found that theories on the teaching process of ancient China included the two-step theory (learn and practice or learn and travel), the three-step theory (learn, think, and travel), the four-step theory (learn, think, practice, and travel), the five-step theory (study extensively, enquire accurately, reflect carefully, discriminate clearly, and practice earnestly), the six-step theory (study extensively, enquire accurately, reflect carefully, discriminate clearly, exercise frequently, and practice earnestly), and the seven-step theory (aspire tenaciously, study extensively, enquire accurately, reflect carefully, discriminate clearly, exercise frequently, and practice earnestly). The author thinks that although the above theories all have merit to an extent, it is the five-step theory that deals with the process of teaching in a conscious and definite way and that is also the most influential theory on the steps of the teaching and learning process in ancient China.

The five-step theory was first presented by the writer of *Li Ji: Zhong Yong* (the *Book of Rites:The Doctrine of Moderation*):

> To this attainment there are requisite, the extensive study of what is good, accurate inquiry about it, careful reflection on it, the clear discrimination of it, and the earnest practice of it. The superior man, if there is anything he has not studied, or if, in what he has studied, there is anything he cannot understand, will not interrupt his labor. If there is anything he has not inquired about, or anything in what he has inquired about which he does not know, he will not interrupt his labor. If there is anything which he has not reflected on, or anything in what he has reflected on which he does not apprehend, he will not interrupt his labor. If there is anything which he has not discriminated, or if his discrimination is not clear, he will not interrupt his labor. If there is anything which he has not practiced, or his practice fails in earnestness, he will not interrupt his labor.

Zhu Xi, a great educator of the Southern Song Dynasty, reiterated and defined the five steps in his *School Regulations of Bailudong Academy*:

> Between father and son, there should be affection; between sovereign and minister, righteousness; between husband and wife, attention to their separate functions; between old and young, a proper order; and between friends, fidelity, all of which are the quintessence and aims of Wu Jiao (the cultivation of the "five constant virtues"). Emperor Yao and Emperor Shun appointed Qi as Si Tu (Minister of the Masses) to execute the cultivation of the five constant virtues. In this respect, learning was to learn the five constant virtues. Further, there were five steps of learning, namely, studying extensively, enquiring accurately, reflecting carefully, discriminating clearly, and practicing earnestly.

What Zhu Xi explained here was the teaching content and teaching process of China's feudal society in ancient times, which was observed by later academics in history and which influenced the development of teaching theories throughout all of feudal society. Additionally, Zhu Xi pointed out that among the above five steps, "Studying, enquiring, reflecting, and discriminating are steps of probing into things to find truth. As for earnest practice, there is a key for each, from self-cultivation to dealing with things and people."

During the Ming and Qing Dynasties, when he interpreted the five-step teaching theory from *Zhong Yong* (the *Doctrine of Moderation*), Wang Fuzhi wrote:

> When you study what you cannot understand, you are in urgent need of enquiring; when you enquire about what you do not know, you are in urgent need of reflecting; when you reflect on what you do not apprehend, again you need to study; when you discriminate what is not clear to you, still you need to enquire; when your practice fails in earnestness, then you should study, enquire, reflect, and discriminate to store up strength to practice. When you encounter what you just have studied, enquired about, reflected on, and discriminated, you should practice what you have got. When you practice hastily with all strength at one time, you fail. You cannot say that what you study, enquire about, reflect on, and discriminate cannot bring you there, but that you should watch your time. If among these steps there is one that is the last one to experience delay, it should be practice.[57]

Wang Fuzhi thought that the five steps of the teaching process had a certain sequence and order of priority. There was an interrelation between study and discrimination, inquiry and reflection, reflection and study, and discrimination and inquiry, as well as a dialectical relationship between these four steps and practice. Nonetheless, practice was considered the most important step in the entire teaching process. All of these elements are a conclusion of the teaching process theories of ancient China.

Modern teaching theories often divide the process of teaching into four basic steps: apperceive one's textbook, comprehend one's textbook, enhance one's knowledge, and apply one's knowledge.[58] Some theories add motivation before the four basic steps and add evaluation following them to form six basic steps of the teaching process. If we make a comparison between China's five-step theory of ancient times and the four-step theory of modern teaching theories, we will find that they are extraordinarily alike. In addition to "aspiring tenaciously" (motivation) and "examination" (evaluation), if we take some other arguments of ancient educators into account, then the seven-step teaching theory of ancient China also has some similarities with the six-step theory of modern teaching theories, as illustrated in the figure below:

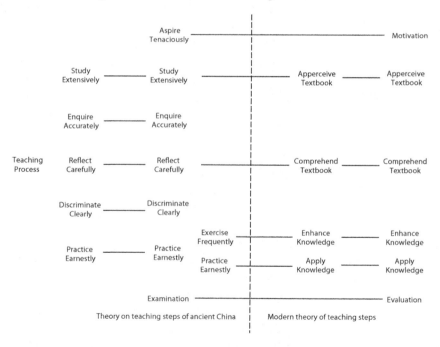

In order to have a comprehensive understanding of ancient China's theory on the steps of the teaching process, we will focus on analyzing seven steps: aspire tenaciously, study extensively, enquire accurately, reflect carefully, discriminate clearly, practice earnestly, and examination. We will then examine the interrelation between the various elements in each step.

1. Aspire Tenaciously

"Zhi" means motivation or resolution. Zhu Xi explained it as "where the heart goes."[59]

Wang Fuzhi interpreted it as "what the heart expects"[60] or "the master of the human heart."[61] When Chen Chun, Zhu Xi's brilliant disciple in his later years, explained Zhi, he said:

> Zhi is like direction, which the heart fully devotes itself to. If someone is devoted to the Way, that is to say his heart is committed to the Way; if devoted to study, his heart is committed to study. Zhi is what one desires and wants to obtain at any price. It cannot be called Zhi if the slightest trace of retreat or giving up is shown.

Zhi here is a strong motivation and persevering will.

Though educators in ancient China did not view aspiration as one of the specific steps of the teaching process, they did regard it as a significant precondition:

Mo-tse said, "His wisdom will not be far-reaching whose purpose is not firm."[62]

Zhang Zai said, "In all learning, for he who would be an officer, the first thing is [the knowledge of] business; for scholars, the first thing is the direction of the mind." This means that those who are officers should be taught the knowledge of their business, and those who are not officers should be taught the correct direction of the mind. The correct direction of the mind is one of the chief regulations in teaching.[63]

Lu Shiyi said, "Zhi is the vanguard of the journey of the Way. Only if the vanguard is brave will the rear army progress quickly; only if one is steadfast, resolved, and determined will his learning achieve greatness."[64]

Wang Fuzhi said, "One should first determine goals and then learn and think toward achieving them. Thus, his talents and intelligence will increase every day. Finally, he will become wealthy in knowledge. If he is determined and steadfast, then Qi (natural energy) will be refreshed every day and will not tire by following his resolution."[65]

In the eyes of ancient educators in China, Zhi was one of "the chief regulations in teaching" and the "vanguard of the journey of the Way." Setting aspirations was the precondition for "learning and thinking," and had, in fact, already been looked on as an indispensible part of the teaching process.

Attaching great importance to setting aspirations was a fine tradition of the ancient teaching theories of China. For example, Confucius not only demanded in the process of moral education that disciples should "be devoted to the Way," but also contended in the process of his teaching that disciples should "be committed to study" in order to motivate them. He taught his disciples that "The commander of the forces of a large state may be carried off, but the will of even a common man cannot be taken from him."[66]

Zhang Zai of the Northern Song Dynasty also thought highly of setting aspirations. He not only considered setting aspirations as a prerequisite of the teaching process, but also saw it as the sole and decisive factor, by saying that "leaving aside whether his Qi is good or bad, for one who is devoted to study, aspiration is the only determining factor."[67] This means that aspiration was considered to be more important than aptitude. Wang Fuzhi even said that "The difference between man and animals lies merely in will. If one does not hold steadfast to will, doing things at his best, then is there any difference between man and animals?"[68] This statement regarded will as one of man's essential defining features.

Educators in ancient China not only emphasized the significance and necessity of setting aspirations, but also defined two key requirements. The first was that one should have high and sublime aspirations. For instance, Zhang Zai said, "It is extremely bad for a learner to aim low and have light Qi, because when one aims low, it is for him to become content; when one is easily satisfied, he will make no progress."[69] This means that if one did not aim high, he would not progress. Wang Fuzhi also explicitly pointed out that the higher learners' expectations were, and the stronger their motives were, the greater the achievements they would make:

A learner's knowledge and magnanimity rely on his aspiration. If his aspiration is not high, he will achieve no deep knowledge; if his aspiration is not deep, then he will not become magnanimous. One who expects little can achieve his goals by just floating on water, and thus he surely will have no deep knowledge; one whose desires are shallow may be complacent for the moment, and thus he certainly will not have a noble and open heart."[70]

The second requirement for setting aspirations was that one should aspire in a steadfast and single-minded manner. For example, Zhu Xi said, "Being steadfast and striving all along, there is no need to worry about not making progress, is there?"[71] Wang Fuzhi also disapproved of capriciousness and changing one's mind frequently, saying, "Aspiration originates from one's devotion to study and ends up following one's heart. Once it is set, it cannot be changed and will be achieved."[72] He also said, "One's doings are diverse and not identical, but his will must be steadfast and consistent. There is never a man with two wills. That one devotes himself to this and meanwhile that cannot be claimed to be will but is nothing to do with will at all."[73] He meant that if one devotes himself to learning one thing today and another thing tomorrow, then he is a man without will.

2. Study Extensively

China's ancient educators paid a great deal of attention to extensive learning in the process of teaching and considered it to be the foundation of successful teaching. For instance, Confucius advocated that his disciples hear much, see much, and extensively study all learning. He said, "Hearing much and selecting what is good and following it; seeing much and keeping it in memory—this is the second style of knowledge."[74] He also said, "Hear much and put aside the points of which you stand in doubt, while at the same time speaking cautiously of others. Then you will have few occasions for blame. See much and put aside the things that seem perilous, while at the same time being cautious in carrying the others into practice. Then you will have few occasions for repentance."[75] Further, he illustrated the significance of extensive study with his own experience: "I have spent the whole day without eating, and the whole night without sleeping, occupied with thinking. It was of no use. The better plan is to learn."[76] He believed that sheer thinking without perceptual materials was of no benefit.

Wang Fuzhi of the Ming and Qing Dynasties summed up his experience of extensive learning and repeatedly advocated that learners hear much, experience much, and read extensively. He held that "The principles of all things should be learned in order to be known and studied extensively to be discriminated."[77] In addition, he thought that, in the process of teaching, learners cannot be conceited but should learn from predecessors; if one did not learn extensively, it would be difficult for his thoughts to be deep due to a lack of source materials. Thus, he remarked, "I do my best to find out the principles of things and make a comparison with predecessors' respective findings to verify whether my discoveries are classic principles. If there is no verification, then these discoveries need to wait. So learning must be extensive."[78]

Ancient educators in China also noticed the relationship between extensive and intensive learning in the process of teaching. For example, Mencius contended that "'in learning extensively and discussing minutely what is learned, the object of the superior man is that he may be able to go back and set forth in brief what is essential."[79] This advocated that extensive learning must be combined with intensive, succinct study. This idea was further interpreted by Wang Fuzhi, who said, "'Jiang Yi' means to outline the contents of extensive learning in brief, which is not to say that one's learning is extensive only for this moment, but rather that one's learning will become what is set forth in brief. Brevity is based on erudition, and erudition needs to be brief. Thus, the goal is to condense the contents of extensive study, and then learn extensively and discuss minutely what is learned. The merit of extensive learning is brought into play by summarizing. Not summarizing all one's learning is a false, tiring, and consuming way of learning. Why bother to do so?"[80] He thought that extensive learning and setting forth all learning in brief were not mutually exclusive, but dependent on one another and able to help each other forward.

As is said in "brevity is based on erudition, and erudition needs to be brief," if one does not make efforts to condense, outline, and systematize the contents of learning, one will not have a wealth of knowledge. Similarly, if one does not make efforts to learn extensively, read widely, and practice unceasingly, one will not have the ability to be succinct.

In order to make it easier for students to acquire knowledge, educators in ancient China paid more attention to intuitive instruction. For instance, *The Records on the Subject of Learning* writes that "the best teaching method is to make analogies" and "when he can vary analogies in his teaching, he can be a master indeed," which holds that vivid and felicitous analogies have a positive influence on students' acquisition of knowledge. Thus, intuitive language was one of the key teaching features in ancient China. A statistical study on analogies in *Mencius* revealed that of all 261 chapters, there are 93 chapters using 159 analogies altogether.[81] China's ancient cultivation of literacy was characteristic of intuitiveness, which offered precious experience for later generations. Further, educators were also aware of intuitive pedagogy in the teachings of natural science. For example, Sun Simiao, a famous medical scientist of the Tang Dynasty, elaborately drew a large colored wall map of acupuncture, *Ming Tang Tu*, when he was teaching medical science. In addition, Liu Hui, a great mathematician during the Three Kingdoms period, also insisted on "using figurative speech to explain principles and drawing pictures to illustrate structures" in his teaching of mathematics.[82] Both are models of intuitive instruction.

3. Enquire Accurately

Enquiring accurately, or interrogating and questioning, is also an important link in the teaching process and the key to the effect of education. China's ancient educators focused much on this stage. For example, Confucius sighed that he could not help the students who could not discover or propose any questions in learning: "For those who do not ask 'how to do,' I do not know how to do with them."[83] Therefore, he not only requested of his students that they should "not be ashamed to ask those who are inferior to them,"[84] but also practice in person to "consult for every matter."[85] Zhang Zai described asking questions as one of the standards of evaluating teaching and learning.

> People do not have questions because they do not take practical actions. If they are involved in practical activities, they will surely have doubts and questions....If you have understood the meaning of the whole passage but one chapter or section, you will still have questions. The things which you do not know are what you should ask the teachers and try to understand. If you do

not have any questions, it means only that you do not carefully think about what you learn.[86]

Zhu Xi described asking questions as a standard for evaluating one's progress:

People who do not have questions when reading should be taught to bring up questions. Those who have questions should learn to solve them, which is progress.[87]

Of course, interrogating and questioning are not the aim, for interrogating is to acquire actual knowledge and questioning is to remove doubts. Questioning is simply "the chance of awareness."[88] Wang Fuzhi pointed out the defect of questioning in order to question:

People who are quick-minded and assertive tend to believe themselves rather than ancient people. But they are occupied with preconceptions and fail to recognize that ancient people have already found the answers through trial and error. But people who only imitate the ancient ones want to reap reward without exerting effort. Those who understand things in a contorted way may find things right at the beginning, but may change their minds later, which is very dangerous.[89]

These words are quite penetrating and get to the core of the topic. It is well known that in the teaching process, students mainly focus on booklore, which is highly simplified and generalized. The well-chosen knowledge has been filtered by history. If one questions in order to question and is too opinionated, he may go astray and waste energy. Therefore, actual teaching is a process of leading students from a state of not having questions to asking questions, and finally to answering questions. So Zhu Xi said:

At the beginning of reading, one may not have questions. Then he may gradually begin to have questions. In the middle of reading, he may have questions in every section. If he continues to read, the questions will gradually be answered. He can achieve mastery through a comprehensive learning of the subject with all the problems being solved, and this can be regarded as learning.[90]

Wang Fuzhi provided a similar and very interesting expression:

As one puts more and more time into learning, he will witness the process of going from having no questions to having many questions. But when he answers his questions, his faith in the truth will be much firmer. Those who have questions do not doubt the reasons; they may simply doubt the expressions of the reasons. Those who do not have questions do not take the truth for granted. They observe carefully and search for the truth. When they have understood all things, they will surely have no questions at all.[91]

Wang Fuzhi's statement not only discusses the teaching process from not having questions to the emergence of questions and then to answers, but also illustrates that the key to discovering and solving problems in teaching practice is to "examine carefully" and to "carry out firmly."

4. Reflect Carefully

Ancient Chinese educators held the idea that the teaching process could not stop at the level of "extensive learning" and "interrogation," but should be promoted to the level of reflecting carefully, or deliberation, which laid emphasis on the function of thought. For example, Confucius advocated the combination of learning and thinking and proposed the famous statement that "learning without thought means the waste of labor; thought without learning is perilous."[92] He thought that if a person learned without thinking, he would still be confused and would gain nothing, no matter how extensively he read or how penetrating his questions. Zhu Xi stated vividly that if one read without thinking, he would not know the meaning of what he read…it is like having someone watch your house, but he is not a member of your family, and he does not truly care for you.[93] He thought that if people did not think deeply and carefully, they would not truly master knowledge.

Wang Fuzhi also pointed out the dialectical relationship between learning and thinking: "One cannot focus on one aspect and neglect the other, but should combine the two to achieve success."[94] When he criticized the mistake of separating learning and thinking made by the "obstinate ones," who learned without thinking, and the "quick and assertive ones," who thought without learning, he pointed out that learning and thinking are unified and necessary links in the teaching process. Learning and thinking must go hand in hand. The more knowledge you have, the more profound your thoughts will be. When you encounter problems, you will have to be more diligent to solve them. He said, "Learning is not an obstacle to thinking. The more you read, the more penetrating your thoughts will be. What is more, learning contributes to the correct way of thinking; if you are confused, you should be more diligent."[95] In addition, he said, "Learning comes from gathering acquired knowledge. If one puts the old and new materials together, he will know more. Thinking is a result of one's continuous observations. What a person knows is from his careful observations of small things."[96] It follows that learning must be innovated in the process of succession, and thinking should involve noticing the small things and be deepened constantly.

Because deliberation was an important phase in the teaching process in ancient China, educators laid great emphasis on inspiring the thinking of students in the teaching practice and encouraged students to "draw inferences about other cases from one instance," "hear one point and know the ten sequences," "study the past and foretell future changes," and think actively.

They also regarded the enlightenment of students' thought as a teaching guideline. For instance, Zhu Xi paid much attention to leading students to "think deeply"[97] and guiding them to the right way of thinking. He said, "You need to think and rethink; think when you walk and sit. If you do not have the result in the morning, you have to think about it at night. If you still do not have the result at night, you should rethink it tomorrow. If you think in this way, there is no reason that you can't come to understand the problem."[98]

5. Discriminate Clearly

In the teaching process, discriminating clearly means that students should form specific concepts and grasp exact knowledge. Both discrimination and deliberation belong to the phase of mastering knowledge, and these terms refer to students' mental activities. Discrimination is a specific request of thinking, a further step of deliberation, and the inevitable outcome. Wang Fuzhi demonstrated the relationship between deliberation and discrimination in the book *Collected Reviews of the Four Books*:

Extensive reading, interrogating, and sincere behavior belong to learning, whereas deliberation and discrimination belong to thinking. The one who discriminates things thinks of certainty, and the one who thinks deliberately considers reasons. People who are certain of things ask for clarity, and people who are uncertain of things discriminate them in order to understand them fully. People who ask for reasons do not have enough evidence, so they think deliberately and carefully. People who do not ask for reasons deliberately know that everything in the world is created equally, and they are completely indifferent to worldly temptations. But they are unable to verify the truth. Thinking has two phases, which are both necessary.

Wang Fuzhi divided the teaching process into two major parts: learning and thinking. The "learning" part had three phases, while the "thinking" part had two phases. The first stage of thinking was to "ponder over the certainty," which is to know "what it is" after thinking and to discriminate the external links of things. The second stage was to "think about the reasons," which means to find out "why it is so" after thinking and to get to know the intrinsic nature of things. The former requires "discrimination," whereas the latter requires "deliberation." It is not hard to see that Wang Fuzhi changed the sequence of discrimination and deliberation in the book *The Doctrine of the Mean*. In fact, the two are inextricably interwoven. It can also be said that the whole thinking process is spiraling, which means that one first discriminates (understands), then thinks deliberately (to know the reasons), and then discriminates things again (to master knowledge).

Ancient Chinese educators also focused much on the meaning and function of discrimination in the teaching process. For example, Zhu Xi said, "If you can discriminate things well, you will not have bad judgment, and you can put your judgment into practice without question."[99] In other words, only after discriminating and mastering the exact and concrete knowledge, rather than the uncertain, can we put knowledge into practice effectively. Therefore, discriminating is a key link to using reliable knowledge acquired through extensive reading, interrogation, and deliberation.

Ancient Chinese educators paid attention to guiding students to discriminate things in the teaching process. First, one was to exclude subjective biases. For example, in *The Analects of Confucius*, students were asked "not to speculate without evidence, not to affirm absolutely, not to be inflexible and stubborn, and not to be self-righteous."[100] Second, students were to compare and differentiate. For example, Wang Chong said, "If you use the blade of a knife to cut another, you will know whether they are sharp or not. If two arguments are put together, the right and wrong can be easily seen."[101] Zhu Xi said:

> If you read only the words, the ideas of different great masters will have similarities and differences, which are quite conspicuous. If one says something in one way, you may be prone to his idea and think in his way. If another person says something in another way, you may be influenced by his ideas and think in another different way. After listening to the ideas of the two people, you should think about their ideas carefully and determine who is better.[102]

Through comparison, it is possible to discriminate the sharp from the blunt, to understand right from wrong.

6. Practice Earnestly

Practicing earnestly can be divided into two stages: constant practice and devoted actions. Constant practice refers to timely and continuous review and practice of acquired knowledge in order to grasp it completely. Ancient Chinese educators emphasized constant practice. They not only stressed the significance of practicing the knowledge, which we have become familiar with, but also described the effect of practicing new knowledge and understanding it. For example, Confucius said, "Is it not a pleasure to study and practice what you have learned?"[103] Further, he said, "If a person can learn something new every day and not forget anything each month, he is studious."[104] He also said, "A man who is able to review past knowledge in order to acquire new knowledge is qualified to be a teacher."[105]

Zhu Xi described the motivation of constant practice. He said:

> Learning to people is as flying is to birds. Constant study is like the continuous flight of birds. Yue means happiness. So after constant study and repeated review, learners will become very familiar with the knowledge, and they will be quite happy. After they are absorbed in studying, they cannot stop learning.[106]

It follows that through constant practice, one can become quite familiar with past knowledge and become so pleased that he will have the desire to learn new things. Due to the importance of constant practice, ancient educators advocated "to learn and constantly review what one has learned" and "to gain new insights through restudying old material" as key principles in teaching.

Ancient Chinese educators also focused on the ways of teaching students to practice constantly in their teaching activities. They helped students learn to memorize and consolidate knowledge. For instance, in the book *Guanzi: The Duty of Disciple*, people were asked "to learn in the daytime and to review at night; to abide by the rules and not to slack"; *Guoyu (the History of the States): The History of Lu* stated that "young people from rich families are to learn lessons in the morning, take lectures to understand new knowledge in the daytime, review what they have learned in the evening, introspect whether they have made mistakes until they are satisfied at night, and only then can they rest."

This idea is similar to the proactive inhibition and retroactive inhibition in modern pedagogical psychology, which claims to make full use of the best time in the morning and in the evening to study, memorize, and review. Another example is that Zhu Xi said, "Reading aloud can help thinking, because when people are reading aloud, they are memorizing the words in their hearts. If they simply read without thinking in the mind, no matter how hard they read, they are unlikely to memorize the knowledge clearly."[107] "If they can read fluently and think about questions intently, they will naturally memorize the knowledge by heart and will never forget."[108] This is to say that reading aloud and thinking can help people memorize things.

The knowledge people have acquired after discrimination and constant practice should ultimately be put to use. If one does not know how to use his knowledge, it will be meaningless, even if he is wealthy in knowledge. As a result, ancient Chinese educators laid great emphasis on practice, which they thought was the exact foothold of studying, and the climax of the teaching process. Confucius once said, "Though a man may be able to recite the three hundred poems, yet if, when entrusted with a governmental charge, he knows not how to act, or if, when sent to any quarter on a mission, he cannot give his replies unassisted, not-withstanding the extent of his learning, of what practical use is it?"[109] This means that although one is very familiar with *The Book of Poetry*, if he is not capable of finishing the political task delivered to him and cannot negotiate indepen-dently when he serves as an envoy abroad, the knowledge he has acquired means nothing to him. Xuncius also pointed out clearly that the fundamental aim of studying is to use what you have learned. He said:

> The process of studying stops at the level of practice, which helps people under-stand the truth. These kinds of people are called wise men, and they are kind and righteous in nature and clear about what is right and what is wrong. They practice what they preach, and they make judgments without mistakes. There is nothing else to say because all things are included in the process of practicing.[110]

In the book *Answers to Cao Yuanke*, Zhu Xi wrote, "The ultimate purpose of study is to practice. If you know all things without practicing, you will be no different from the ones who know nothing at all. However, if you practice without knowing the reasons, you are unlikely to know about the meaning of the result." He not only opposed practicing without knowing, which may lead to a state of blindness, but also opposed knowing without practicing, which makes one no different from the ones who know nothing. Wang Fuzhi was against the idea of discussing teaching without practicing. He claimed that "one can achieve success if he both learns and practices."[111] He focused much on the use of knowledge and believed that only through practice can knowledge be reflected. He stated that one must practice in order to examine whether he has truly grasped the knowledge. He said:

> Those who know how to handle something take advantage of their practice; those who have to practice something cannot rely on their knowledge. Practice can gain people knowledge, whereas knowledge itself may not make people's practice feasible....Knowledge can go along with practice, whereas practice may not happen together with knowledge. People should approach things widely and learn from them in order to gradually understand the general rules. So should the learning of the general rules be the start of learning? The learning of the noble man should not be detached from practice, nor should knowledge be regarded as the only necessity.[112]

Wang Fuzhi once used chess as an example to illustrate the significance of practice in teaching. He said:

> Studying is much like playing chess. If you focus only on studying books about how to play chess instead of playing with others, it will be quite hard for

you to learn it well. You have to play with others in order to gain knowledge from practicing, which cannot be gained from books. Further, if one puts his whole heart into studying books about playing chess, he has already been in the phase of practicing.[113]

Wang Fuzhi thought that in the process of learning to play chess, one could not play well if he had only read books he hoped to copy blindly. Only when he both reads the book and practices with others can he learn the game well and put his knowledge into use effectively.

7. Examination

From the theory of the modern teaching process, examination and evaluation are indispensable elements of the teaching process. Through examination and evaluation, teachers get to know how well their students are mastering knowledge and skills, which informs future teaching. Although the five-phase theory of the ancient Chinese teaching process does not include examination, ancient Chinese educators had a certain understanding of it from their theory and practice.

For example, in the Northern Song Dynasty, Zhang Zai said, "Teachers have to know the easy and hard parts of the study and the specific conditions of each student. From each student's understanding about what he has learned, teachers can tell who has mastered the knowledge better."[114] In his opinion, teachers should know how well their students grasp the knowledge and the general development of their virtues in order to have a well-thought-out plan about the next stage of teaching. *The Records on the Subject of Learning* also recorded the examination and evaluation of teaching in our schools in the antediluvian period.

Students enter college when they are at a certain age, and the country checks their study and grades every other year. In the first year, the ability to analyze sentences and paragraphs and one's ambitions are checked; in the third year, attentiveness and harmonious relationships with surrounding people are checked; in the fifth year, the extensiveness of one's knowledge and one's intimacy with his teachers are checked; and in the seventh year, the abilities to conduct research and distinguish friends are checked. Those who are qualified, reach the level of "initial success." Within nine years, students should comprehend by analogy. In addition, politically, they should be firm and reach the level of maturity. Those who are qualified have made great achievements. They are then able to educate other citizens, delight close friends, and be admired by distant ones, all of which are the guidelines of the Great Learning.

According to the textual research and illustrations of Mr. Gao Shiliang, the above section refers to the evaluation system of college education in the antediluvian period.[115] This describes the first stage of college education. Those who are qualified reach the level of "initial success." The second stage requires students to comprehend by analogy and hear one point and know ten sequences. In addition, politically, they should be firm and reach the level of maturity. Those who are qualified have made "great achievements." Obviously, the evaluation system mentioned here is quite complete, with a clear outline of the content, time span, and requirements. However, the exact method of evaluation is not clear, perhaps because it would have been assumed in ancient times.

From the Han Dynasty, the evaluation system in China gradually became complete, and there are records of the methods of examination and evaluation. For example, in the Han Dynasty, the Imperial College adopted the method of "setting subjects to express strategies" to examine students every year. There were two kinds of test according to degree of difficulty: Jia and Yi. Test papers were sealed. Students could choose one of the two tests or both when they were examined. There were two possible grades: pass or fail. Those who passed the test were offered an official position and could graduate from school. Since the Sui and Tang Dynasties, people began to use the imperial examination system, and a rather strict and complete testing system was formed, including such elements as oral testing, learning by rote, written testing, questions on politics, and poetry and prose, which we will study in Chapter Eight. Inside schools, the evaluation system became more and more complete and intensified. For instance, in the Tang Dynasty, central schools had tests every ten days, every year, and when students graduated. Medical students had tests once a month, each quarter of a year, and at the end of a year. There were also tests every ten days, with the goal of checking the progress of students' studies. Students were marked as passing or failing, and failing students would be punished.

The tests at the end of a year included ten questions. Students who could answer eight questions correctly were considered the better ones; those who could answer six correctly were considered intermediate; and those who could answer only five correctly were considered lower and were required to study again. This three-level scoring method was still in use at the end of the Qing Dynasty.

Interestingly, in the teaching process of ancient Chinese folk education, in small libraries, home schooling with a private tutor, and even academies of classical learning, there were few tests and marking methods similar to those of the official schools. However, the lack of an evaluation system did not impede teachers from assessing the progress of their students. They came to know their students through observing their speech and behavior, questioning them, and doing research.[116] Therefore, teachers could still teach students in accordance with students' aptitude and exchange ideas with them.

The discussions about the teaching process of ancient Chinese educators are so accurate and detailed that they are the greatest in the world. The five-phase theory has been especially described in quite a systematic and clear way, which is rare and commendable. If we count from the time of the book

The Doctrine of the Mean, Chinese educational theory began to appear two thousand years earlier than the Western theory of Herbart, and 1,800 years earlier than Comenius's *Magna Didactica.*

The Principles and Methods of Teaching

Teaching principles are general theories to guide the teaching process and also the basic requirements for the work of teaching, and teaching methods, which describe how to complete teaching tasks, are general terms for teachers' working methods and students' learning methods. Teaching principles and methods are formed in the process of teaching practices, and as such, they are conclusions and generalizations about teaching practices and experiences.

Educators at all times and in all countries propose several quite valuable teaching principles and methods in their education practices, especially the Western educators of contemporary times. For example, Comenius once put forward the principles of direct perception and advancement in an orderly fashion. Dewey brought forward the principles of learning from practice, interests, and motivation. Bruner described the principles of motivation, procedure, structure, and reinforcement. Bahkob proposed the principles of superior difficulty and high speed. In terms of teaching methods, there are numerous. Just to name a few, there are the "midwifery" model of Socrates, the discovery approach of Bruner, the example teaching method of Wagenschein, the suggestive teaching method of Lozanov, and the outlining of key points using signs proposed by Andrianov. What is worth thinking is that although these modern teaching principles and methods were proposed within a certain historical context and under particular philosophical ideas, if we carefully examine the discussions of teaching principles and methods of ancient Chinese educators, we can find some archetypes and inspirations. Therefore, it is relevant and meaningful to systematically study the theories of ancient Chinese teaching principles and teaching methods.

There are more than one hundred teaching principles and methods proposed by ancient Chinese educators. The major ones offer help after students have been thinking about things, to advance in a systematic order, to gain new insights through restudying old material, to learn that teaching others teaches yourself, to educate students in accordance with their aptitude, to teach in a timely fashion, to study earnestly and think carefully, to be determined from the beginning, to be willing to accept new ideas and think repeatedly, to put oneself in a situation to observe and experience, to study diligently, to behave well and set a good example for other students, to read comprehensively and make brief conclusions, to combine learning and thinking, to combine entertainment and diligent work, to unify learning and doing, to learn in order to practice, to seek knowledge independently and improve the ability to self-study, and to discuss with others and discriminate things. Some of these have been mentioned in the analysis of the theory of ancient Chinese teaching processes, and some will be discussed in more detail in Chapter Seven, "Reading Methods in Ancient China." Here the most essential teaching methods will be discussed.

Ancient Chinese teaching principles can roughly be divided into three major areas: the teaching principles of teachers, the learning principles of students, and the shared principles and methods of both teaching and learning.

1. Teaching Principles and Methods

1) Heuristic Education

The principle of offering help after students have been thinking about things can also be called the heuristic education principle, which means to arouse the initiative and enthusiasm of students during the teaching process, to inspire their thinking activities so that they will be thoroughly acquainted with knowledge, and their intelligence will be developed. It is the great educator Confucius who first came up with this principle in ancient China. He said:

> I do not open up the truth to one who is not eager to acquire knowledge, nor do I help anyone who is not anxious to explain knowledge himself. When I have presented one corner of a subject to someone, and he cannot learn from it the other three, I do not repeat my lesson.[117]

According to the explanation of Zhu Xi, "fen" means "the mind seeks for the reasons but cannot find them," and "fei" means "one wants to speak out but does not know how to express himself." So the above words of Confucius are to say: during the teaching process, do not guide students until they want to understand but fail; and do not enlighten students until they want to express themselves but fail. If you tell a student about the east, but he cannot deduce the west, south, and north from it, you should no longer teach him. Because the heuristic education principle emphasizes the initiative and enthusiasm of students and is not like the method of forcing study, which puts students in a negative and passive situation, it has endured ever since its proposal by Confucius. It was inherited and developed by every subsequent generation of educators and became one of the most influential teaching principles of ancient China. Wang Fuzhi, a great thinker of the Chinese ancient academy, also illustrated this principle systematically:

> If teachers instruct students who are neither eager to gain knowledge, nor anxious to explain themselves, teaching will be a waste of time and energy, and will have no benefits at all.[118]

Teachers ought to teach everything to students, but they can keep some things to themselves. This can help students understand on their own. Teachers should have enlightened students and tell them what they do not know. However, teachers should not be in a hurry. They must wait for the students until they have the determination to understand all things. When learners are anxious to know, they will be happy to listen to teachers and will be excited to be exposed to new materials. If students do not want to know things, they will not focus on their study and will not put effort into it. What is more, they will find the words of their teachers redundant. When teachers give lectures, they should know whether a student has the ambition and ability to search for knowledge. If a student is willing to learn, his teacher will guide him to the right way of studying. If one is not willing to learn and teachers hurry to teach him everything, he will only know the superficial ideas without thinking more profoundly. In this case, it will be better not to tell him.[119]

Wang Fuzhi believed that there were two forms of heuristic education: "to teach everything" and "to not teach everything." But these two have the similarities that students should have "the ambition to find out the reasons," they should have anxious expectations, and they should be prepared for study. Only when students are motivated to "try to find out the reasons but fail and become angry with themselves," and "cannot make up their minds and cannot speak out," can teachers enlighten and guide them appropriately. Only in this way can teaching be to the point and effective. Otherwise, if students "do not think about the problems independently," and do not achieve the level of wanting to know the reasons desperately, they will "waste time and not study attentively" and "know nothing at all," and they will either care for nothing or know nothing about the reasons, and get nothing in the end, even if their teachers are always explaining things to them.

Heuristic education can be carried out in many ways. For example, it is said in *The Records on the Subject of Learning*:

> Teachers should be good at leading students. They guide students instead of forcing them to follow, which makes the relationship much closer. They are strict with students without making them feel depressed, which is helpful for students to develop freely. They enlighten students rather than tell them the results directly, which inspires students to think independently. The intimate relationship, the free environment, and independent thinking are components of good education.

"Teachers should be good at giving systematic guidance, and students should be fond of learning." As explained by Dai Xi in the Southern Song Dynasty, "Yu" means "to enlighten." There are three ways of achieving enlightenment. The first is through "harmony," which means that teachers can handle the bilateral relationship between teaching and learning well and guide students rather than force them to follow. The second is by being "amiable," which means that although teachers should be strict with students, they should not exert too much pressure on students for fear that students may become afraid of learning new things. The third is "to inspire thinking," which means that when teachers begin to give lectures, they should begin with only the introductory parts, rather than the entire contents, in order to make students remain active.

This method of enlightening students actually reveals the principle of combining the guiding role of teachers and the initiative of students in the teaching process. When talking about the principle of "psychological disposition," modern American educator Jerome Bruner said in *On the Principles of Teaching*, "Since learning and solving problems are decided by individual exploring activities, teaching should improve and regulate the exploring activities chosen by students."[120] This view is similar to the expressions in *The Records on the Subject of Learning*.

Generally speaking, the major teaching methods used by ancient Chinese educators in heuristic education include the following elements.

First, people should be good at questioning and answering. For example, Confucius said, "Am I knowledgeable? No. A countryman asked me a question that I could not answer. But I asked him from the two ends of his question, and then he was quite clear about the problem."[121] This means that we can ask the questioner for the pros and cons of his question. *The Records on the Subject of Learning* has more penetrating insights:

> Teachers who are good at raising questions are like workers who cut down hard trees. They start from the fragile parts and gradually cut the branches. If the questions raised for students gradually progress from easy to difficult, learners will accept them happily and try to understand the meaning of each question. However, teachers who are not good at raising questions are simply the opposite. It is also like striking bells. If you hit a small one, you will hear small sounds; but if you strike a large one, loud voices will be heard. Teachers should give responses according to the degree of difficulty of the questions. All of these are the methods of teaching and learning.

Teachers should give responses according to the degree of difficulty of the questions. Teachers should progress gradually and act as the sound of bells. Students can make use of the continuous melodious sound waves to ponder repeatedly until they fully understand.

Second, teachers should leave adequate time for learning. The educators of ancient China opposed the teaching method of paying attention to all sides and taking in everything in a glance. For instance, in the Eastern Han Dynasty, Wang Chong wrote:

> The words of wise men cannot be understood completely. The reasons they state cannot be fully grasped immediately. If you do not comprehend, you should ask him to explain more clearly. If you cannot understand completely, you should bring forward questions to try to grasp the meaning. Gao Yao stated the principles of governing a country in the presence of Emperor Shun, but his words were superficial and rough. After the questioning and argument of Emperor Shun, his thoughts were more penetrating, and his ideas were clearer. Because of this kind of questioning, the words of Gao Yao became more profound and clear.[122]

This paragraph emphasizes the function of repeated questioning and argument. The questions of Emperor Shun made the words of Gao Yao become more profound due to inspiration, and more cleare due to continued questioning. From another perspective, this paragraph also demonstrates that not telling everything can arouse the enthusiasm of listeners so that "simple words may have complex meanings," and learners can deepen their understanding.

Third, students should draw inferences about other cases from one instance. When Confucius came up with the principle of heuristic education, he presented the requirement of inferring other things from one fact, which is actually a method of analogical reasoning. It is like hearing one point and from it knowing ten sequences and inferring the future by analyzing the past. This is a method of "associating similarities."

In teaching practices, ancient Chinese educators always used the enlightening way, such as the discussion about being "poor but not flattering"[123] between Confucius and Zigong, and the discussion about "the dimples of her beautiful smile"[124] between Confucius and Zixia.

2) Teaching Students in Accordance with Their Aptitude

Teaching students in accordance with their aptitude is not only a moral education principle, but also a teaching principle. As a teaching principle, it means to organize teaching work with a definite purpose according to the individual needs and age differences of one's students. As mentioned earlier, the principle of teaching students in accordance with their aptitude originated with Confucius, who was quite adept at following this principle in both moral education and intellectual education. For example, Confucius said, "People who are at the intermediate level can be taught profound theories, whereas people who are below the intermediate level can hardly understand profound ideas."[125]

This means that the requirements for teaching should be individualized according to the different intelligence levels of one's students. Those students who are above the intermediate intelligence level can be taught more profound knowledge, whereas those who are below the intermediate intelligence level cannot be taught the same knowledge.

All educators in each generation after Confucius focused on the application of this principle in their teaching. For instance, *The Records on the Subject of Learning* states:

Nowadays, teachers simply read books and fill students with knowledge. They are eager to pursue the fast pace of progressing without considering the adaptability of students. As a result, learners lose their passion and sincerity for studying, and teachers fail to teach students in accordance with their aptitude. Teachers violate the rules of educating students and fail to achieve the requirements of teaching.

The book also stated:

Generally, teachers only focused on reading the words written on bamboo slips learned by students, always asked them questions they could hardly understand, and talked verbosely. When they were giving lectures, they did not consider the receptive ability of students, so that learners could not study wholeheartedly. Teachers failed to teach students in accordance with their aptitude, and students could not show their individual talents. Therefore, teachers violated the rules of teaching, and learners could not make smooth progress.

In the work of teaching, there are five main ways that ancient Chinese educators made use of the principle of teaching students in accordance with their aptitude.[126]

First, teachers should instruct students according to their intelligence level. For instance, according to the variability of students' intelligence level, Confucius came up with the idea that some students "can study together but may not reach the same level at the same time," some students "can reach the same level at the same time but may not be able to study together," and some "can study together but may not be able to flexibly adjust to changing circumstances."[127]

Mo-tse also gave the analogy of cutting a dress according to one's figure to refer to teaching students in accordance with their aptitude. He said, "Teachers should instruct the well-educated with more profound knowledge, and teach people who have little literacy with simpler knowledge. They should help develop the advantages of people, and treat those who have self-esteem respectfully."[128] In studying skills, Mo-tse also considered students' different abilities. "Several people asked Mo-tse to be taught shooting, but he said, 'No. People should know what they are capable of, and do what they are able to do.'"[129]

Second, teachers should instruct students according to their knowledge level. Modern pedagogical theory points out that the knowledge students have already acquired restricts new teaching content, methods, and speed, and ultimately influences the effect of teaching. China's ancient educators also realized this problem in some way. They not only tried to determine the intellectual level that students had already achieved, but also taught them according to their acquired knowledge level. For example, Xuncius said, "A short rope cannot fetch water from a deep well, and people with little knowledge are not able to discuss the words of wise men."[130] Further, he said, "Shallow things cannot measure deep ones; foolish people are not capable of discussing with the wise ones, and one can never talk with frogs from a shabby well about the fun of roaming the East China Sea."[131] All of these are metaphors which show that teachers should not give lectures on profound and difficult subjects to students who lack the requisite background knowledge. Ancient educators noticed the link between acquired and new knowledge, so they brought forward the idea of "gaining new insights through restudying old material," which will be discussed later.

Third, teachers should instruct students according to the age of their students. Ancient educators in China thought that the educational content and teaching methods should be different according to the age of their students. For example, Zhu Xi said, "Children should be taught basic codes of ethics and form good behavioral habits to master the fundamental cultural knowledge and skills. Young people should be well polished and be cultivated into helpful talents for the country."[132] This means that primary learning is mainly the education on "doing concrete things," such as the ways of cleaning, dealing with people and things, and etiquette. However, the Great Learning mainly teaches students "reasons" for things, such as searching for the truth of everything in the world, cultivating one's moral character, managing state affairs, and appeasing the citizens of the country. Primary learning aims at behavior training, whereas the Great Learning focuses on theory teaching. If teachers do not follow this method, they will have to put in two-fold efforts but only will get half the result.

If children do not gain the knowledge of primary learning, they will not restrain themselves and cultivate their minds, and thus they will not have a foundation for the Great Learning. When they grow up, if they are not exposed to the Great Learning, they will not understand the principles and reasons for things, and they will only have the achievements of primary learning no matter what they do.[133]

Talking about this problem, Wang Fuzhi commented, "Children who are above six years old have the basis to be taught the six classical arts. But if they are very young, they cannot be instructed in these things. If students are forced to learn, they will not understand the profound reasons. What is worse, they will be smart but narrow-minded and live in a shiftless way. They will be trapped in superficial ideas and will not be able to comprehend the essence of knowledge. As a result, only when students are capable of understanding knowledge can they be enlightened and can they make great achievements."[134] This means that if teachers fail to take into account the age of their students and teach small children profound and difficult concepts, the teaching will not be as effective as expected and will actually have negative effects.

Fourth, teachers should adopt individualized instruction according to students' specific talents. Ancient Chinese educators thought that in the teaching process, students' talents should not be neglected and they should not be taught in the way of "cooking in one pot." According to *The Analects of Confucius*, due to students' individual talents, Confucius offered four subjects: moral conduct, speech, government affairs, and literature, and he taught his students according to what subject suited each best.

Mencius divided his students into "virtuous people," "talented ones," "those who are capable of answering questions," and "those who influence others and lead others to imitate them." He taught his students according to which type each belonged to.

In the Northern Song Dynasty, a specialized form of instruction called the "Suhu methodology" came into being. It got this name because educator Hu Yuan put this methodology into practice in Suzhou and Huzhou. He separated school into two departments: "The Argumentation of Confucian Classics" and "Governing Affairs" (similar to that studied in modern colleges). "The Argumentation of Confucian Classics" was the study of the classics of the Confucian school, such as the Six Classics, whereas "Governing Affairs" focused on the study of military affairs and public security. "There are people who are fond of Confucian classics, people who like weapons and battles, people who are fond of literature and art, and people who are righteous. People of specific types should gather together and be instructed in the same things."[135] Hu Yuan also adopted the methodology of combining primary and auxiliary courses, which meant that, on the basis of one's mastery of a primary subject, students should then take an auxiliary course. This teaching methodology was greatly influential and is very effective. Later on, Hu Yuan was promoted to take charge of the Imperial College, and his teaching methodology was officially named the Method of the Imperial College.

Fifth, teachers should carry out teaching according to students' learning characteristics. Students differ not only in such aspects as intelligence, knowledge level, age, and talent, but also in the characteristics of how they learn. In teaching, this factor must be taken into consideration for the better development of every student. Ancient Chinese educators were aware of this fact, as indicated by one line in *The Records on the Subject of Learning*: "Among learners there are four defects....Some err in the multitude of their studies; some, in their fewness; some, in the feeling of ease [with which they proceed]; and some, in the readiness with which they stop." The teacher must make himself acquainted with these kinds of errors. Some students bite off more than they can chew without thoroughly understanding; some students are satisfied with a superficial understanding and a narrow range of knowledge; some are not consistent in their learning; and some are content with their present level and seek no further development. With the knowledge of these different characteristics, the teacher can achieve the best teaching effects through individualized ways of addressing these problems.

3) Timely Teaching

There are principles for ascertaining the best time for aspects of moral education like "restraint before occurrence" and "educating children to develop sound habits." Similarly, to determine the best opportunity is also a significant point in teaching; this is called the principle of timely teaching. This idea was first seen in *The Records on the Subject of Learning*: "The timeliness of instruction is to teach just when it is required," and "Instruction given after the appropriate time is done with toil and carried out with difficulty." "Just when it is required" means that special content should be taught within a specific learning period, neither too late nor too early. Yet the wording in *The Records on the Subject of Learning* is measured. It says that the loss of the prime opportunity does not necessarily lead to a total failure, but it will make it "too hard to succeed." The practice of modern foreign language teaching has also proved the conclusion in *The Records on the Subject of Learning*. For example, the time before the age of 12 is generally believed to be the best period for language learning, because the two cerebral hemispheres are not yet highly differentiated, and thus the advantage of language learning is guaranteed. After this period, one can also learn a foreign language well, but it will take more time and effort.

The study of the timeliness of instruction has already been embarked on in the field of modern educational psychology. Although few satisfactory results have been achieved so far, research, such as Piaget's division of stages, including the pre-operational stage, the concrete operational stage, and the formal operational stage, as well as Bruner's teaching content structure, are inspirational achievements. Chinese educators in ancient times certainly could not have conducted thorough research on the problem of the timeliness of instruction, but their explorations were by no means few. Due to the limitations of the historical time, most results were only the conjecture of the expert or based on individual experience. For example, *Bao Fu* (*Teachers for the Emperor or Princes*), written by Jia Yi in the Western Han Dynasty, proposed early childhood education for the reason that "when the mind has not been imprisoned by many external things, the enlightenment effect of teaching can be realized in a much easier way." Yan Zhitui in the Northern Zhou Dynasty believed that the key period for learning is between the ages of 7 and 19. "After 20, if you set aside the books you have recited for just one month, your memory will lapse to a blank."[136]

In *On Children's Education*, Lu Shiyi considered the age of 15 to be a critical point:

> Everyone is born with memory and perception. Before 15, with the mind uninfected by material desire and unrestricted by knowledge, one is more potent in memory than in perception. After 15, gradually becoming infected by desires and enlightened by knowledge, one's mind is ruled more by perception than by memory. Thus, all the books worth reading should be finished with a sound understanding before 15.

Ancient Chinese educators did not discuss the content of teaching in detail. They just claimed that practice (behavioral training) should be emphasized in childhood learning, whereas advanced learning should put emphasis on knowledge and rules, which was discussed in the previous section.

2. The Principles and Methods of Learning

Since students' learning was a priority of China's ancient teaching theory, ancient educators gave a detailed discussion on learning principles and methods in teaching. A research study entitled "China's Ancient Educators' Discussion on Learning"[137] discussed several points, the most significant of which will be discussed below.

1) Seeking Knowledge and Understanding It by Oneself

China's ancient educators believed that students' initiative and enthusiasm should be brought into full play during the teaching process, and that only when students sought for and attained understanding on their own could they truly master it. As Mencius once remarked:

> The noble man makes his advances in what he is learning with deep earnestness and by the proper course, wishing to get hold of it in himself. Having got hold of it in himself, he abides in it calmly and firmly. Abiding in it calmly and firmly, he reposes a deep reliance on it. Reposing a deep reliance on it, he seizes it on the left and right, meeting everywhere with it as a fountain from which things flow. It is on this account that the noble man wishes to get hold of what he is learning in himself.[138]

Mencius held that if a student wanted to make the greatest achievements in the right way, he must be proactive to get hold of, or understand, what he is learning. Only in this way could he make a comprehensive study and become a thorough master of his knowledge and then put it into practice. It would appear that everything would go well for such a student eventually.

Zhang Zai, a Confucian scholar in the Song Dynasty, also had the opinion that a student should develop the habit of "seeking knowledge by himself" during the learning process. He wrote, "The pleasure of learning is rooted in the learner himself. One who seeks knowledge by himself can obtain the truth and pleasure of learning. Getting hold of what he is learning, he abides in it calmly and firmly."[139] In this sense, only when a person seeks what he is learning and gets hold of it by himself can he arouse a great interest in it and consolidate what he has learned.

China's ancient educators felt that the key in carrying out the principles and methods of teaching was that one should thoroughly reflect on what he is learning and digest it, which means one should not learn for learning's sake, or read for reading's sake, but he should assimilate and digest what he has learned, and understand its roots and branches.

Wang Tingxiang, a scholar in the Ming Dynasty, once wrote:

It is not very well thought out if one learns abundantly without deep thinking. Only after he thinks about it and understands it can it be the truth. A vague explanation may not be quite reasonable; however, it is brilliant when one masters knowledge after putting it into practice. This is why the noble man has a wide range of studies, but pays more attention to his inner cultivation. He understands what he has learned but values it highly when he puts what he has learned into practice.[140]

Wang Tingxiang believed that "the thought of what one is learning and the mastery of it" was an essential stage if one wanted to "acquire knowledge abundantly" and then "put it into application" in the end.

In the Qing Dynasty, Dai Zhen once wrote on the subject of Mencius's thoughts:

Blood and Qi are nourished by food. Only when food is transformed into nutrition can it become your blood and Qi, and then it will not be food any more. So it is people's wisdom to knowledge....It can be said that the learning of knowledge is like food; you must pay attention to comprehending knowledge instead of learning it by rote. Otherwise, you will only superficially know the knowledge you have forced in and will not acquire a thorough understanding of it. However, having got hold of it in yourself, you will be able to abide in it calmly and firmly. Reposing a deep reliance on it, you will seize it on the left and right, meeting everywhere with it as a fountain from which things flow. At that point, you could be as smart as a sage.[141]

Dai Zhen held that, as food and drink can be absorbed by the body and converted into blood and Qi after digestion, learning can be turned into wisdom after digestion in the same way.

As a matter of fact, teaching had already been divided into two levels: knowing and understanding. Further, it is well known that teaching can be divided into three levels: memory, understanding, and thinking, based on modern foreign teaching theories.[142] Bloom classified teaching objectives into three domains: cognitive, affective, and psychomotor. The cognitive domain has six subdomains: knowledge, comprehension, application, analysis, synthesis, and evaluation. AuSubel, according to how students study, divided teaching into acceptance and discovery, and according to teaching content, divided it into mechanical teaching and meaningful teaching.[143] In this way, "knowing" is equivalent to AuSubel's acceptance level and mechanical learning, and "understanding" is equivalent to AuSubel's discovery level and meaningful learning. It is worth mentioning that Wang Yangming once put forward a theory similar to Bloom's three domains:

One friend asked, "I read books but I cannot remember all the contents. What should I do?" The teacher responded, "If you know the meaning of those books, why do you bother to memorize the contents? You should be aware that knowing ranks only second in importance. Of primary importance is that you should make your heart and head bright. If you want only to memorize the contents, you will not understand them. If you seek only to understand those contents, your heart and head will not be bright."[144]

The three levels of memorizing, knowing, and understanding essentially correspond to the memory, understanding, and thinking levels of modern teaching theory. However, Wang Yangming did not give a detailed explanation of his three levels, and for him, learning's ultimate end was nothing more than to "make one's body bright." This is where his defect lies.

2) A Combination of Pleasure and Motivation

Based on the theory of a combination of pleasure and motivation, joyful feelings and a consistent interest should be integrated with enduring perseverance so as to make sure that pleasure and motivation are inseparable. This will help students develop a strong impetus for study.

Educators in ancient China gave a high priority to cultivating students' consistent interests and joyful feelings in their teaching activities. For instance,

Confucius argued, "Knowing it is not as good as loving it; loving it is not as good as delighting in it."[145] Once Ye Gong asked Zilu about Confucius, but Zilu could not answer him. Confucius told him, "Why did you not just tell him that I am a man who, in eagerness for study, forgets to eat, in his enjoyment of it, forgets his problems, and who is unaware of old age setting in?"[146] From his words, we see that Confucius himself was a man who "in eagerness for study, forgets to eat, in his enjoyment of it, forgets his problems," and who also asked his students to love and find pleasure in studying. He struck a balance between work and leisure.

Zhang Zai in the Song Dynasty held the same opinion: "One who delights in learning will be engaged in study vigorously and will not give up halfway. In the end, he will make progress."[147] *Lv's Commentary of History* states:

> A sensible teacher can make his students feel at ease, joyful, relaxed, calm, and solemn, as well as serious when instructing. With those six points made, the road to evil will be blocked and the road to justice clear....It is human nature that people do not like doing difficult things, and they do not take pleasure from them."[148]

These words are worth analyzing. On the one hand, this passage points out that people will not feel happy for what they worry about and cannot make any achievement in doing things they cannot take pleasure in. This is also true of teaching. In this sense, experienced teachers should make their students feel at ease, joyful, relaxed, calm, and solemn, as well as serious, which will help them to develop a strong interest in and positive feelings toward study. On the other hand, including stability, pleasure, relaxation, and calm with seriousness and strictness, those six elements together will promote a man to succeed in studying. It can be deduced that only by combining interest and hard work can teaching be highly effective.

Ancient Chinese educators also attached importance to developing students' tenacious will and a spirit of pursuing knowledge during teaching practices. Students' learning is hardworking, so it cannot be as comfortable as walking in a garden or as relaxed as seeing an opera in a theater. It is neither like driving a horse on flat land, nor like sprinkling water by a seaside. Only one who does not fear toil, perseveres in his aim, and climbs along the steep mountain road (of learning) is likely to reach the top and see the bright light.

Confucius valued highly the qualities of diligence and tenacity. He once encouraged his students, saying, "I have not yet met a man of true goodness but would be satisfied to meet a man of constancy."[149] He also taught his students to march forward courageously and never give up halfway. He said,

"The execution of learning may be compared to what may happen in piling a mound. If there was but one basket of earth to complete the work, and I stop, the stopping is my own work. This may be compared to throwing down the earth on level ground. Alhough but one basketful is thrown at a time, advancing with it is my own going forward."[150]

Zhang Zai held that the biggest mistake one could make in studying was nothing but to "give up when he is confronted with difficulty."[151] "Learning is like climbing. No one will not stride forward when the road is smooth; however, some people stop when faced with a rugged road. It is time to muster up one's courage to move on."[152] Therefore, one who is motivated and tenacious can "advance forward continually."[153]

Speaking of the relationship between people's motivation and confidence, he said:

> A lack of endeavor and perseverance underlies the reason one cannot stay confident and have a clear direction. One should follow a right way and keep pursuing it when studying. It is like a flowing river, rushing forward, day and night. He will be then full of confidence, bear a clear way in mind, and naturally attain rich knowledge.[154]

The order of learning is from self-encouragement, to self-confidence, to self-understanding, and at last to self-achievement, according to the natural logic of Zhang Zai's teaching theory. Su Shi, a great man of letters in the Song Dynasty, wrote an ever lasting, passionate thesis in *View on Chao Cuo*: "People in ancient times who could have great success not only had extraordinary talent but also had gritty ambition."

Wang Fuzhi emphasized both pleasure and motivation. He developed a teaching theory in a clear and systematic way, namely, the teaching process not only included one's positive and cheerful emotion, but also was supported by one's exertion and tough will. In his point of view, on the one hand, motivation was an essential part of the teaching activity: "If one is not industrious but relies on his teacher to lower requirements to fit him, he will be reduced to an ignorant and incapable man in his life."[155] On the other hand, pleasure could not be separated from motivation. If one exerted himself in studying without any pleasure, he would not endure for a long time:

> As for the motivation explained in *The Doctrine of the Mean*, it indicates that an industrious learner, who is able to learn, enquire, retrospect, discriminate, and practice earnestly, will not be content with just motivation and tenacity. What is more, since sincerity and decency are what one cultivates in tranquility, to urge one to acquire will make him feel uneasy and go astray from these traits. Further, the effort of motivation cannot take effect without

pleasure. The way of educating children should model that of the sages: if one does not delight in what he is learning but is motivated to learn, he will not persevere for a long time.[156]

How can pleasure be the foundation of diligence? Wang held that it hinged on the traits and function of people's feelings: "If one is in harmony with his surroundings, he will not be against it. If one feels joyful, he will not become bored with it." Only when a person regards studying as a pleasure can he "make achievements with pleasure,"[157] fearing no suffering or difficulty.

3) Learning to Meet Practical Needs

Based on the the teaching theory of learning to meet practical needs, students are required to apply what they have learned to practical use and put knowledge into practice, which resembles modern educational principles. Ancient Chinese educators emphasized the teaching principles and methods of learning to meet practical needs. The concept of "practicing earnestly" has already been addressed in this chapter. However, in terms of the important role the principles and methods of learning to meet practical needs played in ancient China's teaching theories, a few more words should be added for further discussion.

There are three reasons Chinese educators in ancient times attached such great importance to the principles and methods of learning to meet practical needs. First, its importance is decided by the objective law of the dialectical relationship between learning (knowledge) and practical needs (practices). Ancient educators believed that learning and practical needs (knowledge and practice) could promote each other mutually. Practical needs (practices) guided by knowledge acquired from purposeful learning can end in effective results. In contrast, practices without the guidance of knowledge will be blind actions. In the same way, wise ideas and thoughts come out after being put into practices. In contrast, knowledge separate from practical use will be empty. Zhu Xi made an incisive statement on this relationship: "One who engages himself in practice will know more. The more intensively one gains knowledge, the more smoothly he will act.[158]

Practice is the root of study:"If one only knows how to act but never does act, he will be the same as a man who knows nothing. If one is anxious to act without knowing why, he will have no idea what he will get."[159] The first sentence of this quote states that learning (knowledge) and practical needs (practice) promote each other mutually; the second sentence explains that the purpose of learning lies in practical use. One is better off not learning something if he acquires knowledge but does not put it into action. In this way, two sides must be united during teaching: putting knowledge into practice and combining knowledge with practice.

Second, the fundamental motivation and ultimate purpose of learning is to address practical problems. Ancient Chinese educators believed that the ultimate purpose of teaching was to allow students to use what they have learned. As Wang Chong, a philosopher in the Eastern Han Dynasty, said:

One who stresses making a thorough mastery of what he is learning will always give importance to putting it into practical use. If one could only read poems and classic works fluently, even in large numbers, he would be the same as a parrot. He could expound on the meaning of those classics, and even write good articles, but he still would have no distinguished talent and thus could not be capable (of being burdened with great tasks).[160]

Wang Chong pointed out that what mattered most in teaching was to digest all subjects so that one could apply what he has learned to practical use. One who is only capable of reading or reciting thousands of poems and books is no more than a parrot, simply repeating what the books say.

Huang Xi, a scholar in the Northern Song Dynasty, made a further point that if one learned something without using it, he would completely miss the true meaning of learning; however, the ultimate goal of teaching was to enable students to bring what they have learned into practice. He said, "A man who has a life but never learns is no better than one who never was born. Learning something without understanding it is equivalent to not knowing. One who knows something but does not put it into practice had better not learn. It is of utmost value when one learns something and brings it into practical use."[161]

Third, there was opposition to two academic trends in ancient times. It is well known that there existed two influential academic trends in Chinese history, namely, metaphysics in the Wei and Jin Dynasties and Neo-Confucianism in the Song and Ming Dynasties. Although these trends, to some extent, positively influenced the development of ancient China's academic thoughts, and played a role in changing and improving the model and level of thinking, there still exist some weaknesses in these trends, which cannot be ignored.

One is that in these trends, theory is detached from reality. For example, impacted by the fashion of the elegant arguments of metaphysics in the Wei and Jin Dynasties, a large number of scholars were ignorant of reality and talked hollowly:

Scholars of that time spoke emptily without devoting themselves to practice. If asked how to build a house, they could speak with fervor and assurance even though they had no idea that the lintel should be placed horizontally and the short supports on the beam vertically. If asked how to plant, they could speak big words without knowing that glutinous millet should be cultivated earlier and common millet later. As it is much easier to harangue and compose poems or prose, absurd things took place.[162]

This is what Yan Zhitui revealed. Li Gong, a scholar in the Qing Dynasty, criticized unsparingly the empty and shallow academic trend that had begun in the Song and Ming Dynasties:

> Smart and great men in the world perhaps all fell into the trap of thinking that Zen (deep meditation) could make them feel good both mentally and physically. Therefore, they wrote resplendent articles with no real connotation. In the late Ming Dynasty, no official could be relied on in governmental agencies, and no official worked in earnest. Senior officials sitting in their offices read *The Commentary of Zuo*. When the troops and horses of enemies came to the gate of their capitals, they were still talking about strategies of how to govern a country. Despite being incapable of being senior officials, they deemed making great achievements and performances to be petty things. They wrote books day and night, saying, "It is the very thing to hand down for posterity." As a result, their deeds led to natural disasters, the country's destruction, and people's deaths. Oh, how poor it is! Who on earth should be blamed? It is no wonder why Mr. Yan cried out the reasons within.[163]

Under such circumstances, these trends bear a historical significance, emphasizing the importance of learning to meet practical needs. This is both a principle and a method of teaching. Educators in ancient China valued two points when implementing their teaching practice. First, they advocated that the knowledge one mastered could meet practical needs and could be used to tackle practical problems. Liu Zhiji, a historian in the Tang Dynasty, argued:

> If one who learns for a thousand years and reads a huge pile of books cannot recognize a gentle and upright man, or realize his own mistakes when faced with conflict, he is "a man with a bookcase" or "an owner of books," as Ge Hong (a Daoist preacher in the Eastern Jin Dynasty) described. "Then even though you know a lot, what good is it?" Confucius remarked. That is the type of person they discussed.[164]

This means if a learner cannot apply what he has learned to practical use, but feels good seeing reasonable things or does not know why it is wrong when seeing unreasonable things, he is nothing other than someone with useless book knowledge, or a "walking bookcase."

Second, ancient Chinese educators proposed that "knowledge should be earnestly practiced for what it preaches."[165] This means that learners should improve their morality and culture, as has been discussed within the topic of moral education in Chapter Four.

3. Shared Principles and Methods Between Teaching and Learning

Educational activity is a bilateral act of teaching and learning. Apart from the three teaching principles and methods discussed above, with a focus on teaching and learning, respectively, there are three further principles and methods shared by teaching and learning.

1) The Mutual Promotion of Teaching and Learning

In the course of teaching, teachers and students, based on each other's role, promote each other and improve mutually through joint activities.

Mao Lirui, a notable Chinese educator, once said:

> It is praiseworthy that the principle of the mutually beneficial relationship between teachers and students is originally a Confucian teaching theory and was never mentioned in foreign teaching theories. Teaching literally seems to oppose learning, but they actually supplement each other. One should be taught to learn. One cannot acquire any knowledge without instruction. It is rare that one can be self-taught without the aid of a teacher. Instruction requires both the teacher and the student to learn. Teachers are inspired by their students, and engage in further studies in order to improve themselves as teachers.[166]

These words clearly illustrate the principles and methods of mutual promotion between teaching and learning in Chinese ancient teaching theories.

Starting with Confucius, China's ancient educators thought highly of the mutually beneficial relationship between teaching and learning. For example, Confucius himself noticed that teachers and students could learn from each other by exchanging views and mutual inspiration. He "taught his students without weariness, guiding them a step at a time,"[167] and gave considerate instruction and help to them. Meanwhile, he was adept at learning from his students. He once praised one of his students, "Ah, Shang, you uplift me,"[168] and "When doing something together as a threesome, there must be one who will have something to teach me."[169]

The Records on the Subject of Learning described the principle of the mutually beneficial relationship between teachers and students and expressed this thought in a clear manner, saying, "When one learns, he knows his own deficiencies; when one teaches, he knows the difficulties of learning. After one knows his deficiencies, he is able to turn around and examine himself; after one knows the difficulties, he is able to stimulate himself to effort. Hence it is said, 'Teaching and learning help each other.'"

In view of how to carry out the principles and methods of teaching and learning, Chinese educators in ancient times made suggestions and comments as described below.

First, emphasis should be put on the teacher's instruction. As Xuncius said, "One who does not obey his teacher's instruction and discipline rites, but always believes himself to be right, will accomplish nothing but absurd things, becoming like a blind man trying to distinguish between colors or a deaf man trying to discern sounds."[170] Further, he said:

> A knowing man could become a criminal and a brave man an immoral person if they do not obey what their teacher instructs. This is because they may use their knowledge in wrong ways and what they observe will be ridiculous. On the contrary, if one does as his teacher guides, he will be quick to know sense, and his courage will help him gain prestige. Thus, he will be able to use his abilities to behave well and quickly come to a conclusion based on his observation. This is a valuable quality for a man to have. If he does not, it will be the biggest misfortune in his life.[171]

As far as Xuncius was concerned, it is of great value that a man who is taught by a teacher and knows laws and rules can become a brilliant and accomplished gentleman. Wang Chong believed that teachers' advice played a significant role in students' development and growth: "A learner should spare no effort on studying and improving himself under the guidance of his teacher."[172] Han Yu, a great writer of the Tang Dynasty, made an incisive and vivid statement on teachers' instruction in his book *On the Teacher*:

> In ancient times, those who wanted to learn would seek out a teacher, one who could propagate the doctrine, impart professional knowledge, and resolve doubts. Since no one is born omniscient, who can claim to have no doubts? If one has doubts and is not willing to learn from a teacher, his doubts will never be resolved. Anyone who was born before me and learned the doctrine before me is my teacher. Anyone who was born after me and learned the doctrine before me is also my teacher. Since what I desire is to learn the doctrine, why should I care whether he was born before or after me? Therefore, it does not matter whether a person is high or low in position, young or old in age. Where there is the doctrine, there is my teacher.

Alas! The tradition of learning from the teacher has long been neglected. Thus it is difficult to find a person without any doubts at all. Ancient sages, who far surpassed us, even learned from their teachers. People today, who are far inferior to them, regard learning from the teacher as a disgrace. Thus, wise men become wiser and unlearned men become more foolish. This explains what makes a wise man and what makes a foolish man.

Han Yu held that the reason that the teacher was able to propagate and impart professional knowledge and moral education lay in the fact that he had learned and understood the doctrine earlier than his students. All men, the sages and the fools, should respect their teachers and honor the truth alike, and ask for knowledge from their teachers with an open mind. This is a relatively systematic argument on the nature of a teacher.

Second, emphasis should be placed on "a friend-like relationship between teachers and students." This statement advocates that teachers and students should learn from each other's strong points to offset one's weaknesses and improve mutually. *Yanzi Chun Qiu* (the *Spring and Autumn Annals of Yanzi*): *Inner Chapter Admonition II* states, "Many people learn together, and the one among them who can hold on to the last minute can be your teacher." Du Fu wrote in *Six Four-Line Poems*, "One should learn from different teachers." Liu Zongyuan, a man of letters in the Tang Dynasty, suggested clearly, "We should get rid of the definition of teacher and learn from everyone for the teacher's sake. Teachers and students learn from each other, which can save us from the worldly burden and benefit us. Since ancient times, no man of reason would reject such an idea."[173] The idea of a friend-like relationship between teachers and students builds on the mutually beneficial relationship between teachers and students, and it "ushered in a new way in ancient teaching theory and aroused people to think."[174] Wang Fuzhi completely grasped its meaning and proposed, "Teachers and students establish their relationship based on the learning of knowledge" and "help each other in the moral aspect."[175] He believed that teachers and students could exchange ideas not only on erudition, but also on morality.

Third, emphasis should be placed on encouraging students to surpass their teachers. Students should be encouraged to learn from their teachers and then to surpass them. Xuncius was the first to suggest such an idea: "A notable man said, 'There is no end to learning. Indigo blue is extracted from the indigo plant but is bluer than the plant it comes from. So is the ice colder than the water.'"[176]

Xuncius himself was a good practitioner of this thought. He had gone far away to Jixia Academy (a famous institution of Qi in the Warring States Period) three times, where he learned from various schools. He accepted Confucian theories, as well as theories from Daoism, Legalism, and other schools. Naturally, he epitomized all thoughts of different schools during the Pre-Qin Period.

Han Yu agreed that students learned from their teachers and would surpass them one day in the future, which was exactly the goal of education. It was understandable that students sought instruction from their teachers with the aim of succeeding them in mind. "If one expects that his article is better than others' and is quoted by others, he has already made it."[177]

Zhang Zai in the Song Dynasty agreed that the goal of students eventually surpassing their teachers was an inevitable trend: "Presently, you learn from other people and will become better than them in the future. It is a natural trend."[178]

2) Making Gradual Progress

The principle and method of making gradual progress requires a systematic teaching plan according to the scientific knowledge system and students' intellectual abilities. Chinese educators in ancient times attached importance to this teaching theory. For example, Confucius' students commended him, saying, "My master skillfully guides his students a step at a time."[179] We can see that Confucius was good at guiding his students step by step based on his teaching materials and instructing them to study in a gradual and systematic manner. They grew more interested in what they were learning and reached a state in which they could not give up.

Mencius aired his views when he tried to decipher Confucius' exclamation about flowing water:

> There is a spring of water; how it gushes out! It rests neither day nor night. It fills up every hole and then advances, flowing into the four seas. Such is water to have a spring! It was this which he found to praise.[180]

> Flowing water does not proceed until it has filled the hollows in its course. The student, who has set his mind on the doctrines of the sage, does not advance to them but by completing one lesson after another.[181]

Mencius held that teaching should without doubt advance like flowing water, day and night, but should also be carried out step by step, like flowing water filling up every hole on its way and then advancing. Only by doing this can drops of knowledge be accumulated bit by bit into a sea and can a student become accomplished. He added that if a teacher rushes for a quick result, failing to follow a certain order while teaching, he will inevitably achieve no success. This means that "he who advances with haste will retire with speed."[182]

The theory of making gradual progress can also be seen in *The Records on the Subject of Learning*. In this book, it is written, "The communication of lessons in an undiscriminating manner and without suitability produces damage and disorder and fails in its aim." With sublime words, this statement had a far-reaching meaning. "An undiscriminating manner" refers to the teacher giving lessons in a disorderly and unsystematic way, while failing to proceed in terms of the inner system and degree of difficulty of the teaching content.

In fact, the process of teaching is based on rules:

Taking the *Analects of Confucius* and *Mencius,* for instance, one should read the former first and then the latter. He should move on to the next only after understanding the first. For another example, when one reads a book, he should read it systematically, in the order of its chapters.[183]

These words reveal that the principles and methods of making gradual progress depend on the logic of knowledge itself.

"Without suitability" indicates that teachers do not take students' age and intelligence level into account when selecting teaching content. Wang Yangming said:

We must vary our topics accordingly when discussing with others. For example, a sapling needs water in a certain amount. When it grows larger, a certain amount of water is again required. From its sprout to its arm-length thickness, water is required in a limited amount. If the little bud is poured over with a bucket of water, it will drown.[184]

A baby in its mother's womb is only pure Qi, knowing nothing. When he is born, he can cry, then smile, and later on, recognize his parents and siblings and stand up, walk, hold, and carry things. As time goes on, he can do everything. This is because his energy grows and his physical strength improves, and he becomes smarter and smarter day after day. These achievements do not come out all at once when he was born. All things have a fundamental process.[185]

This actually indicates that the principles and methods of teaching and learning depend on students' physical and mental development. Wang believed that people's development was similar to the growth of a sapling, from small to big, and from immature to mature. Pouring a whole bucket of water over the sapling is like trying to impart advanced knowledge to a newborn baby. This runs counter to the teacher's desire and brings only harm.

As for how to put the theory into practice, educators made several suggestions as follows.

First, one should build a solid foundation. As Laozi said, "The tree that fills the arms grows from the tiniest sprout; the tower of nine stories rose from a [small] heap of earth; the journey of a thousand li (500 meters) commenced with a single step."[186]

Zhu Xi originated this thought and also expounded it at large, giving examples. He said, "Learning is like climbing a pagoda, one step after another. You can see the top step without the necessity to ask other people. If you never take a step but only suspend your foot in midair and think wishfully about taking a step, it is the same as remaining on the bottom step."[187] He thought that learning was like climbing a pagoda; those who wanted to reach the top when at the bottom without taking a step were just engaging in "wishful thinking."

Second, one should start from the easy and progress to the difficult. *The Records on the Subject of Education* pointed out long ago that teaching should be carried out from easy to difficult and from simple to complicated: "The skillful questioner is like a workman applying himself to deal with a hard tree. First he attacks the easy parts and then the knotty. After a long time, when the pupil and the master talk together, the subject is explained."

The Records on the Subject of Education also states, "The son of a good furrier is sure to learn how to make a fur robe. The son of a good maker of bows is sure to learn how to make a sieve. Those who first yoke a [young] horse place it behind, with the carriage in front. The superior man who examines these cases can instruct himself in [the method of] learning." This shows that an experienced furrier will teach his son to make a fur robe if he passes down his craftsmanship to his son. An experienced maker of bows will teach his son to weave willows into a sieve. If a young horse is trained to drive a cart, it will be guided by an older horse and run after the cart. Only by learning from the easy to the difficult can one turn difficulty into easiness later.

Third, one should optimize the teaching plan. This requires the teacher to make a specific plan for his teaching schedule and teaching content in advance and evaluate how well his teaching goes. Indiscriminate scheduling or having no general ideas for teaching content in mind should be avoided. Zhu Xi illustrated the shortcomings of not having a clear plan with a metaphor:

A man who advances without order is like a starving man coming to a restaurant. He will gobble up fish or meat, cakes or biscuits, whether in a dish or in a bowl, into his stomach without chewing carefully or swallowing slowly. Although he will get full, he will not have a clue of what he has eaten or the taste of it.[188]

In other words, random teaching is similar to a starving man walking into a restaurant.

3) Reviewing Past Knowledge to Learn New Knowledge

The principle of reviewing past knowledge to learn new knowledge asks students not only to review and consolidate what one has learned, but also to comprehend it in order to obtain new meaning or gain inspiration, which can be an impetus to pursue new knowledge. Chinese educators long ago explored this principle and method.

For example, *The Analects of Confucius* make a specific presentation in the very beginning: "Is it not a pleasure to study and practice what you have learned?" Also, in *The Analects of Confucius: Wei Zheng* (*The Practice of Governance*), Confucius stated clearly, "Reviewing what you have learned and learning anew, you are fit to be a teacher." Confucius believed that teachers should grasp the principle and method of reviewing past knowledge to learn new knowledge. It is worth noting not only for the teacher but also for the student. In practice, Confucius required his students to obey this principle in their learning. Zeng Can "each day examined himself in three ways,"[189] one of which was that he examined whether he had reviewed what his teacher had taught. Another student, Zixia, said, "Someone who is aware every day of what he lacks, and every month does not forget what he has developed, can be called 'loving to learn.'"[190]

How can one put this principle and method into practice? Ancient Chinese educators gave some valuable advice.

First, one should combine studying in college and at home, and emphasize the complementary benefits of regular subjects and exercises in his spare time. *The Records on the Subject of Education* stated clearly:

> In the system of teaching at the Great College, every season had its appropriate subject, and when the pupils withdrew and gave up their lessons [for the day], they were required to continue their learning at home. If a student does not learn [at college] to play in tune, he cannot enjoy his lutes; if he does not learn extensively the figures of poetry, he cannot enjoy the odes; if he does not learn the varieties of dress, he cannot take part in different ceremonies.

Apart from lessons during class, students should be given certain homework to help consolidate what they have learned and become skillful, such as by practicing elemental motions for musical instrument tuning, practicing songs, and doing cleaning after class. All these practices are significant for the tuning of musical instruments, as well as mastering the rhythms of poetry and the rules of rites.

Second, one should combine "reviewing what has been learned" with "acquiring the new," and emphasize reviewing in order to learn the new knowledge. Lu Ji, a writer in the Jin Dynasty, wrote in his *Essay on Literature*, "Inherit the old to innovate; follow the turbid to make it clear."

Zhang Zai said, "When one cherishes a doubt over the truth, he will remove the old views to fill in new ideas. If a new thought occurs, he should write it down immediately."[191] He taught his students to discard their old views if they found something wrong in their books and to then seek new ideas. Students were to note them down as soon as they gained a new understanding.

Zhu Xi gave his students the clear-cut instructions to not be conservative or adhere to past practices and to learn to break down outdated views and be innovative: "A learner cannot stick to old knowledge. He has to cast it away to catch a new idea. It is just like letting out the dirty water to let clear water in."[192]

Fang Yizhi, a scholar in the Ming Dynasty, commented that the key of reviewing the old to learn the new lies in continual learning, instead of a negative adoption of the old knowledge: "Learning is to absorb the accumulated wisdom from the ancestors and to renew the outdated constantly; thus, the older knowledge will become updated. Therefore, one should strive to gain [new knowledge], instead of plagiarizing others' views." Since new knowledge cannot be copied from others' old views, one has to make repeated studies based on existing wisdom in order to reach a state of being "self-accomplished" and thus acquiring new knowledge.

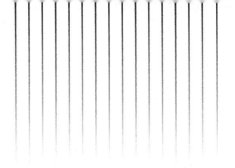

6

Thoughts on Teachers
in Ancient China

Teaching is one of the most ancient professions in the world. No society can do without teachers, who accelerate the delivery of predecessors' knowledge and experiences to new generations, acting as a bridge for the continuation and development of human society. Just as Russian educator Konstantin Ushinsky said:

> If a teacher does not lag behind the process of modern education, he will believe that he is an active and positive member of a large institution that overcomes the ignorance and vices of human beings, an intermediary between all the noble and great figures in history and the new generation, a preserver of the sacred teachings from those who fight for truth and happiness. He feels that he is a living link between the past and the future….His career, although ordinary on the surface, is one of the greatest careers in history."[1]

Similarly, the seventeenth-century Czech educator Comenius said, "Is there any better and greater contribution to our country than teaching and educating the youth?" He also defined teaching as "the most glorious profession under the sun."

How did the ancient educators of China discuss teachers? And what was the status and the role of teachers in China's ancient society? This chapter intends to introduce and analyze these topics.

The Changing Status of Teachers in Ancient China

In the history of ancient China's educational thought, there have always been disputes about the status of teachers. Some people think that it is ancient Chinese tradition to respect teachers and their teaching.[2] But some believe that teachers were never respected, especially in ancient China, only having undisputed authority in the teacher–student relationship.[3] How should we view this issue? We should start with an examination of the emergence of the teaching profession in ancient China and how the status of teachers changed over time.

In the earliest populations of ancient China, there were no specific educational activities. So-called education among primitive people was carried out in the community: "Communication, teaching on production and life experience, and the education of offspring all rely on the collective."[4]

After moving from a primitive society to clan communes, Chinese society witnessed the emergence of "the custom of electing clan chiefs from the same family in every clan, which brought about the initial tribal dignitaries."[5] These "tribal dignitaries," clan chiefs, or elders were charged with the responsibility for education and thus became the first "part-time teachers." There are many records in ancient books.

When Fu Hsi, a legendary emperor in ancient China, who was believed to be a god of philosophy as well as a god of fishery and husbandry, was the sovereign, there were many beasts in the world, so he taught people how to hunt.[6] When Fu Hsi died, the times of another mythical emperor, Shen Nung, inventor of Chinese medicine and farming, flourished. He cut wood into a plow and burned wood into a handle for the plow, then taught people the benefits of this tool.[7] Yao, a legendary monarch in ancient China, employed Qi (the ancestor of China's farming civilization) to teach people to live on the mountain, build dwellings according to the landform, and study planting technologies…so Yao appointed Qi as Minister of Agriculture.[8] The Minister of Agriculture taught the people to sow and reap, cultivating the five kinds of grain. When the five kinds of grain were brought to maturity, the people were able to subsist.[9]

These statements reflect that the educational activities of China's first "part-time teachers" were basically conducted for the purpose of improving productive labor.

At the end of the clan commune period, with the development of social production and the expansion of the social division of labor, differentiation occurred in education, that is, specialized schools for training the children of tribal dignitaries appeared. The "knowledge of Chengyun" and the "knowledge of Yuxiang" were the original such schools. At that time, there were two types of teachers in these schools. One was the tribal dignitary, who was both administrative leader and part-time schoolteacher, signifying "the unity of authority and teachers."[10] The other was the highly respected elder, who was selected and acted as a full-time teacher.[11] Therefore, the first full-time teachers were seniors and elders, and they not only taught the children of the noble class the practices of shooting, manners, and music, but also explained good words, deeds, and human relations to the emperor, feudal princes, officials, and nobility by "begging the old for their wise counsel" and through "conversation at general reunions"[12] in the ceremony of respecting elders. At this time, teachers were certainly respected, and the reason was likely the unity of authority and teachers.

The unity of authority and teachers was directly succeeded by the slave society of the Xia Dynasty, the Shang Dynasty, and especially the Western Zhou Dynasty (from the eleventh century BC to 771 BC). Throughout that period, the combination of education and politics and the unity of authority and teachers gradually improved. The educational model of "learning in the government," namely educational institutions established in the government, came into being.

Teachers in the Western Zhou Dynasty were divided into two kinds: one for state schools, the other for local schools. Among teachers for state schools, the Grand Director of Music (also called the Music Master, who was the ritualist responsible for religious sacrifices and national ceremonies) was mainly in charge. Those inferior to him were the Lower Director of Music, the Greater Assistant, the Smaller Assistant, the Grand Perfecter (of Instruction), the Flute Masters, the Subdirectors, the Grand Tutor, the Assistant Tutor, the Educational Officer, and the Educational Minister, all of whom had their respective duties.[13] These teachers were both music officers in the government and teachers of the nobility.

Among teachers for local schools, the Minister of the Masses (the chief of civil administration officials) was mainly in charge. Those inferior to him were local administrative officials at various levels, such as the Rural Teacher, the Rural Senior Official, the Governor, the Township Official, the Grand Preceptor, and the Master of the Child. There were also retired senior officials and scholars working as teachers, called "Civil Masters" or "Masters of the Child."[14]

The educational system of the unity of politics and pedagogy and of authority and teachers in the Western Zhou Dynasty was the political and ethical basis of Chinese educational thought and paved the way for an improvement in the status of teachers as well. This meant that when teachers were also political officials, they were recognized and respected by people; otherwise, it was hard to guarantee their status. Thus, in the realm of pedagogy, "official-oriented" thought came into being.

When the wheel of history rolled to the Spring and Autumn Period and the Warring States Period, great upheavals and revolutions happened in society, with three of the most obvious changes occurring in the field of education: the decline of state-owned schools, the rise of private schools, and the establishment of the scholar-official class. Due to the fact that slaveholders had to concentrate on military rivalry in the circumstances of lords vying to be part of the hegemon and being too busy to pay attention to educational enterprises, the phenomenon of the decline of state-owned schools occurred: "Education is no longer a noble's patent; the popularity of private school makes civilians also have a chance to receive education."[15]

In order to meet social needs for education, private schools were thus born. Although now it is hard to verify who the founder of private school education was in Chinese history, it is widely accepted that the emergence of private schools as a new form of schooling in China's educational history should be attributed to Confucius. The appearance of private schools not only broke the authority's monopoly on education—"learning in the government"—and provided opportunities for newly rising businessmen, landowners, farmers, and handicraftsmen to be educated, but also gave birth to the first educators in the history of China who made teaching their profession. Moreover, the rise of the scholar class[16] and private schools were mutually promoted, contributing to the flourishing of educational enterprises at that time.

During the Spring and Autumn Period and the Warring States Period, because teachers were more or less in a close relationship with authority and politics, the status of teachers was still generally high. *Discourses on Salt and Iron: Discourses on Confucianists* records the situation of the State of Qi attaching great importance to scholars, including teachers:

> In the State of Qi, King Xuan likewise encouraged the Confucianists and honored the learned. The followers of Meng Ke [Mencius] and Chun Yukun accepted salaries of the Senior Grand Officer [an official post in ancient China] but without holding regular appointments. It seems that at the gate of the Qi's capital, there assembled over a thousand of these officers.

Teachers in the Ji Xia School (the Capital School), the highest institution of learning at that time, surely acted as a "think tank" for the king of Qi State.

But it was also during this time that the status of teachers began to be questioned, with their status falling completely under the control of the governors. Let us take a look at Confucius' experience. Confucius is the first great educator in Chinese history, as well as the paragon of all teachers. Sima Qian, a great historian, writer, and thinker in the Western Han Dynasty, once made a brief summary of Confucius' life:

> Confucius was born poor and humble. When he grew up, he worked as a minor official in the Ji family, an accurate and fair teller of money and grain. Then he was appointed as a minor official managing a ranch, and cattle multiplied

there. Thus, he rose to the position of Si Kong (Minister of Industry). Later, he left the Lu State and suffered being cast out in the State of Qi, was expelled by Song and Wei, was besieged in the land of Chen and Wei, and eventually returned to Lu State.[17]

During his brief and busy life, Confucius had a successful official career for a time when he was appointed as Si Kong and Da Si Kou ("Minister of Justice") by the Lu State, meanwhile taking on the duties of the Prime Minister, and was well known. But due to his "disagreeable" thoughts, the authorities chose not to tolerate him, and thus he resigned and went traveling. Confucius' teaching cause then never ceased from his thirties onward.

Nonetheless, against the historical background of the time (although he was respected as "the exemplary teacher for all ages" and as a sage), he had a bitter taste of misery and hardship when he resigned and went traveling. He experienced attacks from thugs, was snubbed by sovereigns, and faced slander from people and the despondency of his disciples. All these events surely exerted a great influence on the formation of Confucius' pessimistic mood of world-weariness in his later years.[18] In the end, Confucius was "dejected and frustrated, like a homeless dog" and "died in Queli" suddenly after hearing the bad news of his disciple Zilu's death in the Wei State.[19]

Let us now look at the experience of Xuncius, a great thinker from the end of the Warring States Period. In Chinese history, Xuncius is the first educational thinker who gave a full description of the status and role of teachers, exalting teachers to an unprecedentedly high status. He put forward the idea explicitly at a comparatively early time that the role of teachers was closely related to the rise and fall of the nation, the life and death of the legal system, and the good and evil of the human heart by saying, "When a country is on the verge of great florescence, it is certain to prize its teachers and give great importance to breadth of learning. If it does this, then laws and standards will be preserved."

"When a country is on the verge of decay, then it is sure to show contempt for teachers and slight its masters. If it does this, then its people will be smug. If the people are smugly self-satisfied, then laws and standards will be allowed to go to ruin."[20] He thought that only by valuing teachers could the social system and law grow sound and be observed by the people. Therefore, Xuncius said:

Ethical codes have three roots. Heaven and earth are the root of life. Forebears are the root of kinship. Lords and teachers are the root of order. Were there no heaven and no earth, how could there be life? Were there no forebears, how could there be issue? Were there no lords and teachers, how could there be order? Were even one of these three lost, there would be no peace and security for man. Thus, rituals serve heaven above and earth below, pay honor to one's forebears, and exalt rulers and teachers, for these are three roots of ethical codes.[21]

This was the first time teachers were juxtaposed with heaven, earth, lords, and forebears. The exalted status of teachers lay in the supremacy of ethical codes, but if there were no teachers, how could one know about ethical codes? Therefore, Xuncius further said:

it is through ritual that the individual is rectified. It is by means of a teacher that ritual is rectified. If there were no ritual, how could the individual be rectified? If there were no teachers, how could you know which ritual is correct? When what ritual mandates, you make so in your conduct, then your emotions will find peace in ritual. When what your teacher says you say also, then your knowledge will be like that of your teacher. When your emotions find peace in ritual and your knowledge is like that of your teacher, then you will become a sage.[22]

Xuncius meant that ethical codes were used to rectify people's ideology and behavior, and teachers were the ones who advised whether one's thoughts and behavior lived up to the requirements of rituals. Thus, it was ultimately the responsibility of teachers to see ethical codes put into practice. So it was no wonder that Xuncius regarded having a teacher as the key to success when he said:

Thus, if a man who is intelligent lacks teacher and model, he will certainly become a robber. If he is brave, he will surely become a murderer. If versatile, he will certainly cause disorder. If a precise investigator, he will surely create anomalous results. If a discriminator, he will certainly advance extravagant schemes. An intelligent man who has both teacher and model will quickly become comprehensively skilled. If brave, he will quickly become awe-inspiring. If versatile, he will quickly complete his tasks. If a precise investigator, he will soon exhaust things. If a discriminator, he will soon discover the principle of things. Accordingly, having a teacher and model is man's greatest treasure, and lacking a teacher and model his greatest calamity.[23]

Xuncius, an educator who thought highly of teachers and the teaching model, had a very similar life experience to that of Confucius. He also had been successful for a time when the Ji Xia School was prospering and thriving. He was not only the oldest and most qualified master among scholars, but also respected and favored by the lord of the Qi State, appointed as "Ji Jiu" (a post in Ji Xia School usually held by a senior master who communicated with heaven on behalf of the community) three times and "Coaching" (a title conferred on a person who was not native but held a high post). However, when the political situation of the Qi State changed, he had no choice but to leave for the Chu State.

Xuncius was slandered in the Chu State and not appointed to a high position. When he later returned to Ji Xia School, he had to take a post where "the wise had no opportunity to reflect, the able had no opportunity to govern, and the worthy had no opportunity to serve," "with his fame and reputation being not plainly evident, his followers not legion, and his glory and brilliance not widely known."[24]

Therefore, when teaching became an independent occupation from the system of the unity of politics and pedagogy and authority and teachers, the status of teachers became insecure. Whether the status of teachers was high or low often reflected a certain political situation and was even controlled by the likes and dislikes of the governors. Only when teachers were the "bond" of the ethical and political relation network in feudal society could they be preferred and appointed to significant positions,[25] which can be seen in the difference in how scholars, including teachers, were treated between the Western Han and Eastern Han Dynasties.

Most of the founding heroes of the Western Han Dynasty were outlaws and scoundrels, while during the revival period of the Eastern Han Dynasty, generals all had the mien of scholars, owing to a different social climate….So for a certain time, the emperor and his subjects were of similar disposition and likings, which led to the expression, "like emperor, like subjects."[26]

It is surely a little partial of Zhao Yi to attribute the different attitudes of the founding monarchs of the two Han dynasties toward Confucianists, saying that "the emperor and his subjects were of the same style" and "their disposition and likes would have some similarities." In saying this, he ignored the influence of the social and historical background. However, it is reasonable to a certain degree that he realized the different essences of the founding emperors and subjects of the two Han dynasties and the distinction between their attitudes toward Confucianists. It has been recorded that Liu Bang, Emperor Gaozu of Han, "spurned scholars" and even took off the hats of Confucianists and threw them into excrement and urine,[27] which was the utmost insult to intellectuals.

In contrast, Emperor Wu of Han ordered that all prefectures should have educational officers and "establish the post of Boshi on the *Five Classics*, responsible for enrolling students and preparing classified examinations of archery for them, and prized with salaries. This order had been executed for over a century until the time of Emperor Ping of Han Liu Kan, when there were multitudes of educators and branches of doctrines, one classic could be explained with more than one million words, and there were over one thousand masters."[28]

Actually, the reason for Liu Bang's slighting of Confucian scholars was that it was warriors who made the greatest contributions to the foundation of the Han Dynasty, while Confucian scholars seldom took part in battles or got involved in military and political affairs directly. Therefore, naturally, Liu Bang made light of Confucian scholars. Nonetheless, until the time of Emperor Wu of Han, scholars had been gaining dominant status in society and were directly involved in politics. During the early Eastern Han Dynasty, Emperor Guangwu, Ming, and Zhang, among others, all treated scholars with due respect, and often they themselves were born to a scholarly family, such as Emperor Guangwu. After the Han Dynasty, the status of teachers again fell into question, and this continued through to the Wei and Jin Dynasties, reaching a very precarious point in the Tang Dynasty. As Han Yu said, "Since the Han Dynasty, schooling had been declining, but still there were people who taught classics and imparted professional knowledge and skills, which, however, have never been heard today."[29]

Liu Zongyuan also wrote that "Since the Wei and Jin Dynasties, people have been more unwilling to follow a teacher. Nowadays, it is not heard that there are teachers. If there are any, people will laugh at them and think of them as madmen. Only Han Yu has taken in students regardless of social opinion and being jeered and insulted, and he has written *On the Teacher*, being a serious teacher."[30] In the Tang Dynasty, the status of teachers had already lost its past sacred halo, the essential reason for which was the separation of politics and pedagogy and between authority and teachers. Also, teachers became estranged from social and political life. A further significant reason that cannot be ignored is the influence of the imperial examination system.[31]

We know that the imperial examination system created a type of socialized education, in which all scholars had only one goal to assiduously strive for: knocking open the "door" of the imperial examination, through which only a very small number of "lucky dogs" could proceed, namely, the so-called "only one ten thousandth being recruited into the service of the imperial government through the imperial examination."[32] But as a scholar who failed the imperial examination, one would be disappointed in himself and disdained by others if he picked up his previous profession as a farmer, businessman, or craftsman. So those who could not knock open the door of the imperial examination had to choose teaching as their career. After the birth of the imperial examination system, most teachers were scholars frustrated by it. As a result, the status of teachers fell sharply.

Until the Yuan Dynasty, the status of teachers in China continued its disastrous fall, nearly being reduced to the lowest level of society.

Zheng Sixiao said, "According to Tatar, the social hierarchy from high to low, respectively, is governors, minor officials, monks, Daoists, doctors, craftsmen, hunters, artisans, Confucian scholars, and beggars."[33] Xie Fangde wrote in *Prologue to Seeing Fang Zaibo Off Back to the Three Mountains*:

Those entertainers of the Yuan Dynasty who acted in poetic dramas and mocked Confucian scholars said that "According to the decrees and regulations of our great Yuan, people are classified into ten classes. The first two classes are governors first and officials second They are put in the first places for they are superior. The reason for their being superior is that they are of benefit to the nation; the last four classes are artisans as the seventh, prostitutes the eighth, Confucian scholars the ninth, and beggars the tenth. They are put in the last places for they are inferior. The reason for their being inferior is that they are of no benefit to the nation.

This indicates that the social status of scholars, including teachers, was actually inferior to those of craftsmen and prostitutes and only higher than that of beggars. Moreover, Zheng Banqiao, a painter of the Qing Dynasty, also described the teacher's life under another's roof:

Teachers are originally inferior in status and depend on others for a living. Half-starved and idle, I am a teacher at ease with no fetters and no yokes. Father and brother blame my idleness when there are few classes, and students bear grudges against me when I am strict with them. Fortunately, I do well in my official career now, covering up half the shame of my past as a teacher.[34]

These words illustrate the difficult and miserable life of those poor scholars who worked as teachers in private schools or as abecedarian teachers for a living. Therefore, in China's feudal society, people often regarded being a teacher as the last thing for a scholar to do, and there was a popular saying complaining that "as long as there are two dou (a measure for grain) at home, never work as a teacher."

But among ordinary people and in the field of education, teachers were often still esteemed, and this tradition was never lost, even when the rulers degraded teachers to the bottom of society. Thus, although the status of teachers went through many changes in ancient China, falling from the zenith to the nadir, the tradition of educators, educational thinkers, and even the public singing highly of and showing respect to teachers has never become extinct.

The Functions of the Teacher

In the first part of this chapter, we briefly studied the historical changes in the status of teachers in ancient China.

We will now analyze the interpretations of the role or functions of teachers of ancient China's educators. Sayings on the functions of teachers in ancient China have three aspects as follows.

1. The Function of Teachers: Propagating the Way

The "Dao" (the Way) is a basic conception in ancient Chinese philosophy that first appeared during the Spring and Autumn Period when renowned statesman and thinker Zichan put forward the idea that "the way of heaven is distant, while the way of man is near. We cannot reach the former."[35] "The way of heaven" here means the law of celestial bodies' movements, whereas "the way of man" signifies the principles and rules of being a human. Later generations of Confucians defined each step of the Way as a code of ethical principles. For example, Dong Zhongshu of the Western Han Dynasty pointed out that "the Way originates from heaven and will not change if heaven does not change."[36] Therefore, "propagating the Way" was to teach political and ethical morality, which was the foremost function of ancient education in China and the primary task of teachers at that time.

Very early on, this idea was put forward explicitly by Ma Rong of the Han Dynasty. He said, "Teachers are those who illustrate ethics and virtues to students with analogies."[37] Zheng Xuan, a master of Confucian classics in the Eastern Han Dynasty, had a similar saying: "Those who teach people the Way are called teachers,"[38] which meant that the most important task and role of teachers is to propagate political and ethical morality. During the Tang Dynasty, Han Yu made an incisive summary of teachers' functions in his book *On the Teacher*: "Teachers are those who propagate the Way, impart professional knowledge, and remove confusion."

In the Tang Dynasty, poet Han Yu's view of propagating the Way was to teach the political and ethical morality of feudalism. "Imparting professional knowledge" was to give lectures on Confucian classics, such as the *Book of Poetry*, the *Book of History*, the *Book of Changes* and the *Spring and Autumn Annals*. "Removing confusion" was to answer all difficult questions that students encountered in their learning of the Way and professional knowledge. Of these three, propagating the Way was the root, with imparting professional knowledge and removing confusion being auxiliary to guarantee the smooth procession of propagating the Way. This was further explained by Yang Jian of the Song Dynasty from his perspective of the idealism of the mind.

For example, he said:

> Being a teacher is to propagate the Way. The Way cannot be obtained from the outside but is got by enlightening the mind. So is it possible for a teacher to teach students the Way by instilling things from the outside without touching and enlightening the mind? If possible, it is merely a repetition of the Way inherent in the mind. If a teacher ignores his students' thoughts, then what is taught is all other for students because it has nothing to do with them.[39]

This means that the teacher's role is to enlighten and revitalize the Way innate in students' minds.

Wang Fuzhi, who lived during the Ming and Qing Dynasties, also attached great weight to the propagation of the Way, believing that the foremost aim of the Great Learning was to "teach people to cultivate themselves and regulate others so as to accomplish virtues to become a great man."[40] However, he disapproved of the idea of understanding the Way only through the mind advocated by the School of Mind. He contended that one should combine "observations" with "potential abilities."

2. The Function of Teachers: Developing Talents

In the history of Western educational thought, it was the French educator Rousseau who advanced the proposition that "education makes a man." In Rousseau's view, children were considered to be men liberated from the restraints of society and parents. He thought that real education was the development of children's natures, which was a drastic change in pedagogy and established the principles of modern education.[41]

Although ancient Chinese educators did not make such a proposition in an explicit way, similar ideas had been expressed throughout history. Xuncius, living during the Pre-Qin Period, held that teachers were a decisive factor in shaping students' characters by saying, "So having a teacher and a teaching model is man's greatest treasure, and lacking a teacher and a teaching model his greatest calamity. If a man has neither teacher nor model, then he will exalt his inborn nature; if he has both, he will exalt accumulated effort."[42]

Yang Xiong of the late Western Han Dynasty thought highly of the role of teachers in developing talents as well. He exclaimed, "Teacher! Teacher! You are the crucial factor in children's fates,"[43] which deemed that, to a certain extent, teachers took charge of students' lives and had a great influence on their future. *Baihu General Views (Debates on Unifying the Cardinal Principles of Confucian Classics in the White Tiger Pavilion)*, compiled by Ban Gu of the Han Dynasty, pointed out that if there were no teaching, man would only be a natural being in the biological sense. Only by being educated by teachers to grasp the cultural heritage of human and social moral rules could man become a real social being in the sociological sense. "So although man is human-natured, still he needs to follow a teacher."[44] In the Song Dynasty, Zhang Zai's words were very close to Rousseau's famous proposition:

Learners should establish their human nature. They should be educated to become benevolent and know why man is man. Thus, learners are educated how to be men.[45]

Although the statements of Ban Gu and Zhang Zai cannot be exalted to the same status as Rousseau's thoughts, in terms of time, they were made over 1,600 and 700 years earlier, respectively, than Rousseau's.

Furthermore, Liu Zongyuan of the Tang Dynasty and Lu You of the Song Dynasty exemplified teachers' importance in developing talents through their own experience and lessons they learned from experience. Liu Zongyuan wrote:

> When I was young, I loved music and met someone learning to play the Qin instrument (a seven-stringed zither) without the instruction of a master. Sometimes he would take a music book and read it; thus he could know how to place his fingers on the Qin. He would practice playing the Qin from very early until night. When it was very dark, he would light a candle, and if the candle ran out, then he would play on mats. Thus he learned for ten years and thought that he was perfect. Then he left for a big city and played the Qin before a seated audience. The audience guffawed, "Hey, what a noise! How odd his tempo is!" At last, he was so ashamed that he went back. When I grew older, I loved handwriting and again met someone learning handwriting without the instructions of a master. He had to learn from old books and bent over a desk to practice. He was as diligent as the man who practiced playing the Qin and had persevered for even more years. Then he took out his works and said, "My handwriting could not be better." Those who knew calligraphy laughed at him and said, "The handwriting is loose in form and reverse in streaks." At last, he was spurned by the world and returned ashamed. Those two men both made their greatest efforts to learn but were not recognized by people. Why? Because there was no teacher to guide them, so they did not learn the quintessence that cannot be acquired if not taught. Therefore, even though they learned day and night, year by year, they grew not closer but further from the quintessence.[46]

Liu Zongyuan meant that if one had no guidance from a teacher and explored only by himself, he often could not understand the key knowledge and would achieve only half the result with double the effort, or even achieve nothing, thus having difficulties in developing his abilities. So Liu Zongyuan said in his *Admonition on Having Teachers and Friends*, "What can I do without being taught? How can I become an able man without being educated?"

Lu You of the Song Dynasty had tasted the bitter consequences of not having a teacher to instruct him. He said in his *A Reply to Zhu Bu Liu* (Zhu Bu is an official post in ancient China),

When I was close to the age of 20, I began to focus on learning from the ancients. However, at that time, I had no teacher or friend to ask for help. I had no one to ask questions when I read some profound thoughts. So I had to guess the general meaning by myself. Sometimes I might get the right answer and sometimes the wrong; at times, at first, I may have doubted that I was wrong, but at last I believed that I was right; at times, at the very beginning, I may have understood the meaning very easily, but gradually I found that my understanding was not proper, and this happened often. And eventually, I still did not know what the truth was.

Lu You believed that if one wanted to master the knowledge of a subject, one could not do so without a teacher's guidance.

During the Ming and Qing Dynasties, Huang Zongxi pointed out when illustrating the function of teachers, "Present or past, there is great learning and small learning, but there never has been one who can make achievements without having a teacher,"[47] deeming that one will not succeed in his studies or develop his talents if not educated by a teacher.

3. The Function of Teachers: Rectifying Deviations

"Rectifying deviations" means that teachers can not only develop students' flawless characters, turning them from natural beings into social beings through educational activities, but also rectify their deviant behavior, changing them from unqualified social beings to well-qualified social beings. This idea was reiterated time and again by the authors of *Lv's Commentary of History*.

Lv's Commentary of History stated that it was certain that one would develop into a great person who was wise and virtuous if he had good qualities and was well taught: "I know of no such thing that a learner who has an erudite teacher as well as talents will not become a sage."[48] Meanwhile, the authors also emphasized the role teachers played in rectifying people's misconduct. They pointed out that some well-known and virtuous men of the Warring States Period were people who should have "received penalty, been killed, or spurned"; however, they were not punished or abused but became "famous and eminent all over the world," the reason for which being that "they had been educated," thanks to the rectifying education of teachers. For instance, Zi Zhang had been a "vulgar philistine from the Lu State," Yan Zhuoju had been a "chief robber on Liangfu Hill," Duangan Mu had been a "market middleman from the Jin State," Gao He and Xian Zishi had been "grumpy and atrocious men from the Qi State," and Suolu Shen had been a "very cunning man from the east,"[49] but they all were transformed into celebrities of unquestioned moral rectitude and high morality by studying under masters such as Confucius, Zixia, Mo-tse, and Qin Guxi.

The Ways to Be a Teacher

What qualities should a teacher have in the process of exercising the teacher's functions and achieving educational goals? In other words, what are the requirements for being a teacher? In 1952, the American Educational Research Association (AERA) listed a teacher's abilities as follows: (1) the teacher's influence (upon the level students will reach and the achievements they will make all their lifetime, and upon the level students will reach when studying in other schools afterwards, upon the achievement of educational goals set for students now); (2) parents' satisfaction with their child's teacher; (3) educational administrative departments' and the school president's satisfaction with the teacher; (4) the teacher's advice, values, and attitudes; (5) the teacher's knowledge of educational psychology; (6) the teacher's mood and ability to adapt to society; (7) the teacher's knowledge of setting a syllabus; (8) the teacher's knowledge of the subject he or she teaches; (9) the teacher's interest in the subject he or she teaches; (10) the teacher's performance during internship; (11) the teacher's performance in his or her major of educational studies; and (12) the teacher's intelligence. Although ancient Chinese educators' expositions were not as comprehensive or "modern," they still created a system of their own with distinguished characteristics. This next part intends to make an analysis of the ways to be a teacher in ancient Chinese educational thought from three perspectives.

1. An Outline of the Ways to Be a Teacher

In ancient China, the most concise summary that expounded on the ways to be a teacher was from Confucius, who discussed "learning without satiety," and "instructing others without becoming wearied." He said:

> The silent treasuring of knowledge, learning without satiety, and instructing others without becoming wearied: which of these belongs to me?[50]
>   The sage and the man of perfect virtue: how dare I rank myself with them? It may simply be said of me that I strive to become such without satiety and teach others without weariness.[51]

If we carefully analyze the connotations of "learning without satiety and instructing others without becoming wearied," we will find that it is a good summary of the ways to be a teacher, as well as a great contribution to the educational theories of ancient China. Until this point, there had been no other saying more concise and precise than this eight-word outline from Confucius in stating a teacher's basic qualities.

Let us take a look at "learning without satiety" first. If one wants to a teacher who deserves the title, he must keep learning and studying without satiety. Only by learning continuously and tenaciously can one become erudite and sublime. A teacher who is slack in learning is naturally not capable of being a model for others.

Throughout history, Confucius is the epitome of those who "learn without satiety." In his teaching career, he did not stop learning even for a brief moment. He said, "I am not one who was born in the possession of knowledge; I am one who is fond of antiquity and earnest in seeking it there,"[52] considering that there was no one who was as fond of learning as he from far or near.[53] He learned diligently and enquired often, studying wherever he went. He was "not ashamed to ask and learn from his inferiors," as "anyone could be his teacher." He kept learning even in his later years, saying, "If some years were added to my life, I would start the study of *Yi* at the age of 50 [the *Book of Changes*], and then I might come to be without great faults."[54] He summarized his life as follows: "At fifteen, I had my mind bent on learning. At thirty, I stood firm. At forty, I had no doubts. At fifty, I knew the decrees of heaven. At sixty, my ear was an obedient organ for the reception of truth. At seventy, I could follow what my heart desired, without transgressing what was right."[55]

Confucius's "learning without satiety" not only made him an erudite and versatile figure in history, but also set a good model for educators throughout future generations.

In the history of China, there were many teachers who studied diligently, leaving behind stories praised far and wide. For instance, it was recorded that at the age of eight, Zhu Xi, a great educator of the Song Dynasty, wrote, "If one does not do so, one is not man" after reading the *Classic of Filial Piety*. At age ten, he was "in such joy that words failed him" when he read "The sage and we are the same in kind" in *Mencius*.[56] When studying under Li Dong, he also focused on learning, forgetting food and sleep, and thus was lauded by Li Dong several times for "sparing no efforts to learn, being warmhearted, and having awe for righteousness, which was rarely seen in peers."[57]

Next, let us look at "instructing others without becoming wearied." The aim of a teacher's being well-learned is to do well in teaching. If one wants to be a teacher who deserves the title, in addition to "learning without satiety," he has to work hard, "instructing others without becoming wearied." Only by being devoted to the cause of education heart and soul can one do well in educational work. It is impossible for one who is tired by educational work to be an excellent teacher, and it is often the case that such a teacher will mislead and do harm to his students.

Throughout history, Confucius is also the paradigm of those who "instruct others without becoming wearied." Whoever asked for instruction received instruction from him without reservation. However hard circumstances were, he kept giving lectures. For example, while being besieged in the Song State, he continued to "lecture on the *Book of Rites* to his disciples under a big tree";

even while running out of food in the Chen State, he still "gave lectures, recited poems, sang songs, and played the Qin to his disciples without stopping."[58]

When Confucius praised Yan Yuan, he said, "Never flagging when I set forth anything to him—ah! That is Hui [Yan Hui, a student of Confucius]."[59] He also said, "I have talked with Hui for a whole day, and he has not made any objection to anything I have said—as if he were stupid."[60] To some degree these words certainly reflected Yan Yuan's sincere attitude toward studies, but meanwhile they were also a manifestation of Confucius' spirit of "instructing others without becoming wearied." If there was no Confucius' "instructing others without becoming wearied," it would be hard for Yan Yuan "never to flag" and "not to make any objection," for which Yan Yuan had a deep feeling. Further, he thought that it was the Master's spirit of "instructing without becoming wearied" with "orderly and skillful methods" that made him reach the point that "when he wishes to quit, he cannot do so" in both studying and the cultivation of morality.

Confucius' spirit of "instructing others without becoming wearied" has always been the paradigm of the spirit of teachers throughout Chinese history. For instance, the *History of the Song Dynasty* writes that Cheng Yi, a neo-Confucianist and educator in the Northern Song Dynasty, "instructed others without becoming wearied all his lifetime, so he had the largest number of students, whose alumni were well-known scholars." When Zhu Xi, a great Chinese educator in the Song Dynasty, was teaching in the Bailudong Academy, he also "instructed students without becoming wearied, because as soon as holidays came, students were filled with confusion to remove and difficult questions to ask. If he went on a holiday, enjoying roaming along streams and among rocks, he would return to the academy after just one day."[61]

The *Year Book of Zhuzi* contains the records of Zhu Xi concerning himself with the teachings of the Yuelu Academy by sparing time from his busy political work:

> The master worked hard in the daytime to cope with affairs in governing the county. At night, he gave lectures, discussed with students, and answered questions, showing no weariness. He taught students to be practical and internalize what they had learned by applying their knowledge to life, not to ignore and disdain trivial things and matters just by their side, and not to admire and pursue things too lofty to achieve. This advice was said so sincerely and cordially that all those present were deeply moved.[62]

Moreover, "learning without satiety" and "instructing others without becoming wearied" are closely related and help each other forward. As early as over 60 years ago, concerning the issue of learning, Mao Zedong stated,

"The enemy of learning is complacence. If one wants to learn something, he has to start with not being smug. Pertaining to oneself, he should 'learn without satiety' and as regards others, he should 'give instruction without becoming wearied,' an attitude we should have."[63] Indeed, it is true that when a teacher learns without satiety, he will teach others without becoming wearied; similarly, when a teacher instructs others without becoming wearied, he will learn without satiety.

2. The Basic Qualities of a Teacher

Educators in ancient China not only described the ways to be a teacher, but also described the basic qualities and major capabilities of a teacher in great detail, which enriched the connotations of the ways to be a teacher. Xuncius said:

> There are four techniques for being a teacher, but a superficially broad general acquaintance is not one of them. One who requires deference, is majestic in manner, and instills a fearing respect may properly be regarded as a teacher. One who is white-haired with age and is trustworthy may properly be regarded as a teacher. One who, in reciting and explaining, neither transgresses nor errs may properly be regarded as a teacher. One who recognizes the distinguishing characteristics of things in making assessments may properly be regarded as a teacher.[64]

Xuncius meant that the basic qualities of a teacher had four manifestations: first, majesty, making students defer to the teacher; second, trustworthiness, having a rich teaching experience; third, the ability to impart knowledge in a systematic and orderly way; fourth, proficiency in distinguishing the characteristics of things in textbooks and explaining sublime words that have deep meaning. Dong Zhongshu, a great expert on Confucianism in the Han Dynasty, expounded on the idea that an excellent teacher should have five basic qualities:

> One who is good at being a teacher should perfect his morality and be virtuous. He also should be careful with his behavior and regulate his time well. He should teach with propriety, being neither more nor less and neither fast nor slow. He should neither be in haste in teaching nor feel it a suffering to pause for the moment. He should examine what has been done and thus accomplish his undertakings. Therefore, he will not labor and become weary physically, ending up with the accomplishment of his teaching work, which is wise, and we should follow suit.[65]

That is to say, a teacher should be both talented and virtuous, possessing the power to influence students with his own personality and being competent in his work. A teacher should pay attention to the characteristics of his students' ages, having a good knowledge of their psychology. A teacher should act according to his own abilities, proceeding step by step in an orderly way. A teacher should pay attention to the regulation and evaluation of his students but not inhibit their interests and initiatives. A teacher should teach according to the traits of his students' characters, based on a close and deep observation of their doings.[66]

In summary, the basic qualities of a teacher should be displayed as defined below.

1) Being Impartial and Treating All Students Fairly

Teachers should be impartial to all students, rather than being snobbish. Confucius attached great importance to this idea when performing his duty as a teacher. However, Chen Kang, a student of Confucius, questioned the fairness of Confucius and guessed that he might be giving special tuition to his son Bo Yu. Once, Chen Kang met Bo Yu, asking, "Have you heard any lessons from your father different from what we have all heard?" Bo Yu replied frankly, "No."[67]

The author of *Lv's Commentary of History* also thought teachers should not be concerned about whether a student's family background was noble or humble, rich or poor. If teachers fawned upon students from rich and powerful families, but suppressed, embarrassed, or detested students from poor and humble families who were diligent in learning, they would set students against teachers emotionally, resulting in "both a failure in education and an abolition of teaching principles."[68]

2) Being Strict with Oneself and Making an Example of Oneself

Teachers should be strict with themselves and be a model of virtue for others. Concerning this, Confucius said, "He who requires much from himself and little from others will keep himself from being the object of resentment."[69] Confucius thought highly of the modeling effect of teachers, holding that examples were always more efficacious than precept and advocating "education without precept."

Dong Zhongshu advocated that teachers should be careful with their words and deeds in case of having a bad influence on their students. Dong said, "A man of complete virtue hates it very much if he confuses students with unrealistic words....All teachers cannot be too cautious or careful."[70]

Yang Xiong regarded teachers as models for all people, so he held that teachers should help students to change by setting themselves as examples. Wang Anshi, a scholar in the Song Dynasty, also held the same opinion, saying, "Teachers are those who can be a model for others."[71] People who are most suitable are selected to be teachers. He said, "Those scholar-officials who have both ability and political integrity and have had experience as officials can be teachers."[72] When talking about the educational methods for teaching "filial piety and fraternal duty," Wang Fuzhi, a scholar during the Ming and Qing Dynasties, wrote:

> Filial piety and fraternal duty cannot be explained in words. They form one kind of human nature. It would be pedantic and unrealistic to explain it with words. If students are taught this way, they just feign and cannot master the knowledge. Therefore, the kings of ancient times who could practice what they preached could educate all people. They made all people behave well voluntarily. Therefore, although people were not taught to show filial piety and comply with fraternal duty, they were willing to do so. We are no match for our ancestors when it comes to helping our juniors make progress.[73]

In Wang Fuzhi's opinion, to conduct the education of filial piety and fraternal duty, teachers could teach students only by setting an example, not by explaining the concept to them. Through the effect of setting an example, students followed the virtue voluntarily.

3) Possessing Stable Emotions and a Dignified Manner

Teachers should be good at mastering their tempers, rather than being rash or reckless. Confucius said:

> The noble man has nine things which are the subjects of thoughtful consideration. In regard to the use of his eyes, he is anxious to see clearly. In regard to the use of his ears, he is anxious to hear distinctly. In regard to his countenance, he is anxious that it should be benign. In regard to his demeanor, he is anxious that it should be respectful. In regard to his speech, he is anxious that it should be sincere. In regard to his doing of business, he is anxious that it should be reverently careful. In regard to what he doubts, he is anxious to question others. When he is angry, he thinks of the difficulties [his anger may bring]. When he seeks to gain, he thinks of righteousness.[74]

Confucius was also "mild, yet dignified; majestic, yet not fierce; respectful, yet composed." He was always in a good emotional state. Zhu Xi required teachers not to be swayed by their emotions; only with "a light temper and an upright mind" could one be "complete in the character and tranquil in emotion." Zhu said, "Scholars should pay more attention to cultivating temperament and should control their emotions. Nowadays, people regard virtuous men as having no emotions. In fact, it is not that they do not have emotions, but that they are able to control their emotions."[75] In *Jing Zhai Zhen* (*Maxims Written in Jing Zhai*), he once proposed such requirements for all people:

> People should be well-dressed and keep a dignity in their looks. People should live without flippancy and should worship the gods. When walking, they should be sure-footed; when bowing, their gestures should be respectful. People should choose places to walk, and walk in curved lines like ants to show respect. When going out, they should behave to every one as if receiving a great guest; when doing things, they should behave as if assisting at a great sacrifice. Do always tremble with fear [be careful], and do not take things too easily.[76]

What an interesting yet serious scene!

Being Cheerful and Optimistic

Teachers should be optimistic and should infect students with positive emotions. Confucius was such an educator. Once, the official She asked Zilu, a student of Confucius, about Confucius, and Zilu did not answer him. When Zilu returned home, he relayed the interaction to Confucius. Confucius said, "Why did you not say to him, 'He is simply a man who, in his eager pursuit of knowledge, forgets his food, who, in the joy of its attainment, forgets his sorrows, and who does not perceive that old age is coming on?'"[77] Being so optimistic, although Confucius had only "coarse rice to eat, with plain boiled water to drink, and with just a bended arm for a pillow," he still "had joys in the midst of these things."[78]

Cheng Hao, a famous educator in the Song Dynasty, was also optimistic, sanguine, and kind to his students, making his students feel as though they were "sitting comfortably in the spring breeze" when with him. In *Learning Plans for Clarifying Truth*, Huang Zongxi recorded the following story: "Once, You Dingfu [a neo-Confucianist in the Song Dynasty] visited Guishan. Guishan asked him where he came from. Dingfu said, 'I just came back from the spring breeze and harmony.' Guishan asked where this was. Dingfu said it was a place where he learned truth."

Being Honest, Modest, and Courageous Enough to Correct Mistakes

Teachers should be honest, modest, and courageous enough to correct their mistakes. It is said in *Xuncius: Zidao* that Confucius once told Zilu:

> A man of virtue, when he knows a thing, is to hold that he knows it; and when he does not know a thing, is to allow that he does not know it—this is the rule of discourse. When he can do a thing, he will do it; and when he cannot do a

thing, he says he cannot—this is the rule of behavior. If a man knows the rule of discourse, he is smart; and when he behaves in accordance with the rule of behavior, he is virtuous. A smart and virtuous man is perfect.

Teachers should be honest when it comes to knowledge and competence. Meanwhile, teachers should also be willing to take advice. Confucius said, "When I walk along with two others, they may serve me as my teachers."[79] Mencius said, "The problem of men is that they like to be teachers of others."[80] When students act better than teachers, teachers should be modest enough to consult and learn from their students.

In the Northern and Southern Dynasties (AD 420 to 589), a man named Li Mi "received education from Kong Fan, an expert in linguistics and philology." Years later, Li Mi excelled his master, so Kong Fan learned from Li Mi in turn. Their story became a favorite tale at that time. It is said in *The History of the Northern Dynasty: The Biography of Li Mi* that "Blue is extracted from the indigo plant but is more blue than the indigo plant. Similarly, the teacher–student relationship is not eternal. The man who knows more serves as the teacher."

Wang Tong, a scholar during the Sui Dynasty and the Tang Dynasty, taught others when he was only fifteen years old: "Countless people came to learn from him, the number nearing almost a thousand."[81] Even noted public figures, such as Li Jing, Fang Xuanling, and Wei Zheng, came to him for advice.

Teachers should also have the courage to correct their mistakes. There is an apt saying from Zigong, a student of Confucius. Zigong said, "The faults of the noble man are like the eclipses of the sun and moon. He has his faults, and all men see them; he changes again, and all men look up to him."[82] If a teacher has faults, he should not be afraid for people to see his faults or be afraid of having his authority undermined; as long as he corrects his mistakes, people will still admire him, and he can raise his prestige.

3. The Main Capabilities of Teachers

In order to do educational work well and improve the quality of education, teachers should possess certain capabilities, further to the basic qualities described earlier. According to the opinions and practices of ancient Chinese educators, teachers should have the following capabilities.

1) Being Adept at Learning the Capabilities of One's Students

The precondition for achieving success in educational work is to understand one's students. Soviet educator Nadezhda Krupskaya once said, "Only when teachers are sensitive can they see and detect changes of children's minds.... If we do not understand children's characteristics at different ages, we will not know what children of different ages are interested in and how they come to know the environment. It is then impossible for us to succeed in our educational work."[83]

Ancient Chinese educators also paid attention to this matter. In Confucius' educational work, he was adept at getting to know his students in different ways. He "listened to them" and "watched their behaviors," he observed their words and deeds in daily conditions, and he focused on their behavior under special circumstances. He analyzed his students' external behaviors and also had insight into their inner worlds, which dominated their behaviors; he paid attention to what students had done in the past, made clear what they were doing at present, and even forecast their futures.[84]

Lu Jiuyuan in the Song Dynasty was also a master who knew his students well. He claimed, "I know nothing but the defects in people's minds."[85] In terms of the educational process, he said, "There is no need to have school regulations. If students have few faults and I point them out, they may be shamed and become ill at ease. If students do not realize their faults, I will make a careful and detailed analysis to make them know."[86]

2) Being Adept at Inspiring and Enlightening

Confucius gave a clear proposition that teachers should cultivate talents with the teaching principles of inspiring and enlightening, and he paid great attention to this in his own educational practices. He consciously seized opportunities to enlighten and inspire his students in order to get twofold results with half the effort by making them comprehend and feel enlightened through analogy. Confucius' method, which "sets it forth from one end to the other and exhausts it," is one example. When students asked Confucius questions, Confucius would not say what he thought at once. However, he would first start from the questions. Those who proposed questions were asked to give their opinions. Then Confucius would counter with questions dialectically to determine the nature and content of the questions. The questioners would at last know there must be a reasonable answer, and the conclusions would be drawn forth naturally.

Mo-tse, the famous Chinese philosopher of the Warring States Period, also paid attention to the methods of inspiring and enlightening students. In his teaching, Mo-tse often gave concrete examples to explain the attributes of things. He often asked his students questions, such as "Why?," "By what?," and "How do you know?" in order to inspire his students to think for themselves.

3) Being Adept at Teaching Students in Accordance with Their Aptitudes

Different students have different psychological make-ups, so teaching students according to their aptitude requires a deep understanding of students' mental activities. The capability to teach students according to their aptitudes is an essential part of the cultivation of teachers. In Chapters Four and Five, we introduced this essential component of teaching and moral education in ancient China. Here we will look at some more examples.

For instance, Zigong and Zilu both asked Confucius what qualities a man must possess to entitle him to be called a scholar. Confucius gave them two different but equally practical answers according to their different qualities. He told Zigong, "He who, in his conduct, maintains a sense of shame, and when sent to any quarter will not disgrace his prince's commission, deserves to be called a scholar."[87] According to Zhu Xi, the reason Confucius said so was that Zigong was eloquent, but Confucius wanted him to know that eloquence was not the only deciding factor in being a scholar. To Zilu, Confucius said, "He must be thus: earnest, urgent, and bland." This was because Zilu was rough and rash, and needed to be taught to be earnest, urgent, and bland so that he could possess the qualities of a scholar.

Wang Fuzhi also stressed that students with different characteristics should be taught differently. He said, "The talents of students are different, and their characteristics can be rigid or tender. Teachers should adopt different educational methods to correct students' bad conduct to help them achieve moderation."[88] Wang Yangming in the Ming Dynasty discussed this question from the perspective of the age of students. Wang thought that in educational activities, if teachers neglected the level of psychological development of students or students' different ages, they would lose their initiative and would not achieve the best educational results. What was worse, they might hamper students' intellectual development. Wang gave an example, saying:

> We must vary our topics accordingly when discussing with others. For example, a sapling needs water in a certain amount. When it grows larger, a certain amount of water is again required. From its sprout to its arm-length thickness, water is required in a limited amount. If the little bud is poured over with a bucket of water, it will drown.[89]

That is to say, too much advanced knowledge will be harmful to young students. However, it also demonstrates a lack of capability in teaching students according to their aptitudes if teachers teach knowledge that is too simple to senior students with a high level of understanding.

Wang Yangming gave another example to explain this:

> Taking walking as an example, he who has exhausted all his mental constitution and knows the Way of Heaven is like a young and strong person who can run up and down for thousands of miles. He who preserves his mental constitution,

nourishes his nature, and knows the way to serve the way of Heaven is like a little child who is just learning to walk in the courtyard. He, regardless of age, who waits in the cultivation of his personal character for whatever issue is like a swaddling baby who is just learning to stand and take steps by leaning on a wall. If he can already run up and down for thousands of miles, then there is no need to let him learn how to walk in the courtyard, for it is no problem to him at all. If he already can walk in the courtyard, then there is no need to let him learn to stand and take steps by leaning on a wall, for it is no problem to him at all. However, to learn to stand and take steps is the basis for learning to walk in the courtyard; to learn to walk in the courtyard is the basis for running up and down for thousands of miles. These skills originate from the same place.[90]

If you make adults learn like children, it is inevitable that you will make them detest and neglect your teaching.

4) Being Adept at Language Expression
Being adept at language expression is also an important capability to improve educational quality. The research of Soloman (1964), Hiller (1971), and others revealed the significant relationship between the clarity of teachers' verbal expression and the academic performance of their students. Educators in ancient China also proposed several requirements for teachers' verbal expression capabilities.

For example, in *The Records on the Subject of Education*, teachers are asked to be concise as well as refined and proper when speaking. Teachers were also supposed to be able to explain a problem through just a few examples.[91] Xuncius also thought that teachers should be good at giving examples when explaining things. He said, "Explain a thing by giving examples, and clarify a thing dialectically."[92] Further, he said, "Brief explanations can help people see clearly, clarifying the main reason can help people understand complicated affairs, and seizing the fundamental elements can help people know the essential significance."[93]

Being adept at proposing questions was also considered part of teachers' verbal expression capabilities. *The Records on the Subject of Education* states:

Good questioners are like those lumbering a stout tree. They start with the easy parts and then move on to the joints of the tree. And gradually, they split the tree. Good answerers are like bell ringers. If the bell is knocked lightly, the sound will be small; if the bell is knocked hard, the sound will be large; if the bell is knocked slowly, the sound will be slow.

This is the so-called way to progress in learning.

Many educators in ancient China were also good at verbal expression. For example, the words of Confucius were quite vivid. From *The Analects of Confucius*, we can see that Confucius was adept at using astronomical phenomena, physical and chemical materials, the vital phenomena of plants and animals, the production of agriculture and the handicraft industry, and poems and proverbs of the time to explain his political opinions and ethical thoughts, to answer questions, or to explain certain principles. Further, he was adept at using facial expressions to enhance the effect of his words. Sometimes he gave just a soft smile; sometimes he drew a long breath and sighed; sometimes he was serious in speech and manner; sometimes he was humorous and made jokes. All these were helpful ways to improve the level of verbal expression and educational quality.

4. The Teacher–Student Relationship

The teacher–student relationship is one of the most basic interpersonal relationships and one kind of emotional relationship based on mutual understanding. It is formed during the course of communication between teachers and students and directly influences the educational effect.

Educators in ancient China discussed the teacher–student relationship in many ways, focusing on the following two aspects.

1) Teaching and Learning Benefit Each Other Mutually

As mentioned earlier, *The Records on the Subject of Education* first put forward the concept that teaching and learning can benefit each other mutually. It is said in *The Records on the Subject of Education*:

> If you do not taste the cuisine, you will not know its flavor; if you do not study, you will not know the benefit of the best knowledge. Therefore, only by learning will people know their lack of knowledge; only by teaching will people have confusion about what they thought and what they knew. If people find they have a low level of knowledge, they will spur themselves to study harder; if people feel confused, they will impel themselves to study further. Therefore, it is said that teaching and learning benefit each other mutually. It is the very reason!

This first revealed the interrelationship, influence, and mutual promotion between teaching and learning and showed that teachers and students are indivisible in educational activities.

In *On the Teacher*, a classic work, Han Yu in the Tang Dynasty explained why there was mutual promotion between teaching and learning from another perspective. In this work, Han Yu said:

> Sages do not have fixed teachers. Confucius learned from Tanzi, Changhong, Shixiang, and Laodan. Those people were not as virtuous as Confucius. However, Confucius said, "When walking along with two others, they may

serve me as my teachers." Therefore, students need not be inferior to teachers, and teachers need not be superior to students. One might learn the doctrine earlier than others and might become a master in a specific field. It is just like this.

Taking Confucius as an example, Han Yu described three basic aspects of the teacher–student relationship. First, it is not necessary that "students be inferior to teachers"; in fact, they may surpass their teachers. Second, it is "unnecessary that teachers be superior to students in all fields," so teachers should be modest and learn from the people around them, including their students. They should be insatiable in learning and should always endeavor to do still better. Third, "one might learn the doctrine earlier than others and might become a master in a specific field." The time it takes for students and teachers to learn "the doctrine" may vary, which may result in their achieving different merits in different fields and skills at different times. Therefore, no one can always be in the position of the teacher. Teachers are those who learn earlier and those who are masters in specific fields. From these points, we know it is truly important that students learn from teachers, for only under the guidance of teachers can students develop healthily. However, teachers should not pride themselves on being teachers or neglect the opportunity to learn from their students. Therefore, the teacher–student relationship is a two-way relationship.

2) Respecting Teachers and Loving Students

Another key component of the teacher–student relationship is respecting teachers and loving students. In ancient China, although the status of teachers in society fluctuated, in the process of education, the teacher–student relationship maintained a good tradition. Therefore, in the long history of thousands of years, there are many moving stories about respecting teachers and loving students. The following section will analyze this from two perspectives.

(1) Respecting Teachers   *The Records on the Subject of Education* states, "As for the rite of great learning, when emperors summon teachers, they do not let teachers face the north (the etiquette of officials in feudal times toward the emperor) and will forgo formalities in order to honor the teacher and respect his teaching." Zheng Xuan in the Han Dynasty stated, "The reason emperors do not make teachers stand in the position of officials is to show their respect for teachers and teaching."[94] Of course, to respect teachers is to take the doctrines seriously, for teachers are the people who teach them.

In the Wei and Jin Dynasties, the social status of teachers was negatively impacted. Many people felt it a shame to be a teacher. Han Yu in the Tang Dynasty made tart criticism about this unhealthy trend. He said:

Sages in ancient times far exceeded ordinary people, but they took others as teachers and learned from them. Nowadays, people are far behind sages, but they feel it a shame to learn from others. That is why the wise are getting wiser, and the stupid are getting more stupid.[95]

Respect for teachers consisted of the following aspects.

Bearing the Guidance of Teachers in Mind   In ancient China, students were willing to accept instruction from their teachers. For example, some students of Confucius said they would "make it their business to practice what Confucius told them"; some prepared to "recite what Confucius said for their whole lives"; some recorded Confucius' instructions on their belts. Once, Confucius said, "I would prefer not speaking." When hearing this, Zigong was very anxious and said, "If you, Master, do not speak, what shall we, your disciples, record?"[96] In ancient China, students' pursuit of teachers' instructions was heart-warming. For example, the book *The History of the Later Han Dynasty: The Biography of Li Gu* recorded that Li Gu "was a studious child who often walked far away to search for teachers."

In *The History of the Song Dynasty: The Biography of Yang Shi*, there was a popular story called "Standing in the Snow to Wait upon Master Cheng Respectfully." The story describes that once, Yang Shi went to meet his teacher, Cheng Yi, but Cheng was taking a nap in his chair. Even though it was snowing, Yang Shi and You Dingfu stood outside the door and waited until Cheng woke up. At that time, the snow on the ground was more than a foot deep.

Song Lian, a famous scholar, also wrote about his experience when learning from teachers. He wrote:

I once walked a hundred miles away with Confucian classics to consult a senior scholar who was learned and had moral integrity. He enjoyed high prestige and commanded universal respect, so his study was full of students who had gone to consult him. Never was he mild and roundabout, nor did he look gentle. I stood beside him, waiting. I proposed my problems and asked for the truth. I stooped and pricked up my ears when listening to him. Sometimes, if I was reprimanded, I would be more respectful, submissive, and courteous. Never dared I retort. Instead, I would go to ask him again when he had calmed down. Therefore, although I was slow, I still learned something.[97]

In *Guangzi: Discipline for Students*, it was seen as the basic duty of students to bear their teachers' guidance in mind. The book stated:

Teachers give guidance, and students follow it. Students should be modest and courteous, so that they can learn things thoroughly. When students see good qualities, they should follow them. When they see righteousness, they should carry it out by actual effort. Students should be gentle and show filial piety and fraternal duty. Students should not be arrogant and imperious or count on strength. Their will should not be hypocritical or evil, and their behavior should be upright.

Teachers and Students Should Share Joys and Sorrows   In the educational history of China, it is often seen that students and teachers shared joys and sorrows. Among the students of Confucius, there were many following him, sharing their joys and sorrows with him, and protecting him. For example, although Confucius often criticized Zilu (also called You) as a man more brave than wise, Zilu always followed Confucius, actually acting as his guard. It was no wonder that Confucius said, "My doctrines make no way. I will get upon a raft and float about on the sea. He that will accompany me will be You, I dare say."[98]

Another time, Confucius left Chen for Wei, but met people from Pu along the way who stopped him from passing. Gongliang Ru, a student of Confucius, used his own cart to escort Confucius and engaged in a furious battle against the Pu people. At last, Confucius left the city from the eastern gate safe and sound.

When Zhu Xi, a famous educator of the Southern Song Dynasty, died, someone wrote to the emperor and lodged a false accusation, saying:

Hypocrites from all directions gathered in Xinzhou and planned to attend the burial ceremony for their teacher. In their gathering, they talked only about the right and wrong of people and criticized politics. I hope Your Majesty can send me to restrain them.[99]

Emperor Ningzong then sent out an imperial decree to restrict the scale of the burial ceremony. However, the number of mourners was still in the thousands.

During Wang Fuzhi's educational career, in the Ming and Qing Dynasties, Wang "had meals with his students in the day and burned the midnight oil with his students at night." At that time, he "was poverty stricken and in want of books, paper, and pens, so he often borrowed these things from his friends and disciples. When he finished writing, he would teach the knowledge of his writings to his students." He almost depended on his students' sponsorship of his academic activities. He began to teach when he was 36 years old. From that time on, most of the source of his income was from his students. However, despite the difficulties and hardships, in simple and humble huts and thatched cottages, he and his students still shared the joy of searching for knowledge and seeking truth.

Maintaining the Dignity of Teachers   Educators in ancient China paid much attention to the dignity of teachers. For example, *The Records on the Subject of Education* states, "In learning, it is most difficult to respect teachers. Only when teachers are respected can truth be respected; then people will respect knowledge and take learning seriously."

Xuncius also stressed the dignity of teachers and thought teachers should have prestige. He said, "Speaking without praising teachers is disrespectful; educational staff who do not revere their teachers are betrayers. Wise and able emperors will not give posts to these two kinds of people, and officials will not speak to them even if they meet along the way."[100] Therefore, Xuncius thought having prestige was one of the essential conditions "to be suitable as a teacher."[101]

The authors of *Lv's Commentary of History* further developed this thought. They thought students not only should follow the guidance of their teachers, but also should use their teachers' words to explain things and should develop their teachers' instruction.[102] They also thought students should "be respectful and polite, have pleasant smiles, be cautious when speaking, and be neither too slow nor too fast when walking."[103]

In ancient China, there were many favorite tales about students protecting the dignity of their teachers. For example, Shusun Wu, a senior official in Lu, once told others, "Zigong is superior to Zhongni [Confucius]." When Zigong heard this, he thought the words were not practical and were harmful to Confucius' prestige. In order to clarify the fact, he said:

> Let me use the comparison of a house and its encompassing wall. My wall only reaches to the shoulders. One may peep over it and see whatever is valuable in the apartments. The wall of my Master is several fathoms high. If one does not find the door and enter by it, he cannot see the ancestral temple with its beauties, nor all the officers in their rich array. But I may assume that they are few who find the door. Was not the observation of the chief only what might have been expected?[104]

Zigong thought Shusun Wu's words were totally nonsense because he did not know Confucius at all. Another time, Chen Ziqin, addressing Zigong, said, "You are too modest. How can Zhongni be said to be superior to you?" Zigong said to him, "For one word a man is often deemed to be wise, and for one word he is often deemed to be foolish. We ought to be careful indeed in what we say. Our Master cannot be attained to, just in the same way as the heavens cannot be reached by the steps of a staircase."[105]

Zigong also said, "It is of no use doing so. Zhongni cannot be reviled. The talents and virtue of other men are hillocks and mounds, which may be stepped over. Zhongni is the sun or moon, which is not possible to step over."[106]

Zigong tried hard to protect his teacher's dignity. It is no wonder Sima Qian said that Zigong played an important role in making Confucius well known in the world.[107]

Virtue Is More Valuable than the Teacher   The act of respecting and loving teachers is not equal to being obsequious to teachers and doing the bidding of teachers. Students should have the courage to point out their teachers' shortcomings and mistakes and have the courage to exceed their teachers. It was Confucius who first said, "Let every man consider virtue as what devolves on himself. He may not yield the performance of it even to his teacher."[108] He thought students and teachers were equal before virtue. His opinion was on par with the thought of Aristotle, who said, "Plato is dear to me, but dearer still is truth."

Han Yu developed Confucius' thought, saying, "Students need not be inferior to teachers, and teachers need not be superior to students." In his work *On the Teacher*, Han Yu said:

> Anyone who was born before me and learned the doctrine before me is my teacher. Anyone who was born after me and learned the doctrine before me is also my teacher. Since what I desire is to learn the doctrine, why should I care whether he was born before or after me? Therefore, it does not matter whether a person is high or low in position, young or old in age. Where there is the doctrine, there is my teacher.

Scholars in ancient China also took this as an important principle when dealing with the teacher–student relationship. For example, Zilu once asked Confucius, "The ruler of Wei has been waiting for you in order for you to administer the government. What will you consider the first thing to be done?" The Master replied, "What is necessary is to rectify names." Zilu thought these words were high-sounding and impractical, so he was outspoken in his remarks, saying, "So! Indeed! You are wide of the mark! Why must there be such recti-fication?"[109] Another time, when Zilu witnessed that Confucius on one hand was "against the traitors," and on the other was wishing to reap some benefits from them, he questioned Confucius: "Gongshan Furao, when he was holding Fei, in an attitude of rebellion, invited the Master to visit him, who was rather inclined to go. Zilu was displeased and said, 'Indeed, you cannot go! Why must you think of going to see Gongshan?'"[110] He meant that the Master should not visit Gongshan even though he had nowhere else to go.

It should be pointed out that respecting teachers was a traditional virtue in ancient China, but it still reflects the feudal ethics inherent in the teacher–student relationship, which is like the relationship between emperor and minister or between father and son. There are many popular stories about putting virtue before teachers, but it is more often that students are submissive and obedient to teachers. A lively, vivid, and democratic educational atmosphere was not common in ancient China. When carrying on the ancient tradition of respecting teachers, we should also give up the dross of these traditions.

(2) Loving Students   Teachers' love for students and the educational cause is the inexhaustible source of educational work. Only when teachers truly love their students can they be concerned with students' physical and mental development, can they dive into textbooks with gusto, and can they continually improve educational methods. Therefore, at all times and in all countries, educators take love as the starting point for teachers to undertake their educational work.

Confucius once said, "Can there be love which does not lead to strictness with its object? Can there be loyalty which does not lead to the instruction of its object?"[111] British educator William Russell also said, "In places where teachers do not have love, students will not fully or freely develop in both character and intelligence."[112] The famous Russian educator Sukhomlynsky pointed out that study in schools was not to transfer knowledge from one head into another head without passion, but was the contact of teachers' and students' souls at all times. That is to say, if teachers and students do not connect in their souls and if there is no love and emotion in each other's company, although the teacher may be wealthy in knowledge and profoundly learned, he will not be able to open his students' minds.

The theories and practices of educators in ancient China who loved their students are as follows.

Loving and Caring for Students   Confucius applied the spirit of loving others when teaching his students. He showed all-around concern for his students in their character, life, and study. He always stayed with his students and talked with them freely and easily. When Ran was ill, Confucius went to ask for him. He took hold of Boniu's hand through the window, and said, "It is killing him. It is the appointment of heaven, alas! That such a man should have such a sickness! That such a man should have such a sickness!"[113] When Yan Yuan "died young unfortunately," Confucius was extremely grieved and shouted to the sky, "Alas! Heaven is destroying me! Heaven is destroying me!"[114] He wailed for him exceedingly, and the disciples who were with him said, "Master, your grief is excessive!" He responded, "Is it excessive? If I am not to mourn bitterly for this man, for whom should I mourn?"[115]

The authors of *Lv's Commentary of History* also advocated that teachers should "treat students as themselves and place themselves in their students' position,"[116] holding that this was essential to building a good teacher–student relationship. They thought people always liked, praised, and helped those who shared the same will with them.[117] If not, they would contract enmity.

Fully Trusting Students   In educational work, it is the golden law and precious rule to respect and trust students. Sukhomlynsky said, "The deeper I can reach into children's inner worlds, and the better I can understand their thoughts and emotions, the clearer I see the important rule in our educational work that when influencing children's inner worlds, never can we harm their self-respect, which is the most sensitive part of their hearts."[118] The practices of educators in ancient China fully reflected this golden law and precious rule. Confucius trusted his students very much. *The Analects of Confucius: Zi Han* says,

"A youth is to be regarded with respect. How do we know that his future will not be equal to our present?"

In Confucius' opinion, all young men should be regarded with respect. He thought young men had an unlimited future of development and the future was sure to exceed the present. When Gongye Chang, one of his students, was put in jail, he believed this student was innocent and offered to marry his daughter to Gongye Chang.[119] He believed that every student had certain talents. He said, "In a kingdom of a thousand chariots, You might be employed to manage the military levies"; "In a city of a thousand families, or a clan of a hundred chariots, Qiu might be employed as governor"; "With his sash girded and standing in court, Chi might be employed to converse with visitors and guests";[120] and "There is Yong; he might occupy the place of a prince."[121] In the case that others would not believe Ran Yong had this ability, Confucius said, "If the calf of a brindled cow be red and horned, although men may not wish to use it, would the spirits of the mountains and rivers put it aside?"[122] He took the cow as an example to say that, although Ran Yong was born humble, he was virtuous and smart and was therefore capable of occupying the place of a prince.

Being Strict with Students   Loving students not only is caring for them, respecting them, and trusting them, but also involves being strict with them. Russian educator Leonid Zankov had an insightful comment on this topic. He said, "Teachers' love for children is not only treating them kindly, which is of course needed, but to love students is to offer vigor, talents, and knowledge without reservation in order to have the best effect in teaching, educating students and helping them develop mentally. Therefore, teachers should combine their love for students with reasonably strict requirements."[123]

Educators in ancient China also had strict requirements for their students. For example, although the students of Confucius were all studious,

Confucius was very cautious about praising "studious" students, except Yan Yuan. However, he said, "Such was Hui that for three months there would be nothing in his mind contrary to perfect virtue." Never did he think his students were already perfectly virtuous. When he saw his students' faults and short-comings, he would give no leeway and would criticize them. For example, he always criticized Zilu, saying:

How uncultivated you are, You![124]
    You has more than his own share of energy.[125]
    You is fonder of daring than I am. He does not exercise his judgment upon matters.[126]

Zai Yu, a student of Confucius, was asleep during the daytime. Confucius was angry at him and said, "Rotten wood cannot be carved; a wall of dirty earth will not receive the trowel." Although the comment was harsh, we see from this a glimpse of Confucius' strict requirements for his students.

Mo-tse was also strict with his students. For example, Qin Guxi served Mo-tse for three years, even developing calluses on his hands and feet and a tan on his face, but he was still under Mo-tse's control like a servant and dared not ask what he wanted to know.[127]

Encouraging Students to Become Useful People   The primary purpose of caring for, trusting, and being strict with students is to encourage them to become useful people. Therefore, Comenius, an educator from the Czech Republic, defined schools as "factories to manufacture useful people."[128]

Educators in ancient China paid great attention to cultivating talents. Mencius once referred to teaching talents as one kind of happiness in life. Hu Yuan, an educator in the Song Dynasty, also said:

In order to govern a country, talents are needed. In order to cultivate talents, education is needed. It is the teacher who does the educational work; it is the officials of the county who develop and extend education and make all people know it; and the foundation of education is the school.[129]

Yan Yuan in the Qing Dynasty clearly stated, "People say teaching is a post with very little to do, but they do not know that talents are the fundamental element of governance and that schools are the centers for the development of talents."[130]

In educational practices, educators in ancient China also made efforts to encourage students to become useful people. For example, Confucius often encouraged students to have more confidence and courage to make progress.

He said, "Is virtue a thing remote? I wish to be virtuous, and virtue is at hand."[131] He also said, "Is anyone able for one day to apply his strength to virtue? I have not seen the case in which one's strength would be insufficient."[132]

Zhu Xi also asked his students to have confidence in becoming useful people and to exert themselves constantly, but not to be afraid if they had poor qualities or weak foundations. He said, "Although all people are kind, they have different physical endowments, so some people learn the doctrines early, others late; some people feel it easy, others difficult. However, as long as people exert themselves constantly, they all can achieve the same goal."[133]

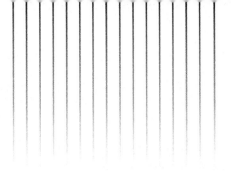

7

Reading Methods in Ancient China

Reading methods have always been a "neglected" aspect of the history of ancient education in China. Further, they were seldom discussed in various works on the history of China's educational thought. However, reading plays a very important role in educational activities. As early as the 1920s, Yang Xianjiang, a Marxist educator, pointed out the necessity of studying reading methods and held that they were an inevitable requirement for modern education. He pointed out:

> The necessity of studying reading methods lies in the importance of reading and our hope for effective reading. There are methods of writing as well as teaching. How can we neglect the methods of reading? Within the previous passive education environment, in which students simply listened to their teachers, educators could avoid discussing reading methods. However, under the circumstances of modern education, in which students are required to have the ability to study all knowledge by themselves, the study of reading methods has become necessary accordingly."[1]

Ancient Chinese education attached great importance to guiding students' reading. In particular, after the rise of academies in the Song Dynasty, educators began paying more attention to guiding students to learn knowledge from books (mainly the Six Classics) by themselves, and began summarizing a set of reading methods. For example, Zhu Xi emphasized the function of reading, saying:

> The exploration of knowledge is first of all to probe into the reasons; the key to probing into the reasons lies in reading.[2]
> The methods the sages teach us are all in the Confucian classics; people with lofty ideals should naturally clarify them with careful reading and questioning.[3]

It is because ancient reading methods are a summary of ancient thinkers' and educators' reading and study experiences and the essence of ancient education that they undoubtedly deserve a place in China's educational history. Wei Zhengtong, a scholar in Taiwan, China, discussed reading methods as a specific topic in his book *The Wisdom of the Chinese*.[4] It is now urgent for us to also study this subject.

Guidelines for Reading Methods

The guidelines for reading methods can also be called the basic principles of reading. Zhu Xi in the Song Dynasty gave the most detailed explanation. He pointed out clearly in *Mencius Variorum*:

> It is true in the learning of art that there must be certain methods to achieve success; teachers cannot teach well without using proper methods, and students cannot learn efficiently by abandoning appropriate ways. Then how can it be wrong in the pursuit of the doctrines of the sages?

Zhu Xi held that anything could be done successfully via certain methods. There were teaching methods for teaching as well as learning methods for learning. Without specific methods, neither teachers' teaching nor students' study could be efficient and would ultimately accomplish nothing.

On the basis of summarizing his predecessors' reading experience and his own practice of long-term and arduous study, Zhu Xi described some insightful reading methods, which were compiled in the *Reading Methods of Zhu Xi* by his disciples shortly after his death. According to Cheng Duanli, a scholar living at the beginning of the Yuan Dynasty, who recorded in his book *The Annual Schedule of Reading of Cheng's Family School*:

> By assembling Zhu Xi's daily instructions and selecting their essence, his disciples summarized six principles of reading methods: learning progressively, studying earnestly and thinking carefully, ruminating with an open

mind, combining reading with one's own experience, working harder at crucial moments, and reading with an undivided mind and steadfast ambition.

These six reading methods, which exerted a tremendous influence, were the guidance or principles of ancient reading methods and were looked up to as standards by later scholars. The following section analyzes and comments on each method.

1. Learning Progressively

As a tenet of teaching and one of the guiding principles of reading, the progressive principle meant that reading was a systematic process that should be conducted according to the book's logical order and the learner's level. Zhu Xi explained the principle with an example: "Reading is like climbing a mountain. Most people want to go up high, but one can never reach the top of the mountain if he or she does not begin at the foot."[5]

Why should we read step by step? Zhu Xi said:

Generally speaking, the deficiency of most modern scholars who discuss the way of learning lies in their high objectives. They always think that the fast way of achieving success in both learning and teaching is taking a shortcut and beginning from advanced knowledge, instead of learning step by step. In my view, this method is fickle and unwise, for it neglects and abandons all subtle and delicate points that are worth pondering in the tortuous process of learning.[6]

Zhu Xi held that the above reading method "refused to begin at the foot of the mountain" and that "wanting to take a shortcut and beginning from advanced knowledge, instead of learning step by step" was the biggest problem of learning and "a misleading trap."[7] Therefore, Zhu Xi endorsed the idea of "more haste, less speed" put forward by Confucius and the reading method of "learning step by step" proposed in *The Records on the Subject of Education*. He believed that only by climbing step by step from the foot of a mountain in a down-to-earth way can one finally reach the peak.

How does one read step by step? Zhu Xi said:

For example, one should first read *The Analects of Confucius* and then *Mencius* if one wants to read these two books. As for any book, one should read in accordance with the order of sections and chapters in the book, instead of disrupting the beginning or end. Exploring the meaning of each word as well the purpose of each sentence, one should arrange his schedule according to the estimation of one's ability and adhere to it strictly, refusing to move forward until he has determined the meaning of previous content, daring not to be overly ambitious to move on until he has thoroughly comprehended what he has already read. This is called reading step by step.[8]

According to Zhu Xi, the progressive principle consists of three main components. First, one should pay attention to the connection between old and new knowledge during the reading process, and lay a solid foundation, "moving forward after understanding the previous content." Take *The Analects of Confucius* and *Mencius*, for example. One is unqualified to read *Mencius* before mastering *The Analects*.

Second, one should read according to his ability, and read materials at his knowledge and intelligent level: "Just like shooting a bow, one should use just a four-dou-strength bow ("four-dou" is a measure of grain) if he has the five-dou strength to shoot a bow, for in this way he can control it. Now some learners read without estimating their abilities, which can lead to the panic of not comprehending the book."

Third, one should strengthen the process of reviewing and consolidate what he has learned. Zhu Xi opposed the reading method of "trying to read an unread book blindly without thinking of deducing or reviewing the content of what he has read." In a letter answering Zhang Jingfu, Zhu Xi said, "Learning without review or practice, one can neither consolidate knowledge nor stabilize himself; reviewing but in an intermittent way and making efforts off and on only leads to failure." He believed that the consolidation of mastered knowledge could be realized through frequent and constant practice and review, and one could gain new insights through restudying old materials.

2. Studying Earnestly and Thinking Carefully

Studying earnestly and thinking carefully refers to the combination of memory and thought. According to Zhu Xi's explanation, studying earnestly requires one to "understand and remember a book completely, with its contents available at one's fingertips,"[9] "so that it seems that all words are written by the learner."[10] Thinking carefully demanded that one "ruminate on the deep meanings of a book over and over again, instead of reading for just the literal meaning,"[11] "so that the learner can understand the meaning of the book as thoroughly as the writer."[12] Thus, compared to Confucius' proposition that "Learning without thought is labor lost; thought without learning is perilous," this reading method is more specific and thorough.

Why should we study earnestly and think carefully? Zhu Xi said:

Scholars should be quite familiar with what they have learned so that they can have knowledge at hand when needed; otherwise, spending time on speculation only suspends one's thinking and makes one's thought different from that before.[13]

Generally speaking, when reading, one should read over and over again to master the book, so that one can understand the book as if innately. As with eating fruit, eating voraciously means one cannot taste its flavor; only by chewing slowly and savoring every bite can one taste its flavor: sweet, bitter, or spicy. This is called knowing the flavor, as well as understanding the idea of a book.[14]

In Zhu Xi's view, perusal was the precondition for learners to commit what they had learned to memory, so that "the content would present when needed." Only with solid memory could the learner think carefully and comprehend the learning material thoroughly. Otherwise, reading would be equal to swallowing whole dates: eating the dates but not tasting their essence; reading in this way would be harmful to one's learning. According to Zhu Xi, the purpose of perusal was not just to keep the content in mind, but to extract and apply knowledge and serve the mind. This was a superior point of view. He thought the reason for some readers' inefficient reading was a lack of effort in careful thinking and earnest studying. He said:

When reading, one should first bear the main body of text and notes in mind, understanding the annotations, events, names and meanings of subjects, and origins of quotations, as well as relationships among these factors, as if they had been written by the reader. Then one is qualified to ponder the idea of the book and develop insightful opinions. Otherwise, perfunctory learning and making empty talk is not learning for oneself, but for dealing with examinations.[15]

Zhu Xi further discussed the dialectical relationship between perusal (memory) and thinking (mind) during the reading process:

When reciting, a way to help the memory is to think constantly in the heart. One can never remember in detail if he only reads with the mouth and does not think in the heart.[16]

Think after reading, read after thinking, and the reader will naturally understand the idea. If reading without thinking, one cannot understand the idea; if thinking without reading, one cannot feel at ease even though he understands the writer. Just as you cannot ask a person you have hired to guard your house to do anything else for you, the master cannot order a person at will. If one studies the book by heart and also understands its idea thoroughly, he can naturally keep the idea in mind and will never forget it.[17]

He argued that perusal (memory) was the foundation of thinking (mind), so memory could "help the learner think." Thinking was the condition for perusal, so one can "hardly remember" without thinking. Thinking on the basis of memory, and trying to remember with the help of understanding, the collaboration of memory and thinking could help learners reach the state of "thoroughly understanding the essence of a book and never forgetting." This argument is undoubtedly more profound and reasonable than some propositions in Western learning theories, such as the viewpoints of the association school and the cognitive school, which emphasize only one aspect, either memory or mind.

How can we achieve perusal? Zhu Xi said, "I always advocate we should read with three organs: the brain, eyes, and mouth. Without using the brain, we cannot read carefully; without the concentrated attention of the brain and eyes, we only read literally and recite mechanically; reading this way, we can hardly remember the content for very long."[18] Therefore, when reading, we should use the brain to activate the mind so that we can keep the contents of the book in mind, we should use the eyes to read intently, and we should use the mouth to read aloud. Among these requirements, the use of the brain is the foundation, but the other two are also important. Following on this concept, Hu Shi, a modern scholar, put forward the idea of "using hands when reading." Together with Zhu Xi's thoughts, this method was called "reading with four organs."

For successful perusal, repeated reading was also demanded. Zhu Xi said, "Read over and over again," and "Do not stop reading even when you have understood the idea, for the meaning you understand after reading one thousand times is different from that after reading ten thousand times."[19] He also said, "Reading one hundred times is naturally better than reading fifty times; two hundred times is better than one hundred times."[20] Emphasizing perusal is no doubt reasonable, but overemphasizing it would be as mechanical and stiff as the law of frequency put forward by American educational psychologist Edward Thorndike.

How can we think carefully? Zhu Xi believed the key was to ask and answer questions. He said,

"Efficient reading is to find questions when everything seems understood, and to find answers when there are questions."[21] He considered reading to be a process from the absence of doubt to asking questions and then to answering questions.

How can we raise questions? As far as Zhu Xi was concerned, questions could not be fabricated; painstaking effort was the only way to pose worthwhile questions: "Questions come from hard work."[22]

How can we answer questions? Zhu Xi described two methods. The first was "interrogating oneself," which meant to check whether one's own questions were well grounded. He said, "A weakness of humans is that they tend to doubt only others' opinions but never question their own ideas. If one interrogates himself as he would question others, maybe then he will be able to see right and wrong more easily."[23]

The second method for answering questions was "interrogating mutually with the points of all schools." Zhu Xi said:

> When reading, the most worthy part lies in discerning the differences between thoughts of various schools. First, ask persistently why one school holds a particular viewpoint, and then ask why another school holds a different viewpoint. Then compare their words and make a thorough exploration. In this way, one can certainly find the truth.[24]

He pointed out here that, when faced with different theories, one should first discover their arguments; then, through his own study and thinking, compare their differences and similarities, the strong and weak points of each theory; and finally put forward his own opinions. It was insightful of Zhu Xi to regard raising questions as the core of thinking and to propose effective methods to remove doubts and answer questions.

3. Ruminating with an Open Mind

Ruminating with an open mind means that the reader should read with an open and quiet mind and ponder the purpose of a book over and over again. Zhu Xi once said, "There is no other efficient reading method than being modest and ruminating on the reading material repeatedly."[25]

Why should we ruminate with an open mind? Zhu Xi said:

> One must read with modesty.[26]
> An open and quiet mind is the basis of probing the truth.[27]
> To get the truth, one must ponder over and over.[28]

Zhu Xi thought that only by ruminating and studying carefully with an open and quiet mind could the reader "learn something in his heart" and "clearly understand the deep meaning."[29] Therefore, ruminating with modesty was an important psychological condition when reading and learning.

How can we ruminate with an open mind? Zhu Xi put forward the following five suggestions.

First, avoid forming an opinion or judgment too early. Zhu Xi said, "One should read with an open mind, continuing to read the next paragraph even when you have understood the possible meaning, instead of forming your opinion immediately; just as if you were listening to a lawsuit in which the judgment will not be made until the litigation is complete."[30]

Zhu Xi thought it was impossible for the reader to understand the real meaning of a book if he had formed an opinion or impression in his mind early on. He criticized the style of study at the time, which involved some scholars speculating subjectively and putting forward their own ideas at the very beginning of reading. He said, "Now people tend to give their own ideas before reading and impose their ideas on ancient writings. Reading in this way just popularizes their own opinions, so how can they come to understand the ancients' ideas?"[31] Only through respecting the original works and exploring the real meaning of a book can the reader benefit from reading.

Second, the learner should never feel self-contented. Zhu Xi was opposed to the bombastic and domineering reading atmosphere of his time. He said, "It is true that scholars should never be satisfied with themselves."[32] He had two fears for reading, "arrogance" and "parsimony": "Arrogance and parsimony mean that one holds what he has learned tightly and does not share with others and that one arrogantly pretends that he has mastered knowledge he does not actually understand. The former is called parsimony and the latter arrogance."[33] Therefore, having conceit means that self-contented learners make grand gestures and act arrogantly; stinginess means that self-approbated learners monopolize knowledge without sharing it with others. People with these two negative qualities are naturally unable to learn with an open mind.

Third, avoid giving strained interpretations and drawing far-fetched analogies. Zhu Xi criticized the scholars of his time, saying, "Now people tend to hold an opinion before reading, and then use the words of the sages to prove their ideas. If there are discrepancies, they just make forced analogies."[34] He held that the reading method of "drawing a far-fetched interpretation from all possible trivial and tiny aspects" and casually making forced analogies could only lead readers off track. So he also said:

Now some learners draw conclusions from far-fetched interpretations or believe rumors without verifying facts. Therefore, although they read classic books every day, they have no idea of the meaning of those books. What they read are just writings with meanings fabricated according to their own opinions. How can they make progress through this way of learning?[35]

Fourth, avoid expecting results at the beginning. Zhu Xi said, "One should read and explore the idea of a book with an open and sprightly mind, and should not expect to achieve success at the beginning."[36] In his opinion, requirements and expected effects should not be decided subjectively before gaining some understanding of a book. Otherwise, "One might feel worried if he cannot achieve the goal in a short period of time," which will lead to haste and ineffective results.

Fifth, avoid being careless and impatient. Zhu Xi said, "One should make great efforts to read carefully, because carelessness and impatience ultimately lead to nothing being accomplished. For example, when reading *The Analects of Confucius*, one can naturally understand the truth by comparing the opinions of various schools."[37] Reading experience at all times and all over the world has proved that carelessness and impatience are the enemy of reading, and a quiet mind and diligent study are the only ways to achieve good results.

4. Combining Reading with One's Own Experience

Combining reading with one's own experience means that one should rely on his own efforts to read and understand a book, emphasizing absorption and the use of knowledge. Zhu Xi said, "The way of learning truth is to practice the truth personally and to gradually integrate and finally absorb it. But now people separate themselves from the truth and make the two aspects of truth and practice irrelevant. Scholars should practice the words of the sages personally."[38] He thought when reading, one should ponder the points of the book over and over again instead of only "reading literally, rushing to finish before a deadline, and thus neglecting the true wonder of a book," or being satisfied with just the literal meaning.

Why should we combine reading with our own experience? Zhu Xi said:

Learning is actually hard. If one does not make efforts at the level of writings, he will be at a loss as to how to start; if he learns mechanically from every single word and sentence but does not practice them in person, he still will not benefit from learning.[39]

One cannot just seek principles from books when reading; he should explore the truth by combining what he has read with his own reality. After the Qin and Han Dynasties, scholars tended to focus on books for answers even when there were no previous records of their problems, instead of trying to find solutions from their realities. They sought the so-called truth through the misuse of some sages' ideas of their own realities even though the words were inappropriate.[40]

Zhu Xi thought one would learn nothing if he limited himself to principles in books without thinking them over in relation to his own reality and experience, the practice of which would bring no benefit. Of course, the experience Zhu Xi was speaking of mainly referred to the experience of the ethics and morals of feudal China, which is the aspect we should abandon.

How can we read based on our own reality and experience? Zhu Xi put forward three valuable propositions in this regard.

First, learn by oneself. Zhu Xi thought one should learn by himself instead of relying on others: "Help from teachers and friends can only instruct one at the beginning and help to judge the effect at the end. The main work should be completed by oneself with great effort."[41] This means that the help from teachers and friends is necessary but limited. Help at the beginning may indicate the right way and method to learn, and help at the end may judge whether the learner's comprehension is correct, but the main work of learning must be done on one's own. Zhu Xi once told his students, "Practice is more complex and difficult than the words I have said. Reading and exploring the truth by your own effort requires your own perception, experience, and observation, as well as rumination. I am just a teacher leading you along the road, judging your learning outcomes, and giving you help when there are questions."[42]

Second, combine learning with reality and practice. Zhu Xi opposed the reading method of "exploring truth only from books and neglecting to learn from personal practice." He said with deep feeling, "Now most people simply learn the words they see on paper and stop thinking when they understand their literal meaning, but they do not try to acquire knowledge from their own experience and practice. What is the use of learning in such a manner?"[43] He also pointed out that "only by thoroughly understanding the lines in a book and by observing in practice can one calm the mind and gradually come to understand the truth." Otherwise, even though one "learns widely and recites many books every day,"[44] he still will not benefit from study. Therefore, the combination of a solid understanding of the content of a book and the learner's reality is the only way to make reading efficient.

Third, be self-confident. Zhu Xi said, "When reading, one cannot echo whatever others say without judgment. Only by ruminating with a quiet mind can one find the truth. If someone said sand could be eaten, and I parrot this, does this make sand edible?"[45] He was against the attitude of going with the tide, for doing so only makes one a poor parrot who cannot achieve any success.

5. Working Harder at Crucial Moments

Working harder at crucial moments means that one should read with indomitable will, high spirit, and great effort. Zhu Xi once described the state of hard working at crucial moments:

> Extend the timeframe and seize the day to learn. One should learn with indomitable will. A careless and sloppy attitude is of no use. In addition, learning methods such as being so immersed in work as to forget meals and seeking pleasure in order to free oneself from care are terrible behaviors that we should abandon![46]

Why should we work harder at crucial moments? Karl Marx said in the preface to the French version of *Das Kapital*, "There is no royal road to science, and only those who do not dread the fatiguing climb of its steep paths have a chance of gaining its luminous summits."[47] This is a profound explanation of the reason for working harder at crucial moments. Zhu Xi also provides a vivid explanation:

> Increasing strength at the critical moment is very much required during the process of learning. This means one should make more effort when strength is running out, so that one can continue to study and make progress. Learning is like going upstream; the boat easily moves at full speed in smooth water, but in rough water, the boatman should pole with all his strength without slowing; otherwise the boat will not be able to continue upstream.[48]

Studying is like rowing a boat against the current. In Zhu Xi's opinion, when traveling upstream, all efforts will be wasted if the paddler does not work hard. Studying should be the same.

How do we work harder at crucial moments? Zhu Xi provides a sound psychological explanation:

> When reading, one should achieve mastery through a comprehensive study of the subject…what the reader needs to do is bury himself in study without thinking back and forth, so that he will ultimately succeed. These are all excuses: saying that he has not done this before, it is late, there is not enough time, this is difficult, he is a slow person, and he is forgetful. Instead of being overcautious and indecisive, one needs to simply put all effort into reading, instead of pursuing speed, and then he can achieve something after a short period of time. We should understand that a short period of time might delay our whole life, and we might become old unknowingly.[49]

Zhu Xi encouraged people to absorb themselves in books, instead of being overcautious and indecisive, worrying about this or that with hesitation. Great effort should be made, no matter what a man's quality is. He said, "As for learning, in order to succeed, even a smart person should make painstaking efforts; how can someone who is mediocre achieve success if he does not work hard?"[50] Even a smart person should work harder to gain knowledge, let alone one who is less intelligent.

Therefore, Zhu Xi asked people to build self-confidence and felt that neither a shallow foundation, a late start, a slow disposition, nor a poor memory could be obstacles to study. Only "through working wholeheartedly with determination and courage, like a soldier rushing full-steam ahead when the drum beats, regardless of what may happen on the front, can one obtain achievements."[51]

Working harder at crucial moments also required people to read with a resolute and daring spirit and refrain from a loose and capricious attitude toward reading. Zhu Xi said, "Reading words is like a valiant general commanding troops, fighting hard, and like a strict official judging a case, interrogating until the end; one should read with the spirit of never giving up."[52] Further, he said, "Reading is like fighting on the battlefield; one rushes forward to the beat of the drum without thinking of surviving. One can achieve success in learning only by moving forward perseveringly."[53] This means one should read in a state of excitement and tension, investing all energy, "so he may forget to eat when hungry and to drink when thirsty," and finally moving forward steadfastly and achieving the effect of "leaving the trace of a hit after drubbing and the trace of blood after slapping," achieving obvious effect with solid work.

6. Reading with an Undivided Mind and Steadfast Ambition

One should read with a quiet and undivided state of mind and steadfast ambition: "One should keep an undivided mind even when he is free, and avoid putting oneself in a land of nothing. When handling affairs, one should focus on dealing with matters; when reading, one should focus on books. One should command the mind perfectly, no matter whether in motion or at rest."[54] One should "move forward with a resolute will."

Why should we read with an undivided mind and steadfast ambition? Zhu Xi said:

An undivided mind is a person guarding an entrance.[55]
An undivided mind is a guiding principle of learning.[56]
The key to learning lies in steadfast ambition and has nothing to do with the degree of talent.[57]
One should first be determined in his heart before working; without ambition, one cannot succeed.[58]

Zhu Xi regarded the "undivided mind" as "a person guarding an entrance." This proposition is similar to the concept of attention in modern psychological theory to a certain degree. Ushinski, the famous Russian educator, once said, "Attention is the only portal through which one can feel the impression of the external world or the state of the nervous system."[59] Professor Yan Guocai, a Chinese psychologist, also thought that attention was the organizer and sustainer of intellectual activities; only with the participation of attention could human intellectual activities take place and develop smoothly and effectively.[60] What does ambition mean? Zhu Xi said it was "the ideal in the heart."[61] According to his brilliant disciple Chen Chun's explanation, "Ambition is also the ideal." He said, "For instance, having the ambition of studying doctrines means that doctrines occupy one's whole heart; having the ambition of learning means one wants to learn with one's whole heart." Further, he said, "Continuing to explore at all times and determining to realize the ideal is called aspiration."[62] This shows that ambition is similar to how modern psychology views aspiration and motivation.

Attention and ambition are two important factors in learning psychology. Zhu Xi paid much attention to these two factors, which, together, can be called "the first consideration to find the truth." This view holds that these two psychological qualities are more important than other qualities. An undivided mind was seen as the guiding principle, with ambition as the foundation, and both were seen to play an important part in study activities. This was a very insightful view.

How should we read with an undivided mind and steadfast ambition? Zhu Xi said:

An undivided mind requires one to restrain his heart when reading.[63]

It is easy for one to focus on a book and study every word and sentence at the beginning. However, it is necessary to restrain the heart and read meticulously with a pure and quiet mind, not being distracted by all the sounds under the sky.[64]

There is no need to say more on reading with an undivided mind. Ruminating with a serious and strict mind, changing one's facial expressions, adjusting one's train of thought, cleaning one's hat and clothes [being well-dressed], and making oneself appear honorable are nothing but decoration.[65]

With ambition, one will bear his goal in mind constantly, never tiring of it.[66]

Zhu Xi thought that an undivided mind and steadfast ambition were different from the Buddhist view of "the state of sitting alone with merry expression, hearing nothing, seeing nothing, and thinking nothing."[67] It required the convergence of body and mind; the constant review of books; "keeping one's spirit up and sitting up straight";[68] and "focusing on thinking inside and avoiding fidgeting outside."[69] The key to an undivided mind and steadfast ambition was to have great ambition, which should "exceed the surface of things,"[70] and to "keep moving forward with a determined heart."[71] An undivided mind needed honesty and "should remain constant through all situations."[72] In Zhu Xi's opinion, an undivided mind was the precondition for steadfast ambition. He said, "It's just empty talk if one sets up great ambition… but reads in a careless way and spends the day idly."[73] With respect to specific practices, Zhu Xi thought one should prepare himself mentally and physically, gathering the untamed mind in concentration. Reading with a distracted mind would only lead to futile actions and wasted time and energy, so it was better to read when one was concentrated.

The reading methods Zhu Xi put forward were not only the guiding principles of ancient reading methods, but also a valuable, instructive, and precious legacy of ancient China's education theories.

The Essence of Reading Methods

Beyond the reading guidelines described above, ancient Chinese educators also put forward several original reading methods. Zhou Yongnian in the Qing Dynasty described some of these in detail in *Reading Tactics of Excellent Predecessors*. We will now analyze some of these original reading methods.

1. The Method of Establishing the Outline and Exploring the Subtle Meaning

The method of establishing the outline and exploring the subtle meaning was put forward by Han Yu, an educator in the Tang Dynasty, in *Explaining Questions on Learning*:

> One should regularly chant and recite texts from the Six Classical Arts and write a commentary on the writings of the ancient philosophers. When reading, one should note down the outline and the subtle meaning of the words with the desire to leave out nothing, lighting a candle when the sun goes down and working hard all the year round.

According to Han Yu's method, one should first classify the books to be read and then read with various methods according to their different natures and categories. When reading books recording historical facts, one must be able to outline the contents of the books; when reading theoretical books, one should be capable of seeking the profound ideas in them. Therefore, the key to establishing the outline and exploring the subtle meaning is to grasp the key points and derive the essence of a book's contents.

The method of establishing the outline and exploring the subtle meaning of a book is enhanced by using one's hands frequently. Li Guangdi, a scholar in the Qing Dynasty, once said in response to Han Yu's reading method:

> The key lies in the two actions of taking notes and writing down thoughts. Reading only with the eyes and mouth is not better than taking notes when reading, for the mind must be moving along with the hands when you are writing. Reading twenty times is not better than writing one time. Moreover, it is not possible to read and think carelessly when required to establish the

outline or explore the subtle meaning. If one can compare similarities and differences, judge right and wrong, write down his own questions, and adhere to the argument during this process, he can naturally improve his thought further and remember the truth more firmly.[74]

Li Guangdi's comment not only indicates that the method of "using one's hands" is far more efficient than that of reading and reciting, but also points out that using one's hands is in fact a direct promotion for reading. Under the pressure of establishing the outline and exploring the subtle meaning, one must read carefully and think seriously; otherwise one cannot successfully finish the required task.

2. The Method of Solving Problems One by One

The method of solving problems one by one was described by Su Shi, a great writer in the Song Dynasty. It was derived from the idea of "focusing on attacking one side when the enemy disperses its forces" from *The Art of War.* This means that when troops are "under attack from all directions," the army should concentrate on the superior force and destroy that of the enemy one by one, "attacking the weak with the strong," instead of dividing forces and sallying out in all directions, thus risking meeting huge forces with few troops. Su Shi created the reading method of destroying the enemy one by one based on Sun Tzu's military strategies and tactics. He said:

When I was young, the topics I remembered from the imperial civil service examinations were similar to those of previous years. At that time, there were cases of examinees writing wonderful articles on a few difficult topics and being directly taken away by the chief examiner. Such things never happen again nowadays, and even if they do, there is little help. Hence that is not an ideal shortcut. Talented as you are, along with strong competence and many years' accumulation of knowledge, surely you can have your own way to get a high score, but in fact, this is destined by fate. However, I think if young people want to win some academic achievements, they should read a book more than once, completely and thoroughly. The knowledge in a book is as rich as the sea, containing all kinds of things. But with limited energy, one cannot take all of these things in, and instead takes only what he really wants. Therefore, one should have a clear objective in his study. If you want to learn how to administer state affairs well and ensure national security, you should regard this as your objective, work hard on it, and cast away distracting thoughts. If you want to be erudite and informed, you need to have this objective in mind. These are two examples for you; other things are the same. Inflexible as it is, one day, when you do achieve your goals, you will be able to handle all kinds of situations. Those who read cursorily cannot be mentioned with you in the same breath. What I recommend is far from efficient; hence it may sound ridiculous.[75]

In Su Shi's view, books were all-encompassing and of rich contents. Even a single book covered a wide range of knowledge. Therefore, one could only "explore one aspect of a book at once," concentrating on one particular question. For example, if one wanted to know the relationship between the rise and fall of dynasties and sages, he should focus on studying just this subject in one reading, instead of considering many questions at once, such as events, quotations, decrees and regulations, or cultural relics. Only in this way could one get fruitful results step by step.

3. Banqiao's Reading Method

Banqiao's reading method was put forward by Zheng Banqiao, a poet and painter in the Qing Dynasty, who not only was a master of poetry, calligraphy, and painting, but also had original and incisive opinions on reading methods.

First, he proposed remembering with forgetting. It was considered that the reason why Zheng Banqiao had remarkable talent and unique style in poetry, calligraphy, and painting was that he was perspicacious and had a good memory. But he said disapprovingly, "The thing I like least is a photographic memory. As to the *Four Books and Five Classics,* I have forgotten some things. There is nothing else, but those which need to be forgotten must be forgotten, and those which should not, shall be embedded in memory forever."[76] He thought there was no need to commit everything to memory. Rather, it was necessary to remember the knowledge one needed and to forget useless information.

It was true that Zheng Banqiao had a good memory. Once there was a person who contested with him to recite Confucian classics. He "wrote from memory, three to five papers of words a day, sometimes one or two papers, sometimes seven or eight, and sometimes, when he was seized by a whim, he wrote twenty to thirty papers; hence, he finished all within two months. Although the words he wrote had differences in calligraphy, there was no error in any sentence or phrase."[77] But his secret to memory was simply the reading method of remembering with forgetting. He thought that remembering useless information was just like "storing smelly oil and spoiled sauce in a ratty cupboard, which was so filthy that no one could bear it."[78]

This conclusion coincides with some research results in modern psychology. Memory psychologists consider that remembering and forgetting have an inherent connection of dialectical unity. Forgetting is not always negative. Only by actively forgetting something (this is called "eliminating noise" from the viewpoint of information theory) can one remember things (useful information) efficiently. If we could only remember but not forget, everything we have ever seen and heard would fill up our brain, the treasury of our memory would overflow with waste, and thus our thoughts imaginations would not take wing. Therefore, there is scientific ground for Banqiao's reading method of remembering with forgetting.

Second, Zheng Banqiao proposed the method of learning and questioning. Zheng Banqiao thought that careful thinking and asking questions were important in reading, and that only with learning and questioning could one achieve fruitful results. He felt that reading without thinking and learning without questioning were both useless. He said:

> The phrase "learning knowledge" should be comprehended from two perspectives: learning and questioning. Learning without questioning only makes today's learners mediocre, even if they have read large volumes of books. Yun Xi, also known as Master Qiongya, is an inquisitive scholar, who tends to ask dozens of people questions again and again until his questions are answered and he understands all principles thoroughly. Therefore, his articles and viewpoints are as penetrating and perspicacious as viewing a blazing fire.[79]

Banqiao advocated the ancient reading method of attaching importance to questioning, studied the inherent meaning of "learning knowledge," and held that without asking questions, a reader was just a mediocrity even if he had read tens of thousands of books. He advocated perseverance in asking questions until reaching the truth. This is quite similar to the function of the question step of the SQ3R reading method, which involved the five steps of survey, question, read, recite, and review and was popular abroad in the 1980s. The study of modern reading methods has repeatedly proved that only an emphasis on asking questions and finding answers can make the activity of reading meaningful, targeted, and critical; and only through questioning can one clear his confusions and acquire new knowledge. This can be called a golden rule among reading methods.

Third, Banqiao proposed absorbing and abandoning. He thought reading should be creative and selective, with one absorbing but also abandoning to fly one's own colors. He followed this method in painting, too. For example, when he learned to paint orchids and bamboo from painters Shi Tao and Li Fangying, he did not copy blindly or imitate utterly, but explored the essence in the process of absorbing and abandoning on his own.

Why should we both absorb and abandon knowledge in our reading? Banqiao described two reasons. First, the purpose of reading was to master knowledge. Without the ability to master knowledge, the result of much reading was like an upstart unsure of how to spend money. He said, "Reading tens of thousands of books but having no thoughts of one's own is like an upstart suf-fering for the pain of spending money."[80] Therefore, only mastering knowledge could make one achieve the state of being "free from the constraints of the ancient scholars and having agreement between the temperament and the spirit. Then works will be copious and fluent and conform to the current style of writing."

Second, he said that the purpose of reading was to create, but not to follow the established rules and imitate the ancients with every step. He said, "When learning, there is no need to focus on all of the content; absorbing half and abandoning half were enough. This is not because one does not want to gain knowledge of all the content, but that one is unable to do so. Besides, it is not necessary to do so. There is a poem that says, 'When learning from others, instead of taking in all the information, one should explore and think with his own mind. If a person is reluctant to learn from the people around him, then when can he travel afar to pursue knowledge?'[81] On this basis, he also put forward that reading content should be chosen carefully, with quality more important than quantity. He said, "For instance, in the 130 articles of *the His-torical Records*, the best is "The Chronicle of Xiangyu," in which the most won-derful and moving parts deserving repeated reading are "The Battle of Julu," "Dinner at Hongmen," and "Meeting in Gaixia." If one reads every article and memorizes all the words in *The Historical Records*, he is merely a mediocrity!"[82] He gave another example, saying, "Only idiots read every sentence in the *Five Classics*, the *Traditional Twenty-One Histories*, and *Twelve Buddhist Scriptures*; only fools learn every school of poetry from all dynasties, that is, the Han Dynasty, the Wei Dynasty, the Six Dynasties, the Three Periods of the Tang Dynasty, and the Northern and Southern Song Dynasties."[83]

On the issue of reading, Zheng Banqiao also emphasized the concen-trated mind and the abandonment of fickle attitude. He stressed the impor-tance of a good study environment, saying that "reading at a neat desk before a bright window is a great joy in the world."[84] He pointed out that readers should "study assiduously and determine and analyze the essence" of a book in order to appreciate its essential ideas.

4. The Method of Intensive Reading

The method of intensive reading was proposed by the scholar Li Guangdi of the Qing Dynasty. He wrote:

> Memory is needed in reading, and it cannot be easily acquired. To improve one's memory, one should adopt the method of intensively reading a book. No matter whether the book is thick or thin, once one has thoroughly compre-hended the book, understanding the underlying meaning of every word, and

being able to distinguish right from wrong and good from bad among various theories, he will be able to base his comprehension of other books on this one. One cannot get any help from his friends if he treats them all the same. Therefore, in leading troops, he should have several hundred loyal soldiers who are prepared to die; in making friends, he should have a handful of companions who are congenial to him. In this way, he will have many people to help him when needed. The reason lies in the fact that those whom he holds dear have others whom they hold dear. The same is true with selecting a book. Once a book is utterly understood, other books of the same type can be understood, as well. Nevertheless, the book must be of significance, or it will be useless, which is also like leading troops or making friends. What is the use of getting close to cowardly soldiers or making friends with rascals?[85]

Li Guangdi believed that this method not only contributed to improving one's memory, but also acted as a "foundation" for him to absorb the knowledge of other books. He held that a book that was going to be intensively read must be carefully selected. It should be beneficial for him, allowing him to lay a solid foundation to understand other books. He must concentrate and be careful when reading, "understanding the underlying meaning of every word and being able to distinguish right from wrong and good from bad among various theories." After being intensively read, a book can be regarded as the foundation of learning, and knowledge will snowball.

5. The Method of Consecutive Reading

The method of consecutive reading was proposed by Xing Maoxun, a teacher of the Qing Dynasty, and was briefly introduced in *The Method of Teaching Children*, written by Wang Jun.

Xing Maoxun often said that his teacher adopted the method of consecutive reading to teach reading. Consecutive reading means that one reads one page of material on the first day, and then reads that page, as well as a new page, on the next day. On the third day, the first two pages must be repeated. By the eleventh day, one can stop reading the first page and start from the second page. From then on, he reads ten consecutive pages every day, and each page of material is read ten times. In this way, even mediocre and unwise people can come to understand the material in their hearts.

Actually, this approach to memorizing what has been read is similar to the revolving memory method of modern times. In this method, one does some reading on the first day, then reads something new on the second day while also reviewing the previous day's reading. On the third day, he reads new material and again reviews what he read the first two days. Again, by the eleventh day, he can stop reading the material of the first day and start with the material read on the second day. In this way, he will read ten pages each day, and each page will be read ten times, allowing it to be fully absorbed, even by untalented ones.

6. The Method of Gradual Accumulation Through Intensive Learning

The method of gradual accumulation through intensive learning, put forward by Ye Yisheng, a writer of the late Ming and early Qing Dynasties, was recorded by Zhang Erqi, a scholar of the Qing Dynasty, in his book *Chitchat of Hao'an*:

> Ye Yishen of the Licheng [the city of Li] proposed an effective way of memorizing. He said that he had been born a slow learner, so he wrote down whatever he liked when reading a book. Then he read the notes several times and pasted them on the wall, sometimes ten notes a day, but at least six or seven. After he closed the book, he would go through the notes on the wall three to five times a day intensively, trying to memorize them all and never missing one word. When the wall was completely covered with notes, he would remove and collect the notes he had pasted on the first day, and the vacant places would be covered by new notes. He kept doing this without taking a day off. In this way, he collected some three thousand notes in a year. Several years later, he became very rich in knowledge. It was often seen that some people who extensively read books did not make further progress, as they had discerned little knowledge, which never stayed in their minds after a few days. This way of reading a book is inferior to that of gradual accumulation through intensive learning.

Contrary to such reading habits as skimming the surface, this method emphasizes a small amount of persistent absorption. The method of gradual accumulation through intensive learning states that, when reading a book, one should note down all the passages, paragraphs, mottos, or aphorisms he likes, and then read and recite them ten times. After that, he should paste these notes on the wall. The number of notes should be kept between six and ten or more a day. Whenever he gets tired and needs a moment of rest, he may walk around, reading the notes on the wall several times a day until he has completely memorized them. Then he can remove and collect these notes, and replace them with new notes. By this means, more than three thousand wonderful notes can be accumulated in a year, and a splendid amount of knowledge can be acquired in several years. It was by this approach that Ye Yisheng became a famous learned dramatist playwright with a brilliant literary grace.

7. The Method of Circling and Smearing

The method of circling and smearing was described by Wang Jun in his book *The Method of Teaching Children*. He held that our mind and hands should work together when reading so as to gain better understanding and memory. In the book, he wrote:

> After students are enrolled in school, ink is needed in every subject. In reading every passage, they need to circle and smear with ink so as to lay a solid foundation for learning. Once they have made progress, they should circle what they have smeared and smear what they have circled by themselves. Further, whenever an idea occurs to them when they are reading a piece of material, they should write it down to be altered and smeared in the future. If a piece of material remains clean, without even a mark on it after being read, it indicates that the reader did not concentrate on the reading at all.

The method of circling and smearing involves two steps. First, when reading a piece of material, one should circle the high points and smear the unsatisfactory parts according to his own understanding and perspective. As he deepens his learning, he might "smear what he has circled and circle what he has smeared." As a result, he makes a little progress every time when he actively circles and smears. This is the way "to lay a solid foundation for learning." Second, one should make notes, commentaries, and annotations in his reading materials. If a book "remains clean, without even a mark on it," it shows that the reader "did not concentrate on the reading at all."

8. The Method of Pondering and Applying the Knowledge of a Book

When reading a book, one must know the method of pondering and applying its knowledge. When one starts to read a book, he should ponder and pursue an understanding of the essence of the book. After he finishes reading it, he should put the knowledge of it to use. The method of pondering makes the essential ideas of a book accessible; the method of applying leads to a thorough use of these ideas. If one barely ponders, he fails to embrace the core ideas of ancient people; if he seldom practices, he gets conquered by the literal language. One can hardly obtain the essence of reading until he knows how to ponder and how to use the knowledge of a book.[86]

In fact, this method focuses on the two steps of reading. The first step is to ponder, to some extent "making the essential ideas of a book accessible." Readers must carefully reflect on the profound meaning of the book. The second step is to apply, which means that readers must avoid being slaves to a book, "being conquered by the literal language." They should make "a thorough use," applying what is learned from books in real life.

Lu Longqi of the Qing Dynasty further developed this approach into the idea of combining reading with being a man. He said, "Reading a book and being a man are not two separate things. Applying what is learned from books to ourselves forms the law of being a man, and people who follow this approach to reading become good readers. If one does not put the lines of books into practice, reading and being a man will be two different things for him, and he will be considered merely a man who has read nothing."[87] To some extent, "making the essential ideas of a book accessible" (reading) and "making a thorough use" (being a man) are unified by "applying what is learned from books to ourselves." This is the right way to read.

The Essentials of Reading

There has been an immense amount of research and discussion on the reading methods of ancient China. However, few valuable opinions were included earlier. Therefore, we should discard the dross and select the essential elements, and transcribe some mottos on reading in the hope of remedying defects.

Books Should Be Read with Doubts

Mencius was the first to propose the idea that doubting is essential in reading and that it is better to be without books than to give entire credit to them. He said:

> It would be better to be without *Shangshu* than to give entire credit to it. In the *Successful Completion of the War*, I select two or three passages only, which I believe. The benevolent man has no enemy under heaven. When the prince the most benevolent was engaged against him who was the most opposite, how could the blood of the people have flowed till it floated the pestles of the mortars?[88]

He quoted the example of King Wu of the Zhou Dynasty bringing the Shang Dynasty to an end to doubt the authenticity of the content of *Shangshu*. He also presented the idea that people could not readily believe and excessively depend on books. Later, this idea was further developed by Wang Chong of the Han Dynasty. He wrote:

> Mediocre people tend to believe in books that are actually groundlessly produced. They think that anything that has been recorded on bamboo slips and silk fabrics was made by sages and men of virtue who never make mistakes. Therefore, they believe whatever is in the books and read and recite them. Once they happen to read right and correct ones, which are different from the groundless books they prefer to believe, they would say that the former kind is valueless and incredible. As a matter of fact, since secrets can be unveiled and hidden truth can be judged, how can those people make such a general rumor in unison that the clear records in correct books, which can be easily

judged to be right, do not echo truth? The reason is that they do not attach much importance to or deeply think about their reading.[89]

In other words, not all printed things echo the truth. We should not "believe whatever is in books and read and recite them." We ought to think when reading any book. We must extract the essential knowledge of books, use it in a specific way, and distinguish the right from the wrong by ourselves.

Zhang Zai of the Song Dynasty also shared his insightful view in this respect. He said:

People who read little are not able to find truth and acquire essential knowledge. Reading books is to maintain a sensible mind, and people who do not read for some time will lose their cultivation of morality and virtue. People who read often can see through things; on the contrary, people who do not read are ignorant of reason and truth. When reading a book, one must often recite and ponder or sit meditating at night to obtain the essence of the book. One may not remember what he has read if he does not recite. But once he has understood the general idea of a book, it will be very easy for him to memorize it. So readers will have their own doubts explained and know what is beyond their reach. They make progress when they come to understand good things in a book; and they can also be enriched when they turn to doubt seemingly undoubtable things.[90]

In Zhang Zai's opinion, the key to reading is to "doubt seemingly undoubtable things," and the aim is to "have doubts explained." Therefore, we must balance the dialectical relationship between memorizing and thinking in the process of reading books so as to make progress.

The above idea of Mencius's was further developed by Lu Jiuyuan, who also put forward the method of doubting:

It is necessary to believe things in the ancestors' books, but we cannot mindlessly believe them all. The philosophical connotation of these books must be taken into consideration.[91]

From Lu Jiuyuan's point of view, the standard to judge whether knowledge in a book can be trusted is its "philosophical connotation." The fact or falsehood of a book, whether it speaks of reason or some other topic, can be identified by its "philosophical connotation."

Books Should Be Read Intensively

The methods mentioned above, such as the method of gradual accumulation through intensive learning, all stress the importance of intensive reading.

In this regard, two other statements may be quoted. One was proposed by Zhuxi of the Song Dynasty. He said:

> One should read carefully instead of skimming, should read something that can be easily understood instead of obscure things, should read by a regular, rather than an opportunistic, schedule, and should read something at hand instead of pursuing what is beyond reach.[92]

The other statement was put forward by Ji Yun of the Qing Dynasty. He said:

> Reading mechanically results in failure, and reading seldomly can also lead to failure.[93]

Both statements advocate the method of intensive reading, step by step, without craving only the quantity of books.

Books Should Be Read Proficiently

Educators in ancient times attached great importance to proficient reading, especially to memorizing and reciting. Proficient reading was considered especially important for beginners. Zhang Zai said:

> Classics must be memorized. Even though one has the wisdom of Shun and Yu, he cannot possibly be eloquent and will turn out to be less functional than the deaf and blind who express their ideas through gestures. Thus one should state what he has memorized, and then he can put things he has stated into action. Therefore, beginners must recite and memorize books.[94]

As for those who read a lot of books but cannot remember much, it is because they are unaware of the philosophical connotation of the books. If they manage to figure it out, they will obtain an extraordinary memory. Confucius adopted a fundamental philosophical connotation to see through things. Therefore, scholars should patiently pursue the profound essence of a book so that they can naturally become wise enough to see through things and have all their doubts settled. This is philosophical connotation.[95]

Confucius held that memorizing was of great significance to verbal expression and action. Therefore, people must "patiently pursue the profound essence of a book."

Lu Jiuyuan believed that the key to memorizing was repeated comprehension. Readers should read from shallower to deeper and from easier books to more difficult ones. He said to his students:

Learners should first comprehend easy content over and over again to a proficient level, and then they can effortlessly understand difficult content. However, if they read obscure parts at the very beginning, they will not have a good knowledge of it.[96]

He also quoted a poem in instructing his students:

One should avoid reading in a rush and should calmly appreciate the connotation of the work instead. Facing intangible points, he might as well skip; as for the points that are relevant to him, he should carefully ponder. He can remain energetic if he masters his own mind, but if he blindly goes after others' opinions, he may only find himself having wasted a lot of time. I would like to send these sentences to you as advice and hope you do not let others' ideas ruin your own thoughts.[97]

Lu Jiuyuan thought that another crucial point in memorizing was carefulness without going too far:

The way of reading lies in a calm attitude and careful appreciation without any curtness involved. It is the truth that the pursuit of learning should be as unhurried as the cultivation of sentiment. It is necessary to read plenty of books, but what is more important is the assimilation of knowledge. Follow the truth, and one can learn with pleasure.[98]

He also said:

When reading a book, after getting a general meaning of it, one should patiently read it without imposing any subjective opinion on it, or it will do no good in absorbing knowledge, cultivating good habits, pushing him forward, and getting him hardened. When facing points that are not understandable, it is acceptable to let them slide, and he may base his connotation of the book on what he has understood. In this way, he can gradually accumulate more day by day and one day become an erudite person. When he reads in retrospect the previously unknown points, he will immediately find them understandable and clear.[99]

Huang Tingjian thought that proficient reading lay not only in books but also away from books. He said:

There is an ancient saying that says, "Centralize all troops in one direction in a battle and have them chase after their enemies for one thousand miles, and they will eventually win the battle." One may find reading interesting when he reads industriously. When he stops to take a short rest, he may think over the aftertaste of it. As time passes, he will appreciate the efforts made by ancient people. Therefore, one should proficiently read one or two books. After that he will be able to comprehend other books even if he reads just several parts of them.[100]

That is to say, when reading a book, one should fully concentrate and "centralize in one direction"; during a break, one should re-ponder what he has just read; thus, he will utterly embrace the knowledge.

After carefully reading a book, one should not only seize the essential elements but also have a general knowledge of the entire book. As Zhang Zai said:

It is unwise for one to read a book in a rush, or he will fail to understand its essence. One should also gain a general idea of what the book discusses. Language in a book is like a finger pointing in a certain direction. One can see things afar by following the direction. However, if one limits his view to the finger instead of looking past it to get a panoramic view, he will lose the direction, which is equal to children's way.[101]

He also said, "In reading a book, one should draw a conclusion about what is discussed in it so as to unveil the author's intention."[102] Lu Jiuyuan explicitly stated that "In reading a book, one must read the literal meaning. But if he stops there, he is equal to children in learning. He should also pursue the book's intention."[103] These scholars held that the main purpose of reading was not only to take in the literal meaning of a book, but to develop an understanding of a book's "intention." If one knows only the literal meaning of a book, he is no better than children in reading books.

Modesty Must Be Valued in Reading

It was commonly agreed by educators in ancient times that readers should have a modest attitude. Yan Zhitui wrote:

Learning is to seek beneficial knowledge. I have met someone who is very arrogant, disrespects elders, and looks down upon his peers because he has read dozens of books. Others hate and detest him as enemy and owl. I think people like him are even inferior to those who do not read.[104]

Yan Zhitui thought that people should not satisfy themselves with merely reading several books. If they think highly of themselves, and even disrespect elders and show contempt for their peers because of having read many books, they fail to meet their original goal of benefiting from reading. On the contrary, they actually ruin themselves through reading. In this case, it would be better if they had never read any books.

> When reading classics, one should first read and ponder what can be easily obtained from the books. One should neither neglect understandable content nor satisfy himself with what has been acquired. If he sticks to these suggestions for a long time, he will benefit much from them. Whenever he is faced with confusing points, he had better not mindlessly search for the answers, because he will dismiss all these doubts when he makes progress in reading easy content in the future.[105]

Yan Zhitui held that in reading books, especially the classics, two attitudes should be abandoned, namely, "ignoring what is easy to understand and boasting about what has been read," which would most probably lead people toward careless reading and gaining nothing in the end. So people must be modest in reading, learning, and introspection. When one encounters any doubts, he should gradually address the doubts, instead of either hesitating to press ahead or blindly determining to figure them out. In this way, he can clear his doubts and make continuous progress.

Practice Should Be Valued in Reading

Educators in ancient China also valued practice in reading. For example, the famous poet Lu You of the Song Dynasty mentioned in *To My Son and Nephew: Written on a Winter Night*, "Reading is not enough; a better understanding requires personal practice." He held that knowledge acquired through reading cannot be completely understood without being practiced.

Yan Zhitui of the Northern Qi Dynasty comprehensively elaborated this thought. He wrote:

> The purpose of learning is to broaden our mind and sharpen our insight, which is conducive to our practice. As for those who do not know how to serve their parents, they should learn from ancient people who comprehend their parents' minds, bear their unpleasant looks, and politely and industriously present sweet and soft things to them. Thus, they will become prudent and do whatever their parents want them to.

As for those who do not know how to serve the emperors, they should learn from ancient people who responsibly abide by their obligations, never hesitate to sacrifice themselves in dangerous situations, and dare to expostulate for the benefit of their own country. Thus, they will become loyal and crave to make their due contributions.

As for those who are arrogant and extravagant, they should learn from ancient people who are modest, economical, humble to improve their virtue, polite to set a good example, and respectful to strengthen themselves. Thus they will become aware of their defects and become restrained.

With regard to those who are mean, they should learn from ancient people who are unselfish, value friendship while putting aside their own interests, keep away from proud and boastful people, and help the poor. Thus they will feel shameful and become generous.

As to those who are bad-tempered and violent, they should learn from ancient people who keep a lower profile and remain tolerant, respectful, and open-minded. Thus, they will feel exhausted and upset, with their body feeling uncomfortable.

As to those who are timid, they should learn from ancient people who are not scared of death, tough in mind, upright in action, reliable, and stick to their goals. Thus, they will become energetic and indestructible. The same is true with anyone else. Even though they cannot be thoroughly reformed, they can at least correct their bad habits.

> What has been learned can work in all aspects once it is practiced. However, for many scholars, words speak louder than action. They are not loyal to their emperors, filial to their parents, benevolent to others, or helpful to friends. In settling a case, they do not know its reason; in governing a small county of only hundreds of households, they cannot administrate the people; when asked about building a house, they mistake a lintel over the door and a short support on the beam; when asked about ploughing work, they are bewildered by the planting time of millet and wheat. They are no help in handling affairs of national defense and administration. All they can do is enjoy their casual chats and recite poems. Most probably these are the reasons why they are ridiculed by warriors and local officials.[106]

Yan Zhitui thought that the fundamental purpose of learning was to acquire knowledge and then to put it into practice. Disadvantages, physical or mental, can be changed and corrected through reading a certain sort of book.

According to Chen Que, a scholar of the late Ming and early Qing Dynasties, whether one reads carefully and effectively can be measured by whether he knows how to use what he has learned. He said

> Those who do not apply what they have read have actually never read. I often say the six words "prudent in saying, moderate in eating" to my son He. I do

not know whether he has engraved the words in his mind. But if he refuses to follow his father's instruction, how can he become a learned man? I never like superficial and ostentatious things. All I need to do is watch his everyday actions. If he shows even a tiny bit of prudence, I can say that he has made progress, and I will be very pleased. Even if he becomes a renowned celebrity in the future, I will not appreciate it."[107]

Yan Yuan of the Qing Dynasty also pointed out that "It is of no use to only think, talk, and read something. One needs to be able to apply what one has read when needed."[108] This is what really counts.

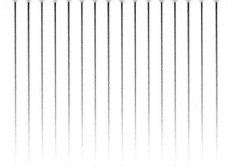

8

The Imperial Examination and Ancient China's Education

In the history of Chinese education, the imperial examination system probably exerted the greatest influence on education, schooling, intellectuals, and even ancient culture. Ever since it was created in ancient China's feudal society, the imperial examination was endowed with incredible power to recruit the talented, and passing it was considered the ultimate goal by scholars. Mr. Jin Zheng said:

> During the long period of feudal society, very few of the great politicians, thinkers, writers, historians, and experts in other fields who made tremendous contributions to enriching and developing Chinese culture did not step into the upper class through the imperial examination. On the other hand, the majority of those who had an enormous negative impact on the development of Chinese culture during the same period of time also experienced the examination. If intellectuals are the cultural representatives of a nation and a society, the mental outlook and spirit of Chinese intellectuals generation after generation were created by the imperial examination system.[1]

The imperial examination system was indeed nurtured by the system of ancient Chinese cultural education. Both its function of reinforcing ancient Chinese cultural education and its influence on the behavior of the people of modern China should not be neglected.

The Creation of the Imperial Examination

With regard to the issue of when the imperial examination system was created, it is widely recognized that it came into being in the Sui Dynasty, which is supported by many famous experts on educational history, such as Gu Shusen and Mao Lirui.[2]

However, others hold that the imperial examination did not originate in the Sui Dynasty.[3] Actually, the differing opinions are related to different understandings of what the fundamental characteristics of the imperial examination system are. We will not attempt to determine exactly when the system came into being, but rather research its origins diachronically.

The imperial examination system grew out of the intellectual selection system. *Encyclopedia Britannica* reads, "The earliest examination system we have unearthed is China's selection system (1115 BC) and its related examinations, which were regularly held (202 BC)." This possibly refers to the intellectual selection of the Western Zhou Dynasty and the recommendation and interview system of the Han Dynasty. Indeed, it is recorded that there was a system of local recommendation and examination in the Western Zhou Dynasty, which means that talents selected through the township test would be recommended successively to the central government. Every three years, a township examination was held to select township intellectuals: "Talents who are superior in terms of virtue, character, morality, and skills will be selected."[4] Typically, those who had been recommended to the central government would be tested by the kings of Zhou: "Feudal kings recommend talented people to the king, whose archery will be tested by the king himself."[5] The way that ancient tribes advocated martial arts was to some extent inherited from choosing talents through a test of archery.

During the Warring States Period, the heredity system gradually eroded, and a system of scholars rose rapidly. Therefore, the system of selecting intellectuals through recommendation and examination was gradually improved, and increasingly, more people had the opportunity to be chosen. Liu Bang of the Han Dynasty, having learned a lesson from the first emperor of Qin and Xiang Yu, who refused to employ scholars, ordered officials at different levels to recommend talented people in 197 BC. He stated:

> I will grant those wise talents who are willing to make their due contribution for the country respected and honorable status. This order must be spread far and wide to make my message known by the public. Officials at all levels, from royal doctors, prime ministers, feudal kings, and imperial ministers to county chiefs, must personally visit and invite eligible talents to work as politicians. Furthermore, officials must also dispatch civil vehicles to send the talents to the mansions of prime ministers and have their appearances, characters, and ages recorded.[6]

Liu Bang, Emperor Gaozu of Han, prescribed in this order that officials in both central and local governments should recommend intellectuals. If they failed to promote any known talents, they would be removed. Once they discovered a person with ability, they were to personally visit and invite the eligible talent to work as a politician, and then dispatch a civil vehicle to send the selected talent to the mansions of prime ministers. Further, they were to record his appearance, character, and age. This form of recommendation was similar to the selection of scholars from grass roots in later imperial examinations, that is, the system of recommendation and interview of the Han Dynasty. This developed into a fixed system during the regime of Emperor Gaozu of the Han Dynasty.

Liu Bang ordered that local governments of all prefectures were to recommend filial and incorrupt people to the central government according to their respective population ratios. Generally, one in every two hundred thousand people was to be recommended. That meant that every prefecture was to select between one and six candidates. He also stated, "Officials who do not follow the order and fail to recommend filial talents will be punished in the name of disrespect. Officials who fail to select incorrupt intellectuals are incompetent and will be removed."[7] Further, other subjects, such as Xiu Cai (talents, assessed in the imperial examination at the county level) and Ming Fa (the study of laws and decrees), were also included in the system. After being recommended and interviewed, the selected individuals were to take examinations set by the royal court, including essay examinations and a random choice of questions to be answered.[8] Many similarities can be found between the system of recommendation and interview and the imperial examination system in terms of both form and content. Nevertheless, the two systems have different natures. That is, while the imperial examination system was based primarily on examination and was supplemented by recommendation, the system of recommendation and interview follows an opposite track, and all candidates would be selected: "People who are able to take the essay examination will certainly be employed. But they will take different levels of official positions."[9]

The system of recommendation and interview to some degree made positive contributions, but it also brought about some problems. For instance, it accounted for mutual support between people and groups. Consequently, people elected by local governments were from notable families. It was possible that both hypocritical and articulate individuals could be selected by false pretenses, which caused the emergence of so-called "misnomers." Ge Hong of the Jin Dynasty criticized the system, saying:

At the end of the Han Dynasty, during election time, the talented and the poor could by no means live up to their expectations while official positions were occupied by misnomers. Those who had social relationships were regarded to be intelligent; otherwise, they were considered stupid.[10]

As a result, people who were claimed to be scholars could not read; people who were claimed to be filial evicted their fathers; people who were claimed to be incorrupt and honest were as turbid as mud; and the renowned generals who owned elite houses were as cowardly as chickens.[11] The above comments mean that those "scholars" who were supposed to be good at writing could not even read; those so-called "filial" people drove their fathers out; people who had a reputation for being incorrupt and honest were as dirty as mud; and the crowned "generals" living in luxurious houses were no braver than chickens. These remarks wonderfully criticized the "misnomer" situation inherent in the system of recommendation and interview.

Cao Pi, one of the sons of Cao Cao, adopted the idea of the "nine-rank system," proposed by Chen Qun, who was then Director of the Board of Rites. He assigned "Zhongzheng" officials in all prefectures to inspect, investigate, and evaluate local people, who were then divided into nine different ranks from upper to lower in terms of their talent and virtue. Certain individuals would then be recommended as would-be officials by the Zhongzheng officials to the Ministry of Official Personnel Affairs. The nine-rank system played an active role in changing the system of recommendation and interview that had been manipulated by established families. However, it did not improve the fundamental system of selecting talents, because most Zhongzheng officials were powerful bureaucrats, who thus continued to promote individuals from distinguished families. Therefore, the system gradually evolved into yet another recommendation system in the Han Dynasty. The so-called system of "no impoverished ones in the upper class and no distinguished ones in the lower class"[12] is a good proof of this.

The division of the country since the Wei and Jin Dynasties came to an end in the Sui Dynasty, and some important reforms also took place in the system of selecting officials. Of note, Emperor Wen of Sui abolished the nine-rank system and established the position of Zhou Du (head minister of a state or a county) to introduce talents without grading them. In the eighteenth year of the founding of the Sui Dynasty (AD 598), Emperor Wen ordered, "All fifth-ranked officials in the central government [in a system of nine ranks], governors, and prefectural governors must select talents in terms of their talent and virtues."[13] In AD 607, Emperor Yang of Sui ordered officials to "select talented and competent people" in terms of ten characteristics: being filial, moral, righteous, and honest, demonstrating integrity, persistence, and academic excellence, with an aptitude for writing, and being strategically superior and physically strong.[14] Two years later, this list was reduced to four characteristics: "Talents should be elected on the basis of four characteristics, namely, academic excellence and talent, physical strength, being industrious and competent in political issues, and being morally upright, without fear of power."[15]

It was recorded in *The Old Book of Tang* that Jin Shi, the highest imperial examination, was set by the regime of Emperor Yang of Sui when the essay examination was the only component. Further, Liu Su said in *A New Account of Tales of Great Tang*, "Two subjects, Jin Shi and Ming Jing (proficiency in Confucian classics), were set in the Sui Dynasty." These records became proof for later generations that the imperial examination system originated in the Sui Dynasty. Yet there are a few points which need further discussion. First and foremost, no record on the setting of Jin Shi and Ming Jing in the Sui Dynasty can be found in the *Annals of Emperor Yang* and *History as a Mirror*, which shows that even though the system had been established by this time, it did not have a significant influence at that time.

Second, even if the above two subjects were indeed established in the Sui Dynasty, they essentially bore no difference from the previously mentioned settings of two subjects, ten subjects, and four subjects; therefore, this new system did not break away from the idea of subject division or the setting of the essay examination under Han's recommendation and interview system.

Third, according to general public opinion, there were three key features of the imperial examination system. First, people could "independently apply to take the examinations." Regardless of family background, social status, and economic situation, intellectuals could apply independently to take the examinations, free from the requirement of recommendation by representatives of local or central governments. Second, the examinations were to be held regularly without any orders from the emperor. Third, the examinations were held strictly, and whether examinees matriculated depended entirely on the quality of their essays.[16]

However, the Sui Dynasty's talent selection system did not feature the three aspects described above. People who took the examinations were to be recommended by local officials and could not freely apply for participation; the examinations were held irregularly under the emperor's provisional orders; and the examinations were not strictly supervised, in either the Sui or the Tang Dynasty. Further, it is said that during the short regime of the Sui Dynasty, "the election of intellectuals and talents" lasted for only about ten years, without developing in scale or influence.

Nevertheless, the Sui Dynasty's official selection system was formed during the transition period between the recommendation and interview system of the Han Dynasty and the imperial examination system of later generations; therefore, it had a significant influence on the formal birth of the imperial examination system in the Tang Dynasty. So it can be said that the imperial examination system in ancient China was established in the Han Dynasty, well developed in the Sui Dynasty, and fully formed in the Tang Dynasty.

There are two major signs of the formal establishment of the imperial examination system in the Tang Dynasty. One is the order of selecting talents promulgated by Emperor Gaozu in AD 622, who pronounced "self-recommendation" and "self-application"[17] to be legal. This meant that poor scholars of the lower class could individually apply to take the examination. The second sign was the explicitly stated order that "Once scholars and those who have taken the Ming Jing, Xiu Cai, Jun Shi (an imperial examination higher than Xiu Cai but lower than Jin Shi), and Jin Shi examinations have a good reputation in their counties, they can take the examinations held by county governments and then be tested by state governors. Matriculated eligible individuals would be recommended to the central government every October."[18] In this way, the timing of the examinations was fixed.

Changes to the Imperial Examination

After its formal establishment in the Tang Dynasty, the imperial examination experienced gradual development and continuous reform and amendment, which can be described by a process of moving from being prosperous to being well developed to being decadent. The Tang Dynasty's examination system involved various subjects. It was recorded in *The New Book of Tang: Treatises on Official Selection*:

> The subjects include Xiu Cai, Ming Jing, Jun Shi, Jin Shi, Ming Fa, Ming Zi (handwriting examination), Ming Suan (arithmetic examination), Yi Shi (an examination of one's mastery of a certain history), San Shi (an examination of one's mastery of three history books: *The Historical Records*, *The Book of Han*, and *The Book of the Later Han*), Kai Yuan Li (an examination of one's mastery of rites), Dao Ju (selecting talents from those who were proficient in Taoism), and Tong Zi (selecting talents from those who were proficient in classics, aged between 12 and 16), among which Xiu Cai, Ming Jing, Jin Shi, Ming Fa, Ming Zi, and Ming Suan were permanent subjects. In Xiu Cai, examinees would answer five questions on strategies for policy and would be graded according to their proficiency in both liberal arts and science. People who were graded from B to A+ passed the examination.[19]

Due to the emphasis on talent and erudition, the examination was so demanding that very few examinees were accepted. Further, only a few positions were available, and officials were hardly ever promoted; thus, scholars were not keen on the examination but preferred to take the subjects of Ming Jing and Jin Shi.

In the subject of Ming Jing, "examinees take the gap-filling test of Confucian classics first and then take the oral examination, including ten questions on the classics. Examinees must correctly answer at least three questions. All of the examinees would also be graded at four different levels."[20] The purpose of this test was to evaluate the examinees' proficiency in Confucian classics, such as the *Book of Rites, Commentary of Zuo,* the *Book of Odes,* the *Rites of Zhou, Ceremonial Etiquette* (medium classics), the *Book of Changes,* the *Book of History, Commentary of Gongyang, Commentary of Guliang* (small classics), *Tao Te Ching,* and *Filial Piety* (upper classics). All these were included in the exam. A great number of scholars preferred this exam for its low requirement.

In the subject of Jin Shi, "examinees will be tested on Tie Jing (帖经, a fill-in-the-blank test on the classics) and essay writing and will then take an essay examination on strategy. Essays should be comprehensive in content and elegant in diction. Essays on strategy should feature reason and appropriateness."[21] This subject stressed poetry, prose, and political essays. Since officials elected through this subject were more likely to be promoted, it was taken by numerous participants: "The number of applicants is no less than one thousand and can be more than two thousand."[22]

There were five major methods of examination: an oral test, Tie Jing, Mo Yi (writing Confucian classics from memory), Ce Wen (questioning strategy), and Shi Fu (writing of poetry and prose). Oral tests were taken on the spot, but there is no record that describes their content. The four remaining methods of the examination can be described as follows.

1. **Tie Jing:** This was an important method, which would be adopted in all subjects in the Tang Dynasty. During the exam, "a certain classic, except for one line, will be covered up. Examiners will then cut a piece of paper into pieces to cover certain words of the uncovered line. Generally, they will cover three words with the pieces of paper, but possibly four, five, or six at any time."[23] This is very similar to the modern gap-filling test, which emphasizes examinees' proficiency in the classics and critical analysis.

2. **Mo Yi:** Examiners asked a question according to Confucian classics, and then examinees wrote down a commentary, added notes, or described the context of the testing lines. This method is similar to the modern short-answer format, also evaluating examinees' proficiency in Confucian classics and critical analysis. For example, if examinees are told, "Please write down the line that follows "To those who are polite to the emperor, he will treat them like a filial son supporting his parents," examinees should first know that this line is from *Commentary of Zuo,* and then they need to write the line that follows: "to those who are rude to the emperor, he will kill them like an eagle chasing after a sparrow." Thus, they get the correct answer.

Sometimes this method was also used in the oral test, which was called "Kou Yi" (answering questions on Confucian classics from memory).

3. **Ce Wen:** This method followed the method of extracting questioning of the Western Han Dynasty. Examinees were required to devise strategic solutions to address real-world issues in politics, governing, education, and production. This method was practically political questioning. Part of every subject, scholars spared no effort to collect and memorize the test questions, as well as the essays of previous matriculated scholars, in order to prepare for their exams.

4. **Shi Fu:** Gradually, Ce Wen became a mere formality. So the Tang government set a test of poetry and prose. Examinees were required to write a poem and a piece of prose that reflected not only their historical knowledge and ideological level, but also their knowledge of literature and their writing ability. They were limited to writing a twelve-line five-character hexameter. The rhyme of the poem was also limited. In producing a piece of prose, examinees needed to use rhetorical devices, such as analogy and quotation, and rhythm was also limited.

Since intellectuals in the Tang Dynasty could "apply individually to take the imperial examination," the urgent demand for ordinary landlords and poor scholars to participate in governing the country was met, promoting the imperial examination to its golden era in the Tang Dynasty. Even Emperor Taizong of Tang, when he saw new selected scholars gathering to check the admission list, pleasantly commented, "Talents around the country are coming to work for me!"[24]

Of course, there were disadvantages to the Tang Dynasty's imperial examination system, which cannot be ignored. First and foremost, unlike the system of covering up the names of examinees and transcribing their examinations, examinees' names and handwriting remained clear on their test papers in the Tang Dynasty, which created conditions for chief examiners to cheat by showing favoritism.

Second, the Tang Dynasty's government adopted an approach of "Tongbang," in which chief examiners provided a list of examinees ("Bangtie") according to their reputation in society for reference when they decided who would pass the examination. These examiners could assign specific officials to carry out the so-called "Tongbaotie" investigation. However, during the investigation, social celebrities and royal officials played a significant role in recommending scholars, and they even had the power to decide on the matriculation list before the official exam. This meant that some examiners engaged in undesirable behaviors, such as "Xingjuan,"[25] that is, helping others during the examination or accepting bribes. All these prove that the Tang Dynasty's imperial examination system was influenced by the Han Dynasty's system of recommendation and interview, as well as the nine-rank system of the Wei and Jin Dynasties.

Third, the Tang Dynasty's imperial examination began to exert an impact on school education, causing contradiction between the two sides. In the early Tang Dynasty, school education took an important place in the society. However, during the regime of Empress Wu, schooling was gradually neglected while the imperial examination gained in importance. Fewer people who had been educated in school could pass the examination, and it became harder and harder for accepted ones among them to get promoted, leading to the social conduct of "People taking pride in obtaining an official position in Jingzhao and Tonghua through the imperial examination and therefore refusing to receive a school education."[26]

What is more, functioning as a "baton," the imperial examination could greatly influence the teaching objectives, content, and methods of schooling. For instance, education institutions in the Tang Dynasty, such as the Imperial Academy, the Imperial College, and the national school Si Men Xue, organized their teaching according to the requirements of selecting talents by testing their knowledge of nine Confucian classics in the imperial examination.

Drawing lessons from the Tang Dynasty and the Five Dynasties Period, the Song Dynasty emphasized the governance of a country by civil officials and made a series of improvement and reforms to the imperial examination. The first one was increasing the quota of scholars allowed to take the imperial examination, referred to as "opening up the imperial examination threshold to the public so that everyone has equal opportunity and ceases being a treacherous fellow." As the record goes, for the 22 years during the reign of Emperor Taizong of Song, nearly 10,000 successful candidates were selected in the highest imperial examination, whereas just over 6,000 candidates were selected throughout the entire 290 years of the Tang Dynasty. This helped to ease the problem of the shortage of talents at the very beginning of the Song Dynasty. However, the surplus of selected candidates left the hidden peril of the bureaucratic redundancy of officials.

The second reform made to the imperial examination system in the Song Dynasty was improving the treatment of successfully selected candidates. The Song Dynasty inherited the practices of feasting and publishing a list of successful candidates from the Tang Dynasty. For example, in the second year of "Rejuvenating the nation through peace," during the reign of Emperor Taizong of Song, he conferred over 500 successful candidates, gave a grand banquet at Kaibao Temple, and composed poems for them. At the same time, the system for obtaining an official position upon successful completion of the examination was established, and the final assessment formalities of the Ministry of Official Personnel Affairs were removed.

The third reform to the imperial examination system in the Song Dynasty was the establishment of a complete legislative system against embezzlement and malpractice for the imperial examination. Preferential recommendation was forbidden, and the popular practice of having candidates recommended by officials and celebrities was abandoned. Restrictions were placed on the Privileges of the Chief Examiner (the appointed official in charge of the imperial examination), such as "avoiding contact," whereby clan members and relatives of the examiner were examined at another venue, and "locking the venue," whereby once the chief examiner was designated, he was to live in the examination compound to be secluded from the outside world. He was forbidden contact with his family in order to shun pleas. Also, several deputy examiners (temporary examiners) were engaged to restrict and supervise each other. Further, two practices were adopted to effectively rule out interference from the rich and powerful, curbing the harmful practices of corruption, pleading, and forming cliques to pursue selfish interests. These included "sealing," whereby personal information such as names, hometowns, families, and other revealing information was kept sealed, and "transcription," whereby examinations were transcribed to prevent examiners from recognizing the handwriting of examinees. A transcription council was established in the year 1015. Thus, after the improvement of the imperial examination in the Song Dynasty, the ancient imperial examination system entered a stage of maturity.

Reform of the imperial examination system in the Song Dynasty strengthened its function in social and political life, broadening the social foundation of the examination. With the promotion of rulers, almost all intellectuals regarded the examination as the only way to gain wealth and obtain official positions.[27] It is worth mentioning that research theories on imperial examination education began to develop, and many people commented on the reform of the imperial examination, including Fan Zhongyan, Wang Anshi, Sima Guang, and Su Shi.

At the beginning of the Yuan Dynasty, the imperial examination was not given much attention. The first imperial examination of the Yuan Dynasty was held 80 years after the establishment of the nation with the aim of gathering and attracting intellectuals from the Han ethnicity to devote themselves to the nation.

There were two conspicuous characteristics of the imperial examination in the Yuan Dynasty. First, there was an unfair preferential policy toward some ethnicities. The imperial examination was held every three years and was divided into a provincial examination, a metropolitan examination, and a final examination presided over by the emperor. At the provincial level, the Mongolians and the Semu were examined only in the argumentation of Confucian classics and the strategy of country governance, whereas people of the Han ethnicity were required to take an additional examination in which they were required to compose one poem and one article. One hundred candidates out of 300 were selected in the provincial examination. However, there were only 25 selected among each of the Mongolians, Semu, Han, and people from the south, which meant that candidates of the Han ethnicity and those from the south had half the chance of being selected, because their populations were several times larger than those of the Mongolians and the Semu. When the list of those selected was published, it was divided into two columns to show the differences among the ethnicities. Conferring official positions also embodied ethnic inequality. Positions of selected Mongolian and Semu people were higher than those of the Han ethnicity and those from the south.

The second characteristic of the imperial examination in the Yuan Dynasty was that the Four Books and Five Classics, annotated by Neo-Confucianists, became the main content of the imperial examination.

When Emperor Renzong of the Yuan Dynasty lifted the ban on the imperial examination in the year 1313, he described the new rules of the system:

> In the first session of the examination, the Mongolians and the Semu will be questioned on the contents of the Classics, *The Great Learning*, *The Analects of Confucius*, *Mencius*, and *The Doctrine of the Mean*, as well as the variorum edition of Zhu Xi. Papers whose meanings are profound and whose diction is graceful shall be chosen. The second session of the examination will focus on current events. Papers should exceed 500 words. As to candidates of the ethnicity of Han and those from the south, they will take examinations on two questions, one pertaining to the Confucian Classics, *The Great Learning*, *The Analects of Confucius*, *Mencius*, and *The Doctrine of the Mean*, and one on the strategy of governing a country. They should conclude with their own work of interpretation, to exceed 300 words, on Zhu Xi's content of *The Book of Poetry*, Cai Chen's part of *Shangshu*, or Zhu Xi's and Cheng Yi's parts of *The Book of Changes*.[28]

Honoring Cheng's and Zhu's Neo-Confucianism via the imperial examination played a significant role in establishing the status of Cheng's and Zhu's Neo-Confucianism in the late period of feudal society and became a model for later generations.

In the third year of the Ming Dynasty (1370, the Year of Hongwu), Emperor Zhu Yuanzhang led the convocation of the imperial examination and stated, "All civil officials from both majority and minority ethnic groups shall be selected through the imperial examination. No candidate can obtain an official position without success in the imperial examination."[29]

Although there were several changes, the system of selecting officials through the imperial examination did not undergo vicissitudes. The system became quite complex in terms of layers, levels, and stipulations. Candidates in the Ming Dynasty had to go through five levels of the imperial examination. The first level was for candidates to be tested at the regional level of the county. Those who passed were called pupil candidates.

The second level was for candidates to be tested at the prefecture level. The tests were divided into two categories: a test according to year and a test based on subjects. The test according to year was held annually for pupil candidates as an entrance test for academies. After being admitted, they were recognized as official students. They could also then be called scholars, or Xiu Cai, those who had passed the imperial examination at the county level in the Ming and Qing Dynasties.

Tests based on subjects were for the Xiu Cai who had studied in academies. The qualified ones were allowed to attend provincial examinations. Unqualified ones were not considered official students.

The third level was the provincial examination, also called "Dabi," which was held in the examination compound of each province three times a year. Since the examination was held from 11 p.m. to 1 a.m., 5 a.m. to 7 a.m., 11 a.m. to 1 p.m., and 5 p.m. to 7 p.m. from August 9 to 15 according to the Chinese lunar calendar, it was sometimes called the imperial examination held in autumn. Successful candidates in this examination were called "Ju Ren." The top candidate was called "Jie Yuan."

The fourth level was the metropolitan examination, which was held in the capital by the Ministry of Rites in the year following the provincial examination. Since the examination was taken from February 9 to 15 according to the Chinese lunar calendar, this examination was sometimes called the examination held in spring. Qualified candidates from this examination were called "Jin Shi," and the top candidate was called "Hui Yuan."

The fifth level was the final imperial examination presided over by the emperor and was held one month after the metropolitan examination, on March 5, in the royal palace. The main contents were strategies for coping with current events, and topics were decided by the emperor. In this examination, no candidates would be eliminated. All candidates would be ranked. The first three candidates were "Yi Jia" (一 甲), who were "Zhuang Yuan" (first place), "Bang Yan" (second place), and "Tan Hua" (third place). The top three were considered "Jin Shi Ji Di" (the most successful candidates in the examination). Several candidates were "Er Jia," who were "Jin Shi Chu Shen" (qualified as being successful in the highest imperial examination). Others were "San Jia," who were "Tong Jin Shi Chu Shen" (also qualified as being successful in the examination). All candidates would be conferred official positions.

One of the main characteristics of the imperial examination system of the Ming Dynasty was the adoption of stereotyped writing, which consisted of eight parts. Thus, this stereotyped writing was also called the eight-part essay. The essay was made up of fixed paragraphs, such as the interpretation of the theme, further elaboration of the theme, the beginning of the body, the beginning of the discussion, the body of the discussion, and the conclusion of the discussion. The interpretation of the theme involved explaining the theme of the piece in two sentences. The ensuing four sections were made up of coupled argumentative sentences, and the four sections were divided into eight parts. This eight-part essay nailed down the form, genre, language, and number of words used to select the intellectuals, although it was impractical and rigid. Thus, the imperial examination system gradually lost its vitality. A powerful official of the Qing Dynasty, Ortai, said, "The eight-part essay is useful for its function in governing intellectuals and stimulating elites."

The Qing Dynasty modeled the imperial examination system of the Ming Dynasty, yet the imperial system gradually degenerated. Because the eight-part essay was an important part of the imperial system, many candidates gained success in unfair ways. Candidates from wealthy families hired famous intellectuals to write more than ten essays ahead of the exam and ordered their intelligent servants or maids to memorize them rather than reciting the classics by themselves. Themes largely conformed with articles composed by famous intellectuals. There was not much difference in style, structure, or difficulty. It was the same with the Four Books (*The Great Learning, The Doctrine of the Mean, The Analects of Confucius,* and *Mencius*). After the list of successful candidates was released, the cunning candidate would be successful ever after.[30] Ordinary candidates would collect composed essays of previous candidates and buy anthologies to pass the exam, like the *Authorized Anthology of the Eight-Part Essay,* which was compiled by Fang Bao. This anthology was similar to the compilation of keys to examinations in the modern world, also called "Fang Gao" or "Wei Mo."

Meanwhile, corruption and embezzlement became more severe. Although the central government exercised harsh punishment, they could never stop it entirely. There were many means of cheating, such as bribery, currying favor with authority figures for personal gain, carrying notes secretly, hiring someone to take the examination in one's place, intentionally switching students' names on examinations (usually one was the best and the other far worse), secretly sharing answers during the examination, asking another person to take the examination in one's place, and intentionally providing false household registration information. The imperial examination became entirely a gateway to fame and status. The degradation of the imperial examination system predicted its doom. In 1906, the Qing government was forced to abolish the imperial examination. Therefore, the imperial examination system, which had lasted for over 1,000 years, ceased to exist just six years before the feudal and despotic Qing Dynasty perished.

Positive and Negative Aspects of the Imperial Examination System

The imperial examination system led a paradoxical existence in ancient China and played a contradictory role in ancient education. As Mr. Wang Bingzhao stated in *Free Talk About the Imperial Examination System*, the imperial examination helped maintain a balance between central authority and individual initiative in various regions. However, it bred the social morality of "honoring learning higher than anything in the world" and the erroneous belief that success in the examination would lead to success in all areas of life, generating the bad habits of corruption, embezzlement, and bribery. The imperial examinations linked reading, examinations, and the appointment of officials, and connected the cultivation, selection, and appointment of intellectuals. The imperial examination system came to rule over education and academies, which thus became mere accessories to the imperial examination system. The imperial examination system overcame the preference of moral quality and families, but the selection of officials based solely on knowledge never materialized. On the contrary, the imperial examination system was led into the dead end of recital, rote learning, and copying. The imperial examination system established standard content, criteria, and procedures; however, it encouraged formalization, dogmatization, and inflexibility.[31]

But is there a certain connection between the aforesaid positive and negative aspects of the imperial examination system? How can we analyze the influences of the imperial examination system on ancient education? How can we study the historical reasons for and the cultural background of the imperial examination system from boom to bust?

1. The imperial examination system established in China was the earliest and most complete system of developing civil servants in the world, and it played a role in maintaining unity and stability within society in ancient times.

It is universally acknowledged that the civil servant systems of Western countries have the characteristics of open competition, equal opportunity, and merit-based employment. Although the social foundation for the ancient Chinese imperial examination system and the Western civil servant system in modern times are totally different, the characteristics and philosophy of the latter can be detected in the imperial examination system. Thus, academia both at home and abroad holds that the civil servant system originated in ancient China. As Professor Allen Campbell, Chief of the General Personnel Office during the administration of U.S. President Carter, lectured in Beijing in 1983, saying, "When I received the invitation from the United Nations to lecture on the civil servant system in China, I was stunned to realize we owe the foundation of the civil servant system to China. And it was recorded in all the textbooks of political teaching in the Western world."[32]

In the Western world, from ancient Greece to the Middle Ages, there existed no exact records of written testing. It first appeared in European universities in the eighteenth century. During the Middle Ages, aristocrats and civilians were two distinct hierarchies. Civilians from lower strata had no opportunity to step into the upper class. However, the imperial examination system in China allowed learners to register for the examination regardless of birth, social status, or wealth, breaking down many, though not all, barriers. Although it was a flawed system in some ways, learners had more opportunity to achieve official positions in an equal way. In the social environment of the time, this was a significant reform and an issue which all countries in the world paid close attention to. Especially in the eighteenth and nineteenth centuries, the system became a model for change in Western countries. These countries created civil servant systems by imitating China's imperial examination system. When we come to the masterpieces of the enlightened thinkers of the Western world, nearly all the great intellectuals admired and appreciated the imperial system in China (although they observed China with "rose-colored glasses"). As Matteo Ricci, an Italian missionary in the late Ming Dynasty, pointed out, "Another main difference between China and the Western world, which is worth our attention, is that the country is governed by the intelligentsia, commonly called philosophy. They manage the whole country in an orderly way."[33]

Among the old capitalist countries, France began to carry out the examination of civil servants in 1791, and the United Kingdom established an examination system in 1853. If we consider the imperial decree on selecting officials in the fifth year of Emperor Gaozu of the Tang Dynasty (AD 622) as the founding of China's imperial examination system, we can consider that the civil servant system of China was established 1,100 years earlier than that of the Western world. If we consider the imperial examination system as originating with the recommendatory system of the Han Dynasty, when, in the year 178 BC, Emperor Wen of the Han Dynasty issued an order to recommend kind, outspoken, and moral people, then China's civil servant system was actually established nearly 2,000 years earlier than that of Western countries. Therefore, it is by no means an exaggeration to claim that China established the earliest and most complete civil servant system in the world.

The imperial examination system formed a system whereby the "intelligentsia were not defined by regional restriction, family interests, or armed strength."[34] To a large extent, this broke the monopoly over the system by wealthy and powerful aristocrats, acceded to the common landowners' demand for participating in politics, and paved a broad way for intellectuals who were also common landlords and ordinary civilians to obtain official careers. Further, the spiritual cohesion and sound social foundation that a unified country needs gradually came into being, thus playing a considerable role in maintaining social unity and stability.

In ancient society, wealthy and powerful aristocrats who relied on region and heredity were the greatest barrier to the unity of a country. They set up separate regional regimes, proclaimed themselves emperors, took control of royal courts, and threatened royal power; therefore, they were one of the main causes of social disunity. For example, the nine-rank system implemented in the Northern and Southern Song Dynasties, which was beneficial to the wealthy and powerful aristocrats who were so determined by heredity, led to the longest separation in China's history. The imperial examination system "naturally denied aristocratic politics" and deprived the wealthy and powerful aristocrats of their privileges, diminishing their power. Although poor intellectuals from the middle and lower classes had little chance to enter politics directly, it was still possible. However, they were under the control of the highest royal power. At the same time, "civil politics established a sociopolitical ideology commensurate with themselves—Confucianism—and selected civil officials to raise them up with a common faith, thus influencing the whole society,"[35] and made unity and stability the key features of a new powerful national mentality. In this way, a threefold force of central authority, intelligentsia, and Confucianism, which was formed via the imperial examination system, exerted great influence on the long-term unity of ancient Chinese society.

2. The imperial examination system expanded the social means to attract and introduce talents in feudal countries and had a significant influence on discovering and cultivating talents.

The imperial examination system broke the political monopoly of hereditary-based control by wealthy and powerful aristocrats and gave ordinary intellectuals access to the regime, guaranteeing the quality and quantity of talents. (Of course, most civilians from the lower classes were unable to participate in the examination for lack of education, and many intellectuals were degraded after they achieved their goals and began their official careers).

In particular, at the beginning of its maturity in the Tang and Song Dynasties, the imperial examination system was dynamic and lively and attracted poor intellectuals from the middle and lower classes to enter the governing class, generating a large number of talented individuals in succession at that time, for example, Lu Zhi, Pei Du, Liu Yan, Han Yu, Liu Zongyuan, Bai Juyi, Liu Yuxi, and others in the mid-Tang Dynasty, and Fan Zhongyan, Ouyang Xiu, Huang Tingjian, Qin Guan, Liu Yong, Shen Kuo, Su Song, Wang Anshi, Sima Guang, the Su brothers (Su Shi and his younger brother, Su Zhe), Zhou Dunyi, Shao Yong, Zhang Zai, the Cheng brothers (Cheng Hao and Cheng Yi), Zeng Gong, and others in the Northern Song Dynasty. All of these individuals succeeded in the arena of the imperial examinations and then gained the chance to display their talents and put them to good use. To some extent, the imperial examination system offered them a platform to showcase their talents. Foreigners could also participate in the imperial examinations, and Abe no nakamaro (Zhao Heng) from Japan; Kim Keji, Choe Chiwon, and Tsui Yan from Korea; Li Yan from Da Shi (currently an Arabic region), and others all succeeded in the imperial exam one after another. The policy of opening the examination system to the world indeed played an active role in discovering and cultivating talents.

3. The imperial examination system influenced literature and historical science in ancient China. It led directly to the prosperity of poetry in the Tang Dynasty and of articles in the Song Dynasty. It bred the diligent practice of ancient intellectuals.

The imperial examination system focused primarily on literature and historical science. For example, the imperial examination system in the Tang Dynasty was centered on poetry and prose. After the time of Tian Bao (742 to 756), it was authorized that when a candidate failed the test of classics, he could make it up in the poetry test. So the quality of examinees' poems often directly impacted their test score. Sometimes the role of the poems was decisive. By this means, candidates attached great importance to the creation of poems. The largest number of poets in Chinese history thus played a decisive role in the prosperity of poems in the Tang Dynasty.[36] As to the 50,000 poems collected in the *Complete Tang Poems*, they outnumbered three to one the total volume of poems of the more than 1,600 years from the Western Zhou Dynasty to the Sui Dynasty. In the poetic circles of the Tang Dynasty, "at the peaceful and splendid time, many talents were recruited as officials, all having outstanding talents, and they were like stars in the Milk River,"[37] talented poets like Li Bai and Du Fu stood out, and numerous renowned masterpieces of various styles emerged. This time was completely exceptional in China's history.

The imperial examination system formed a direct link between learning and a political career, galvanized ancient intellectuals to study diligently, and made intellectuals walk on a path of assiduous study to obtain an official position. Thus, widespread stories were passed down from ancient China, like studying tirelessly by tying one's hair to a beam and jabbing one's leg with an awl, digging a hole in the wall to borrow a neighbor's light to study by, reading by the light of bagged fireflies, waking up to study as the cocks crow, hanging up curtains to seclude oneself from the outside to study, and burying oneself in studies without one look at the garden. To date, the diligence of Chinese students is still admired and praised by intellectuals throughout the world.

4. The imperial examination system strengthened the ancient intellectuals' pursuit of fame and fortune, largely decaying their minds and devastating their spirits and personalities.

The nature of the imperial examination system can be defined as "he who excels in learning can be an official," which meant that the purpose of learning was to seek political success. Although only a small proportion of intellectuals became officials, success in the imperial examination system demonstrated the likelihood of becoming an official. This vague possibility obsessed the ancient intellectuals: "Although one failed in one part of the examination, one could gain ground in another part. One examination after another, people turned old in a flash."[38] Pu Songling of the Qing Dynasty vividly described how the imperial examination system decayed intellectuals' minds and devastated their spirits in the story "Wang Zi'an" from *Strange Tales from a Chinese Studio*:

> There were seven metaphors to describe the situation of a Xiu Cai when he took the imperial exam: When an intellectual entered the examination compound, he was bare-footed and held a basket, like a beggar. When the examiner called the roll, the examiner's attendant scolded the intellectual as if he had been a prisoner. The intellectuals walked into the room, with their feet visible through a slot in the door. They were like the late-autumn bees. After they walked out of the compound at the end of the examination, they were dejected and depressed as if the color of the sky had altered. The intellectuals were like sick birds outside their cage. When they waited for the good news, they were alert and had illusions. At one moment they dreamed of constructing a building within a flash. The next moment, they had a bad dream of a skeleton rotting within a breath. Then they would become uneasy as if they were tied monkeys. All of a sudden, a man on horseback delivered the news that the intellectual was not on the list. Then the intellectual's expression changed as if he had died. It was as though he had been bitten by mosquitoes that had fed on poison, and he became senseless. When he lost his ambition the very first time, he would abuse the chief examiner. If he failed the essay, he would burn all of his stationery, which would at least diminish his anger and resentment. He would continue to stamp on them and throw the fallen pieces into ditches. From then on he would live in the mountains wearing his hair down and facing the stone wall. He was determined to chase people away if they showed him any essays related to the imperial examination system. However, as time passed, his anger and resentment vanished, and he was overwhelmed with itches. At this time, he was like a bird which had broken through its egg and had started to build a new nest.

Ancient intellectuals squandered their life trying to master the imperial examination system, adhering to it and depleting their efforts. Moreover, some candidates resorted to any means to take a shortcut to fame and political power. According to *The Collected Tales of Tang*, under the reign of the emperors of the Ming Dynasty, there were a large number of intellectuals. Over 1,000 intellectuals participated in the metropolitan examination. Candidates within the examination compound visited each other and formed gangs to exclude other candidates. Well-known candidates were elected as the heads of the gangs. Candidates from the powerful and wealthy families always followed the pattern of blocking the sight of the examiners. Those candidates who failed in the exam would make noises. As for those poor intellectuals who had neither wealthy nor powerful families to depend on, they could merely bow servilely to ask someone to make recommendations. Bribing the chief examiner and referrer and cheating in the exam were common among the powerful and wealthy.

Xu Dachun, at the beginning of the Qing Dynasty, depicted and satirized intellectuals under the imperial system:

> Intellectuals are the worst because their articles are like mud. The government intends to recruit talents; however, it turns out that examinees are resorting to cheating means. Defining the theme with three sentences, analyzing the theme in another two sentences, and raving from the beginning to the end will gain access to success. Do they know the Three Books, *Tong Dian*, *Tong Zhi*, and *Wen Xian Tong Kao*, and the Four History Books, *The Historical Records*, the *Book of Han*, the *Book of the Later Han*, and the *Records of the Three Kingdoms*? Do they know when the Emperor Hanzu and the Emperor Tangzong reigned? On their desk lie good articles, yet they still buy the tools to cheat. Their backs become stooped, and their mouths open and close as if they were immersed in learning, but they are simply repeating old knowledge. Does it taste good? They just idle away time and life. But they gain official positions by cheating. Indeed this is the bad fortune of the royal court![39]

Zhou Jin, Fan Jin, and others in *The Scholars*, created by Wu Jingzi, were typical of learners under the imperial examination system.

5. The imperial examination system diminished the educational function of academies and exerted a negative influence on the purpose of education, teaching content, and teaching methods.

The educational functions of academies were diverse, as political, economic, cultural, and psychological issues were taught. Education impacted society and individual students via these functions. But the imperial examination system diminished the educational function of academies, thus devaluing the education affiliated with them. Thus, the waxing and waning of influence between the imperial exam system and academies lasted during the later period of feudal society. In the early period of the Song Dynasty, Fan Zhongyan devised the reform of the imperial examination system and the establishment of academies as follows:

> At present, if an academy has a good teacher, he can teach the Six Classics and pass down the principles of statecraft and the ways of governing citizens. Yet the government selects officials based on poems and articles and arranges tests according to the righteousness of Moyi (quick written answers upon reading text perfectly). The intellectuals always give up their principles and follow less worthy ones. Although intellectuals crowd the royal court, the talented ones are in the minority. After all, the country is at risk, and there is a shortage of talented people. Thus, education should be made a priority and a pillar of industry for the economy. People with industrial minds should be selected, and perhaps the plight can be improved.[40]

Although Fan Zhongyan and Wang Anshi both introduced the reform of academies, the Ming and Qing Dynasties had a rule that "academies have to serve the imperial system"; thus, academies were doomed to decline. Academies fell to the role of "grooming talents to cope with the imperial examination system" and thus became affiliated with the imperial examination system. Accordingly, Tang Chenglie of the Qing Dynasty stated in *On the Academy*, "A country establishes academies, and they are guided by the imperial examination system, so there is no true edification. Then citizens will not study." This is the so-called "prosperity of the imperial exam system and perishing of the academies."[41]

Under the imperial examination system, the educational goal of the academy was to prepare intellectuals for the imperial examinations. The content and method of the imperial examinations became the general focus of the academies' teaching content and the measure by which students' learning was assessed. For example, in the Tang Dynasty, the curricula of the Imperial Academy, the Imperial College, and the national school Si Men Xue were arranged according to the nine classics studied in the imperial examination system. The nine classics were divided into great, intermediate, and small classics. If the candidate had to know two classics, one was to be a great classic and the other a small one or two intermediate ones. If the candidate had to know three classics, he was to know a great one, an intermediate one, and a small one. If the candidate had to know five classics, he was to know all the great classics, as well as *The Analects of Confucius* and *Filial Piety*. During the Qing Dynasty, "for the implementation of selecting talents via the eight-part essay, the eight-part essay flourished whereas the influence of the Six Classics faded. The eighteen-examiner system became widespread, whereas the *Twenty-One Histories* fell."[42]

Beginning in elementary school, candidates had received instruction in the structure and composition of the eight-part essay. Orthodox classics of

Confucianism were neglected and could not be listed in the curricula. Academies became the pre-school for the imperial examination system. If the academy could not meet the needs of the imperial examination system, the academy would be ignored. So, candidates would register in an academy and then go back home to study the eight-part essay.

6. The imperial examination system contributed to extreme autocracy, encouraged the pervasive consciousness of the "official rank standard," and left feudal society stagnant for a long time.

As Mr. Jin Zheng said in *The Imperial Examination System and Chinese Culture*, the development of the imperial examination system was also the development of the centralized feudal monarchy. The increase in the emperor's power was in step with the decrease in the power of the wealthy and powerful aristocrats whose power was based on heredity. On one hand, this was helpful for the society's unity and stability. On the other hand, it facilitated the extreme autocracy of the power of the emperor. Officials who had achieved their political careers by way of the imperial examination system relied on the results of examinations in the name of the emperor instead of on hereditary status and privilege, so they naturally feared and depended on royal power. Likewise, the emperor controlled the whole official class through the imperial examination system and then controlled the whole society through the officials. The French Enlightenment thinker Montesquieu once said, "Powerful people will continue to exert their power until they are stopped." Thus, the "abuse of power should be prevented, and power should be restricted with power." But in the structure of an ancient centralized country, there existed no power higher than the imperial power. So the emperor, with supreme power over everything, could randomly enrich or impoverish and honor or trample his people, and control the country within his hand and mobilize civilians as servants.

Since the imperial examination system connected learning with being an official, learning was no longer a way to entertain, refine one's temperament, obtain knowledge, and develop intelligence. It became a tool to enter politics. Once the candidate (Ju Ren or Jin Shi) succeeded, he could enjoy enormous fame and wealth. Thus, "official-oriented" thought emerged at first among the representatives of culture and then throughout society. One characteristic of official-oriented thought was a strong desire for a powerful political position. The second was being in awe of officials, absolutely obedient to officials, and behaving according to officials' facial expressions. Mr Li Dazhao stated:

> Chinese people have a hereditary nature in dealing with examinations. Be it activity, culture, system, or career, it is a kind of examination or test. This means saying words by heart to pander to examiners. People even regard time, thought, cultural activities, and social psychology as the content of an

examination. Words they say and articles they compose are silent papers trying to figure out the examiners' thoughts, having nothing to do with their real lives.[43]

The third characteristic of official-oriented thought was the "dream of being an honest official with integrity," that is, longing for an honest official to manage society. This is the reason Bao Zheng and Hai Rui were highly praised throughout the ages. "Longing to be an official" was fundamental. If the ideal of "being an official" was undermined, "fear of officials" ensued, and the "dream of being an honest official with integrity" faded.

There were many factors that contributed to the longtime stagnation of ancient China's feudal society, and the imperial examination system could be counted as one. The imperial examination system was open to the general public, and equal competition made the intelligentsia submerge themselves in political careers and never consider reforming. The imperial examination system contributed to complete political organization, which controlled and improved society. The whole country performed simple and easy tasks and repeated them again and again, maintaining the frozen long-term stability, but also stagnation, of society.

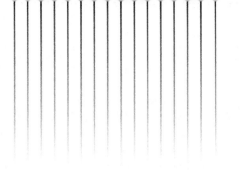

9

The Academy and Ancient China's Education

The academy of classical learning is an achievement of vigorous development in the history of ancient China's education. As a special educational form and system, the academy blossomed under the historical circumstances of the decline of state-owned and private schools. In some ways, it was the beginning of educational reform in ancient China.

The academy experienced both boom and bust after the Song Dynasty, and it withered with the rise of modern schools. Yet, as a unique educational institution in ancient times, it not only produced intellectuals and talents generation after generation, but also formed a sound tradition of teaching and management. Great educators after the Song Dynasty were all associated with academies. When Zhang Zhengfan, an expert on educational history, commented on academies, he pointed out that academies "exerted a profound influence on education, society, politics, and academic thinking. In terms of education, academies were far superior to modern universities for their splendid seats, free ways of teaching, unity of instruction and lessons, providing education for all people without discrimination, teaching students according to their aptitude, emphasis on creativity, and initiative."[1]

When Chairman Mao established the Hunan Self-Study University for educating officials in Changsha, he advocated that we should draw lessons from the management of academies in ancient times. He also stated that "absorbing the strength of ancient academies into modern schools and adopting voluntary ways to study science of all types could reveal truth, cultivate talents, popularize culture, and circulate science throughout society."[2] It can be seen that academy education had become an integral part of Chinese education and a valuable treasure in the realm of Chinese educational thought.

The Origin and Rise of the Academy

Strictly speaking, the academy came into being in the Song Dynasty. But the word "academy," which referred to a place for the official collection and collation of books or a private school, first appeared in the Tang Dynasty.[3] *The New Book of Tang: Treatises on Art and Culture* explained the origin and process of the authority involved in establishing the academies:

> Emperor Xuanzong of the Tang Dynasty designated Ma Huaisu, Zuo Sanqi Changshi (an imperial advisor and attendant), and a scholar from Zhao Wen Guan (the Institute for the Glorification of Literature) as envoys to rectify the books, along with Zhu Wuliang, You Sanqi Changshi (an imperial advisor and attendant), as well as a scholar from Chong Wen Guan (the Institute for the Promotion of Literature). They gathered in the east of the capital and collated books in Qianyuan Palace. Zhu Wuliang suggested that the choice of books should be based on the works of Prime Ministers Song Jing and Su Ting, such as stories from the time of Zhenguan (the name of the era of the Tang Dynasty when the emperor was Li Shimin) and that civilian transcriptions should also be included. When they went back to the capital, the books were relocated to Lizheng Hall in the East Palace, and a compound for collation was established in the Zhuzuo (Works) Yard. Later expansions of Ji Xian Academy (the Academy for Intellectuals) were established outside Guangshun Gate of the Daming Palace and Mingfu Gate of the Eastern Capital (Luoyang). Intellectuals came to read here.

From this, we can see that official academies were similar to royal libraries.

Meanwhile, quite a few private academies began to emerge in civil society. Chen Yuanhui and others read about 11 academies from *Complete Tang Poems*.[4] Wang Jingdi discovered "a total of 11" from local chronicles.[5] However, there may have been more than 11 academies. These private academies were always named after a person, such as Li Mi Academy, Zhao Kunji Academy, and the Shen Bin Academy for Successful Intellectuals. These features were the same for both local and private academies. Unlike official academies, whose goal was to collect and collate books, private academies featured individual teaching and lectures given by professors; for example, "Liu Qingxia lectured in Huang Liao

Academy" and "Chen lectured the students of Song Zhou Academy." Although these academies could not be compared with those of the Song Dynasty, they were the origins of future educational institutions.

Until the beginning of the Song Dynasty, academies developed rapidly, but they then fell into a pattern of gradual decline for the following three reasons. First, state-owned schools fell into disrepair, and intellectuals became frustrated by the lack of schools. From the end of the Tang Dynasty until the time of the Five Dynasties, the country was in tumult, schools were left in ruins, education declined, and learners longed for schools in which to study. At the beginning of the Song Dynasty, the country returned to peace, and society called for talents, reigniting the impetus for intellectuals to seek education. New educational institutions basing themselves on the private academies of the past and substitutes for official education came into being at the right moment.

Second, the government sponsored and protected academies. At the beginning of the Song Dynasty, academies filled the gap in official education and met society's need for developing talents, so academies received government funding. Many academies received honored books, honored tablets, and farmland from the emperor. For example, in the year 977, Bailudong Academy received the printed version of nine classics from the emperor; in 1009, Yingtianfu Academy received an honored tablet; and Yuelu Academy received honored books in 999 and a tablet in 1015. Maoshan Academy received farmland from the emperor in 1024. The government not only gained control of academies by becoming their sponsors, but also transformed some private academies into official institutions.

Third, Buddhists influenced the academy system by giving lectures. Since the end of the Han Dynasty, when Buddhism was introduced to China, it had become increasingly influential. Buddhism prospered in the Wei and Jin Dynasties and reached its peak of influence during the Tang Dynasty. Disciples of Buddhism often built temples in places of interest and in forests as places for them to learn, practice, and give lectures. This had a certain influence on the choice of location for academies in the early Song Dynasty, with many being established in places with picturesque scenery.

The Records of Bailudong Academy, composed by Lv Zuqian, a scholar of the Song Dynasty, explained why academies thrived in the early Song Dynasty:

I was pleased to know that at the very beginning of the state when wars and conflicts had just ended, there were not many scholars, and learning gradually became popular. Confucian scholars mainly stayed in mountains and forests and lectured in their leisure time. By and large, there were over 100 scholars. Songyang Academy, Yuelu Academy, Zhuiyang Academy, and Shidong Academy were the four famous academies at the time.

Zhu Xi also mentioned academies at the beginning of the Song Dynasty in *Records of Renovating Shigu Academy*: "State-owned schools of the previous dynasties were in ruins, and learners were anxious for places in which to learn. So they chose places of interests and built fine houses for teaching. Meanwhile, the emperor praised and granted awards to academies, such as Cishan Academy, Yuelu Academy, and Bailudong Academy." Along with the academies mentioned above, Shigu, Maoshan, Hualin, and Leitang were also famous academies.

The Development and Evolution of the Academy

Academies started to become renowned at the very beginning of the Song Dynasty, yet they declined afterward. One of the main reasons for this decline was the impact of the imperial examination system. In the early Song Dynasty, the imperial examinations were held on a very small scale. During the reign of Emperor Taizu of the Song Dynasty, there were only 11 or 12 candidates. Thus, the royal court granted awards to academies. With the expansion of the imperial examination system, academies became of minor importance to the government. The imperial examination system was particularly emphasized during the rule of Emperor Zhenzong, who encouraged and guided learners with *Encouraging Learning*:

> To be better off, you need not invest in fertile lands, for books will promise a bumper harvest. To own a home, you need not collect huge logs, for books will build a luxurious mansion at your feet. To find a wife, you need not seek a professional matchmaker, for books will pair you with the fairest. To travel, you need not anticipate being a lonely walker, for books will arrange an impressive parade of entourages and carriages like a moving forest. If one wishes to realize these life goals, he had better pore over Confucian books with great interest.[6]

Due to the fact that the imperial examination system was greatly emphasized, learners began to chase after fame and wealth and chose not to study in academies located in serene settings in mountains and forests. Further, the promotion of academies during the times of Qingli, Xining, and Chongning in the Song Dynasty had a great effect. Although the drawbacks of the imperial examination system were righted and social reforms were made, official schooling continued to thrive and private schools fell. The government did not care about, and had no time to care about, the development of academies. The most severe move was to stipulate that scholars could not participate in the imperial examination system until they had studied for 300 days in official institutes, which essentially cut off the student resources for the academies. At the time, the life scholars dreamed of was entering official schools, succeeding in the imperial examinations, and pursuing higher official positions and salaries in the end.

Therefore, as two educational systems which coexisted in Chinese feudal society, academies and the imperial examination system restricted each other and experienced boom and bust in turn.

Academies in the Northern Song Dynasty remained in ruins for 145 years. It was when Zhu Xi renovated Bailudong Academy in the Southern Song Dynasty that academies began to prosper again. In 1179, Zhu Xi was head of Nankang County. Directly after he came to office, he asked about the ruins of Bailudong Academy by announcing his question to the public and investigating it himself. He wrote, "Remember the prosperity of the academy that year; there were many scholars." Under the supervision of Zhu Xi, Bailudong Academy was preliminarily renovated in the following year and began to give lectures. Zhu Xi also gathered land and books, hired scholars, recruited students, defined rules, and even lectured in the academy, making it renowned and influencing the development of academies in the Southern Song Dynasty to some degree. Other academies were subsequently renovated or newly established. It took only 20 years for academies to establish a new image of flourishing and thriving all over the land.

Of course, it was not the case that the success of academies in the Southern Song Dynasty should be completely attributed to Zhu Xi. Objectively speaking, their success was based on the demand of the time.

First, the renewal of academies met the demand to disseminate academic thought. In the Northern Song period, academic thought was rather active, but scholars were typically accustomed to systematic personal exploration or the teaching method of one-on-one instruction. So when the Neo-Confucian philosophers were well prepared and became theoretically and organizationally mature, it was urgent for them to disseminate their academic thoughts, expand their influence, and strengthen their personnel massively.

As a result, the masters of Neo-Confucianism were involved in using or establishing academies to recruit students and cultivate their successors and disseminators. For example, Zhu Xi, Lu Jiuyuan, and Lv Zuqian, the three most renowned masters of Neo-Confucianism at the time, were all devoted to disseminating their academic thought with their academies as a base.

Second, the rise of academies was the result of the decline of official education. Although the three education reforms of the Northern Song Dynasty had strengthened official education for some time, they eventually failed, with official education turning out to be ineffective.

The decline of official education can be attributed to two underlying reasons: on one hand, the development of official education had made the students of the Imperial College a politically powerful clan that was difficult for the upper-class rulers to control; on the other hand, large-scale official education was a great burden on the expenditures of the dynasty, so funding had to be cut and eventually withdrawn. Zhu Xi once described official education in Chong'an County, Jianning Province:

> Chong'an County had official schools but no fields, so when a virtuous and talented scholar was intended to teach there, they had to cut other expenditures to hire the scholar. And when they were unable to make ends meet for some reason, the students would starve and eventually leave. As a result, the palaces and halls were left collapsed and the rooms deserted. This was the case for the past ten years.[7]

Academies, primarily funded privately, took the opportunity to become a supplement to official education. Further, the corruption of the imperial examination, the advanced printing industry, and lectures given in the academies by famous masters had all inserted strong vigor into the resurgence of the academies in the Southern Song Dynasty. The number of academies skyrocketed to 185 in the Southern Song Period from just 38 in the Northern Song Period.[8]

In the Yuan Dynasty, academies continued to prosper. When Kubla Khan conquered the whole country, many scholars of the former Southern Song Dynasty retreated from official careers to establish academies, recruit students, and give lectures. Therefore, many private academies were established in this period. Further, the rulers of the Yuan Dynasty adopted conciliatory policies and issued an imperial edict ordering, "In places that were civilized by late learned man and traveled by virtuous people, the government will, together with charitable families, fund scholars with money and food and establish academies."[9] Meanwhile, rulers had strengthened their control over academies by putting presidents in charge of them, commissioned by the royal government. Other personnel, such as teachers, administrative officers, and officers in charge of financial affairs, appointed and paid by the Board of Rites and Ceremonies, were also hired. In this way, academies were made official.

Hence, in the Yuan Dynasty, academies began to surge in numbers but greatly decline in quality. Since the presidents in charge were not famous masters or recommended by famous masters, but were provincial graduates, the academic quality of academies was greatly undermined. Moreover, now that they were funded by the government, they had to speak bureaucratically, which was a betrayal of the tradition of the academy as an independent entity.

Under the reign of Emperor Chengzong, learned people were brought together to compile works. Yu Ji once attacked the corrupt practices of the miscellaneous teachers, saying, "If the principle of respecting teachers is established, then there will be many virtuous people. But the teachers in the country now are not qualified to teach. With these people managing students, no one can believe them. In this way, how can the principle of respecting teachers be established?"[10] The bureaucratic tendency of the academy was particularly prominent following the Ming Dynasty when private academies accounted for less than 20 percent of all academies, which undoubtedly exerted a significant influence on the nature and features of academies in the later period of Chinese feudal society.

In the Ming Dynasty, academies underwent a process of developing from a state of decline to thriving and finally to yet another decline. Although the two academies Zhusi and Nishan were established in the early Ming Dynasty, they were nothing but window dressing and were academies only in name. After a 100-year period of stagnation, academies again rose during the periods of Chenghua and Hongzhi. The renowned Bailudong Academy was restored in 1465, the first year of the Chenghua Period. Until the reign of Emperor Jiajing, academies thrived and were popular among scholars, with lectures being given freely.

The academy reached a high point in development and influence during the Ming Dynasty. At the time, the popularity of academies was related to "the decline and destruction of official education and the acute corruption of the imperial examination system" and was especially influenced by the social climate of lecture-giving advocated by Wang Yangming and Zhan Ruoshui, among others. For example, as was stated in *History of the Ming Dynasty: Biography 119*:

> During the period of Zhengjia, Wang Shouren brought students together in the military, and the day Xu Jie was promoted chancellor (head of the officers in ancient China's feudal society), he gave a lecture. The message spread quickly, and the whole country was shocked and intrigued. Retired officials and reclusive elders began to give lectures and establish academies and would often communicate with each other.

According to historical records, Wang Yangming established Longgang Academy, presided over Guiyang Academy, restored Lianxi Academy, and established Jishan Academy and Fuwen Academy. Therefore, it is safe to say that academies became popular wherever he went. Although Zhan Ruoshui did not agree with Wang Yangming in terms of academic thought, he shared his love for academies and said, "Wherever he traveled, he would establish an academy in honor of his teacher Baisha, and he had followers from all places in the country."[11] When the two died, their students established a large number of academies in honor of them. Wang Yangming's students alone established academies in as many as 17 locations, covering the provinces of Jiangxi, Fujian, Zhejiang, Hunan, Guangdong, Anhui, Henan, Shandong, and Jiangsu.

In the late Ming Dynasty, the academy suffered many times and eventually declined from its heyday. Four instances were due to influence from the royal government. The first instance was in 1537, the sixteenth year of the reign of Emperor Jiajing, when You Jujing and Yu Shi (the investigating censor) accused Zhan Ruoshui of "spreading vicious thoughts, recruiting villains, and establishing academies without authorization."[12] Therefore, Emperor Shizong of the Ming Dynasty ordered officials to destroy these academies, which began the history of academies being destroyed.

In the following year, Xu Zan, the Minister of Civil Officials, applied to the emperor to destroy state-run academies, claiming that they were money-consuming and would disturb ordinary people, and his application "was approved by the Emperor."[13]

Then, in 1579, the seventh year of the Wanli Period, Prime Minister Zhang Juzheng, claiming that academies were "places used by gangs to meet and indulge in empty talk" and "would cause social unrest and affect the stability of the monarchy on a large scale and shelter evil and vicious people on a smaller scale,"[14] "destroyed 64 provincial academies, including Yingtian Academy."[15]

The fourth instance of the destruction of academies took place in 1625, the fifth year of the Tianqi Period. After gaining power, the eunuch Wei Zhongxian was dissatisfied with the Confucianists of Donglin Academy, for they "made ironic comments on the empire and officials." Accordingly, he falsified an imperial edict to destroy academies across the country. The academies in the Ming Dynasty were thus greatly undermined and once again fell into decay.

In the early Qing Dynasty, academies continued to be undermined due to the suppression imposed by the royal government.[16] The ban was not officially abolished until the reign of Emperor Yongzheng, when society was again peaceful and officials and ordinary people began calling for the restoration of academies. In 1733, the eleventh year of the Yongzheng Period, the government of the Qing Dynasty ordered all provinces to establish academies "and choose virtuous and talented people within each province to study in academies; they should work hard in their study and devote themselves to practice so as to make achievements and gain success." The academies were funded officially: "The government will make budgets for the academies and help students with their costs so as to guarantee their normal functioning. And when the funding is not enough, government owned funds can be used."[17] At the same time, it was decided that the president in charge of an academy was to be hired by the officials in charge of education within the province, students of academies were to be tested and evaluated by Dao Yuan (a local official) and a chief secretary together within the province, and privately established academies were required to request approval from the government. These measures not only strengthened the leadership of the government over state-run academies, but also made it possible to supervise privately established academies. Since the ban on academies had been lifted, the academy could now continue to develop.

According to records, in the Qing Dynasty, academies became much larger in number and more extensive in geographical distribution. Remote areas, such as Yunnan, Gansu, Xinjiang, and Taiwan, also began establishing academies.[18] The academies of the Qing Dynasty can be classified into four categories. Academies focusing on teaching Neo-Confucianism fell into the first group, such as the Guanzhong Academy, Donglin Academy, and Ziyang Academy in the early Qing Dynasty, which conformed to the teaching method of discussion and debate, following the traditions of the Song Dynasty. The second group contained academies teaching classics, history, poetry, and articles, among which the most famous ones were Gujing Vihara (the School of Interpreting Classics, in Hangzhou) and Xue Hai Tang (the Hall of the Learning Sea, in Guangzhou). These academies advocated free study and the method of teaching students in accordance with their aptitude. The third group of academies focused on the imperial examinations, and made up most of the academies in the Qing Dynasty. They focused on learning eight-part essays and can be considered preparatory schools for scholars wishing to take the imperial examinations. The fourth group of academies consisted of those mainly teaching and learning the modern science of the Western world, such as the Polytechnic Institution in Shanghai and Hebei Academy in Zhili. Although still called academies, they were, in fact, similar to modern institutions of higher education.[19]

In 1901, the twenty-seventh year of the Guangxu Period, the Qing government adopted the ideas of *The Top Priority: To Change the Way of Developing Political Talents*, by Zhang Zhidong and Liu Kunyi, and issued an imperial decree that all academies should be reformed. Those in the provinces were to be transformed into high schools, those in prefectures transformed into middle schools, and those in counties transformed into elementary schools. From then on, the academy system of ancient China, which first appeared in the late Tang Dynasty and lasted for nearly 1,000 years, disintegrated.

However, the spirit of the academy and the experience of running academies never became outdated, but were inherited by later generations, becoming essential to educational thought in China.

The Characteristics and Contributions of the Academy

Although the academy-based education of ancient China underwent ups and downs, it still lasted for nearly 1,000 years with strong vigor and vitality. As a kind of special educational institution of the later period of China's feudal society, the academy emphasized free teaching and learning, attached great significance to academic research, advocated free communication between different schools, and called for mutual respect and love between teachers and students, resulting in official education and the imperial examination system being left behind. It was a splendid era in ancient Chinese education with its unique teaching methods. The rich experience in methodology and school management that the system of academy education accumulated has become an important part of the favorable tradition of China's educational thought.

1. By combining education with academic research, academy education played a key role in preserving, creating, and disseminating culture.

As stated above, the early academies were places for official book preservation and book revision. They were also places for private individuals to collect books and study. For example, the Lizheng and Jixian Academies of the Tang Dynasty organized a group of scholars and officials responsible for compiling books, including Xue Shi (a scholar-official), Zhi Xue Shi (a scholar-official of a lower rank), Shi Jiang Xue Shi (a scholar-official working as a consultant for the emperor), compiling officials, collating officials, and librarian officials, to "print and compile classics so as to determine theories that could help to strengthen the country."[20] They not only were responsible for revising and collating books but also acted as consultants to learners. Hence, they had to concentrate much of their attention on research and boasted high-level academic ability. As for private academies, which usually had rich collections of books, they also attracted numerous hard-working students to enquire about, read, and discuss books. Therefore, academies were born with a highly academic focus.

Academies have been an important cultural platform for learned people since the Song Dynasty, and the conception and formation of their thoughts can be generally attributed to their unique atmosphere, rich collections of books, as well as the discussions between teachers and students. The origins of many important academic works were owed to the lectures given in academies. For example, when Zhu Xi was teaching at Bailudong Academy, he began with teaching the first chapter of *The Doctrine of the Mean*, and his teaching materials also included *Certain Questions About the Great Learning* and *Questions from the Class of Bailudong Academy*. Therefore, it was assumed that *Notes on the Four Books*, Zhu Xi's classic, was "based on the teaching materials used in his accumulated years of teaching practice and was compiled into a complete work after further revision and collation."[21] Due to the invention of typography in the Song Dynasty, academies were gifted with the ability to engrave and print books, in addition to the book collection, revision, and collation they were already doing, which not only was a reflection of their teaching level and research achievements, but also helped disseminate academic information, enrich teaching content, and therefore promote the development of academies and the dissemination of culture.

In the Song Dynasty, "academy books" became widespread, and academies became a significant publishing and printing force in ancient China. The books compiled and printed by the ancient academies can be categorized as follows. First, there were the important ancient classics, for example, the *Guangya Series of Books* by Guangya Academy, which compiled a complete series of historical books since the Tang and Song Dynasties. The second group consisted of the research results of the scholars of the day. For example, *Xue Hai Tang's Interpretations on Classics* by Xue Hai Tang (the Hall of the Learning Sea) contained 180 books commented on and annotated by the classics teachers, totaling 1,400 volumes. *The Collected Works of Xue Hai Tang* compiled the academic works of 500 people. The third group consisted of historical records and documents about the academies. For example, *Yuelu Academy in Pictures* by Sun Cun and *Records of Bailudong Academy* by Liu Jun, as recorded in *History of the Ming Dynasty: Records of Arts and Literature*, contained important historical records about academies printed by academies. The fourth group consisted of the teaching and research achievements of teachers and students in academies, such as *Enlightenment on the Book of Changes*, which contained the teaching materials of Duo Feng edited by Yuelu Academy, and *Works of Yuelu Academy*, *Articles of Yuelu Academy*, and *Class Discussions of Yuelu Academy*, which were collections of essays from the students of Yuelu Academy.[22] The Zhengyi Academy in Suzhou, with a rich collection of about 60,000 volumes, recorded the reading experience and questions of teachers and students every day and compiled these into *Diaries of Xuegutang* (*Learnings from the Ancients*), which played an important role in promoting the academic research of teachers and students. Education and studies helped each other forward, whereas printing and publication added a driving force and pressure to them, which brought academy education to a higher academic level and made great contributions to the preservation, creation, and dissemination of ancient culture.

2. Academies combined self-study with instruction, attached great importance to inspiring the thoughts of students, and motivated students so that a number of intelligent talents were cultivated.

Since academies were characterized by rich collections of books, the teaching activities in academies were generally centered on books. Students spent most of their time carefully reading books under the instruction of teachers and trying to understand by themselves. Teachers would either explain and analyze the critical points or point out the right direction to students and answer their questions. They would also often teach students according to their abilities.

Zhu Xi once told his students, "When learning, one should not rely on others to point out the essence but should find the answer by oneself."[23] He required his students to pay attention to self-study.

Academy education advocated self-study, which did not mean that students were left alone to do as they wanted. This method actually paid great attention to the instructive role of teachers, which was characterized by two aspects. The first was to guide the students when they were reading. Academies had always attached great importance to guiding students in reading and had specific requirements for students, from which book to read to which to read first, which to read last, which for intensive reading, which for overview reading, which to be recited, and which to be read cursorily. Many teachers would also pass their experience of reading and learning down to their students, such as the *Reading Methods of Zhuzi* and the *Yearly Agenda of Book Reading for the Family School of the Cheng Clan*, mentioned in Chapter Seven.

The other teaching method highlighting the instructive role of teachers was to answer students' doubts and questions. Academy education emphasized that students should be good at raising questions, and students were encouraged to ask and discuss questions. Zhu Xi once told his students, "Those with no doubts should be taught to be doubtful, whereas those with questions should have their questions answered; only when reaching this step, can one really make progress."[24] Further, he said, "When reading books, students must think critically even in ordinary places, and when many doubts emerge, one must concentrate on answering the questions, even to the degree of forgetting to eat or sleep. Only in this way can one make progress."[25] He not only advocated doubts and inquiry, but taught his students methods to doubt.

Many academies would examine and manage the methods of reading and questioning. For example, in the Qing Dynasty, the Longmen Academy in Shanghai stated, "Students should prepare notebooks to write diaries about their behaviors and reading," and "Whenever one has any thoughts or questions, one should record them in his notebook according to date. The records should be true and not falsified, terse and not verbose. One cannot make any excuse for not recording thoughts and questions. And on every fifth day of every month, one should present his notebook to his teacher so as to answer his questions and improve himself."[26] In this way, reading and instruction were well combined.

A number of intelligent talents were cultivated owing to the teaching method of academies, which had motivated the students and combined the self-study of students with the instructions of teachers. For example, in the Song Dynasty, Daoyi Academy cultivated Wu Cheng, a master of Neo-Confucianism, who blended the theories of Zhu Xi and Lu Jiuyuan. Yingtaodong Academy and Zhitai Academy cultivated many famous writers and historians, such as Song Xiang, Song Qi, Huang Zhu, Huang Xu, and Huang Shu, among whom Huang Tingjian of the Poetic School of Jiangxi was one of the best. In the Song Dynasty, the Cheng brothers, Cheng Hao and Cheng Yi, studied for some time in the academy that had fostered Zhou Dunyi and Wang Fuzhi, who also studied at Yuelu Academy. Almost every renowned academy cultivated a number of renowned figures. And many renowned figures never forgot to help their academies, often returning to teach and cultivate further talents after they had become famous. For example, in the Northern Song Dynasty, Fan Zhongyan, a student of Yingtian Academy for five years, spent eight years in the academy teaching and giving lectures after he had become well-known and known as an "outstanding talent."

3. Academies combined teaching with morality education and attached great importance to moral improvement and personality education. Accordingly, a spirit of emphasizing the cultivation of personality was developed.

Mr. Zhang Zhengfan once summarized the characteristic of academy education as "the integrity of teaching and morality education." He said:

> For about 100 years, from the Song, Yuan, and Ming Dynasties to the Qing Dynasty, although there had been changes and supplements to the teaching content and regulations of academies, their purposes remained consistent, that is, to guide people's hearts from going astray by providing academic education and making up for the shortcomings of official schools. That is to say, the true academy education of our country has been the education of personality; as for the proposal of freely doing academic research and the instruction of knowledge, they are merely supplementary.[27]

The characteristic of emphasizing moral improvement and personality education was best reflected in the "school regulations" of the academies. The most representative regulations of academies were the *School Regulations for Bailudong Academy*, formulated by Zhu Xi. In these rules, Zhu Xi outlined education in terms of five basic ethical aspects (there is kinship between father and son, righteousness between emperor and minister, distinction between husband and wife, sequence between senior and junior, and trust between friends), the order of learning, and the essential elements of cultivation (one should speak honestly and act sincerely and respectfully; one should restrain his anger and desire, striving to be good and correct his mistakes), the principles of dealing with things (one should guide himself with moral rules against the pursuit of personal benefit when doing things and should point out the right way without striving for fame and personal benefit), and the principles of getting along with others (do unto others as you would have done to you; when failing to accomplish one's goals, one should turn to oneself to find solutions).

After listing these points, Zhu Xi clearly declared his thoughts on running schools, stating that academies should pay more attention to fostering personality than to strengthening abilities in poetry and prose. He said:

> I had studied privately why the ancient wise man and virtuous man taught people to read and learn, and I found that their purpose was to make people understand ethical rules and principles so as to improve themselves physically and mentally, and then spread this knowledge to others, and not only to teach them to write poetry and prose so as to gain fame and personal benefit.

Zhu Xi's thoughts on running schools had a great bearing on ancient education in China and not only were followed by the academies of different dynasties, but also became the common principles of ancient education. For example, in the Kang Xi Period of the Qing Dynasty, Li Wenzhao, appointed as president of Yuelu Academy, put forward the proposal of "attaching importance to moral qualities and cultivating character and personality" when formulating the guidelines for Yuelu Academy, which can be traced to Zhu Xi.

Further, ancient academies also emphasized the significance of the campus environment for edifying personality and would educate students though the names of stela and the columns of doors, couplets in halls, and the names of rooms and schools. For example, the column of Yuelu Academy was engraved with the couplets "Grounded between Heng and Xiang, the deep waters and hidden mountains can even breed dragons and tigers," and "Inherited from Zou and Lu, through the gate of courtesy and the road of virtues come saints." Donglin Academy, presided over by Gu Xiancheng and Gao Panlong, favored the couplet, "In my ears are the sounds of wind, rain, and reading; of my concern are the affairs of households, the country, and the world." Students benefited from being immersed in such an atmosphere every day.

The tradition of ancient academies of combining teaching with the cultivation of morality and attaching great importance to moral improvement contributed to the trend of the "academy spirit," as it was called by later generations, which had an immeasurable effect on the healthy development of students. For example, the Yuelu Academy cultivated Wu Lie and Zhao Fang in the Song Dynasty, who spared no efforts in fighting against Jin, and patriots Wu Daoxing and Wang Fuzhi in the late Ming Dynasty. In later periods, the academy had other patriotic successors, such as Tang Caichang, Shen Jin, and Yang Changji.[28] Further, Donglin Academy cultivated a group of outstanding scholars who were upright, honest, dignified, and honorable, such as Yang Lian and Zuo Guangdou, under the influence of the righteous and brave Gu

Xiancheng and Gao Panlong, who coached students through their own words and deeds. In the late Ming Dynasty, Donglin Academy also cultivated many loyal, dignified, and honorable figures. Owing to the academy spirit of integrity, Donglin Academy had arrived at the level of "Far or near, all renowned and virtuous figures would respect Donglin Academy, and all learned people in the country would enshrine it."[29]

4. Academies advocated open-door policies and the contention of 100 schools of thought and created the unique rule of assembly and debate, thus combining academy education with social education.

In ancient times, academies often carried out open-door education, with learners not restricted by area or school. If a famous master came to give lectures, students from other academies and from afar would also be admitted. For example, in the Ming Dynasty, when Wang Yangming came to give lectures at Jishan Academy, the number of students reached approximately 300. Students came from many places, including Huguang, Guangdong, Zhili, Nangan, Anfu, and Taihe. In the Shunzhi Period of the Qing Dynasty, Bailugong Academy had grants to accommodate students for lectures and regulated that "our academy has brought talents from all areas of the country, not restricted to one area. So if friends from afar hear the news and would like to come here to pursue knowledge, it would be immoral and dishonorable for us to refuse them."[30] Academies also invited masters from different schools to give lectures and engage in debate.

The rule of assembly and debate created by academies was a model advocating academic competition and information exchange. The so-called assembly and debate was an activity for masters, teachers, and friends or for teachers and students and even scholars in society to convene for free debates and lectures so as to strengthen the quality of education.. The rules of assembly and debate were established by Lv Zuqian, a famous scholar in the Song Dynasty. In 1175, the second spring of the Chunxi Period under the reign of Emperor Xiaozong of the Song Dynasty, Lv Zuqian invited Zhu Xi, Lu Jiuyuan, Lu Jiuling, and their students for an academic discussion in the Swan Lake Temple of Xinzhou. The event was thus called the "Swan Lake Assembly of Debate." The discussion of this assembly focused on "the method of learning." Zhu Xi proposed that learners should "read and see much and then return to the simple and essential," but the Lu brothers believed learners must "first explore and reach their true selves before beginning to read a lot."[31] Lu Jiuling made his point clear with a poem:

> The virtue of respecting the elder has been passed down by ancient saints,
> so even children know to do this. It is a common rule that a house is built on

a foundation and tall hills are built on solid ground. Therefore, we must concentrate on laying a foundation and researching the most essential elements
before understanding the most fundamental theory. We should cherish and
enjoy discussions and debate with friends.[32]

In Lu Jiuling's opinion, the key to learning was to motivate the true self to
understand "the inherent virtue of respecting the elder," just as the construction
of houses and the formation of tall hills require a secure foundation. When Lu
Jiuling had finished just four sentences of his poem, Zhu Xi said to Lv Zuqian,
"Zishou [Lu Jiuling] has already stood by Zijing [Lu Jiuyuan]."[33] When the
poem was finished, the two sides continued their debate, and Lu Jiuyuan and
his brother composed another poem:

It has been a general thought for thousands of years that disasters and tombs
will arouse sadness and an ancestral temple will arouse admiration. Small
streams accumulate into oceans, and lofty Mount Tai and Mount Hua were
formed by small stones. The most basic and simple virtues will eventually
lead to the long-standing and great, whereas a broken cause will, after all,
drift and sink. So if one wants to reach the highest position, he must first distinguish between the true and the false and follow his own heart.[34]

Lu Jiuyuan further argued for the priority and eternality of "the heart." He
believed that grandeur could be reached only by exploring the simple and fundamental power of "the heart," just like the ocean was formed by accumulating
small streams and Mount Tai and Mount Hua were formed with small stones;
whereas the learning method of Zhu Xi was just a "broken cause" and would
eventually drift and sink.

Although Zhu Xi was distressed and unhappy after hearing this poem,
his friendship with the two brothers never wavered. Although their academic
stances never changed, their strengths and shortcomings had been exposed
through the discussion, which became a beautiful tale of the academic competence of ancient times. Three years later, Zhu Xi defended his point of view
with another poem:

I have long admired the morality and thoughts of Lu and am now more concerned after three years' separation. I have sometimes gone out of my house
with my cane and have also gone to climb the remote mountains in a jiaozi
[sedan]. By indulging in learning, together with my foundation of previous
knowledge, I have deepened my understanding and will eventually understand
the fundamental principles. I am afraid if you only follow your own heart, you
will understand no more.[35]

Although Zhu Xi never agreed with the brothers on academic opinions, they admired each other for their morality and composition, and they would not only treat each other politely, but also often praise each other in front of their students. In 1181, Zhu Xi invited Lu Jiuyuan to give lectures at Bailudong Academy. Lu Jiuyuan's speech, "Personal Opinions on the Noble Man's Pursuit of Virtues and the Vile Person's Pursuit of Profits," moved some of the listeners to tears. Zhu Xi also thought Lu Jiuyuan's lectures "could point to the small but intractable diseases hidden in scholars," and felt guilty for not giving so profound lectures in the past. He also asked Lu Jiuyuan to write down a transcript of his speech, which would become the famous *Handouts of the Bailudong Academy*, for which Zhu Xi wrote a postscript.

The method of assembly and debate developed greatly during the Ming and Qing Dynasties. For example, in the Ming Dynasty, Qian Dehong, Wang Ji, and the students of Wang Yangming spared no effort in disseminating Wang's thoughts and theories. According to historical records, it was said that "during Qian Dehong's 30 years in office, he would give lectures every day," and "in Wang Ji's 40 years of retirement, he would not spend a day without giving lectures, and he gave lectures in the two capitals and in areas like Wu, Chu, Min, Yue, Jiang, and Zhe."[36]

Further, clubs were set up in many places, such as the Shuixi Club in Jing County, the Junshan Club in Jiangyin, the Guangyue Club in Guichi, and the Fuchu Club in Guangde. These clubs gradually expanded the lecture-giving of academies to the regional level and became the center of academic activities, thus further expanding the social influence of academies.

In the Qing Dynasty, the method of assembly and debate developed into a complete set of systems, with assemblies of academies in different places having specific principles. For example, Ziyang Assembly followed the principles of "respecting Zhu Xi and worshiping Confucius, restoring the culture of the Song and Ming Dynasties, expounding and propagating Neo-Confucianism, and preserving Taoist traditions." These systems also had detailed regulations. For example, Ziyang Assembly followed regulations outlined in *The Covenant on the Ziyang Assembly*. These systems had fixed dates. For example, Ziyang Assembly had three-day monthly assemblies and three-day general assemblies, with monthly assemblies beginning on the eighth and twenty-third day of each month, lasting from 9 am until 5 pm, and with general assemblies beginning on September 15, the day Zhu Xi was born, and/or March 15, the day Zhu Xi died. These systems had rigorous organization. For example, Ziyang Assembly set up such positions as Hui Zong (supreme leader), Hui Zhang (one dealing with general issues of the assembly), Hui Zheng (one assisting Hui Zhang), Hui Zan (one dealing with chores and student affairs), and Hui Tong (one acting as public liaison to deal with the affairs of the assembly. Finally, these systems had grand ceremonies and special expenditures. Ziyang Assembly was a regional academic seminar based on academies but open to society.

5. By hiring virtuous and prestigious masters and attracting devout and hardworking students, academies not only rose to fame and improved the quality of teaching, but also formed a harmonious relationship between teachers and students.

Academies in ancient China would often attach great importance to hiring a famous master to preside over affairs, since the image of the president (also called a dean, director, or imam) of an academy was the key to deciding whether an academy could become well known, succeed in its teaching, and attract students and scholars from all areas of the country.[37]

Since the Song Dynasty, almost all famous thinkers have given lectures in academies. For example, Lu Jiuyuan gave lectures in Xiangshan Vihara, Zhu Xi in Wuyi Vihara and Bailudong Academy, Lv Zuqian in Lize Academy, Zhang Shi in Chengnan Academy, and Wei Liaoweng in Heshan Academy. In the Yuan Dynasty, Zhao Fu gave lectures in Taiji Academy, Cheng Duanli in Jiaxuan Academy and Jiangdong Academy, and Tong Shu in Luzhai Academy. In the Ming Dynasty, Wang Yangming gave lectures in Longgang Academy and Kuaiji Academy, Zhan Ruoshui in Baisha Academy, Gu Xiancheng and Gao Panlong in Donglin Academy, and Wang Fuzhi in Yuelu Academy. In the Qing Dynasty, Sun Qifeng gave lectures in Baiquan Academy, Huang Zongxi in Jiangyin Zhengren Academy, Li Erqu in Guanzhong Academy, Lu Shiyi in Donglin Academy and Piling Academy, Yan Yuan in Zhangnan Academy, Dai Zhen and Duan Yucai in Shouyang Academy, and Qian Daxin in Zhongshan Academy.

These academies, presided over by famous masters, attracted many scholars who had heard of the quality of these academies and came from thousands of miles away, carrying their book cases and food with them to live there. When some masters left for other academies, many students would follow them and keep them company; some students even raised money to build academies and asked their teachers to live and teach there. So the persistence of academies from generation to generation was inseparable from the amiable relationship between teachers and students when the masters in charge were enthusiastic in teaching and the students were attracted by the masters and humbly pursued knowledge. This was obviously distinct from the official schools of the later period of feudal society.

In *Personal Views on the Imperial Examination System and Schools*, Zhu Xi acutely attacked the drawbacks of the official schools and the imperial examination system of the Song Dynasty:

The so-called Imperial College is just a place for pursuing fame and personal benefit, and those in charge of its affairs are just trying to choose the best for the imperial examinations and obtain their own personal benefit in the dynasty. Those aspiring to virtues and the principles of Confucianism have nothing to learn there. They come just to fill the quota. So when teachers and students see each other, they are just like strangers. Even though they sometimes talk, teachers never teach their students actual virtues, theories, or the arts. Further, the monthly tests and seasonal examinations only help to encourage the students to pursue personal benefit and become shameless. This is far from the original intention of establishing schools to teach people.[38]

Zhu Xi thought the root cause of the cold and distant relationship between teachers and students was that official schools had become subsidiary to the imperial examination system, and "were only places to pursue fame and personal benefit," having no "real education in morality, theories, or the arts." So Zhu Xi worked hard to initiate academy education, which would focus only on exploring theories and self-cultivation, instead of obtaining high positions and salaries.

When Zhu Xi was in charge of the troops in Nankang, he restored the Bailudong Academy and also taught and gave lectures there as a local official: "Once he had time off, he would engage in teaching students and answering questions of students. And when he retired, he would spend the whole day with students roaming along the streams and rocks and then returning in just a day."[39] When he was in charge of military affairs and public security in Jinhu Nanlu in Zhitanzhou, he restored the Yuelu Academy and made time in his busy schedule of political affairs to ask about the education of Yuelu Academy: "He was too busy and tired in the daytime to deal with the affairs of the prefecture, but at night, he would talk with the students and answer their questions with little sign of tiredness. He would always teach the students to learn according to their own abilities and step by step, advising them to be humble in the pursuit of lofty ideals. His advice was so earnest and kind that his listeners were moved to tears."[40] Zhu Xi guided his students patiently and systematically, but he was also strict with them. It was said that he would come to Yuelu Academy every other day to supervise and encourage the students. One day, Zhu Xi checked on two students at random to explain *The Great Learning* and was quite unhappy because they did not understand it clearly and offered a confused explanation. So he ordered the teachers and officials to work out relevant measures within one day for his consultation and decision. He also said angrily to the students, "The academy can originally admit and accept all, but if it remains careless and leaves things as they are, not attempting to improve its students, how can it become well established and maintained?" He even said, "If the students do not work hard to learn, they will be no different from uncivilized and ignorant people."[41] This showed that although the academies of ancient times could not offer their students "background," "fame," or "official positions," the masters were enthusiastic in their teaching, strict with their students, and would never lift their regulations on the students. Thus, academies enjoyed profound and harmonious relationships between teachers and students, relationships that went beyond utilitarianism and were based on attracting students with the masters' personalities and knowledge.

There have been many beautiful stories passed down about the deep and amiable relationships between teachers and students in ancient times. For example, when Zhu Xi, a master of Neo-Confucianism, passed away, Emperor Ningzong of the Song Dynasty ordered a restriction on the scale of the funeral procession, since someone had submitted a request which stated, "Students from all areas of the country have gathered in Xinshang to attend the funeral of the master, and when they gathered, they engaged in discussing the strengths and shortcomings of people and discussing the gains and losses of political affairs. Please order the local officials to restrict them."[42] Despite the restriction, the number of Zhu Xi's friends and students attending his funeral still reached as many as several thousand. This best demonstrates how deep the relationship between teachers and students in ancient times could be.

When Lu Jiuyuan, a master of the philosophy of the mind, passed away during the same period, and had his coffin carried back to his hometown, around 1,000 of his students attended his funeral, which was obvious evidence of their admiration and respect for their master.

In the Ming Dynasty, when his teacher, Yan Shan, was imprisoned, Luo Rufang was not afraid of implications or arousing suspicion. Instead, he sold his estate and property to vindicate his teacher and even served him in the prison for as long as six years at the cost of his opportunity to attend the imperial examination. Later, he earned an official position, but when he retired, he continued to serve his teacher and would bring tea and fruits to him personally. His grandson offered to do this for him, but he replied, "You are not eligible to serve my teacher."[43] From this, it is clear that their relationship had surpassed that of father and son.

Wang Yangming also had a moving relationship with his students. *The Chronicles of Wang Yangming* recorded his equal and amiable attitude toward his students when teaching in academies:

On the Mid-Autumn Day when the moon was as bright as the sun, the master asked his servants to prepare a wine party beside the Bixia Pool for around 100 students. When they became half-drunk, they gradually began to sing songs, and after a while, they either cast pots, beat a drum, or went boating. When the master saw the happy scenes of his students, he left to compose a poem.

This is such a splendid picture of teachers enjoying time with their students! Wang Yangming's enthusiasm for teaching and his amiable attitude toward his students won him the admiration and love of his students. When he was buried after his death, more than 1,000 students came to mourn from thousands of miles away. Later, many of his students set up academies in many places to emulate and memorialize him and to disseminate his theories, which became quite influential.

6. Academies in ancient times emphasized efficiency and effectiveness in their management, with relatively effective management systems, specific regulations, and the policy of involving students in the management of academies.

When academies first appeared, their management systems were rather simple, with presidents being responsible for the organization and management of the academy, as well as the teaching of the academy. Gradually, a management system characteristic of the academy system developed.

Take the Bailudong Academy in the Qing Dynasty as an example. Volume 11 of the *Records of Bailudong Academy* recorded in detail the managerial staff and requirements of the academy:

President (1 person): Hire a famous master in the country to preside over the academy who can support orthodox theories, oppose heresies, understand the reasons of things, and practice with profound knowledge, morality, and virtues. The position can remain vacant if there is no one qualified.

Associate Professor (1 person): Hire a scholar in the province who can thoroughly understand the Five Classics and can practice earnestly. He is mainly responsible for reading and grading the students' articles and analyzing their questions and meanings.

Tangzhang (Administrator) (1 person): This individual is responsible for supervising and checking the assignments and work of students and helping, encouraging, and reconciling the students. He is chosen from the best of the students by the president and associate professor and will be replaced if unqualified or inept.

Steward (1 person); associate steward (2 persons): The steward and associate stewards are in charge of the income, expenditures, food, and affairs, such as restoration and deployment. Those who are talented and honest in the academy will be chosen and will be replaced if unqualified.

Receptionist (2 persons): The receptionists are responsible for receiving guests and those who come to learn from across the country. Those who are refined and elegant in the academy will be chosen and will be replaced according to season.

Director of Classics (5 persons): Every classic of the Five Classics of the Jingyi Zhai (the Hall of Knowledge and Virtues) will be appointed a director.

Directors of Subject Studies (7 persons): Each of the seven subjects (manners, music, shooting, books, math, the calendar, and regulations) of Zhishi Zhai (the Hall of Management Affairs) will be appointed a director.

Yinzan (Host of Ceremonies) (2 persons): These individuals are responsible for "worshiping the saints and leading ceremonies" and are chosen from among those "who are loud in sound and whose pace of walking forward and retreating" is in accordance with courtesy.

Cook (1 person)

Woodsman (2 persons)

Gateman (1 person): The gateman is responsible for opening and closing the gate, cleaning the yard, and being on duty every night to inspect and guard the academy carrying a bell.

Among the above-mentioned 26 persons, 15 were managerial staff (president, associate professor, tangzhang, directors of classics, and directors of subject studies), seven were working staff (steward, associate stewards, receptionists, and yinzan), and four were odd-job men (cook, woodsmen, and gateman). Only the president and associate professors were undertaken by professionals. The cook, woodsmen, and gateman were temporary staff, and the remaining 20 were chosen by the students. Sometimes students were also engaged in editing the records of the academy, inspecting the farmland of the academy, and collecting the rent for the farmland. So to speak, the management of the academy was conducted by the students themselves, which was an efficient use of the human, material, and financial resources of the academy and allowed the students to exercise their abilities, thus improving the efficiency and benefiting the running of the academy.

To strengthen the management of the academy, academies in ancient times formulated a complete set of rules and regulations. For example, Yuelu Academy had 13 kinds of learning regulations, learning rules, and learning maxims and doctrines, totaling as many as 92 in the Qing Dynasty. In 1748, the thirteenth year of the Period of Qianlong, Wang Wenqing formulated the *School Regulations of Yuelu Academy* and *Reading Methods*, and had them engraved in the classroom to encourage the students. The whole passages were as follows:

School Regulations of Yuelu Academy

Students must often visit their parents and should worship the saint on the first and fifteenth day of every lunar month. Students should correct their mistakes and bad habits, be tidy and solemn in their behaviors, and be thrifty and simple in their clothes and food. Students should not waste time on things that are not their business, and when walking and sitting, they must follow the order of ages. It is forbidden to expose the shortcomings of others and to slander others. Dishonest friends must be turned down. Students should not waste time on chatting and meaningless talking. Every day students should read three chapters of the classics and should read several pages of the *Compendium of Materia Medica*. Students should have good knowledge of current affairs and everyday knowledge. Students should read ancient articles and poems and must think and take notes when reading. Schoolwork must be completed on time. Even if students are reading late at night, they should not be late in the morning. When coming up with questions and doubts, students must struggle to find the answers.

Reading Method Formulated by Wang Jiuxi

Six Methods to Read the Classics

First, discover the literal meaning of the words; second, understand the logic and theory contained; third, determine the underlying meaning; fourth, doubt the meaning; fifth, raise different opinions about the meaning; sixth, recognize the true meaning.

Six Methods to Read History

First, remember the facts; second, appreciate and learn the expressive methods of the book; third, explore the reasons for prosperity and turbulence; fourth, consider the historical background and tendencies; fifth, explore the thoughts of the compilers or historian; sixth, form personal opinions and learn lessons from the books.[44]

Some academies also regulated the daily class schedule of students. For example, Longman Academy in the Qing Dynasty regulated the daily class of its students:

Students should prepare notebooks to write diaries about their behavior and reading. In the diary about their behavior, four periods are to be discussed: morning after arising, morning before noon, afternoon, and evening while there is still light. Students should record the main components of their work according to the time of day. In the period between morning and noon, they should work on the classics (once a book is well understood, students can read another) and the laws and rules of life (students should read several chapters every day). In the afternoon, students should read historical books (students get only one book and read from the beginning and must focus) and books of all schools of thought (students should choose among the essential works and should not read useless books) or learn about current affairs (which must accord with the facts); if they have any spare time, students can compose articles (the articles must be reasonable and well thought out) or learn calligraphy (handwriting must be a neat and regular script). In the evening while there is still light, students may prepare for the imperial examination (students should first read reasonable and argumentative articles). Although the arrangement may not be the same every day, this is the typical schedule and spares little time.

Students were to prepare notebooks to write diaries about their behaviors and reading. Whenever one had any thoughts or questions, he was to record them in his notebook according to date. The records were to be true and not falsified, terse and not verbose. One could not make any excuse for not recording thoughts and questions. And on every fifth day of every month, one was to present his notebook to his teacher so as to answer his questions and improve himself. Students were to bear in mind what their teachers had taught. There was a test every month, and by the end of the year, teachers would examine their students' learning and progress.[45]

There were many regulations and restrictions like these, with some perhaps too trivial and some perhaps too rigorous, but their role in guiding students in their learning and moral improvement cannot ignored.

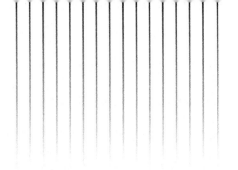

10

Ancient China's
Elementary Education

If we consider that academies were the institutions of higher education in ancient China, then the elementary education of ancient China laid the foundation for modern China's primary education.

What is elementary education? *The Book of Changes: The Diagram of Xu* said, "Elementary education means enlightenment, which means the beginning of things." Kong Yingda's *Annotations of Shang Shu* said, "Ignorance means unknowing. Children are usually ignorant, which makes elementary education for children necessary." Therefore, elementary education means enlightenment education, inspiring education, and fostering the aspirations of children and the elimination of their ignorance.

There are different academic views concerning the appropriate ages for elementary education. For example, some think that it "refers mainly to the primary education of children between the ages of 8 and 15."[1] In fact, the so-called "stage of age" discussed in ancient times is relatively flexible. For example, Wang Jun in the Qing Dynasty said, "Teaching of character is the priority when elementary education begins…when children are around 8 or 9 years old, their intelligence begin to develop, and therefore, the four tones, distinguishing true from false, rhyming, alliteration, and all things like these must be taught."[2] However, Cui Xuegu said, "When we educate children between the ages of 6 and 7, no matter how smart or foolish they are, we should persuade them to study hard and make them realize the significance of learning."[3] Thus, elementary education should begin before the age of 8. It includes not only nursery education, but also the education of children and youth.

Education at this stage plays a crucial role in the course of people's development across their whole lives. British educational philosopher John Locke said, "The little and almost insensible impressions on our tender infancies have very important and lasting consequences."[4]

Bertrand Russell pointed out in *Education and the Good Life*: "Children are born with many instincts and reflections, all of which can be developed into many customs so as to be developed into various kinds of characters. This happens at the early stage of childhood; therefore, it is in childhood that it is most proper to develop a person's character."[5] Ancient educators in China also had an early realization of this fact. In the Southern and Northern Dynasties, Yan Zhitui said, "When young, we are energetic; when growing up, we are interrupted by other thoughts; therefore, it is necessary to be taught early, and we should not miss this opportunity."[6] Shen Li in the Ming Dynasty criticized people who de-emphasized elementary education:

> Elementary education is not only extremely important but also extremely difficult. This is because the course of our lives is based on elementary education, and much time is needed if we want to obtain enlightenment from elementary education effectively. However, common people are ignorant and do not appreciate the importance of elementary education, nor do instructors value it. Further, the ceremonies of householders are simplified and no more than just lesson teaching. But they do not know that elementary education is of great significance or the difficulty of studying. Is it not true that elementary instruction is twice as difficult as college instruction?[7]

Shen Li held the view that college instruction could not compare with the significance of or the energy we should put into elementary education, which was considered the most important and difficult thing. This was because "the course of our lives is based on elementary education." He considered childhood to be the most critical period of people's lives for receiving education.

Elementary education was one of the characteristic elements of ancient China's education. Nearly every educator and thinker has commented on elementary education. Therefore, elementary education is a crucial element of China's educational thought system.

The Content of Elementary Education

China's elementary education in ancient times arose with the pace of China's pedagogy at the time. The book *The History of Zhou*, providing instruction on the recognition of characters, appeared as early as the Zhou Dynasty.[8] Before this time, elementary education was conducted orally.

Until the Han Dynasty, there were "schools," actually libraries,[9] which specialized in delivering elementary education and the relatively standardized materials of elementary instruction. For example, educational books, such as *Cang Jie, Fan Jiang, Ji Jiu (Instant Recognition of Characters)*, and *Wu Shang* were written to teach children to recognize characters, and in the Han Dynasty, *The Analects of Confucius* and *The Classic of Filial Piety* were used as teaching materials for the primary learning stage.

Following the Han Dynasty, elementary instructional materials became wide spread. According to admittedly incomplete statistics, there were as many as 1,215 books for elementary education, including books series.[10] We will now analyze the representative content of ancient elementary instructional materials, from which we can determine many of the rules and implications of elementary education in ancient times. In terms of content, the elementary instructional materials of ancient times can be categorized into five types.

1. Comprehensive Instructional Materials for Elementary Education

Comprehensive instructional materials focused on children's recognition of characters and also imparted some fundamental knowledge. During the Han and Tang Dynasties, the most influential and comprehensive instructional materials for elementary education were *Ji Jiu, The Three-Character Classic, The Thousand-Character Classic*, and *You Xue Qiong Lin (Instructions for Children)*. *Ji Jiu*, written by the eunuch Shiyou in the period of Emperor Yuan of Han, was the most widespread book for character recognition throughout the Han and Tang Dynasties. It included instruction on characters for names, clothing, agriculture, diet, instruments, music, physiology, animals, medicine, and human affairs. The text rhymed and contained no duplicated characters. It included three-character, four-character, and seven-character verses. For example, the tenth chapter on agriculture and diet teaches:

> There are many kinds of plants, including rice, millet, sorghum, and sesame, which can be made into many kinds of food, including dough cake, rice, and bean paste. There are many kinds of vegetables, including okra, shallots, smartweed, perilla, and ginger, which can be made into many kinds of medicine and sauces, including fructus ulmi, fermented soybeans, and fried bean sauce.
>
> Vegetables like rue, garlic, chufa, mustard, and cornel have flavorsome smells. Turnips and myoga are to be stored in winter.

Fruits like pears, persimmons, plums, and peaches ripen when the frost descends. Fruits like jujubes, apricots, and melons taste as sweet as maltose.

Vegetables and fruits are foods that serve as supplements to grains. Now their good flavors will be described for you all.

The Three-Character Classic was the most popular instructional material for elementary education following the Song Dynasty. It was said to have been edited by Wang Yinglin in the Southern Song Dynasty (1127 to 1279). The book discussed the benefits of learning, common-sense knowledge, historical knowledge, morality, and the order of reading. Each sentence contained three words, and all sentences rhymed. The author wrote:

Men at their birth are naturally good. Their natures are much the same. Their habits then become widely different. If foolishly there is no teaching, man's nature will deteriorate. The right way of teaching is to attach the utmost importance to thoroughness. Many years ago, the mother of Mencius chose a neighborhood, and when her child would not learn, she broke the shuttle from her loom. Dou of the Swallow Hills had the right method. He taught five sons, each of whom raised the family's reputation. To feed without teaching is the father's fault. To teach without severity is the teacher's laziness. If the child does not learn, this is not as it should be. If he does not learn while young, what will he be when old?

The Thousand-Character Classic was also a widespread instructional work in ancient China. Its compilation is often related as a magical story. It was said that Emperor Wu of Liang, who wanted to teach his children to recognize Chinese characters, ordered Yin Tieshi to choose 1,000 unique characters to give to Zhou Xingsi to organize into a piece of rhyming text. Zhou Xingsi "finished organizing the characters and submitted his work to the emperor, and his hair became white." One thousand rambling characters, through a one-night effort, became a wonderful and powerful article. *The Thousand-Character Classic* discussed astronomy and geography, history and politics, animals and plants, morality and discipline, and folk idioms and agricultural knowledge, with character recognition the main focus of the content. The beginning of the text reads:

The darkling skies and yellow earth, amid great chaos had their birth. Then Sun and Moon their courses ran; then stars were set and round they span. Then cold and heat arrived by turns, with reaping, keeping, man's concerns. The extra days in leap years strewn, it's Yin and Yang that call the tune. When clouds are formed, the rain is made. When dew drops freeze, the frost is laid. The gold sand streams in gold abound. From Kunlun mountains jade is found. The best of swords is Giant's Might. The best of pearls is Bright-at-night.

For fruit the plum and apple are great. And mustard and ginger are loved on the plate. The seas catch salt where rivers pour. The scaled submerge, the feathered soar. The dragon master, the fire fan; the bird-name giver, the King of Man. Then words appeared the things to note. Then clothes were made the body to coat. To men of worth the power passed down; first Yao, then Shun; each handed the crown.

You Xue Qiong Lin was the largest book of instructional materials for elementary education in ancient times. It was edited by Cheng Dengji in the Ming Dynasty. It was not limited to the length of four- or five-character quatrains, or three- or seven-character quatrains, but contained only sentence pairs. Therefore, the text was relatively flexible and easy to recite. The book discussed astronomy, geography, the seasons, courts, civilian officials, military officers, father and son, brothers, couples, uncle and nephew, teacher and student, friends and guests, marriage, women, relatives, respect between young and old, the body, clothing, human affairs, diet, imperial palaces, instruments, treasures, rich and poor, death and disease, culture and education, the imperial civil examination, handicrafts, artistry, procedures for lawsuits, Buddhism spirits, birds and beasts, and flowers and trees. The book contained 33 chapters in total and was considered an encyclopedia for the education of children. It was also a comprehensive instructional book for elementary education. The chapter "Brothers" begins as follows:

No parents are to be evil to their children, and so precious is the relationship between brothers. We must keep the friendship between fellow countrymen and do no harm to the relationship between brothers and sisters. The harmoniousness among sisters and brothers can accomplish their virtue.

The Book of Lawsuits states:

Common people will complain about injustices they have faced, and wise people consider that it is most precious if there are no lawsuits in society. The monarch in upper society resorts to criminal law cautiously, and criminals are educated so as to do good deeds. In the lower classes, there are no common people who are wronged, and officials can give impartial judgment when they make accusations. Then, even though they may be imprisoned, it can turn out to be a blessing; a drawing on the ground can also become a prison.

Ancient instructional materials for elementary education were comprehensive, rich, and concise. They were well rhymed to be easily recited and memorized. They accorded with the developmental stages of children's physical and mental development and learning, teaching much common sense to children in their process of teaching the recognition of characters.

2. Instructional Materials for Elementary Education Concerning Ethics

Ethical instructional materials focused mainly on the morality of behavior, how to treat others, and ethical cultivation. Ethical education was considered one of the most important points of elementary education. In the Ming Dynasty, Wang Yangming said, "The teaching content in ancient times was about human relations, but later on, people began to recite words and texts, so the instruction of our ancestors disappeared. Loyalty and filial piety, propriety, justice, honesty, and honor should be the main content of the education of children."[11]

The most influential books of the time included *Admonitions for Children*, *Supplement to Children's Manners*, *Admonition of Temperament*, *Disciple Rules*, *Past Excellent Articles*, and *Language for Children*. Among them, *Admonition of Temperament* was the most famous, written by Cheng Duanmeng, a student of Zhu Xi. It was supplemented by Cheng Ruoyong in the Song and Yuan Dynasties, extending it from 30 items to 183 items. It discussed creation, temperament, learning ability, good and evil, moral integrity, and the principles of governance. The book was written with four-word sentences and introduced the knowledge of Neo-Confucianism. Zhu Xi once praised it, saying, "The sentences were thought-provoking, and although the words were small in quantity, it could be considered a grander *Er Ya* [a treatise on word explanations in ancient China]." Some items created in the original works of Cheng Duanmeng were included:

> The heavenly principles are prevalent and are endowed in everything, which is the fate of them. There is no excellence in people's temperaments, which is the feature of people. There is consciousness within ourselves, which commands our temperament and acts as our center. We are moved by others, and the desire is there. We should be concentrated, which shows our respect. To be consistent without other thoughts means to be single-minded. The heavenly fate is popular, which is the natural rule. The dispositions people possess include five characters, which is the heavenly principle. Human beings are sensitive animals with desires. Our organs, such as the ears, eyes, mouth, and nose, can reflect our desires.

The Disciple Rules, edited by Li Yuxiu in the Qing Dynasty, was another very influential book for elementary education in ancient times. There were three words per sentence, and all sentences rhymed for ease of recital. Since it was noted for its content of filial piety and fraternal duty, it was called the "supreme work of elementary education." The whole book was an explanation and development of Confucius' thought that "A young man should serve his parents at home and be respectful to elders outside his home. He should be earnest and truthful, loving all, and become intimate with his innate good-heartedness. After doing this, if he has energy to spare, he can study literature and the arts." After this work appeared, it became quite popular and almost led to *The Three-Character Classic* being forgotten. An excerpt from *The Disciple Rules* states:

All men need love; they are under the same sky and stand on the same ground. A person with lofty virtue enjoys a lofty reputation; a person is not appreciated for the sake of his appearance.

A man with great talent enjoys great fame, and people are convinced by him not because of his big words. If one has talent, he should not be self-centered; if others have talent, do not slander them. Do not flatter the rich, and do not be arrogant when facing the poor; do not dislike old things and prefer new ones. If a man is busy, do not disturb him; if a man is uneasy, do not bother him. If one has shortcomings, do not reveal them; if one has secrets, do not speak out. Thinking highly of others' merits is called kindness; when they know of your praise, think about further encouragement. Discussing others' wickedness is indeed a wicked deed; with this fault increasing continually, mishaps will occur. Advising kindly is to establish virtue; without correction of faults, both the advisor and the advised will be reduced in morality.

Among the instructional materials for elementary education in ancient times, *The Past Excellent Articles*, whose author is unknown, was a further influential book. It became famous and widely known throughout the country beginning in the late Qing Dynasty. This book collected the beautiful words, proverbs, and commandments of ancient society, and discussed diverse topics, reflecting Chinese attitudes toward life and the principles of social conduct. One extract is as follows:

The previous articles with inculcations could broaden our horizons with their accumulation. To view the present requires a review of the past, for past scenes resemble present scenes. We must know ourselves and others and put ourselves in others' positions. We should drink wine with bosom friends and recite poetry with scholars. Although we are acquainted with many people, are there not a few with whom we can share our opinions? Meeting, like knowing each other for the first time, there will be no resentment until later years. Close to the river, we know the characters of fish; close to the mountain, we know the sounds of birds. The mountain stream always ebbs and flows, as do the changeable minds of base men. Gold might become as cheap as iron when someone is unlucky, but when chance is approaching, iron may become as valuable as gold. Restrain yourself when talking with others, instead of making confessions. What you desire might not be realized, but sometime a chance can come when you least expect it.

Taking an overall view of ancient instructional materials for elementary education, we find that they not only included the characteristics of being concise, understandable, vivid, and written to be recited, but also combined ethical cultivation with a discussion of children's daily life, in order to make moral ethics accessible to children. It was of great significance to the improvements in the method and form of children's moral education that feudal dross was excluded from their content.

3. Instructional Materials for Elementary Education Concerning History

Instructional materials for teaching history at the elementary level focused on historical stories or the good deeds of famous people to teach basic history knowledge so as to develop students' sentiment and sense of historical responsibility. Teaching materials of this kind include Li Han's *Knowledge for Children*, Wang Ling's *Knowledge of Seventeen Historical Events for Children*, Hu Yin's *Thousand-Character Historical Account*, Huang Jishan's *Abstract of History*, Chen Li's *Knowledge of Past Dynasties for Children*, Wang Rui's *Knowledge of Past Dynasties for Children*, and Xiao Hanchong's *Longwen and the Whip Shadow*. Zhu Xi's *Children's Education*, Lv Benzhong's *Precept for Children*, and Lv Zuqian's *Supplement to Children's Manners* also included quite a few historical stories and good deeds of historical figures as part of their ethical education.

Some comprehensive reading materials like *The Three-Character Classic* and *The Thousand-Character Classic* also served to provide historical education. Here we will discuss the introduction of three books, including *Knowledge of Past Dynasties for Children*, *Five-Character Lessons*, and *Song of the Titles of Past Reigning Dynasties*. *Knowledge of Past Dynasties for Children*, written by Wang Rui in the Yuan Dynasty, has four characters per sentence and provides a concise narrative of historical events. Zheng Zhensun praised it and said it described "the figures' life, changes in the world, the characters of the emperors, as well as the process of unification, partition, and reunification of the country, in a cohesive organization, with concise language; within less than a thousand words, it includes thousands of years."[12] It describes the history of the Qin and Han Dynasties as follows:

> The Qin Dynasty located its capital in Xianyang, from where it began to take the imperial throne. It conquered and annexed the six states, like a fierce lion; it burned books and buried the literati in pits, changing the system of the Zhou Dynasty as well. Cheng Sheng and Xiang Yu sprang up, but their great deeds lasted for just three generations. Liu Bang-Han Gaozu, who was generous and open-minded, started from Pei County and flourished at the time of Yanzuo.

It became rich and populous at the time of the Empire of Wenjing, the twelfth empire of the Han Dynasty. Two hundred days later, disaster fell on the Confucian scholars. Wang Mang, a new aristocrat, tried to steal the imperial jade seal but failed. The Chimei Army entered and took the imperial throne. There were great men as predicted by prophecy. Emperor Guangwu was endowed by the heavens and was decisive. He gained fame and fortune in Nanyang, eliminating curses. At the time of the thirteenth empire, the dynasty was called the Eastern Han Dynasty (AD 25 to 220). Two hundred years later, this dynasty collapsed because of Emperor Lingxian.

The author of *Five-Character Lessons*, Li Yanji, was a grand scholar in the Ming Dynasty. The book is divided into the records of the Three Kings, the Five Emperors, Tao Tang, the Yu Clan, the Xia, Shang, Zhou, the Spring and Autumn Period, the Warring States Period, the Qin Dynasty, the Western Han Dynasty, the Eastern Han Dynasty, the Three Kingdoms Period, the Western Jin Dynasty, the Eastern Jin Dynasty, the Southern Song Dynasty, the Southern Qi Dynasty, the Southern Liang Dynasty, the Southern Chen Dynasty, the Sui Dynasty, the Tang Dynasty, the Liang Dynasty, the Jin Dynasty, the Han Dynasty, the Zhou Dynasty, the Song Dynasty, the Yuan Dynasty, and the Ming Dynasty. It narrates history from ancient times until the Ming Dynasty and was one of the most comprehensive and rich historical works for children, depicting a clear line of historical development. The book narrates *The History of the Three Kingdoms* as follows:

Cao Cao and Sun Quan rose, contending against each other and rebelling against the Emperor of Han. Cao Pi-son of Cao Cao replaced the previous emperor. He changed the title of the reigning dynasty to Wei and was in command of the troops to destroy the Han Dynasty. Sun Quan named his reigning dynasty Wu. All of these events put China in chaos. Sun Quan placed his capital in Nanjing and drove out its citizens. Liu Bei competed with him, and the Three Kingdoms contended for hegemony. Guan Yu, Zhang Fei, and Zhuge Liang helped the Han Dynasty to keep its status. The country was divided into three parts, and each state fought with the others. This kind of situation lasted for half a century, and led to the country falling into evil days. Finally, the dream of recovering the empire ended in vain.

Song of the Titles of Past Reigning Dynasties was written in the Qing Dynasty by Bao Dongli, who compiled many instructional materials for elementary education concerning historical topics. His other works include *A Brief Abstract of History*, *Collected Compilation for Children's Education*, *Formulas of Provincial*

Names, and *Formulas of 23 Historical Events.* Among these works, *Song of the Titles of Past Reigning Dynasties* is one of the most concise. It states:

> Three emperors were created by Pan Gu, and the achievement of defeating Suiren was unforgettable for people. There were no consistent sayings about the Five Emperors, and the achievements of Huangdi's reign still remain a mystery. There appeared recordings since the years of Zhou Yu, and three emperors appeared in the dynasties of Xia, Shang, and Zhou. Much chaos occurred in the Spring and Autumn and Warring States Periods, and the First Emperor of Qin eliminated traditions fiercely. The Han Dynasty took over the regime and dealt with Xiangyu successfully. Wang Mang usurped the throne and made the Western Han Dynasty perish. The Eastern Han Dynasty prospered under the rule of Liu Xiu. The three kingdoms of Wei, Shu, and Wu experienced a situation of tripartite confrontation. It was rather chaotic in the Jin Dynasty, when six of ten states competed with each other. The Song, Qi, Liang, and Chen Dynasties fought for the southern land, and the Yuan, Wei, Qi, and Zhou contended for the northern territory. The Sui Dynasty lasted for just two generations; it was followed by the Tang Dynasty, which lasted for 300 years.
>
> It was a rare phenomenon when Zhuliang usurped the throne and when the Later Tang Dynasty (923 to 936) perished within a short time like the Zhu and Liang Dynasties. The Jin and Han Dynasties changed their fate soon after; the national power of the Five Dynasties (907 to 960) was gloomy. Then, there were ten states, which set up a separatist regime by force of arms; the Zhao and Song Dynasties then flourished. Only the northern part of the Liao Dynasty was disrupted by the Xia Dynasty, but when the Jin Dynasty rose abruptly, it was difficult for the Liao Dynasty to ward off. The two emperors defended the northern part of ancient China, and the Jianyan Emperor stayed in the southern part of China. Then, the Yuan Dynasty (1271 to 1368), which was vast in territory, was established. It collapsed after less than 100 years, and the Ming Dynasty lasted for a little longer. The morning sun rose up from the Liao Sea, the fire was extinguished, and no light could be seen. The Qing Dynasty took its throne in the Central Plains; culture thrived and governance was peaceful. It has been 4,000 years since the time of Emperors Yao and Shun, and we common people feel lucky to live in this affluent society.

There were some views concerning the exploiting class in historical materials for elementary education. These were also composed in the form of article and couplet, making them easy to remember and especially convenient for systematic learning. In this sense, they are worth discussing. At the same time, these kinds of teaching materials used the least number of words to contain a great deal of information. For example, *Song of the Titles of Past*

Reigning Dynasties used only 266 words to narrate the history from the time of Pan Gu to the Qing Dynasty. The modern historical instructional text *Song of Dynasties* was based on this work.

4. Teaching Materials for Elementary Education Concerning Verses, Odes, and Songs

These instructional materials educated children with appropriate verses, odes, and songs and taught basic writing skills. Although Confucius had advocated the education of poetry many years earlier, the person who truly advocated educating children through poetry was Zhu Xi. His *Enlightenment Poem* was the precedent-setting work for future instructional materials for elementary education on verses, odes, and songs. However, it was not very widely spread because of the heavy influence of Confucian thought. Soon after, many other instructional works of verses, odes, and songs began to emerge, including Chen Chun's *Etiquette Poem for Children's Education*, Wan Huquan's *Rhythmic Song of Instructions for Children*, Hu Yuan's *Poetry of Elementary Education*, and Wang Zhu's *Poetry of a Prodigy*, *Three Hundred Tang Poems*, and *Thousands of Poems*. Of these, Wang Zhu's were the most influential. Wang Zhu lived in the later years of the Northern Song Dynasty. It was recorded that he was good at writing poetry by the time he was 8 or 9 years old, and he was called a child prodigy. People then called his poems the *Poetry of the Prodigy Wang*. However, *Poetry of a Prodigy* also contained poems written by Li Bai and Chen Shubao, the last emperor of the Northern Chen Dynasty. From this, we can see that the book was supplemented by later generations in order to teach children. Much of its content inspired learning, although some content was challenged. For example, the saying that "everything is inferior to learning" was criticized both at the time it was written and by people living in modern times. The four poems encouraging learning in its preface are as follows:

The emperor pays much attention to heroes, and we have been taught knowledge. Everything is inferior to learning.

We must study hard when young, and writing articles can make us stand steadfast. Dignitaries fill the imperial court, all of them scholars.

We can learn well if we are diligent, for there are thousands of books to read under the bright window. It is enough to study for three years, and no one will then laugh at past ignorance.

I was learned and knowledgeable since my youth and possessed high ambition. Others have swords in their hands, whereas I hold brushes as knives.

Among the instructional materials of poetry for elementary education, there were also some books which imparted writing skills to be "referred to in future couplet-composing activities." Examples include Zhu Ming and

Pan Ying's *Rhythm Enlightenment*, Meng Fu's *The Sequel to the Annotations of Enlightenment Couplets*, Si Shouqian's *Parallel Sentences for Children's Education*, Che Wanyu's *Rhythm Enlightenment*, and Zhao Weiyan's *Three-Character Sayings*. Si Shouqian, the author of *Parallel Sentences for Children's Education*, died at the age of 20, leaving only this poem. The poem rhymed every two words, which was suitable for holding children's attention. Several of its sentences are recorded as follows:

> The sky turns warm in the north, and the sun rises in the east. The east wind blows, and the dawn is misty. It is slippery on the bridge because of the frost, and the snow is beginning to thaw. Loyal ministers want to serve the country, and the blush on the faces of beauties sorrowful for the spring starts to fade. Mengzi became a sage for the sake of his mother's moving three times; Zeng Can's achievement should always be owed to the help of the sage.

The Enlightenment of Rhyme was a most influential instructional material for elementary education, combining a rhyming scheme with antithetical parallelism: "They are linked with each other with a light rhythm and a harmonious rhyme, which is easy and interesting for recital."[13] Several sentences are recorded as follows:

> Cloud to rain; snow to wind; evening glow to clear sky; swan geese to flying swallows; birds to singing insects; three-foot swords to six-jun bows; the north to the south of the Changjiang River; man's world is hot, but it is cold in the Moon Palace; smoke-like willow trees along the banks to a garden of red prunus; there is an early-rising traveler with his hair gray, and there is an old man wearing a straw raincoat fishing by the steam in the evening.

From the analysis above, it can be seen that the poetry of elementary education had a strong ethical and educational foundation, designed to influence children gradually and unconsciously to accept feudal ethics, worldviews, and life views, of which many were unacceptable. Most of the poems were to be remembered by heart, namely the saying, "After reading the *Three Hundred Poems of Tang*, you will be able to write a poem even if you cannot recite poetry." This was effective in developing the ability of children to appreciate and write poetry.

5. Instructional Materials for Elementary Education Concerning Scientific Knowledge

These instructional materials focused on the traditionally specialized fields of astronomy, geography, medicine, and biology so as to broaden children's horizons and develop their academic interests. These works include specialized works, such as *Songs of Stepping into Heaven* (on astronomy) and *Mathematics for Elementary Education* in the Song Dynasty, *Enlightenment of Mathematics* in the Yuan Dynasty, *Song of Hygiene in the Tang and Song Dynasties* written in the Ming Dynasty, and *Eclipse Knowledge for Children* (on astronomy) and *Rhymed Song of Classics* in the Qing Dynasty. These works also included comprehensive works, among which the most famous was Fang Fengchen's *Knowledge of Substances for Children*. This book discussed astronomy, geography, mountains, rivers, counties, cities, woods, flowers, grass, farming, seasons, diet, clothing, dwellings, appliances, and animals. The book had a delicate conceptual design and was of practical use, vivid form, and unique style. It was collected as the *Minor Four Books*. Its narration of astronomical phenomena is as follows:

> The sky is superior to earth, which is the law of the universe. The sky is light and clear, and the earth is heavy and muddy. The sun, the moon, and the stars are shining in the sky, making it magnificent. The air is moistened by the rain and the dew and filled with wind. Why do the clouds rise? It is because of the rise of water. Why does the rain fall? It is because there are too many clouds.
>
> Yang and Yin belong to the same system, and the wind circles around them. Yang is the alternate of Yin and breaks into thunder. The rainbow shows when the rain stops, and the lightning strikes when the thunder quakes. The vapor disperses into mist and congeals into hail. The sun will go down when it is up in the middle of the sky; the moon will be eclipsed if it is full in the sky. It waxes and wanes on its own. When the Yang takes the dominant place, the universe becomes broad. Then the sun, the blue sky, the light breeze, and the clear moon will appear.
>
> When the Yin takes the dominant place, it is cloudy, the sunlight is disguised, and the evil stars start to shine. Therefore, the sages disdain Yin and worship Yang. The *Book of Poetry* advocates avoiding snow and frost, and the *Book of Changes* warns about ice and snow.

This kind of common sense in elementary education also provided instruction in ethics, which were stated as follows:

> People live in a group, and therefore need instruction. The lord is kind and ministers loyal, fathers are amicable and sons filial; there is distinction between husband and wife, trust between friends, order among the elderly and the young: all these can then be called human relations.

From a brief review of these five types of teaching materials, we can understand the main content of elementary education in ancient times. They were common in many ways; for example, ethics was included in every subject, which enhanced the infiltration of moral education; further, these works were brief, vivid, and easy to remember. Most were compiled by out-standing scholars, such as the academic masters Zhu Xi and Wang Yinglin, which improved their quality and authority. Some scholars were professional in the compilation of instructional materials for elementary education, such as Bao Dongli in the Qing Dynasty, who compiled many historical works for elementary education.

The Characteristics of Ancient Elementary Education

Ancient scholars emphasized the importance of elementary education. In the practice of providing elementary education, theories and methods with certain characteristics were gradually formed, which educators could refer to and pass on to future generations. Lu Xun once said, "If there is someone who is trying to compile a history and study the methods of educating children in order for us to understand how our ancestors taught, his virtue is no lower than that of Yu (although he might be just a worm)."[14] Seventy years passed, but no one systematically wrote about "the methods of educating children in ancient China," which was rather a pity. Here, I cannot finish this by saying "similar to Yu." The only thing I could do was to attempt to fill in the blanks and conduct my own research on the main characteristics of the theories and practices of elementary education in ancient China. As far as I am concerned, there were five basic characteristics of elementary education in ancient times.

1. Placing Emphasis on Early Education

Elementary education itself was a kind of early education and was to be con-ducted by ancient educators before their disciples reached the age of 15. Ge Hong, who lived in the Western Jin Dynasty (265 to 316), said, "Aspiration fos-tered in youth will be hard to forget, whereas the spirits tend to be distracted when a person grows up; thus, beginning to learn as early as possible is the best choice. When children learn meticulously, their characters will become accomplished, along with the development of habits, which will seem to be naturally formed."[15] Due to the concentrated spirit of children, beginning to learn as early as possible can make it easy for a person to accept all kinds of knowledge, form sound behavioral habits, and set a solid foundation for his development.

The Cheng brothers in the Song Dynasty also advocated early education. They said:

> Ancient people began to learn in their youth, and what they heard and saw were good things. Therefore, when they grew up, they would not see evil things, and thus they tended to make great achievements easily. Nowadays,

what people see in childhood is unkind things, so they tend to speak of those things in their daily life. With one's kindness continuously reduced, how can he learn heavenly principles?[16]

The Cheng brothers thought that learning at a young age was the essential factor for becoming a sage and was crucial for people's development. Without this foundation, it was like "building a house with no foundation, which was difficult to accomplish."[17]

As for the starting point of early education, some educators held that it "starts when one can eat on one's own and speak."[18] For example, in the Qing Dynasty, Wang Fuzhi started from his theory of "habit and the development of character," and proposed that we should educate children from the time they were able to move on their own and speak. He wrote:

People can all be virtuous, it is the nature of humanity; those who become detached from kindheartedness have become so through their habits. Habits are important to people, because the ears are restricted to what they hear, which deprives people of their sensitivity; the eyes are restricted to what they see, which deprives people of their sight; the relationship between father and son is influenced by the ability to speak and walk; the relationship of relatives is enlightened from the awareness of right and wrong. Replacing a person's eyes, ears, or mind, one can see nothing and hear nothing. It is not because they do not want to see or hear, but they have seen and heard what they have never experienced before and are shocked by the inaccessibility to and incompatibility with the new environment. Therefore, it is said that "habits form together with character." The formation of character cannot be changed even by strict teachers or beneficial friends; neither can great reward or punishment rectify them.[19]

Wang Fuzhi held the view that the education of children should be conducted as early as possible, at the beginning of the development of their ability to perceive and speak so as to develop good qualities and behaviors. In fact, this revealed an important rule of education: shaping is easy, but remaking is difficult.

Now because we were shaped since birth, the process of education must begin at the same time. Some educators have advocated starting early education through antenatal training. *Biographies of Exemplary Women: The Mother of the Zhou Dynasty*, written by Liu Xiang in the Han Dynasty, recorded the story of Tairen's (the mother of King Wen) "antenatal training": the mother of King Wen was the daughter of Renshi. Prince Ji married her as the princess consort. Tairen had a character of being upstanding, and she possessed gracious morality. When she was pregnant, she did not see ugly scenes, hear evil sounds, or speak abuses. In this way, she conducted antenatal training. She then gave birth to

King Wen in the toilet. King Wen was born wise and could learn a hundred matters with the teaching of just one matter. The wise men all considered that Tairen was adept at antenatal training. They also said:

> When women were pregnant in ancient times, they did not lie on one side when sleeping, nor did they sit on the edge, nor did they crook their body when standing, nor did they eat spoiled food, nor did they sit sidelong on a mat, nor did they see or hear evil things. They recited poems for blessing, and thus their children would be good-looking and superior in talents. Therefore, when pregnant, one should be careful about her emotions, for emotion might decide good or evil results. People who were born a certain way owe this to the emotions of their mother. The mother of King Wen understood this.

Another educator in the Western Han Dynasty, writing earlier than Liu Xiang, wrote the treatise *Antenatal Training* and advocated "the way of antenatal training should be well preserved for future generations to refer to."[20] Following this, Wang Chong in the Eastern Han Dynasty, Yan Zhitui in the Northern and Southern Dynasties, Zhang Hua in the Western Jin Dynasty, Sun Simiao in the Tang Dynasty, Zhu Xi, the Cheng Brothers, and Chen Ziming in the Song Dynasty, Zhu Zhenheng in the Yuan Dynasty, and Wan Jin and Xu Xiangqing in the Ming Dynasty all made significant contributions to the study of antenatal training.[21] Some of their statements were unscientific in some aspects, but they also made many reasonable comments.[22] For example, some factors, such as "seeing ugly scenes," "speaking abuses," or "being angry" were seen to have a negative effect on the emotions of pregnant women, which might cause unborn infants to be unable to adjust to the environment and have a dislocated central nervous system. This could then lead to the birth of intellectually disabled infants. The noise of "evil sounds" could make unborn infants restless and maladjusted. On the contrary, it was very beneficial to the development of unborn infants if pregnant women played the harp and had a peaceful mood. Therefore, pregnant women were encouraged to create a positive environment for the development of their unborn infants through sound "antenatal training." Ancient thought on antenatal training still needs further exploration.

2. Placing Emphasis on Family Education

In ancient China, families were not only units for production or living, but also the basic units to carry out educational activities. Whether a child goes to school or not, family education is indispensable. For children before the age of primary school, the family is their first school, and parents are their first teachers. Therefore, educators place much emphasis on the educational function of families. Lu Shiyi of the Qing Dynasty said, "Children's education not only includes receiving education in the school but, more importantly, from within the family."[23] Educator Sun Qifeng said, "Teaching children is the most important duty of the family."[24] Ancient educators all regarded family education as the foundation of children's elementary education. Because of this, there are many stories concerning family education popular in China's history, including "The mother of Mencius moved three times to find the proper neighborhood for her son," "The mother of Yuefei tattooed his back," and "Sanniang taught her children." There were also many theoretical articles about family education, such as "Admonitions for the Yan Clan," by Yan Zhitui, "Admonitions for the Yuan Clan," by Yuan Cai, "Admonitions for the Pang Clan," by Pang Shangpeng, "Essential Points of Family Admonitions," by Wu Linzheng, "Five Inherited Regulations by Chen Hongmou," and "Admonitions of Xiaoyoutang," by Sun Qifeng. Further, there were countless verses written as poems by parents to teach their children. In terms of family education, ancient educators emphasized the following elements.

1) Paying Attention to the Influence of Parents on Their Children
Lu Shiyi in the early period of the Qing Dynasty said:

> The education of children requires two parental efforts: the regulation of family and the choice of teachers. If parents are unable to regulate their family, the child will be fond of cruel laughter or hate and will go astray from the right way in certain aspects. Thus, even with a good teacher, it is difficult for the child to be rectified.[25]

This indicated that family education played a crucial role, which cannot be replaced by schooling. If parents cannot regulate their family, even with the instruction of a good teacher, there will be few beneficial effects. Therefore, Lu Shiyi emphasized that parents should influence their children through their own actions:

> We should set an example to our children if we want to teach them. It usually happens that even when a child's father does not intentionally instruct him, his behaviors and temperament will still resemble those of his father to a great extent. This is caused by imitating the actions of his father. When considering the influence they have on their children, parents should always perform self-introspection.[26]

Zhang Lvxiang believed that "it is unwise for parents to educate their children without self-cultivation,"[27] stressing the significance of parents' self-improvement on the education of their children. Why should the significance of parents be stressed? This is because after birth, children have a direct, close relationship with their parents. They are genetically connected with their parents and live together with them all the time, sharing happiness and sorrow. Through what they see and hear from their parents on a constant basis, they are influenced unconsciously. Yan Zhitui called this process "modeling." He said, "The process of modeling takes place from the older generation to the younger generation, from the former generation to the later generation."[28] The process of modeling involves initiative, requiring no compelling force.

2) Advocating the Combination of Love and Education

It is natural for parents to love their children. However, if they do not love their children in the proper way and instead indulge them, the opposite effect will be produced, and children will be influenced negatively.

Therefore, ancient educators placed emphasis on describing the proper relationship between care and education. For example, Yan Zhitui said:

> If parents are serious and strict on one hand while being benign and benevolent on the other hand, their children will be filial, reverent, and prudent. It is improper to love children without educating them. If children are allowed to eat and drink whatever they like, given whatever they want, encouraged what they should be forbidden, and forgiven what they should be punished, they will think it should be like this when they grow up. It will be too late to stop them after they have developed the habit of being arrogant, and then parents' prestige will be impossible to re-establish even if the children are beaten to death. Parents will become increasingly angry and children resentful. When the children grow up to be adults, their morality will already have been ruined.[29]

Yan Zhitui believed it was important for parents to be "serious and strict on one hand and benign and benevolent on the other hand." These two aspects should be integrated with each other and be performed in the proper way. Otherwise, children will be undiscriminating, not knowing what to do and "being reduced to ruined morality."

Lu Shiyi also pointed out that improper education has a life long negative influence on children: "When I see parents teaching their children to beat or abuse others in a joking manner or play with toys that are pleasant to their ears and eyes, I think to myself how they will never grow up to be a talent if they are obsessed with such habits."[30]

The educator Yuan Cai in the Song Dynasty was creative in depicting the relationship between love and education. In his work *Admonitions for the Yuan Clan*, a monograph on family education second to *Admonitions for the Yan Clan*, the following paragraph is thought-provoking:

> When children are still young, parents love them so much as to neglect the flaws in their characters, giving them whatever they desire and tolerating

whatever they do and say. When children make trouble out of nothing, parents blame the babysitter instead of punishing their children. If their children bully other children, they speak ill of the other children instead of scolding their own children. When their children's wrongdoings are pointed out by others, parents will not scold them under the pretext that they are still young. With the passage of time, they will be reduced to indecent morality, which is the direct result of parents' dotage. After children have grown up, parents' care thins little by little to the extent that they will become furious about their children's minor mistakes, overstating them as unforgivable and presenting them to their relatives and friends one by one with some exaggeration. The children are even accused of being immoral and guilty. In fact, the children are not to blame. This is the weak point of parents being unreasonably angry. It often starts from the fault of the mother to care and love improperly. And it is often the case that the father believes whatever the mother says before he investigates the truth. To avoid the potential for negative influence, the father should bear in his mind that he should be strict to his children when they are young and offer them love after they have grown up.

In Yuan Cai's opinion, parents tend to go to two extremes: when children are young, they indulge them in whatever they do and whatever they want; after they have reached adulthood, they are harsh in blaming them for minor mistakes. This is the common fault found in parents who have no idea of the proper ways to educate children and who abuse the love and hate they have for their children. Therefore, they might as well go the opposite way, "being strict with their children when they are young and offering them love after they have grown up," which would help them to develop good behaviors at a young age.

To be honest, the fault Yuan Cai has pointed out can still be found in modern parents. So it is fair to say that his argument is of profound significance. This thought also indirectly reflects his thinking that "children should be taught from a young age."

Apart from the two points mentioned above, China's ancient family education had several other noticeable features. First, family education lasted for a long time, starting from birth and ending with death. In ancient China, family education ran through an individual's whole life. One of the moral principles in ancient Chinese society was "not to go against the will of one's parents." Even when one's parents died, one was still under his parents' influence in an unconscious way and following parents' wishes. The death of our ancestors does not mean the loss of their values, merits, achievements, established family rules, mottos, or commandments. Instead, they continue to function as factors in family education and a powerful source for restraining, encouraging, and fostering the development of later generations.

Second, family education in ancient China placed emphasis on instructing and regulating children's social lives. In ancient China, whether children were at home or far from home, whether they were from the family of a high official in the government or the family of a mediocre farmer, they received the same special attention from their parents. Children's behaviors were under parents' constant regulation and supervision. Seldom would parents turn a blind eye to their children's doings. This was true even after children had established their own families, started their careers, and made brilliant achievements. As is recorded in *Biographies of Exemplary Women*:

> Zi Fa, a general from Chu State in the Warring States Period, ran out of pro-visions when conquering Qin state; he alone enjoyed delicious food while his soldiers ate beans; after returning with a full victory over Qin, his mother refused to see him and said, "You order your soldiers to fight in a dangerous battleground, and you enjoy yourself in a safe place. This is not my son, and you are not allowed to step into my home." It was not until Zi Fa apologized that his mother let him in.

Third, the father played the main role in ancient China's family education. In the ancient Chinese family, the father was the supreme authority. The three cardinal guides and the five virtues as specified in the feudal ethical code ruled Chinese society and governed the social life. It was the behavioral norm in ancient society for "the father to guide his son" and for "the husband to guide his wife." The father's economic position and the moral support given by society decided that the father "is in the ruling position, which does not need to be bestowed by the law."[31] The father had the right to control everything related to the children's lives and to regulate the mother's teaching methods.

In contrast, the mother did not have this authority. Before a daughter got married, she was supported by her father. When she became a wife and mother, she received her daily necessities from her husband. After her husband's death, her son supported her. In short, women were to follow the unreasonable ethic of "being obedient to your father at home, obeying your husband after you get married, and submitting to your son when your husband dies." On the other hand, according to Confucian morality, children were to be respectful of and filial toward the mother.

As a result, the mother was considered second to the main role of the father in family education. Because the mother was "controlled" on one hand but played the second most important role in family education on the other hand, women had the double responsibilities of being "an understanding wife" and "a loving mother." The father was mainly responsible for the success of family edu-cation, which can be proved from the saying that "it is the father's fault for not bringing up children properly," written in *The Three-Character Classic*.

3. Placing Emphasis on Behavioral Education

Based on the physical and psychological features of children, ancient educators stressed the significance of behavioral education in elementary education. Children should be "taught proper behaviors." Zhu Xi, an educator in the Southern Song Dynasty, said:

> Education in ancient times consisted of junior [elementary] education and senior [college] education, which provided instruction in consistent doctrines. Junior education focused on how to behave properly before the king, the father, and the elder brother, whereas senior education focused on the reasons for behaviors. Unlike junior education, senior education focused on why young people should behave a certain way before the king, the father, and the elder brother.[32]

In *Instructions for the Enlightenment of Children*, Zhu Xi wrote, "Children's education is acquired successively from the knowledge of clothing, hats, shoes, talking, walking, sanitation, hygiene, reading, handwriting, and many trifles." Obviously, the main task of children's education was to train their behaviors, equipping them with the knowledge of what to do and how to do it, "forcing them to act." Senior education, on the other hand, focused on explaining the reasons for behaviors, "forcing them to understand."

Lv Dalin, an educator in the Song Dynasty, explained systematically the content of the two levels of education and their dialectical relationship. He wrote:

> Junior education is about learning skills and behaviors, whereas senior education is about improving principles and virtues. Skills include rituals, music, shooting, horseback riding, handwriting, and calculation. Behaviors consist of being filial to parents, kind to friends, harmonious with neighbors, loyal to one's spouse, responsible to society, and pious toward the dead. Doing one's utmost for learning and self-cultivation is virtue, whereas what guides the governing of a state should be principle. Education should be completed step by step from junior education to senior education with no impetuous advance. For one who has finished junior education, he must continue his moral education; for one who has high moral standards, he should also accomplish learning in his junior education.[33]

In Lv Dalin's opinion, the purpose of junior education was to learn six skills and six behaviors, whereas the purpose of senior education was to develop principles and virtues. The former provides the foundation, focusing on improving virtues; while the latter goes a step further, focusing mainly on theoretical instruction. To be a noble person, it is impossible "not to finish junior education"; to be a knowledgeable man is out of the question without "accomplishing senior education." This indicates that elementary education, with behavior training as the focus, is the basis for being a civilized citizen. Owing to this, all textbooks compiled by ancient educators focused on interpreting the basic requirements of behavior training, such as *Instructions for the Enlightenment of Children*, by Zhu Xi, *Etiquette Instructions for Children*, by Tu Xiying, *Schedule of Elementary Education*, by Chen Hu, *School Instructions by Mr. Chen and Mr. Dong*, by Cheng Duanmeng and Dong Zhu, *Daily Etiquette in the Private School*, by Zhen Dexiu, and *Ten Commandments in the Ancient Cave Academy*, by Gao Benheng.

Etiquette Instructions for Children includes three parts: monitoring one's body and mind, caring for one's father and elder brothers in the home and one's teacher and elder generations outside the home, and studying at the academy. All the behaviors in this book are discussed in detail, including washing, dressing, crossing fingers, clenching fists, bending, kneeling, standing, sitting, walking, speaking, listening, eating and drinking, sweeping, answering, advancing and retreating, comforting, greeting, coming and leaving, presenting food, sitting beside others, accompanying, meeting, laboring, learning from the teacher, praying on the first and fifteenth days of the lunar month, serving every morning and night, arranging the room, receiving other people, reading, and practicing calligraphy. The concrete requirements for arranging the room are as follows:

> The student should sit up. Learning tools like the book, writing brush, and ink stone should be placed in their respective places so that they can be easily found when needed. Having finished writing, the student should put his tools back in their original places. And those that he has borrowed from or lent to others should be noted in his book so that they can be returned and will not get lost.

As these specifications were easy for children to follow, they were conducive to training children's behaviors. From the perspective of modern psychology, stressing the training of children's behaviors is in accordance with the rule of children's physical and mental development. In terms of perception and motion, children are adept at representation and imitation, which is of great significance to behavior imitation and acquisition. According to developmental psychologist Jean Piaget, at the age of 7, children enter the concrete operational stage, developing a sense of responsibility and self-discipline and eliminating egotism. When children reach the age of 12, they enter the formal operational stage. In this period, according to Piaget, they develop abstract thought and direct their interests to the future. On one hand, they adapt themselves to reality; on the other hand, they cherish aspirations for the future. Also, they start to learn theoretical knowledge. This clearly shows that at the age of

12, children begin to understand abstract theories. Before this age, they develop their behaviors and habits mainly through representation and imitation. This is in line with the assumptions of ancient Chinese scholars who proposed that elementary education before the age of 15 should "force children to act" and that education after 15 should "force children to understand."

In ancient times, stressing behavioral education was to stress moral and ethical education. In elementary education, moral and ethical education was achieved through behavioral specification and training, which were integrated. Regulations for behavior training included the content of moral education, such as cleanliness, courtesy, discipline, and modesty.

4. Placing Emphasis on Positive Education

Ancient Chinese educators valued the positive guidance of children, hoping to exert a positive influence on them through positive education. Educator Wang Tingxiang of the Ming Dynasty said, "Children are pure in thought. Taught with positive influence, they will definitely be guided properly.... After they have reached adulthood, it will be too late for them to change their bad habits, even if instructed with positive education. Therefore, children should be instructed positively when they are young."[34] "Positive influence" here means positive instruction. In other words, children should be guided with positivity so that they receive the right first impressions. Consequently, they will be educated properly in morality.

Wang Yangming, a philosopher in the Ming Dynasty, elaborated on the significance of positive education from the perspective of children's psychological characteristics as follows:

> Children are probably naturally inclined to play, and they dislike restrictions. They are just like sprouting trees; if you make them smooth, they thrive and flourish; if you impede or destroy them, they may wither. Nowadays, it is necessary to encourage and inspire children to make them cheerful and happy when they are taught so that they can make constant progress. Likewise, if flowers and trees receive timely rainfalls with spring winds, there is not one that does not sprout or grow; thus, it is natural that they grow and thrive rapidly. But if frost falls, they will wither and die within a few days. If students are taught with poetry, not only will their ideas and beliefs be expressed, but their depression and pressure will be released in reading aloud. If they are guided with rituals, they will be reverent and respected and get their blood circulating through moving and their bones strengthened through kneeling and bending. If they are asked to chant poetry, they will increase their knowledge and understanding. Meanwhile, the poems will take root in their hearts through constant reading, and their aspirations will become manifested through reading in measured tones. These were the real purposes of ancient education.[35]

Wang Yangming believed that children's hearts are always open to everything that is beautiful. They should be encouraged step by step and have their interests aroused in a logical manner. They should be treated as by the experienced gardener, who always leaves enough room for the little sapling to stretch in all directions instead of restricting its growth. Like the timely rain and spring breeze, positive education can develop children's interests and respect their natures. Otherwise, they will become timid and overcautious, bearing grudges against their parents and teachers, which will have a negative influence on their health.

Zhang Xingjian, an educator in the Qing Dynasty, stated, "In his childhood, a person is always energetic and vibrant, which resembles the start of spring. Those who are good at teaching will educate children by means of reward and exhortation. Although there might be punishment, it must also be accompanied with the good intention of encouragement."[36] He argued that when the punitive method is the only choice, the teacher should not forget positive education to encourage and comfort his student.

Wang Jun in the Qing Dynasty discussed the significance of positive education on children who are slow-witted and stubborn. He said:

> Confucius is good at encouragement. Mencius believes that the teacher should adopt various methods in teaching. When coming across a student who is slow-witted and stubborn, the teacher should encourage him as often as possible. On seizing the opportunity, the teacher praises him, and he will surely be so happy that he follows whatever the teacher says. However, if the teacher punishes him violently, he will suffer not only physical pain, but also psychological misery, and the teacher will also experience agony.[37]

In Wang Jun's opinion, the "slow-witted and stubborn" children were especially in need of positive education. Only through positive education could they experience joy and pleasure, which in turn would stimulate them to follow the teacher's instruction. On the contrary, if the teacher adopted punitive methods and reduced the students to giving up or rebelling, the teacher would be placed in a dilemma where he could do nothing.

The Methods of Elementary Education

Ancient China emphasized the methods of elementary education, and educators proposed some original ideas on the means of elementary education. Many theoretical books were written, including *The Methods of Elementary Education*, by Wang Rixiu in the Song Dynasty, *Sound Rules of Teaching Children*, written in the Ming Dynasty, *Notes on Elementary Education*, by Chen Fangsheng in the

Qing Dynasty, *Measures of Teaching Children*, by Wang Jun, *Persuading Ways of the Father and Teacher*, by Tang Biao, *Rules in the Private School*, by Zhang Xingjian, and *Key Points in Elementary Education*, by Shi Tianji.

Since enlightenment teachers were the ones primarily responsible for elementary education, their abilities and methods had a direct influence on the result of elementary education. Therefore, ancient educators had high requirements for enlightenment teachers and called for prudence in selecting them. Cui Xuegu in the Qing Dynasty said, "It is hard to be a teacher and even harder to be an enlightenment teacher. If the enlightenment teacher fails in instruction, it will be difficult for students to study well. If he succeeds, it will be easy for students to study later. Therefore, one must be very careful in choosing an enlightenment teacher."[38] He believed that being an enlightenment teacher was the most difficult job because it was the most arduous task and had the most far-reaching influence because the quality of elementary education had a direct influence on the quality of children's later education. Owing to this, far sighted educators in ancient times were critical of the adverse social atmosphere. Zhang Lvxiang in the Qing Dynasty said, "The enlightenment teacher has great responsibility, but the public overlooks his role. In contrast, the knowledge of the imperial examination is shallow, but the public thinks highly of it. They are indeed not aware of the difference."[39] Another educator in the Qing Dynasty, Tang Biao, argued for the necessity of respecting enlightenment teachers in terms of their arduous work, meager salary, and far-reaching influence as follows:

People generally respect teachers of Confucian classics but do not show due respect to enlightenment teachers. When meeting their teachers for the first time, students usually present teachers of Confucian classics with added remunerations, whereas for enlightenment teachers, the remunerations are much fewer. Teachers of Confucian classics are generally pleased with the meals provided by students. However, enlightenment teachers eat by themselves most of the time. Although occasionally the students might treat enlightenment teachers, students' attitudes are not serious and are full of inconsistencies. Students fail to understand that enlightenment teachers experience several times more difficulties than teachers of Confucian classics in the process of educating and supervising students. They keep their eyes and ears on their students without a moment of distraction. After classes, their mouths are usually very dry, and they seem to lose the ability to speak. Further, a person's life knowledge depends on what he learns in the ten years of elementary education. Teachers should constantly admonish students so that they can develop good behaviors concerning speaking and acting, and students should extensively read the Confucian classics. How to write and how to hold the pen should be taught clearly to students. Taking pauses when speaking and the four tones should also be taught. There are also rules regarding the noting of Confucian classics and where to pause when reading unpunctuated ancient writings. Success in these areas is completely attributed to the enlightenment teacher. The role of the enlightenment teacher can only be played by one who is both noble-hearted and well educated, while at the same time diligent and strict. Because enlightenment teachers are so laborious and play such important roles, children should never look down upon them.[40]

Tang Biao not only criticized the adverse custom of not respecting the enlightenment teacher, but also defended the important influence of the enlightenment teacher on children's lifetime education. He proposed that the enlightenment teacher should be lofty in morals, erudite in knowledge, and industrious and strict in personality.

When it came to the specific methods of elementary education, ancient scholars focused on four aspects: learning characters, writing characters, reading books, and writing compositions. This indicated that ancient elementary education was inclined to the study of philology, that is, the study of language in written historical sources, and that ethical education was carried out within this framework. What follows is a brief analysis of the education in philology.

1. The Teaching Method of Recognizing Characters

The first step in elementary education in ancient times was recognizing characters. Cui Xuegu remarked, "When children are five or six years old, it is their nature to stay close to their parents, since they are still young. If you want them to learn, you have to first get them used to sitting quietly and reading characters."[41] Wang Jun also asserted that "children should start learning with learning characters."[42] To improve the efficiency of learning characters, ancient educators established several useful methods.

The first method was to use square woodblocks. Tang Biao said:

When children are three or four years old, they are able to utter a few words and have some basic knowledge. To teach them characters, you can prepare a thousand woodblocks in a box, each carved with a character from *The Thousand-Character Scripture* in red. Children can be asked to learn as many as ten characters every day or as few as between three and five. (The one who learns the most should be rewarded according to the number. It is far better to make children want to learn characters than to punish them.) Then you can ask the children to make sentences with the characters they have learned in whatever order they like. The smart children will learn all of them within a hundred days. With additional study through books like *The Three-Character Classic* and *A Collection of a Thousand Poems*, they can learn one to two thousand characters in a year.[43]

This method is similar to the modern game of the scrabbling board, which allows children to put characters together to make sentences provided that they know the characters, and which provides incentive measures to mobilize their enthusiasm.

The second method of encouraging the learning of characters was to use paper. Cui Xuegu wrote:

What is learning characters by paper? In the period of elementary education, do not try to teach students with textbooks. You can write words on a small piece of paper in regular script. On the back of the piece of paper should be written words having similar pronunciations, like "food" and "foot," and "hear" and "here." If the student is intelligent enough, you can explain these simple words to them in an understandable way. Having learned these words, the student should review them, ten words or more a day. Again and again, they will learn them by heart.[44]

Paper functioned almost the same as woodblocks, stressing the importance of starting with specific words. However, Cui Xuegu proposed that another matched word be written on the back of a piece of paper to learn two words in one recital, achieving the effect of killing two birds with one stone. He also placed emphasis on reviewing to better remember words that have been learned.

The third method of teaching characters was to use books, which was also developed by Cui Xuegu. He said:

What is learning words by book? To teach students using textbooks, the teacher should ask students to learn the words in books one by one. When a student comes across unknown words, a red pen is used to mark them, and an explanation is written in black at the top, which is the best way to memorize new words.[45]

This method is the process of reading books on the basis of knowing the words, marking new words with a red pen, and learning them with a black pen. Therefore, it is a combination of learning words and reading books.

The fourth method of teaching children to read characters is to read after knowing a certain number of words. Wang Jun in the Qing Dynasty devoted much time to studying the recognition of words. He suggested that a student should put his effort into learning words first before attempting to read: "The first thing to do is to learn words. There is no need to hurry in reading. If the student struggles, the teacher can explain the meaning after they have learned 1,000 words. It is not until students have learned 2,000 words that they should be allowed to read books."[46] He believed that learning 2,000 words was necessary before students began to read. From the perspective of modern educational psychology, Wang Jun's opinion is reasonable because one is able to classify words according to the features of characters after learning some words, which emphasizes the rule of word formation and simplifies the process of learning words. Meanwhile, this method highlights the key points, arouses an interest in learning, and improves the efficiency of learning words. After mastering some words, students can set out to read full texts.[47]

The fifth method of teaching character recognition was to start with simple characters that are also pictorial images. Wang Jun wrote:

> The teacher can begin with single characters like pictographs and ideographs. For example, when teaching "sun" and "moon," the teacher can show them the sun and the moon in the sky; teaching "above" and "below," the teacher can illustrate the concept with things above and things below. Having taught single characters, the teacher can then move on to compound characters.[48]

Chinese characters consist of three elements: form, pronunciation, and meaning. With the method of identifying the form, the visual function of characters is emphasized, which contributes to children learning the form and meaning of the character. Further, the compound character includes a radical and a single word. The mastering of some radicals and single words paves the way for grasping many Chinese characters. This is in line with the rule of starting from the simple and moving to the complex, from the easy to the difficult. Meanwhile, in order to make learning characters interesting, ancient educators compiled textbooks on learning characters, which were helpful to consolidate what had been learned and to prepare for primary reading. These textbooks primarily consisted of short, rhythmic sentences, making them interesting and easy to read. The two most popular were *The Three-Character Classic* and *The Thousand-Character Classic*.

2. The Teaching Method of Writing Characters

Teaching students how to write characters was an important task in China's ancient elementary education. Ancient educators suggested that learning to write characters should take place after learning to recognize characters and read books, which is quite different from modern primary education, with its focus on simultaneously learning to recognize characters and to read. Three reasons account for the ancient preference for learning to write characters after first learning to recognize characters and then learning to read. The first is that writing in ancient times required a number of writing tools, like brush, ink, paper, and ink stone. The second is that children are not physically strong enough to control the brush. The third is that writing in ancient times was a practice of calligraphy from the very beginning. Therefore, Wang Jun wrote:

> It is not wise to start learning to write at a young age because children's hands are small and weak, which makes it hard to impart to them the proper way of holding and moving the brush. The right time to learn is at the age of 8 or 9, and it is better to learn the inscriptions of Yuanmita and Zanggongbei. Moreover, children should not learn to write small characters at first. Although small characters are not bad, large characters are better.[49]

The key points of teaching writing in elementary education are as follows. First, teach students the right placement for the body and the fingers and the way to hold and move the brush so that they can improve their basic skills. In *Primary Education*, Cui Xuegu described the proper position for the body: "When writing, one should sit erect, his breast three cun (an ancient measurement unit, about 0.03 meter) away from the table, his face three cun away from his back." He then described the position of the fingers: "The palm should be empty, the thumb stretching out, the index finger stretching down, the middle finger directing inside, the little finger beside, and the fourth finger rising up. The brush should be held firmly and straight in a vertical stroke." He then described the four points of holding the brush: "The fingers should be empty (not touching the palm), round (with the back of the fingers in an arc), straight (with the brush standing vertically), and firm (fingers held tight to the brush). He then described the four points of writing: "The horizontal stroke should be level and the vertical stroke plumb. The simple character should be thick and the sophisticated one thin. The comma should be short and the dot round. The blank should be even and the horizontal rectilinear." He clearly described the essentials of calligraphy in a few words which made the process easy for children to remember. Following these instructions ensured that students would make steady progress.

The second key point of teaching writing in elementary education was to attach importance to the role of teachers. Tang Biao wrote:

> Calligraphy is difficult. Few people can write words well. If the teacher is not skilled in calligraphy, he can ask people who are adept at it to copy the characters. If he is too shy to ask for help for fear that he will be laughed at, he will be caught by his own lies. It is the master's fault if he looks down upon the

teacher for his asking for help. Whether he is a good teacher or not does not depend on his calligraphy but on his teaching method.[50]

Tang Biao thought that it was unnecessary for teachers to write characters well. However, the characters that are demonstrated for students must be the best. Further, teachers must know the proper way to write in order to benefit their students.

The third key point of teaching writing in elementary education was to write just a few characters well. Wang Xuzhong wrote: "When students start learning to write, it is better to write only two words at a time. Only after the two words have been written well should they be taught other words. It will not do any good if too many words are taught at a time."[51] He believed that students should be patient in copying characters instead of advancing with undue haste.

The fourth key point of teaching writing in elementary education was to practice. Tang Biao wrote:

The key point in writing lies in the right way of holding the brush, the palm being empty and the fingers being flexible. Since children are at the beginning of learning to write, the teacher must help them move the brush. It will be hard for students to develop a good habit if the brush is not placed in their palms. Considering this, a small cork or a tiny ball of cloth may be a good choice. Having them put something like this in their palms and having the teacher move the brush, the students will learn how to write words well after they have grown up.[52]

He thought that the key point in learning to write was the "palm being empty and the fingers being flexible." At the very beginning, a small stick can be used in place of the brush. In addition, a small ball of cloth could be put in the palm. The teacher holding the student's hand and moving the stick is conducive to the student's developing the proper habit of writing. Further, it was suggested that students should write words large first and small later; they should start with the M letter lattice first, then squared paper, and then blank paper.

3. The Teaching Method of Reading

Ancient reading methods were discussed in Chapter Seven, but the discussion focused mainly on self-study. It is obviously impossible for children to learn all by themselves. Therefore, it is necessary for teachers to give them instruction. Ancient educators thought it extremely important to stimulate children's interest in reading. Wang Jun wrote:

Students are human beings, not animals like pigs or dogs. It will be as boring as chanting scripture or chewing sawdust if students are taught without explanation. The dull student may accept knowledge obediently, whereas the wise one may not be satisfied. Everyone longs for happiness and hates sorrow. Although studying is not as merry-making as playing games, it has its own pleasure.[53]

Wang Jun proposed that the teacher's vivid and well-organized explanation can help mobilize the student's interest. Consequently, the student will read with relish.

As to the specific methods of teaching children how to read, Cui Xuegu elaborated on them the most systematically and exhaustively. In his book *Children's Education*, he discussed the specific processes and methods involved in teaching children how to read. What follows is a brief introduction to his method.

First, he advised respecting books:

When reading classics by ancient sages, children show no respect for their books. Their ink-stained and broken books are the fault of their teacher. So to protect their books, children should wash their hands after using the toilet. And those who have not combed and washed their hair should also wash their hands before they begin to study. In their daily life, they should not touch their books, especially in summer. When reading, their book should be placed about two *cuns* away from the edge of the desk. When turning pages, they should use the right thumb to lift the page up and then pinch it with the help of the index finger. They should not knead the pages with fingers and nails nor stick them with saliva.

These instructions taught children to develop the habit of loving and respecting books.

Second, he advised clearly seeing every word. He said:

When reading a book, a student should hold a bookmark to point to every word he sees. This requires children to see clearly every word when reading.

Third, Cui Xuegu advised understanding every sentence. He said:

There are sentences that consist of several words, and sentences that consist of just one word. Further, there are sentences that can be treated as one sentence in meaning although they are composed of several sentences. When reading sentences, children should see clearly every word and every sentence so as to understand their meaning. At the end of a sentence, they should make a big dot at the end of the sentence. At the end of a grammatical pause, they should make a small dot inside the sentence.

These methods aimed to instruct children in how to understand the whole text by comprehending the meaning of every sentence.

Fourth, he advised reading aloud. He proposed:

When reading aloud, one should not add a word nor omit a word. One should not read repeatedly. The voice should not be too high or too low. The speed should not be too fast or too slow. The most hateful conditions are that one reads as if cursing or like a frog croaking because of excitement and that one reads like a locust singing or a fly buzzing due to depression. All these should be punished.

These were the special requirements for paying attention to tone and speed while reading aloud.

Fifth, Cui Xuegu advised becoming familiar with poetry. He stated:

The student should read five poems aloud every day, with each poem read 20 times. This adds up to 100 times by the fifth day. In addition, they will be read another 100 times the next day, amounting to 200 readings of each poem. Reading a poem for five successive days will definitely make it easier to read fluently and understand better without any stumbling. The newly learned poem is read for five days, and the previously learned poem is read for another five days, adding up to ten days for each poem. With ten-day reading, one is no longer worried about being unfamiliar with a poem.

This describes the serial reading method, namely, reading a certain amount of material every day, with the newly learned piece being read 100 times and the previously learned piece being read 20 times. From the perspective of the Ebbinghaus forgetting curve, this is in accordance with the memory law.

Sixth, he advised monitoring the student's familiarity. He said:

The teacher sets a goal of five poems and checks which ones the students are not familiar with or unaware of. If the teacher makes things difficult for the students on purpose and if they can recite only two to three poems, this proves that they are not familiar with the book. If there are too many students to check one by one, the teacher can choose some of them at random. This might be a good choice. While the teacher is spared much effort, the students are urged to work hard on a full scale.

Cui Xuegu's words explained that the teacher should check the students' knowledge of a book to know whether they have familiarized themselves with it.

Seventh, he advised organizing the books that one has read. He said:

Students should organize the books they have read in 10 days within one day, concluding in the morning and reading a new book in the afternoon. Books that one has read in 20 days should be organized within two days, concluding on the morning of the second day, leaving the afternoon for reading a new book. Likewise, books that one has read in a month should be organized within three days, concluding on the morning of the third day. And books read within a quarter of a year should be organized within five days. When a book is finished, it should be thoroughly organized. At the end of a year, one should reorganize the books he has read in that year.

This was a requirement for students to organize the books they had read systematically in a timely fashion.

Eighth, he advised writing from memory. He advised:

After learning a new book, the student should cover the book and write it down from memory. He is not allowed to write incorrect words. Coming across the same word, he should not replace it with two dots; instead, he should write it twice. If the text has two passages, he should write one passage at a time.

This was a requirement proposed for writing from memory.

Ninth, he advised reviewing. He said:

One must keep reviewing all the books that he has read without exception. If he has finished reading *The Great Learning* and begun *The Doctrine of the Mean*, the latter is new to him and the former is old…reviewing the old when reading the new makes one familiar with all books.

It was required that children constantly go over what they had previously learned.

Tenth, Cui Xuegu advised recital. He said:

The teacher should pay attention to what the student is reciting. When the student makes a mistake or stops in the middle, the teacher should not let the mistake go or remind him of the next words.

Eleventh, he advised explaining. He said:

When children are 8 or 9, their ability to understand is much better than before. Under this condition, the teacher can explain to him sentence by sentence what he is reading. The wise one can comprehend it soon and the slow-witted can digest it gradually with the teacher's patient expounding.

To help the student better understand the reading material, the teacher should explain it in a timely and patient manner. As a result, "even the slowest student will aim high and be willing to learn new knowledge voluntarily for being given encouraging remarks every day."

4. The Teaching Method of Writing

The teaching method of writing was also called composition teaching and was an important part of elementary education. Detailed descriptions can be found in *The Method of Teaching Children*, by Wang Jun, and *Primary Education*, by Cui Xuegu. The following discusses the conclusion of the key points of these books.

First, students should be instructed in how to examine the topic they are studying. Cui Xuegu wrote: "When teaching students to write a composition, the teacher should make students aware of the purpose of the topic. Every time a topic is presented, the teacher should explain to them every paragraph in detail, where to put more ink and where to touch lightly." Only after the students are able to analyze the topic can they follow the right steps in writing and focus on the topic at hand.

Second, students should decide on the title by themselves and write things they are familiar with. Wang Jun said, "One day, I saw the official He Zizhen teaching his cousin how to write poems. His cousin decided on the title himself based on things around him. This was a good choice." Children will have a lot to write if they are given the freedom to choose topics by themselves, which is helpful in developing their interest in writing.

Third, students should be free in their writing but "restrained" after "self-indulgence." Wang Jun said, "Poems and compositions should be written as freely as a wild horse, which can run, jump, and neigh without constraint. If self-indulgent, students will constrict themselves after some time. Then, even though they are yoked, they will be willing to obey." He agreed that, at the beginning of the writing practice, students should be allowed to write without constraint and free their ideas without limit. After a period of practicing, to improve their writing, teachers should lead them to pay attention to their choice of words, the deletion of material, and the structure of their composition, thus improving their writing from a state of complexity to being concise." He gave an example as evidence:

When Wang Muzhou, from Zhu City, began school at the age of 14, there were more than 1,000 words in each work; when he was 18, his composition ranked the fourth in the imperial examination at the provincial level with 700 words; when he was 40, he became the first in the metropolitan exam with less than 600 words in his writing. This is a good example of restraint following self-indulgence.

Fourth, students should be encouraged and praised when revising compositions. Ancient educators advised that a composition written by a beginner should not be corrected too much. Otherwise, students might lose confidence in their writing. Wang Jun wrote, "It is better to give them freedom, and the more, the better. If an important word is misused, it is better to circle it instead of changing it." Zhang Xingjian also wrote:

> The student will be depressed if his composition is revised too much. The stronger one will be angry, and the weaker one will be disappointed, both putting their work aside and never touching upon it. The teacher puts arduous effort into the work, while the student does not appreciate it. Thus, a great distance lies between the teacher and the student, which cannot be bridged.[54]

Without encouragement and praise, the student will lose interest and confidence in writing. What is worse, the relationship between the teacher and the student will be damaged.

Fifth, teachers should help students overcome the plateau phenomenon in their writing practice. Wang Jun said:

> When students are undergoing the process of changing their writing style, their essays must get worse in quality. On this occasion, it is taboo to criticize or scold them. Instead, the teacher should be tolerant, providing encouragement and support and waiting for him to resolve his writing on his own. Thus, his writing ability will be improved greatly. This process is similar to the growth of the silkworm. At first, it is just an ovum; then it develops a body and a head and is able to move slowly, which is better than an ovum. After some time, a cocoon is made and the silkworm turns into a pupa, looking worse than an ovum. Then it gradually grows into a moth, reaching its final state. If the student's writing ability remains at the same level, he is doomed to be useless. Only after some growth can he progress to be a potential writer. If the student is unfortunate to have a foolish teacher who puts an end to his growth, it is indeed a pity.

These words illustrate the rule of progressing in waves in one's writing practice. A student's practice may remain at the same level without significant improvement or worsening throughout a certain period, which is called the "plateau phenomenon" in writing. When this phenomenon occurs, the teacher should not criticize the student, but should "be tolerant, providing encouragement and support and waiting for him to resolve his writing on his own." Consequently, "his writing ability will improve greatly."

Sixth, teachers should instruct students to read a large number of excellent essays and keep them in mind to accumulate writing material. Cui Xuegu wrote: "The students should read extensively. If they can recite passages of thousands of words every day and always remember them, there is no need to worry that there will be not enough words within their control or that they will have nothing to write. The key is to think over what they are reading." Reading constantly selected excellent essays and memorizing their essence will lead to rich diction and natural writings.

Seventh, teachers should teach their students specific procedures for writing. The fundamental purpose of teaching writing in ancient times was for application in later life and to be successful in the imperial examination. Since the imperial examination has fixed procedures, the teacher was to teach his students specific content at the beginning of their learning to write. Cui Xuegu illustrated in great detail the requirements for writing, that is, the "eight steps" (analysis, introduction, topic, writing the key introductory, second, third, and concluding paragraphs, and writing the conclusion); the "five knowings" (knowing the subjective from the objective and notional words from functional words; knowing the outline; knowing the procedures; knowing the transition; and knowing how to construct words); the "forty-word formula" (starting, suspension, negation and affirmation, the objective and subjective, diverging and concentrating, setbacks, reversals, transitions, holding and freeing, rising and falling, corresponding, disturbing, pausing, embellishing, continuing, overturning, deleting and adding, delaying, inserting, and concluding); and "variations in writing." Although these requirements may seem to be too numerous and scattered with trifles, they still have certain guiding functions.

Postscript

China is one of the oldest civilizations in the world. During its process of development, the Chinese nation created a splendid ancient culture, making significant contributions to the progress of humanity. As ancient Chinese culture was powerful in its unifying force, it has been deemed the spiritual pillar for the continuous development of the Chinese nation.

China is a country with thousands of years of educational tradition. It was also one of the first countries in the world to found schools. China's ancient education was not only an integral part of the splendid Chinese culture, but also the foundation and condition for the survival and development of China's ancient culture. It is due to education's unique function of transmission that ancient culture could exist for thousands of years and continuously gain strength with the passage of time.

In the sea of ancient Confucian classics, historical records, philosophical writings, and miscellaneous works, there are abundant educational thoughts. These precious thoughts are the essential wisdom of educators from generation to generation and the treasures of China's history of educational thought. At the same time, they have also enriched the world's educational sciences.

Since the beginning of the twentieth century, Western education has become wide spread in China. A number of excellent educators, by taking into consideration China's education situation, have conducted wide-ranging explorations into and research on educational theories and practices in the process of evaluating and learning about Western education, adding a new and splendid chapter to the world's educational history.

Up until now, there has not been any book touching upon the issue of the achievements of China's educational sciences in a systematic way. Moreover, most books about educational history center on people's thoughts with wide but unfocused contents, and they seldom contain developmental research on contemporary educational sciences, especially discussions about contemporary educational thought. I made up my mind to write a book discussing the educational thought spanning from the time when characters were born until the1990s. Thanks to the great support of Jiangsu Education Publishing House, this book, *Research on China's Educational Thought: Achievements and Contributions of China's Educational Sciences from Ancient Times to the 1990s* finally comes to press.

I am fully aware of the fact that writing a book with such a wide coverage and spanning such a long period of time is not something I could do on my own, nor does my ability permit. Therefore, the publication of this book would not have been possible without the support of many professors and friends. Professor Yan Guocai from Shanghai Normal University and Professor Chu Peijun from Suzhou University have offered materials to me many times, showing support by continuing to enquire about how much I have done and encouraging me to go on with my work. Associate Professor Yuan Zhenguo from East China Normal University sent me a great amount of materials and manuscripts about contemporary Chinese education, thus saving me a lot of time looking for the information I needed when I wrote the chapter on contemporary education. And some of his research opinions are also included in certain chapters of this book. Their "help for me is as great as the mountain" and the "friendship between us is as deep as the sea." In addition, Professor Shinichi Suzuki from Waseda University agreed that I could use this book as my thesis defense for my PhD at Waseda University, which doubtless served as an important impetus for my writing of this book.

Against the backdrop of a sluggish publication of academic works, it is indeed admirable for Jiangsu Education Publishing House to publish this book at any cost. I would like to pay high tribute to Jiangsu Education Publishing House for its efforts to promote Chinese culture and enrich China's educational legacy.

Zhu Yongxin

Notes

Introduction
1. Gu Mingyuan. *Education Dictionary* (supplemental co-edited edition), p. 776. (Shanghai: Shanghai Education Publishing House, 1998).
2. Zhang Binxian and Chu Hongqi. *History of Western Educational Thought*, pp. 2–3. (Chengdu: Sichuan Education Press, 1994).
3. Zhang Huanting. *Education Dictionary*, p. 763. (Nanjing: Jiangsu Education Press, 1989).
4. Mao Zedong. *Where Do Correct Ideas Come From? Selected Readings of Mao Zedong*, volume 2, p. 839. (Beijing: People's Publishing House, 1986).
5. Wu Shiying. *Compendium of Foreign Education*, p. 365. (Beijing: Education and Science Press, 1995).
6. Friedrich Von Engels. *Introduction to the Dialectics of Nature: Selections of K. Marx and F. Engels*, volume 4, pp. 261–262. (Beijing: People's Publishing House, 1995).
7. Friedrich Von Engels. "Engels to Conrad Schmidt in Berlin," in *Selections of K. Marx and F. Engels*, volume 4, p. 703. (Beijing: People's Publishing House, 1995).
8. Friedrich Von Engels. "Engels to Franz Mehring," in *Selections of K. Marx and F. Engels*, volume 4, p. 727. (Beijing: People's Publishing House, 1995).
9. Zhang Binxian and Chu Hongqi. *History of Western Educational Thought*, p. 6. (Chengdu: Sichuan Education Press, 1994).

Chapter 1
1. The Six Arts have their roots in Confucian philosophy and formed the basis of education in ancient China. The Six Arts consist of rites, music, archery, charioteering, calligraphy, and mathematics.
2. *Huainanzi: Fanlunxun (A Compendious Essay)*.
3. *Shangshu: Against Luxurious Ease*.
4. *Shangshu: Prince Shi*.
5. *Shangshu: Announcement to the Prince of Kang*.
6. *Shangshu: Marquis of Lv on Punishments*.
7. *The Book of Poetry: Greater Odes of the Kingdom—King Wen*.
8. *The Book of Poetry: Greater Odes of the Kingdom—Successor*.
9. *A General History of China's Education*, compiled by Mao Lirui and Shen Guanqun, volume 1, p. 138. (Jinan: Shandong Education Press, 1985).
10. *Shangshu: Against Luxurious Ease*.
11. *The Analects of Confucius: Tai Bo*.
12. *The Note of Learning and Teaching*, middle volume.
13. *The Analects of Confucius: Duke Ling of Wei*.
14. Kuang Yaming. *Critical Biography of Confucius*, pp. 277–278. (Jinan: Qilu Press, 1985).
15. In this sense, Mr. Feng Youlan considered Confucius to have "established or at least promoted the intellectual class, who did not belong to the agricultural, industrial, commercial, or official classes." Cf. Feng Youlan. *History of Chinese Philosophy*, first volume, p. 71. (Beijing: Zhonghua Book Company, 1961).
16. *The Analects of Confucius: Shu Er (Transmission)*.
17. *The Analects of Confucius: Yong Ye (There Is Yong)*.
18. *The Historical Records: The Collected Biographies of Confucius' Students*.
19. *Xuncius: Feishierzi (Critics of Twelve Intellects)*.
20. *Zhuangzi: Abdication of the Crown*.
21. *The Analects of Confucius: Xue Er (Studying)*.
22. *The Analects of Confucius: Yang Huo*.
23. Gao Zhuancheng. *Confucius: The Disciples of Confucius*, p. 4. (Taiyuan: Shanxi People's Press, 1991).

24. Cf. Zhang Ruifan. *Research on China's Education History*, Pre-Qin subsection, p. 124. (Shanghai: East China Normal University Press, 1991).

25. [USSR] N. A. Konstantinov, et al. *The History of Education*, trans. Li Zizhuo et al., p. 23. (Beijing: People's Education Press, 1958).

26. Wang Shunan. "Commentary on The Note of Learning," *Journal of China*, 1913 (5th and 6th ed.).

27. [Japan] Takeshi Taniguchi. *Verification of The Note of Learning: Foreword*, quoted in *Commentary and Annotations on The Note of Learning*, compiled by Gao Shiliang, p. 163. (Beijing: People's Education Press, 1982).

28. Cf. *Famous Educators in the World*, compiled by the Research Office of Comparative Education of the National Institute of Education Sciences, p. 25. (Guiyang: Guizhou People Press, 1989).

29. *The Analects of Confucius: Wei Zheng* (*The Practice of Government*).

30. *Mencius: Jin Xin* (*Exhaustion of the Mental Constitution*).

31. *The Analects of Confucius: Li Ren* (*Living in Brotherliness*); *The Analects of Confucius: Xue Er* (*Studying*).

32. *Mencius: Teng Wen Gong* (*Duke Wen of Teng*).

33. Ibid.

34. *Xuncius: Quanxue* (*The Persuasion of Learning*) said, "Therefore, power and benefit cannot touch him, nor can the strength of numerous people yield him, nor can all the things in the world change his faith, whether he is alive or dead. This behavior can be called virtue and integrity. With virtue and integrity, one can be persevering and then flexible in response. With perseverance and flexibility, one can be called a mature and perfect man. At that time, heaven will show its brightness and earth its breadth. The worth of a noble man lies in his perfect virtue."

35. *Mo-tse: Shangxian Zhong* (*Exaltation of the Virtuous*).

36. *Han Feizi: Wudu* (*The Five Walks of Life*).

37. *Laozi: Chapter 25.*

38. Dong Zhongshu. *Chun Qiu Fan Lu: Shixing* (*The Annotation of Chun Qiu: Human Characters*).

39. Wang Chong. *Lun Heng: Shuaixing* (*On Balance: Human Nature*).

40. *Lun Heng: Shizhi* (*On Balance: Verifying Knowledge*).

41. *Lun Heng: Xiaoli* (*On Balance: Making Use of Abilities*).

42. *Lun Heng: Shizhi* (*On Balance: Verifying Knowledge*).

43. In 1937, the American scholar J. K. Shryock once translated *The Records of the Figures* into a book called *Research on Human Abilities*, published by the American Eastern Institute.

44. *The Collected Works of Ji Kang: Buyi* (*Divination of Doubts*).

45. Yan Zhitui. *Admonitions for the Yan Clan: Encouraging Learning.*

46. *Admonitions for the Yan Clan: Teaching the Son.*

47. Wang Sanpin. *Verification of Ancient and Present Matters.*

48. Yuan Zhong. *Miscellany of Family Court*, volume 2.

49. Complied by Li Jingde. *The Analects of Zhu Xi and His Disciples*, volume 12.

50. Cf. *A General History of China's Education*, compiled by Mao Lirui and Shen Guanqun, volume 3, p. 151. (Jinan: Shangdong Education Press, 1987).

51. *The Collected Works of Lu Jiuyuan: Essay*; *The Collected Works of Lu Jiuyuan: To Li Zai.*

52. *The Collected Works of Lu Jiuyuan: To Shu Ximei.*

53. *The Collected Works of Lu Jiuyuan: Analects.*

54. Ibid.

55. Guo Qijia. *History of China's Educational Thought*, pp. 290–293. (Beijing: Education Science Publishing House, 1987).

56. *The New History of the Dynasty of Yuan: Shihuozhi* (*Records of Food and Goods*).

57. *The Whole Collection of Duke Wang Wencheng: General Ideas of Children's Education After Reading the Work of Liu Bosong and Others.*

58. Li Zhi. *Burning Books: Three Verses for the Two Masters—Huang and An.*

59. Wang Fuzhi. *Views on Reading Zizhitongjian* (*History as a Mirror*).

Chapter 2

1. [Germany] Georg Wilhelm Friedrich Hegel. *Historical Philosophy*, trans. Wang Zaoshi, p. 124. (Beijing: The Commercial Press, 1963).

2. Wei Zhengtong. *Overview of Chinese Culture: Analysis of Traditional Culture.* (Taipei: Buffalo Book Co., 1973).

3. Cf. Feng Tianyu and Zhou Jiming. *The Mystery of China's Ancient Culture*, p. 59. (Wuhan: Hubei People's Press, 1986).

4. *Selected Collection of Lenin*, volume 3, p. 608. (Beijing, People's Press, 1972). (Translation revised according to the retranslated version of the Central Compilation & Translation Bureau.)

5. Cf. Yang Guoshu. "The Formation and Transformation of the Characters and Behaviors of the Chinese," published in *Discussion About Chinese Culture* by Taiwan's Scholars, edited by Zhang Wenda and Gao Zhihui, pp. 209–211. (Harbin: Heilongjiang Education Press, 1989).

6. [United States] Karl August Wittfogel. *Oriental Despotism*, trans. Xu Shigu et al., p. 18. (Beijing: China Social Sciences Press, 1989).

7. Liang Qichao. *The Relationship Between Geography and Civilization*, volume 10 of *The Collected Works of Yinbing Room*.

8. Fei Xiaotong. *Traditional Ethical Concepts and Population Issues of China, Selected Works of Fei Xiaotong*, pp. 499–500. (Tianjin: Tianjin People's Press, 1988).

9. Gao Yabiao and Wu Danmao. *Deep Down in the National Soul*, p. 32. (Beijing: China Federation of Literary and Art Circles Publishing Co., 1988).

10. Mao Zuhuan. *Viewing the Development of Education from the Methodology*, p. 20. (Chongqing: Chongqing Publishing House G, 1990).

11. Selected translation by Ren Zhongyin. *Selected Works of Education Theories of Quintilianus*, p. 168. (Beijing: People's Education Press, 2001).

12. Ibid., p. 159.

13. *The Analects of Confucius: Shu Er (Transmission)*.

14. *The Analects of Confucius: Ba Yi (Eight Lines of Eight Dancers Apiece)*.

15. *The Analects of Confucius: Different Learning*.

16. *Mencius: Gongsun Chou*.

17. *Mencius: Gongsun Chou*.

18. *Mencius: Gongsun Chou*.

19. *Mencius: Li Lou*.

20. Lin Yutang. *Chinese People* (literal translation: *My Country and My People*), trans. Hao Zhidong and Shen Yihong, pp. 83–85. (Hangzhou: Zhejiang People's Press, 1988).

21. Cf. Gao Ruiquan. "The National Mindset and Traditional Educational Model," in *The Transmission and Evolution of Culture*, ed. Ding Gang, p. 11. (Shanghai: Shanghai Education Press, 1990).

22. *The Whole Collection of Marx and Engels*, volume 2, p. 170. (Beijing: People's Press, 1972).

23. *Edition of Masterworks of Western Ethics*, compiled by Zhou Fucheng, volume 1, p. 303. (Beijing: The Commercial Press, 1964).

24. Xu Kangsheng. *Annotations of and Research on the Silk Manuscripts of Laozi*, pp. 68–69. (Hangzhou: Zhejiang People's Press, 1982).

25. *The Analects of Confucius: Li Ren (Living in Brotherliness)*.

26. *The Analects of Confucius: Shu Er (Transmission)*.

27. *The Record of Ideas*, part 9.

28. *Mo-tse: Da Qu (Major Illustrations)*.

29. *Mo-tse: Gui Yi (Esteem of Righteousness)*.

30. [Great Britain] Bertrand Russell. *Wisdom of the West*, trans. Ma Jiaju and He Lin, pp. 10–13. (Beijing: World Affairs Press, 1992).

31. [United States] Quoted from Burks. "Computers and Education," in *Translation Collection of Philosophy*, volume 3, 1984.

32. Jin Yuelin. "Chinese Philosophy," in *Research of Philosophy*, volume 9, 1985.

33. *The Analects of Confucius: Zizhang*.

34. Cf. Gao Ruiquan. "The National Mindset and Traditional Educational Model," in *The Transmission and Evolution of Culture*, edited by Ding Gang, p. 35.

35. *The Analects of Confucius: Wei Ling Gong (Duke Ling of the Wei State)*.

36. *Xuncius: Tian Lun (Statement About Heaven)*.

37. Quoted from Zhang Haishan. *The History of Western Ethical Thought*, p. 35. (Shenyang: Liaoning People's Press, 1984).

38. Cf. *Collection of Famous Works of Western Ethics*, compiled by Zhou Fucheng, volume 1, p. 309. (Beijing: The Commercial Press, 1964).

39. *The Philosophy of Ancient Greece and Rome*, p. 41. (Beijing: China Renmin University Press, 1989).

40. *The Analects of Confucius: Xue Er (Studying)*.

41. *The Analects of Confucius: Ji Shi (Chief of the Ji Clan)*.

42. *The Analects of Confucius: Xian Jin (Those of Former Eras)*: "Zigong asked, 'Zizhang and Zixia, which one is better?' Confucius said, 'Zizhang is excessive, while Zixia is insufficient.' Zigong said, 'So is Zizhang better?' Confucius said, 'Excess is equal to insufficiency.'"

43. *The Analects of Confucius: Xian Jin (Those of Former Eras)*.

44. *The Analects of Confucius: Wei Zheng (The Practice of Governance).*
45. *The Analects of Confucius: Xue Er (Studying).*
46. *Mencius: Gaozi.*
47. Cf. Zhang Haishan. *The History of Western Ethical Thought*, p. 57. (Shenyang: Liaoning People's Press, 1984).
48. Cf. Gao Ruiquan and Yuan Zhenguo. *Theory of Personality*, p. 48. (Shanghai: Shanghai Culture Publishing House, 1989).
49. *Educational Theories of Western Thinkers*, compiled by Xu Buzeng, p. 41. (Beijing: People's Education Press, 1985).
50. [United States] John Dewey. *The School and Society*, ed. and trans. Zhao Xianglin and Wang Chengxu, published in *Selected Works of Dewey's Educational Theories*, p. 33. (Shanghai: East China Normal University Press, 1981).
51. *The Analects of Confucius: Zi Han (The Master Shunned).*
52. [Germany] Georg Wilhelm Friedrich Hegel. *The Philosophy of History*, trans. Wang Zaoshi, p. 95. (Shanghai: Shanghai Bookstore Publishing House, 2001).
53. [Germany] Georg Wilhelm Friedrich Hegel. *Lectures on the History of Philosophy*, book 1, trans. He Lin and Wang Taiqing, p. 10. (Beijing: The Commercial Press, 1981).
54. Quoted from *The Philosophy of Society in Contemporary China*, chiefly edited by Chen Yanqing, p. 108. (Tianjin: Tianjin People's Press, 1990).
55. Lin Shimin. *The Spiritual Features of Buddhism*, p. 21. (Putian, Fujian: Buddhist Books Center of Guanghua Monastery, copy of reproduction, 1988).
56. *The Analects of Confucius: Xue Er (Studying).*
57. *Chu Qiu Fan Lu: Zhong Zheng (The Annotation of Chun Qiu: Emphasis on Political Affairs).*
58. *Collection of Mr. Hui'an: Duke Wen of Zhu*, volume 39.
59. This is the original poem of Mr. Li Dazhao, which in fact also reflected the general mindset and integrity of Chinese intellectuals. Therefore, it is quoted here.
60. Cai Yuanpei. "The Chinese Nation and the Doctrine of the Mean," in *The Brief Documentation of the History of China's Modern Thinking*, chiefly edited by Cai Shangsi, volume 3, p. 503. (Hangzhou: Zhejiang People's Press, 1983).
61. *The Analects of Confucius: Yan Yuan.*
62. *The Analects of Confucius: Yong Ye (There Is Yong).*
63. Jiao Guocheng. *On the Other–Self Relationship in Ancient China*, p. 57. (Beijing: China Renmin University Press, 1991).
64. Yang Bin. "On the Promotion of National Traditional Education and Culture," in *Jiangsu Education Research*, volume 1, 1992.
65. *Guanzi: Ba Yan (Views on the Cause of the Dominant Position).*
66. *Zhen Guan Zheng Yao (Records of Important Political Affairs During the Period of Zhenguan): On Farming.*

Chapter 3

1. *The Analects of Confucius: The Practice of Government.*
2. *The Analects of Confucius: Zilu.*
3. Ibid.
4. *The Analects of Confucius: Yao Yue (Yao Spoke).*
5. *Mencius: Li Lou.*
6. *Mencius: Jin Xin (Make an Effort to Do Good Deeds).*
7. *Xuncius: Da Lue (General Ideas).*
8. *Mo-tse: Shang Xian (Treasure Talents).*
9. *Mo-tse : Lu Wen (Lu's Question).*
10. *Guanzi: Quan Xiu (Cultivation of Power).*
11. *Laozi: Chapter 18.*
12. *History of the Han Dynasty: The Biography of Dong Zhongshu.*
13. Ibid.
14. Ibid.
15. *Lun Heng: Fei Han (On Balance: Refutation of Han Fei).*
16. *Lun Heng: Shuai Xing (On Balance: Human Nature).*
17. *Fuzi: Tong Zhi (General Annals).*
18. *Fuzi: Que Ti (No Title).*
19. Han Yu. "Submission to the Prime Minister," *Collection of Han Changli*, volume 16.
20. Wang Anshi. "The Note of Learning in Cixi County of Mingzhou," in *The Collection of Duke Wen of Wang*, volume 34.
21. Wang Anshi. "Tens of Thousands of Words Submitted to the Emperor," in *The Collection of Duke Wen of Wang*, volume 1.

22. *Cheng's Annotation of the Book of Changes: Ignorance.*
23. Zhu Xi. *Collected Annotations of The Four Books: Collected Annotations of The Analects of Confucius.*
24. *Cheng's Annotation of the Book of Changes: Ignorance.*
25. Ibid.
26. Ibid.
27. *Analects of Zhuzi*, volume 23.
28. *Collection of Cheng Yi and Cheng Hao: Submission to the Prime Minister for My Father.*
29. Wang Fuzhi. *Annotations of The Four Books*, volume 37.
30. Qiu Chun. *Collections of Theses on Ancient Educational Thought*, volume 2, p. 41. (Beijing: Beijing Normal University Press, 1985).
31. Compiled by Li Gong. *A Chronicle of Mr. Yan Xizhai*, volume 2.
32. Yan Yuan. *Xizhai's Essays*, volume 1.
33. *The Analects of Confucius: Yang Huo.*
34. Although on the surface, Mencius's theory of good human nature addressed Gaozi's idea that "there is no good or bad in human nature," his main theoretical foundation was Confucius' propositions that humans are "born with knowledge" and "men are similar by nature; they grow apart through practice." Xuncius's theory of evil human nature directly criticized Mencius's theory, but its theoretical foundation was Confucius' proposition that humans are "born with knowledge."
35. *Lun Heng: Ming Yi (On Balance: The Meaning of Life).*
36. *Lun Heng: Shuai Xing (On Balance: Human Nature).*
37. *The Analects of Zhuzi*, volume 4.
38. Wang Anshi. *The Third Answer to Wang Shenfu's Letter.*
39. In *Views of Nature*, Wang Anshi said, "Those who practice only good deeds are the so-called extremely wise men; those who practice only evil deeds are the extremely stupid men; those who practice good deeds on one hand and evil deeds on the other are the common people. The fame of an extremely wise man, an extremely stupid man, and a common person are defined after their death....When one is unwilling to change, he is then famed as an extremely stupid man, which is defined after his death; it is not what he was invariably born to be."
40. Wang Tingxiang. *Private Collection: Answer to Xue Juncai's Letter About the Theory of Human Nature.*
41. Wang Tingxiang. "Concentration," in *Watching over Words.*
42. Wang Tingxiang. "Formation of Nature," in *Watching over Words.*
43. Wang Fuzhi. *Waiting for Interpretation.*
44. Wang Fuzhi. *Quotes and Annotations of Shang Shu*, volume 3.
45. *Collection of Yan Yuan: Compilation of Nature*, volume 2.
46. Dai Zhen. *Annotations and Verification of Mencius*, volume 2.
47. *Mencius: Gaozi.*
48. Shao Yong. *Yin Chuan Ji Rang Ji* (a collection of Shao Yong's poems): *Ode to All the Pleasant Scenes.*
49. Shao Yong. "The Observation of Things Outside Objects," in *Huang Ji Jing Shi* (a book discussing the origins of the universe, the evolution of nature, and the changes of social history).
50. Originally written by Huang Zongxi and revised by Quan Zhuwang. *Education Cases of the Dynasties of Song and Yuan*, volume 15.
51. *Inherited Records of the Hu Clan.*
52. *Collection of the Cheng Brothers: Remained Records*, volume 2.
53. *The Complete Collection of Duke Wencheng of Wang: Prologue of the Collection of the Ziyang Academy.*
54. *The Complete Collection of Duke Wencheng of Wang: Edition Sequel.*
55. *Xuncius: Persuasion of Learning.*
56. *Xuncius: Confucians.*
57. *Collection of Chen Liang: A Letter to Ying Zhongshi.*
58. Ye Shi. *Records of Practicing and Learning*, volume 14.
59. *A Letter to Xue Juncai.*
60. *Refined Discussion*, volume 1.
61. *The Analects of Confucius: Shu Er (Transmission).*
62. Ibid.
63. *The Analects of Confucius: Xian Wen (Xian Asked).*
64. *The Analects of Confucius: King Ling of Wei State.*
65. *The Analects of Confucius: Xue Er (Studying).*

66. *The Historical Records: Collected Biographies of Confucians.*
67. *The Analects of Confucius: Zizhang.*
68. *Mo-tse: Universal Love.*
69. *Mencius: King Wen of Teng State.*
70. *Zhuangzi: Xiao Yao You (Mental Freedom).*
71. *Han Feizi: Entirety.*
72. *Lun Heng: Chaoqi (On Balance: The Supreme Extraordinary Talents).*
73. Ibid.
74. Ibid.
75. *Admonitions for the Yan Clan: Encouraging Learning.*
76. *Admonitions for the Yan Clan: Engaging in Social Affairs.*
77. Han Yu. "Discussion of Dao," in *The Complete Collection of Han Changli*, volume 11.
78. *School Regulations of Bailudong Academy* (also called *The Doctrines of Bailudong Academy* and *The Announcement of Bailudong Academy*).
79. Wang Anshi. "Tens of Thousands of Words Submitted to the Emperor," in *The Collection of Duke Wen of Wang*, volume 1.
80. Wang Anshi. "The Selection of Talents," in *The Collection of Duke Wen of Wang*, volume 32.
81. *The Collection of Chen Liang: A Letter Written in the Autumn of the Year Jiachen.*
82. *Collection of Ye Shi: Paper Submission—Education of Scholars.*
83. *Xizhai's Essays*, volume 1.
84. *Records of Mr. Yan Xizhai's Words and Behaviors*, volume 2.
85. Ibid.
86. *The Sequel of Records of Thinking on Surrounding Matters*, volume 2.
87. Wang Anshi. "A Discussion of Education," in *The Collection of Duke Wen of Wang*, volume 32.

Chapter 4

1. [Germany] Johann Friedrich Herbart. "The Science of Education and the Aesthetic Revelation of the World," in *A Selection of Educational Works by the Western Bourgeoisie*, edited by Zhang Huanting, pp. 249–250. (Beijing: People's Education Press, 1964).
2. [USSR] Vasyl Olexandrovych Sukhomlynsky. *Advice for Teachers*, ed. and trans. Du Diankun, p. 227. (Beijing: Education Science Publishing House, 1982).
3. Words and phrases containing "De" in the inscriptions of the copper vessels in the Western Zhou Dynasty included Bing De (maintaining morality), Zheng De (rectifying morality), Kong De (great virtue), An De (holding morality), Hu De (great virtue), Lie De (righteous virtue), Jie De (grand virtue), Yi De (the virtue of women), Ming De (illustrious virtue), Ruo De (the virtue of obedience), Shou De (supreme virtue), Yuan De (original virtue), Bing Yuan Ming De (maintaining original and illustrious virtue), Bing Ming De (maintaining illustrious virtue), Jing De (virtue of respect), Jing De (common virtue), and Zhe Jue De (illustrating the morality of the ancestors).
4. Cf. Zhu Qixin "Viewing the Education of the Western Zhou Dynasty from Copper Vessels," in *Education Research*, volume 3, 1984.
5. *The Analects of Confucius: Xue Er (Studying).*
6. Gao Changjiang. "Retrospection of the Culture of Traditional Education," in *Xinhua Abstract*, volume 12, 1987.
7. *The Analects of Confucius: Wei Zheng (The Practice of Government).*
8. *Mencius: Duke Wen of Teng.*
9. *The History of the Han Dynasty: Biography of Dong Zhongshu.*
10. *Lun Heng: Liang Zhi (On Balance: Measuring Knowledge).*
11. *The Whole Collection of Duke Wang Wencheng: General Ideas of Children's Education After Reading the Works of Liu Bosong and Others.*
12. Wang Fuzhi. *The Annotations of the Cultivation of Children of Zhang Zizheng*, volume 4.
13. Wang Fuzhi. *Collected Reviews of The Four Books*, volume 1.
14. *Mencius: Duke Wen of Teng.*
15. *Mencius: Li Lou.*
16. *Xuncius: Encouragement of Learning.*
17. *Collection of Zhang Zai: Analects.*
18. *Shangshu: Duo Fang (Many a Territory).*
19. *The Analects of Confucius: Duke Ling of State Wei.*
20. *The Analects of Confucius: Xue Er (Studying).*

21. *The Analects of Confucius: Taibo.*
22. *The Collection of Zhang Zai: The Study of Classics and Principles: Connotation of Classics.*
23. *Chun Qiu Fan Lu: Bi Ren Qie Zhi (The Annotation of Chun Qiu: Benevolent and Wise)*
24. Liu Shao. *Records of Personages: Eight Observational Methods.*
25. *The Complete Collection of Mr. Yang Yuan,* volume 40.
26. *The Complete Collection of Mr. Yang Yuan,* volume 41.
27. *Annotations of Mencius,* volume 1.
28. *The Collected Works of Lu Jiuyuan: Analects.*
29. Lu Jiuyuan discussed the specific stages of the process of moral education in great
     depth. The following are some significant selections: "'Practice, the foundation of virtue'
     established practice as the foundation of virtue. Fundamental means the origin. Virtue
     will progress through practice. Without practice, how can the virtue accumulate?"
     "'Modesty is the handle of virtue' means to possess without claiming credit or having
     any pride. The modest are not complacent. When one is complacent, one loses his
     virtue. If one's heart is never complacent, his virtue will accumulate continually.
     Therefore, it is said that 'modesty is the handle of virtue.'" "Restoration comes after
     modesty. Restoring oneself when alive means the restoration of kindness. People's
     original nature is good, while evil things can be reflected in substances. Since people
     know the bad side of substances and make retrospections of themselves, it can be
     seen that kindness is the inherent nature of people. To follow our inherent nature and
     improve our morality can gain us nothing but a noble spirit. Therefore it is said that
     'restoration is the root of morality.'" "The combination of the internal and the external
     sides comes after the awareness of restoration. But if one cannot maintain it constantly,
     his morality will not stand firm, and it may in the end become lost though having been
     gained once. Therefore it is said that 'perseverance is the solidity of morality.'" "The
     cultivation of morality for a noble man is to eliminate the encumbrance of morality in
     order to improve it. Therefore it is said that 'to decrease [one's] desires' is the cultivation
     of morality." "The everyday accumulation of kindness will end in abundance. Therefore
     it is said that 'correction is the abundance of morality.'" "Correction is to move
     toward kindness to benefit one's morality; his morality is then improved and becomes
     abundant." "Without going through difficult situations, one's morality cannot be
     exercised. Therefore it is said that 'difficulty is the exercise of morality.'" "It is noble to
     nurse people and benefit things, and this is the morality of a noble man. Therefore it is
     said that 'nobility is the field of morality.'" "Doing like this, one can make a difference.
     Those who can make a difference always act according to circumstances; those who do
     not are just scholars in their hometowns, which is not a great virtue. Acting according
     to circumstances is not following convention or associating with evil, but just acting
     like Yu, Ji, and Yanzi. Therefore it is said that 'compliance is the principle of morality.'"
     Cf. *The Collected Works of Lu Jiuyuan: Analects.*
30. *The Analects of Confucius: Zi Han (The Master Shunned).*
31. *The Analects of Confucius: Shu Er (Transmission).*
32. *Xuncius: Discussion of Names.*
33. *Xuncius: To Overcome Deceit.*
34. *Analects of Zhuzi,* volume 9.
35. Zhuxi. *The School Regulations of Bailudong Academy.*
36. *Mencius: Gongsun Chou.*
37. *Mencius: Jin Xin (Make an Effort to Do Good Deeds).*
38. *The Analects of Zhuzi,* volume 27.
39. *The Analects of Zhuzi,* volume 21.
40. Ibid.
41. *The Analects of Confucius: Yang Huo.*
42. Ibid.
43. *The Analects of Confucius: Xian Jin (Those of Former Eras).*
44. *The Analects of Confucius: There Is Yong.*
45. *The Analects of Confucius: Gongye Chang.*
46. *Records of Mr. Yan Xizhai's Words and Behaviors.*
47. *The Analects of Confucius: Gongye Chang.*
48. Ibid.
49. *The Analects of Zhuzi,* volume 13.
50. *The Analects of Zhuzi,* volume 16.
51. *The Collected Annotations of The Four Books: Annotations of The Analects of
     Confucius—Taibo.*
52. *The Annotations of Mencius,* volume 1.

53. *The Analects of Confucius: Taibo.*
54. Confucius made two entries about the function of moral education in *The Book of Poetry*: "The odes in *The Book of Poetry* serve to stimulate the mind. They may be used for purposes of self-contemplation. They teach the art of sociability. They show how to regulate feelings of resentment. From them you learn the more immediate duty of serving one's father and the more remote duty of serving one's emperor." (*The Analects of Confucius: Yang Huo*). "In *The Book of Poetry* there are 300 pieces, but the design of them all may be embraced in one sentence: 'Having no depraved thoughts.'" [*The Analects of Confucius: Wei Zheng (The Practice of Government)*].
55. *The Analects of Confucius: Shu Er (Transmission)*: "When the Master was in Qi, he heard the Shao and for three months did not know the taste of flesh. He said, 'I did not know that music could have been made so excellent as this.'" "When the Master was in the company of a person who was singing, if he sang well, he would make him repeat the song, while he accompanied it with his own voice."
56. Zhu Xi developed Confucius' thoughts in *The Collected Annotations of The Four Books*: "Among all the odes in *The Book of Poetry*, those with kind content can inspire people's kindness; those with bad content can reduce people's far-reaching ambitions. Its overall function is to rectify people's temperament." Wang Yangming, on the other hand, emphasized the significance of poems in the moral education of children: "The purpose of learning etiquette and poems is to store them in children's minds so that they can learn them unremittingly and have no spare time to think about evil things." (*Practicing the Instructions*, volume 2).
57. *The Annotations of The Four Books*, volume 21.
58. Cf. Qiu Chun. *Collections of Theses on Ancient Educational Thought*, volume 2, p. 89. (Beijing: Beijing Normal University Press, 1985).
59. *The Annotations of The Four Books*, volume 7.
60. *The Annotations of The Book of Rites*, volume 19.
61. *The Analects of Confucius: Shu Er (Transmission)*.
62. *Mencius: Gongsun Chou.*
63. *The Collection of Zhang Zai: The Education of Children—The Most Reasonable Things.*
64. *The Collection of Lu Jiuyuan: A Discussion of The Analects of Confucius.*
65. *The Collection of Thinking and Questioning: The Supplementary Articles.*
66. *The Annotations of The Cultivation of Children by Zhang Zai*, volume 5.
67. *Mencius: Gaozi.*
68. *Mengzi: Gaozi.*
69. *Han Feizi: Annotations of Laozi.*
70. Volume 13 of *The Analects of Zhuzi* states, "Learners should eliminate all their desires and restore the heavenly principles; this can then be called learning." "In the one heart of a person, the keeping of a heavenly nature means the death of human desires; the excelling of human desires means the perishing of the heavenly nature. The heavenly nature cannot coexist with human desires, and this should be learned by the learners."
71. *The Annotations of The Four Books*, volume 11.
72. *The Analects of Confucius: Shu Er (Transmission)*.
73. *The Analects of Confucius: Li Ren (Living in Brotherliness)*.
74. *The Annotations of the Magnificent Phenomena in The Book of Changes: Kan (Difficulties)*.
75. *The Analects of Confucius: Shu Er (Transmission)*.
76. *Mo-tse: Lu Asked.*
77. Volume 9 of *The Analects of Zhuzi* states, "For attaining knowledge and effortful practice, one should keep a balance between the two; otherwise, the biased one would be crippled. For example, Cheng Ziyun said, 'One's cultivation lies in his respect and his learning in his attainment.' He clearly divided the two, which should be sequenced and weighed differently. In terms of the sequence, the attainment of knowledge should come first; but in terms of weight, effortful practice should be emphasized."
78. *The Expansion of the Supplement of The Great Learning.*
79. *The Analects of Confucius: Wei Zheng (The Practice of Government)*.
80. *The Analects of Confucius: Yan Yuan.*
81. *The Analects of Confucius: Li Ren (Living in Brotherliness)*.
82. *The Analects of Confucius: Xue Er (Studying)*.
83. *The Analects of Confucius: Wei Zheng (The Practice of Government)*.
84. *The Analects of Confucius: Xian Wen (Xian Asked)*.
85. Ibid.

86. *The Analects of Confucius: Yang Huo.*
87. Ibid.
88. *The Analects of Confucius: Gongye Chang.*
89. Ibid.
90. *The Analects of Confucius: Duke Ling of Wei.*
91. *The Analects of Confucius: Xue Er (Studying).*
92. *The Analects of Confucius: Zizhang.*
93. *The Whole Collection of Duke Wang Wencheng,* volume 2.
94. *The Analects of Confucius: Yan Yuan.*
95. *The Analects of Confucius: Shu Er (Transmission).*
96. *The Analects of Confucius: Yan Yuan.*
97. *The Collected Annotations of Children's Learning: The Foreword of Children's Learning,* edited by Zhang Boxing.
98. *The Collected Annotations of Children's Learning: Edited Theories of Children's Learning.*
99. *The Whole Collection of Duke Wang Wencheng,* volume 2: *Practicing the Instructions.*
100. Lu Jie. "The Primary Exploration of the Process of Moral Education," in *Educational Research,* volume 2, 1981.
101. *Xuncius: Persuasion of Learning.*
102. *Xuncius: Honor and Humiliation.*
103. *Xuncius: Persuasion of Learning.*
104. *Private Collection: Answer to Xue Juncai's Letter About the Theory of Human Nature.*
105. *Watching over Words: Bao Fu (Teachers for the Emperor or Princes).*
106. *Biography of Virtuous Women: Motherhood.*
107. *The Analects of Confucius: Shu Er (Transmission).*
108. *The Analects of Confucius: Yan Yuan.*
109. *The Analects of Confucius: Ji Shi (Chief of the Ji Clan).*
110. Ibid.
111. *The Analects of Confucius: Xue Er (Studying).*
112. *The Collection of Zhang Zai: The Annotations of Classics—The Essential Principles of Learning.*
113. *School Principles Showing All the Students in Longchang.*
114. *Waiting to Be Solved.*
115. *Annotations of The Four Books,* volume 8. Cf. Qiu Chun: *Collected Theories of the Ancient Educational Thought,* volume 2, pp. 128–129. (Beijing: Beijing Normal University Press, 1985).
116. [USSR] Vasyl Olexandrovych Sukhomlynsky. *The Art of Education,* trans. Xiao Yong, p. 267. (Changsha: Hunan Education Press, 1983).
117. *The Analects of Confucius: Yan Yuan.*
118. *The Analects of Confucius: Shu Er (Transmission).*
119. *Mencius: Li Lou.*
120. *The Analects of Confucius: Li Ren (Living in Brotherliness).*
121. *The Analects of Confucius: Xue Er (Studying).*
122. Quoted from *Selected Annotations of China's Ancient Educational Poems,* ed. Chen Hancai, pp. 107–108. (Jinan: Shandong Education Press, 1985).
123. *The Analects of Confucius: Gongye Chang.*
124. *The Analects of Confucius: Xue Er (Studying).*
125. *The Analects of Confucius: Duke Ling of Wei.*
126. Han Ying. *Anecdotes of The Book of Poetry.*
127. *Mencius: Gongsun Chou.*
128. *The Essence of Life Principles.*
129. Ibid.
130. *Han Feizi: Observation of Behaviors.*
131. *Admonitions for the Yan Clan: Admiring the Virtuous.*
132. *The Collected Annotations of Children's Education: The Foreword of Children's Education.*
133. *Waiting to Be Solved.*
134. Cf. Fu Rengan. *Rendered Translation of The Record on the Subject of Learning,* pp. 31–32. (Shanghai: Shanghai Education Press, 1982).
135. [Czech Republic] *Comenius: Great Didactic,* trans. Fu Rengan, p. 182. (Beijing: People's Education Press, 1984).
136. *Mo-tse: Cultivation of One's Own Character.*
137. *Annotations of Shangshu: The Third Ode of the Five Brothers* (the brothers of Taikang and the son of King Qi of the Xia Dynasty).
138. *Biography of The Book of Changes,* volume 1.

139. *The Analects of Confucius: Yan Yuan.*
140. Ibid.
141. Ibid.
142. Ibid.
143. *The Analects of Confucius: Xian Jin (Those of Former Eras).*
144. *The Analects of Confucius: Yang Huo.*
145. *Mencius: Jin Xin (Make an Effort to Do Good Deeds).*
146. *The Collection of Zhang Zai: Seven Selected Articles from the Analects of Zhang Zai.*
147. *The Collection of Zhang Zai: The Education of Children—Uprightness.*
148. Quoted from *Collected Annotations of The Four Books.*
149. *Collected Annotations of Mencius*, volume 13.
150. *The Whole Collection of Duke Wang Wencheng*, volume 3.
151. *The Annotations of The Four Books*, volume 36.
152. *The Annotations of The Four Books*, volume 15.
153. *The Analects of Confucius: Zilu.*
154. Ibid.
155. *The Analects of Confucius: Duke Ling of Wei.*
156. *The Analects of Confucius: Yang Huo.*
157. *Mo-tse: Gongmeng* states, "Gaozi said to Mo-tse, 'I administer the state affairs and manage the government.' Mo-tse said, 'When saying the word government, one should practice with his action. Now you say it without action, which is your own fault. If you cannot regulate yourself, how can you administer the government?'"
158. *Huainanzi: Advice for Cultivation.*
159. *Huainanzi: Advice for National Prosperity.*
160. *Mo-tse: Gengzhu.*
161. *Mo-tse: Cultivation of One's Own Character.*
162. *Mencius: Jin Xin (Make an Effort to Do Good Deeds).*
163. *Admonitions for the Yuan Clan*, volume 2.
164. *The Analects of Confucius: Xian Jin (Those of Former Eras).*
165. *The Analects of Confucius: Zi Han (The Master Shunned).*
166. *The Analects of Confucius: Xian Jin (Those of Former Eras).*
167. Cf. Xu Mengying. *Primary Research on the Educational Thought of Confucius*, p. 77. (Zhengzhou: Henan People Press, 1982).
168. *The Collection of Zhang Zai: The Annotations of Classics—The Essential Principles of Learning.*
169. Quoted from *Educational Psychology*, ed. Pan Shu, p. 54. (Beijing: People's Education Press, 1983).

Chapter 5

1. Mao Lirui. "A Study on Confucian Teaching Theory," in the *Journal of Beijing Normal University*, volume 6, 1979.
2. *Laozi: Chapter 19.*
3. *Laozi: Chapter 48.*
4. *Mo-tse: Canon II.*
5. *Mo-tse: Explanations II.*
6. Cf. Yan Guocai and Zhu Yongxin. *China's Educational Psychology from a Modern Perspective*, pp. 29–37. (Shanghai: Shanghai Education Press, 1991).
7. *Xuncius: An Exhortation to Learn.*
8. Wang Anshi. "Pity Zhongyong," in *Collection of Duke Wen of Wang*, volume 33.
9. *Annotations of The Four Books*, volume 5.
10. *Collected Reviews of The Four Books*, volume 7.
11. *Collected Reviews of The Four Books*, volume 9.
12. *The Book of Rites: Zhongyong.*
13. *Lun Heng: Shizhi (On Balance: Verifying Knowledge).*
14. *Collection of the Cheng Brothers: Remaining Records*, volume 19.
15. *Records of Personages: Ti Bie (On Individual Differences).*
16. *Collection of Zhu Geliang: Advice to My Son.*
17. *Xizhai's Essays*, volume B.
18. *Collected Reviews of The Four Books*, volume 3.
19. *The Annotations of the Cultivation of Children by Zhang Zai*, volume 5.
20. *Supplement to The Book of Changes*, volume 4.
21. *Other Views on The Book of Changes*, volume 4.
22. *The Analects of Confucius: Yang Huo.*

23. *Xuncius: An Exhortation to Learn.*
24. *Shuoyuan: Jianben* (*Garden of Stories: The Establishment of Foundations*).
25. *Annotations of The Four Books*, volume 10.
26. *Mencius: Gaozi I.*
27. *Xuncius: The Teachings of the Ru.*
28. Cf. *A General History of China's Education*, compiled by Mao Lirui and Shen Guanqun, volume 1, pp. 94–101. (Jinan: Shangdong Education Press, 1985).
29. *Liji·Yueji* (*The Book of Rites: Record on the Subject of Music*).
30. Ibid.
31. *The Rites of Zhou: Offices of Spring—Office of Music.*
32. Lv Simian. *History Before the Qin Dynasty*, p. 457. (Shanghai: Shanghai Classics Publishing House, 1982).
33. *Liji: Jing Jie* cites Confucius: "If they are mild and gentle, sincere and good, they have been taught from *The Book of Poetry*. If they have a wide comprehension [of things] and know what is remote and old, they have been taught from *The Book of History*. If they be large-hearted and generous, even-tempered and honest, they have been taught from *The Book of Music*. If they be pure and still, refined and subtle, they have been taught from the *Yi*. If they be courteous and modest, grave and respectful, they have been taught from *The Book of Rites and Ceremonies*. If they suitably adapt their language to the things of which they speak, they have been taught from the *Chun Qiu*."
34. *Zhuangzi: Tian Yun* (*Zhuangzi: Heavenly Revolutions*) states, "Confucius compiled six classics: *The Book of Poetry, The Book of History, The Book of Rites, The Book of Music, The Book of Changes,* and *The Spring and Autumn Annals*."
35. *The Analects of Confucius: Wei Zheng* (*The Practice of Government*).
36. When talking about the political and diplomatic meaning of *The Book of Poetry*, Confucius said, "Although a man may be able to recite the 300 odes in *The Book of Poetry*, if, when entrusted with a governmental charge, he knows not how to act, or if, when sent to any quarter on a mission, he cannot give his replies unassisted, notwithstanding the extent of his learning, of what practical use is it?" (*The Analects of Confucius: Zilu*). When talking about its function of self-cultivation, he said, "Do you [Kong Li, Confucius' son] give yourself to the 'Zhou Nan' and the 'Shao Nan' [well-known poems in *The Book of Poetry*]? The man who has not studied the 'Zhou Nan' and the 'Shao Nan' is like one who stands with his face right against a wall. Is he not so?" (*The Analects of Confucius: Yang Huo*). When talking about its artistic and political functions, he said, "My children, why do you not study *The Book of Poetry*? The odes serve to stimulate the mind. They may be used for purposes of self-contemplation. They teach the art of sociability. They show how to regulate feelings of resentment. From them you learn the more immediate duty of serving one's father, and the more remote duty of serving one's emperor. From them we become largely acquainted with the names of birds, beasts, and plants." (*The Analects of Confucius: Yang Huo*).
37. From the line of *The Analects of Confucius: Shu Er*, "The Master's frequent themes of discourse were *The Book of Poetry, The Book of History,* and *The Maintenance of The Rules of Propriety*. On all these he frequently discoursed," we see that *The Book of History* was the teaching book of Confucius.
38. Cf. *The Great Educator Confucius*, compiled by Lv Tao, p. 134. (Shenyang: Liaoning Education Press, 1987).
39. *The Analects of Confucius: Wei Zheng* says, "What does *The Book of History* say of filial piety? 'You are filial, you discharge your brotherly duties. These qualities are displayed in government.' This then also constitutes the exercise of government. Why must there be that, making one be in the government?"
40. *The Analects of Confucius: The Ji Family.*
41. *The Analects of Confucius: Taibo.*
42. *The Analects of Confucius: Ba Yi.*
43. *The Analects of Confucius: Shu Er.*
44. *The Historical Records: The House of Confucius.*
45. Guo Qijia. *A History of China's Educational Thought*, p. 24. (Beijing: Education Science Publishing House, 1987).
46. Li Yuese. *Science and Civilization in China*, volume 1, p. 3. (Beijing: Science Press, 1975).
47. *The Analects of Confucius: Zilu* states, "Fan Chi requested to be taught husbandry. The Master said, 'I am not as good for that as an old husbandman.' He requested also to be taught gardening and was answered, 'I am not as good for that as an old gardener.' Fan Chi having gone out, the Master said, 'A small man, indeed, is Fan Xu! If a superior man loves propriety, people will not dare not be reverent. If he loves righteousness,

people will not dare not to submit to his example. If he loves good faith, people will not dare not be sincere. Now, when these things have been obtained, people from all quarters will come to him, bearing their children on their backs; what need has he then of a knowledge of husbandry?'" *Xuncius: Dispelling Blindness* states, "The farmer concentrates on his fields, yet it would be inadmissible to consider him for the position of director of the fields. The merchant concentrates on the marketplace, but it would be inadmissible to consider him for director of the marketplace. The artisan concentrates on his wares, but it would be inadmissible to consider him for director of wares. There are men incapable of these three skills who could be commissioned to put in order any of these three offices. I say that they are men who concentrate on the Way and not merely on things." In other words, the task of school education was to propagate the doctrines of the ancient sages, paying great attention to propriety, righteousness, and trustworthiness, and little attention to tools and skills.

48. Zhao Jibin. *A New Probe into The Analects of Confucius*, p. 187. Quoted from *The Secrets of China's Ancient Culture*, by Feng Tianyu and Zhou Jiming, p. 101. (Wuhan: Hubei People's Press, 1986).
49. *The Analects of Confucius: Zizhang.*
50. *The Analects of Confucius: Wei Zheng (The Practice of Government).*
51. Ruan Yuan. *Biographies of Chouren* (astronomers, experts on calendars, and arithmeticians). Cf. *A General History of China's Education*, compiled by Mao Lirui and Shen Guanqun, volume 1, pp. 196–197. (Jinan: Shangdong Education Press, 1985).
52. *Huang Di Nei Jing: Ling Shu (The Essential Dwelling of the Mind Bears the Name Ling Shu).*
53. According to Encyclopedia Britannica, the first medical school in Europe was established in Italy in the ninth century, about 200 to 300 years later than that of China.
54. It is recorded in history that the earliest textbook of science and technology issued by the government abroad was *Florence Pharmacopoeia*, published in Italy, about 800 to 900 years later than that of China.
55. It was said that Li Shizhen, a great scientist of the Ming Dynasty, compiled *The Compendium of Materia Medica* and submitted it to the imperial government. The Wanli Emperor simply gave a several-letter order that "the book was left to be read and the office of Li (propriety) has known it" and shelved it. Nonetheless, this great scientific book classified and described more than 1,000 types of plants and several hundred kinds of animals and minerals, 200 years earlier than *Systema Naturae* by Carl Linnaeus, "the father of modern taxonomy" in the West.
56. Zhou Dechang. "Ancient Educators' Theories on the Teaching Process in China," in *Educational Research*, volume 6, 1982; Yan Guocai and Zhu Yongxin. *China's Educational Psychology from a Modern Perspective*, pp. 71–89. (Shanghai: Shanghai Education Press, 1991).
57. *Collected Reviews of The Four Books*, volume 3.
58. Cf. *A Coursebook on Pedagogy*, compiled by Chu Peijun, pp. 115–116. (Shanghai: Shanghai Jiao Tong University Press, 1991).
59. *Classified Conversations of Zhuzi (Zhu Xi)*, volume 5.
60. *Shi Guang Zhuan (Essays and Reviews on The Book of Poetry)*, volume 1.
61. *The Annotations of the Cultivation of Children by Zhang Zai*, volume 1.
62. *Mo-tse: Self-Cultivation.*
63. *The Collection of Zhang Zai: Zheng Meng (Curing Ignorance)—Zhong Zheng (Integrity).*
64. Lu Shiyi. *Abstract Records of Critical Thoughts*, volume 2.
65. *The Annotations of the Cultivation of Children by Zhang Zai*, volume 5.
66. *The Analects of Confucius: Zi Han (The Master Shunned).*
67. *The Collection of Zhang Zai: Records of Words II.*
68. *Records of Thoughts and Questions: Inner Chapters.*
69. *The Collection of Zhang Zai: Jing Xue Li Ku (Secrets of Confucian Classics)—Xue Da Yuan (Origin or Essentials of Learning) II.*
70. *Annotations of The Four Books*, volume 9.
71. *Philosophical Views About Nature and Heavenly Principles*, volume 7.
72. *The Annotations of the Cultivation of Children by Zhang Zai*, volume 5.
73. *Si Jie (Waiting to Be Understood).*
74. *The Analects of Confucius: Shu Er.*
75. *The Analects of Confucius: Wei Zheng.*
76. *The Analects of Confucius: Wei Ling Gong (Duke Ling of Wei State).*
77. *Si Jie (Waiting to Be Understood).*
78. *Annotations of The Four Books*, volume 6.
79. *Mencius: Li Lou II.*
80. *Collected Reviews of The Four Books*, volume 6.

81. Cf. *A General History of Education in China*, compiled by Mao Lirui and Shen Guanqun, volume 1, p. 361. (Jinan: Shandong Education Press, 1985).
82. *Annotations of Nine Chapters on the Mathematical Art*.
83. *The Analects of Confucius: Duke Ling of Wei*.
84. *The Analects of Confucius: Gongye Chang*.
85. *The Analects of Confucius: Ba Yi (Eight Lines of Eight Dancers Apiece)*.
86. *The Collections of Zhang Zai: The Study of Classics and Principles—Temperament*.
87. *The Analects of Zhuzi*, volume 11.
88. *A History of Chinese Thought in the Ming Dynasty: Baisha Study Documents*.
89. *Annotations of The Four Books*, volume 6.
90. *Study Documents of the Song and Yuan Dynasties: Studies of Hui Weng*.
91. *The Spreading of The Book of Songs*, volume 4.
92. *The Analects of Confucius: Wei Zheng*.
93. *The Analects of Zhuzi*, volume 10.
94. *Annotations of The Four Books*, volume 6.
95. Ibid.
96. *Supplement to The Book of Changes*, volume 5.
97. *The Analects of Zhuzi*, volume 9.
98. *The Analects of Zhuzi*, volume 120.
99. *Annotations of The Four Books: Annotation of The Doctrine of Mean*.
100. *The Analects of Confucius: Zi Han*.
101. *Lun Heng: Book of Cases*.
102. *The Analects of Zhuzi*, volume 11.
103. *The Analects of Confucius: Xue Er*.
104. *The Analects of Confucius: Zi Zhang*.
105. *The Analects of Confucius: Wei Zheng*.
106. *The Variorum of The Analects of Confucius*, volume 1.
107. *The Analects of Zhuzi*, volume 10.
108. Ibid.
109. *The Analects of Confucius: Zilu*.
110. *Xuncius: The Teachings of the Ru*.
111. *Collected Reviews of The Four Books*, volume 4.
112. *Quotes and Annotations of Shangshu*, volume 3.
113. *Collected Reviews of The Four Books*, volume 1.
114. *The Collection of Zhang Zai: The Education of Children—Uprightness*.
115. Cf. *The Annotations of the Record on the Subject of Learning*, ed. Gao Shiliang, pp. 29–35. (Beijing: People's Education Press, 1982).
116. For example, in the teaching process, Confucius paid much attention to "judging a person not only by his words but also by his deeds." (*The Analects of Confucius: Gongye Chang*). He said, "See a person's means [of getting things]. Observe his motives. Examine that in which he rests. How can a person conceal his character?" (*The Analects of Confucius: Wei Zheng*). This is similar to "the observational method" in modern times. Confucius also focused on how to question a student to get to know him. For instance, he asked students to talk about their ambitions several times to deepen his understanding of Zilu, Zeng Xi, Ran You, Gong Xihua, and Yan Yuan. Fan Chi requested to be taught "husbandry," and Confucius reached the conclusion that "A small man, indeed, is Fan Xu!" (*The Analects of Confucius: Zilu*). This is similar to the "conversation method" in modern times. Confucius also paid attention to investigating in order to grasp the condition of students or to verify one's own expression. For example, he asked Zi Gong about the intellectual level of Yan Yuan. And he said, "When the multitudes hate a man, it is necessary to examine the case. When the multitudes like a man, it is necessary to examine the case." (*The Analects of Confucius: Duke Ling of Wei*). This is similar to the "survey method" in modern times.
117. *The Analects of Confucius: Shu Er*.
118. *Biography of The Book of Changes*, volume 4.
119. *Annotations of The Four Books*, volume 11.
120. Translated by Shao Ruizhen, in the *Journal of Educational Research*, volume 5, 1979.
121. *The Analects of Confucius: Zi Han*.
122. *Lun Heng: Reflections on Confucianism*.
123. In *The Analects of Confucius: Xue Er*, Zigong asked, "What do you think of a poor man who does not grovel or a rich man who is not proud?" Confucius said, "They are good, but not as good as a poor man who is satisfied and a rich man who loves propriety." Zi Gong said, "*The Book of Odes* says, 'Like cutting and filing, grinding and polishing.' Is this what you are talking about?" Confucius said, "Ah, now I can begin to discuss

The Book of Odes with Ci. I speak of various things, and he knows what is to be brought back."

124. In *The Analects of Confucius: Ba Yi*, Zi Xia asked, "What is the meaning of the passage, 'The pretty dimples of her artful smile! The well-defined black and white of her eye! The plain ground for the colors.'?" The Master said, "The business of laying on the colors follows [the preparation of] the plain ground." "Ceremonies then are a subsequent thing?" The Master said, "It is Shang who can bring out my meaning. Now I can begin to talk about the odes with him."
125. *The Analects of Confucius: Yong Ye.*
126. Cf. "Discussion of Individual Differences and Teaching Students According to Their Aptitude," ed. Yan Guocai, *Journal of Shanghai Teachers College*, volume 1, 1984.
127. *The Analects of Confucius: Zi Han.*
128. *Mo-tse: Da Qu.*
129. *Mo-tse: Gongmeng.*
130. *Xuncius: Rong Ru (Honor and Humility).*
131. *Xuncius: Zheng Lun (Correcting Fallacies).*
132. *The Collected Annotations of Children's Education: The Foreword of Children's Education.*
133. Ibid.
134. *The Annotations of The Book of Rites,* volume 12.
135. *Chen Li: Reading Notes of [Chen] Dongshu.*
136. *Admonitions for the Yan Clan: Encouraging Learning.*
137. Fu Sunjiu. *China's Ancient Educators' Discussion on Learning.* (Nanjing: Nanjing University Press, 1997).
138. *Mencius: Li Lou II.*
139. *The Collection of Zhang Zai: The Study of Classics and Principles—Connotation of Classics.*
140. *Watching over Words: Concentration.*
141. *Annotations of Mencius.*
142. Cf. Yan Guocai and Zhu Yongxin. *China's Educational Psychology from a Modern Perspective,* p. 104. (Shanghai: Shanghai Education Press, 1991).
143. Cf. *Educational Psychology: Principles of Learning and Teaching,* ed. Shao Ruizhen, pp. 24–26. (Shanghai: Shanghai Education Press, 1987).
144. *The Practice of Instructions: Record of Huang Xingzeng (V).*
145. *The Analects of Confucius: Yong Ye.*
146. *The Analects of Confucius: Shu Er.*
147. *The Collection of Zhang Zai: The Annotations of the Classics—The Essential Principles of Learning I.*
148. *Lv Shi Chun Qiu (The History of Lv's Clan): Evils.*
149. *The Analects of Confucius: Shu Er.*
150. *The Analects of Confucius: Zi Han.*
151. *The Collection of Zhang Zai: The Education of Children—Uprightness.*
152. *The Collection of Zhang Zai: The Annotations of Classics—The Essential Principles of Learning II.*
153. *The Collection of Zhang Zai: The Education of Children—Uprightness.*
154. *The Collection of Zhang Zai: Hengqu's Views on The Book of Changes—Xi Ci (Cardinal Principles of The Books of Changes) I.*
155. *Annotations of The Four Books,* volume 25.
156. *The Annotations of the Cultivation of Children by Zhang Zai,* volume 3.
157. Ibid.
158. *Collection of Mr. Hui'an: Duke Wen of Zhu—Answer to Pan Zishan.*
159. *Collection of Mr. Hui'an: Duke Wen of Zhu—Answer to Cao Yuanke.*
160. *Lun Heng: Chaoqi (On Balance: The Supreme Extraordinary Talents).*
161. *Views on Previous Theories and Current Governance: On Education.*
162. *Admonitions for the Yan Clan: Encouraging Learning.*
163. *Li Gong: Shu Gu Essays,* volume 4.
164. *Shi Tong (A Book of Historiography Theory): Miscellaneous Essays II.*
165. *Mo zi: Lu Asked.*
166. Mao Lirui. "A Study on Confucian Teaching Theory," in *Journal of Beijing Normal University*, volume 6, 1979..
167. *The Analects of Confucius: Zi Han.*
168. *The Analects of Confucius: Ba Yi.*
169. *The Analects of Confucius: Shu Er.*
170. *Xuncius: Self-Cultivation.*
171. *Xuncius: The Teachings of the Ru.*
172. *Lun Heng: Liang Zhi (On Balance: Measuring Knowledge).*

173. Liu Zongyuan. *A Review of Scholar Yan Houyu's Theory on Teachers.*
174. Zhou Dechang. *A Critical Inheritance of Ancient Chinese Educational Philosophy,*
     p. 131. (Beijing: Educational Science Publishing House, 1982).
175. *The Annotations of The Four Books,* volume 32.
176. *Xuncius: Quanxue (Persuasion of Learning).*
177. *Han Yu: Answer to Li Yi.*
178. *The Collection of Zhang Zai: The Annotations of the Classics—The Essential Principles of Learning II.*
179. *The Analects of Confucius: Zi Han.*
180. *Mencius: Lilou II.*
181. *Mencius: Jin Xin I.*
182. Ibid.
183. *A Complete Collection of Zhu Xi: The Key to Reading.*
184. *The Complete Collection of Duke Wencheng of Wang: Answer to Huang Yifang.*
185. *The Complete Collection of Duke Wencheng of Wang: Practicing the Instructions I.*
186. *Laozi: Chapter 64.*
187. *Recipe of Effective Reading by Ancient Wisdom,* ed. Zhou Yongnian.
188. *Recipe of Effective Reading by Ancient Wisdom.*
189. *The Analects of Confucius: Xue Er* states, "Cengzi said, 'Each day I examine myself in three ways: in doing things for others, have I been disloyal? In my interactions with friends, have I been untrustworthy? Have I not practiced what I have preached?'"
190. *The Analects of Confucius: Zizhang.*
191. *The Collection of Zhang Zai: The Annotations of Classics—The Essential Principles of Learning II.*
192. *Analects of Zhuzi,* volume 11.

Chapter 6

1. [USSR] *Pedagogy,* chiefly edited by Kairov, p. 693. (Beijing: People's Education Press, 1957).
2. Xu Chunsheng. "The Role and Status of Teachers in History," in *Hebei Education Journal,* volume 1, 1981.
3. Zhu Yongxin and Yuan Zhenguo. *Political Psychology,* p. 87. (Beijing: Knowledge Press, 1990).
4. *A General History of China's Education,* compiled by Mao Lirui and Shen Guanqun, volume 1, p. 6. (Jinan: Shangdong Education Press, 1985).
5. Friedrich Engels. *The Origin of Family, Private Property and the State: Selected Works of Marx and Engels,* volume 4, p. 125. (Beijing: People's Publishing House, 1995).
6. *Shizi.*
7. *Cardinal Principles of The Book of Changes.*
8. *Wu Yue Chun Qiu (The History of the Wu and Yue Regions).*
9. *Mencius: Duke Wen of Teng.*
10. *Shangshu (The Classic of History)* states, "Heaven, to help inferior people, made for them rulers, and made for them instructors." Further, "The Di appointed Xie as the Minister of Instruction to set forth the lessons of duty belonging to those five orders, Bo-yi as the Arranger in the Ancestral Temple to direct three [religious] ceremonies, and Kui as the Director of Music to teach their sons."
11. *The Classic of Rites: The Imperial Ranking System* states, "The lord of Yu nourished the aged (who had retired from service) of the state in (the school called) the higher xiang, and the aged of the common people (and officers who had not obtained rank) in (the school called) the lower xiang." Further, "The lord of Yu wore white robes in nourishing the aged...used the ceremonies of drinking entertainment; the sovereigns of Xia used the upper and lower dark garments of undress in nourishing the aged...used those in entertainment after a reverent sacrifice or offering; during the Yin, they used the upper and lower garments, both of thin white silk, in nourishing the aged...used those of a (substantial) feast."
12. *Education System in Past Ages in China,* compiled by Gu Shusen, explains that "begging the old for their wise counsel" means asking for good advice from the elders, and those who could speak would be recorded; "conversation at general reunions" means that one should talk with the elders about five kinds of human relations, namely father–son, monarch–subject, husband–wife, between brothers, and between friends, and conform to these. Cf. *Education System in Past Ages in China,* compiled by Gu Shusen, pp. 16–17. (Nanjing: Jiangsu People's Publishing House, 1981).
13. Cf. *The Classic of Rites: King Wen as Son and Heir* and *The Rites of Zhou: Offices of Spring.*
14. *Interpretations of The Book of History,* volume 5, says, "Doctors retire at age 70 and go to towns. Doctors work as Grand Preceptors and scholars as Masters of Children."

15. Cf. *A General History of China's Education,* compiled by Mao Lirui and Shen Guanqun, volume 1, p. 161. (Jinan: Shangdong Education Press, 1985).
16. Pertaining to the emergence and rise of the scholar class, cf. Yu Yingshi. "The Rise and Development of Ancient Intelligentsia," in *Scholars and Chinese Culture,* pp. 1–83. (Shanghai: Shanghai People Publishing House, 1987).
17. *The Historical Records: House of Confucius.*
18. Cf. Gao Zhuancheng. *Confucius: Confucius' Disciples,* pp. 79–99.
19. *Lun Heng: Xing'ou (On Balance: On Chance and Luck).*
20. *Xuncius: On Compendium.*
21. *Xuncius: Discourse on Ethical Codes.*
22. *Xuncius: Self-Cultivation.*
23. *Xuncius: The Teachings of the Ru.*
24. *Xuncius: The Questions of Yao.*
25. Cf. Zhu Yongxin: *Difficulties and Surmounting—A Commentary on Contemporary Education in China,* pp. 28–30. (Nanning: Guangxi People Publishing House, 1990).
26. Entry from "Most Meritorious Subjects of the East Han Were Like Confucianists" in *Notes on the Twenty-Two Dynastic Histories* by Zhao Yi.
27. *The Historical Records: Biography of Li Yiji.*
28. *Book of Han: Biographies of Confucian Scholars.*
29. Han Yu. *Thirteen Interview Questions for Jinshi* (a successful candidate in the highest imperial examinations).
30. Liu Zongyuan. *A Reply to Wei Zhongli on the Role of Teachers.*
31. Jin Zhongming. "Chinese Traditional Education and Intellectuals," in *The Transmission and Evolution of Cultures,* chiefly edited by Ding Gang, pp. 56–57. (Shanghai: Shanghai Education Press, 1990).
32. Cf. Jin Zheng. *The Imperial Examination System and Chinese Culture,* p. 161. (Shanghai: Shanghai People Publishing House, 1990).
33. *Xin Shi (Heart History),* volume 2: *A Summary Writing on the Cardinal Principles of Righteousness.*
34. *Complete Works of Zheng Banqiao: Poetry and Essays Outside the Corpus— Self-Mockery.*
35. *Zuo Zhuan (Chronicle of Zuo): Eighteenth Year of Duke Zhao.*
36. *Book of Han: Biography of Dong Zhongshu—Measures to Recommend Able and Virtuous Men III.*
37. *Tong Dian (Comprehensive Institutions),* volume 53.
38. *Notes and Commentaries on The Rites of Zhou,* volume 9.
39. *Collected Works of Cihu,* volume 14: *On the Philosophers.*
40. *Annotations of The Four Books,* volume 1: *Great Learning.*
41. [Japan] *The Groundwork for Modern Pedagogy,* ed. Institute of Pedagogy of the University of Tsukuba, trans. Zhong Qiquan, p. 26. (Shanghai: Shanghai Education Press, 1986).
42. *Xuncius: On the Teachings of the Ru.*
43. *Exemplary Sayings: Learning and Practice.*
44. *Baihu General Views,* volume 4: *Pi Yong (Imperial University).*
45. *The Collection of Zhang Zai: Records of Words II.*
46. *Collection of Liu Hedong's Works,* volume 32.
47. Huang Zongxi. *Anthology of Nanlei,* volume 6.
48. *Lv Shi Chun Qiu: Records of Early Summer—Encouraging Learning.*
49. *Lv Shi Chun Qiu: Respecting the Teacher.*
50. *The Analects of Confucius: Shu Er.*
51. Ibid.
52. Ibid.
53. *The Analects of Confucius: Gongye Chang* states, "The Master said, 'In a hamlet of 10 families, there may be found one as honorable and sincere as I but not so fond of learning.'"
54. *The Analects of Confucius: Shu Er.*
55. *The Analects of Confucius: Wei Zheng.*
56. *The Analects of Zhu Xi,* volume 104.
57. *Collected Works of Li Yanping,* volume 1.
58. *The Historical Records: House of Confucius.*
59. *The Analects of Confucius: Zi Han.*
60. *The Analects of Confucius: Wei Zheng.*
61. *Year Book of Zhuzi,* volume 2, compiled by Wang Maohong.
62. *The Chronicle of Zhuzi,* volume 4.

63. Mao Zedong. "The Role of the Chinese Communist Party in the National War," in *Selected Works of Mao Zedong*, volume 2, p. 535. (Beijing: People's Publishing House, 1991).
64. *Xuncius: On Attracting Scholars*.
65. *Chun Qiu Fan Lu: Yubei*
66. Cf. *A General History of Chinese Education*, compiled by Mao Lirui and Shen Guanqun, volume 2, pp. 179–180. (Jinan: Shandong Education Press).
67. *The Analects of Confucius: Jishi*.
68. *Lv Shi Chun Qiu: The First Month of Summer—Wutu*.
69. *The Analects of Confucius: Duke Ling of Wei*.
70. *Chun Qiu Fan Lu: Chongzheng*.
71. Li Tao. *A Continuation of Zi Zhi Tong Jian* (*History as a Mirror*), volume 232.
72. *Collection of Duke Wang Wengong*, volume 34, *Learning Records in Cixi County*.
73. *Annotations of The Book of Rites*, volume 8, *The Imperial Ranking System*.
74. *Analects: Ji Shi*.
75. *Collection of Mr. Hui'an: Duke Wen of Zhu—Reply to Xu Jingguang*.
76. *Collection of Mr. Hui'an: Duke Wen of Zhu—Jing Zhai Zhen* (*Maxims Written in Jing Zhai*).
77. *The Analects of Confucius: Shu Er*.
78. Ibid.
79. *Analects: Shu Er*.
80. *Mencius: Li Lou Shang*.
81. Du Yan. *Biography of Wang Tong*.
82. *Analects: Zi Zhang*.
83. *Collected Educational Works of Krupskaya*. (Beijing: People's Education Press, 1959).
84. *The Analects of Confucius: Wei Zheng* states, "The Master said, 'I have talked with Hui for a whole day, and he has not made any objection to anything I said, as if he were stupid. He has retired, and I have examined his conduct when away from me and found him able to illustrate my teachings. Hui! He is not stupid.' The Master said, 'See what a man does. Mark his motives. Examine what things he rests. How can a man conceal his character?'"
85. *Collection of Lu Jiuyuan*, volume 35.
86. *The History of the Song Dynasty: The Biography of Lu Jiuyuan*.
87. *The Analects of Confucius: Zi Lu*.
88. *The Annotations of the Cultivation of Children by Zhang Zai*, volume 4.
89. *The Complete Collection of Duke Wencheng of Wang: Reply to Huang Yifang*.
90. *The Complete Collection of Duke Wencheng of Wang*, volume 2.
91. *The Record on the Subject of Education* states, "Teachers are asked to be concise and to the point, refined and appropriate when speaking, and teachers are supposed to explain a problem though just a few examples."
92. *Xun Zi: Non-Phase*.
93. Ibid.
94. *The Annotations of The Books of Rites*, volume 36.
95. Han Yu. *On Teachers*.
96. *The Analects of Confucius: Yang Huo*.
97. Song Lian. *A Letter to Mr. Ma from Dongyang County*.
98. *The Analects of Confucius: Gongye Chang*.
99. *Chronicles of the Song Dynasty*, volume 80: *The Merits and Demerits of the Doctrines*.
100. *Xun Zi: Da Lue*.
101. *Xun Zi: Zhi Shi*.
102. *Lv Shi Chun Qiu: Respecting Teachers*.
103. Ibid.
104. *The Analects of Confucius: Zizhang*.
105. Ibid.
106. Ibid.
107. *Historical Records: Biography of Merchants* states, "Zigong gathered the horses and carried silks and coins to pay tributes to the dukes. Wherever he went, the king there would stand up to treat him as a valuable guest. Therefore, the one who transmitted the fame of Confucius was just Zigong. So was Confucius' fame increased because he took advantage of Zigong's power?"
108. *The Analects of Confucius: Duke Ling of Wei*.
109. *The Analects of Confucius: Zilu*.
110. *The Analects of Confucius: Yang Huo*.
111. *The Analects of Confucius: Xian Wen*.

112. Bertrand Russell. *Education and the Beautiful Life*, quoted in *Selected Works of the Schools of Thought of Modern Western Bourgeois Education*, trans. and ed. Education Department of East China Normal University and Education Department of Hangzhou University, p. 104. (Beijing: People's Educational Press, 1980).
113. *The Analects of Confucius: Yong Ye*.
114. *The Analects of Confucius: Xian Jin*.
115. Ibid.
116. *Lv Shi Chun Qiu: Wu Tu*.
117. Ibid.
118. [USSR] Vasyl Olexandrovych Sukhomlynsky. *Do Trust Children*, trans. Wang Jiaju, p. 3. (Beijing: Education Science Publishing House, 1981).
119. *The Analects of Confucius: Gongye Chang* states, "The Master said of Gongye Chang that he might be married; although he was put in bonds, he had not been guilty of any crime. Accordingly, he gave him his own daughter to be his wife."
120. *The Analects of Confucius: Gongye Chang*.
121. *The Analects of Confucius: Yong Ye*.
122. Ibid.
123. [USSR] Zankov, *Talks with Teachers*, trans. Du Diankun, p. 30. (Beijing: Education Science Publishing House, 1980).
124. *The Analects of Confucius: Zilu*.
125. *The Analects of Confucius: Xian Jin*.
126. *The Analects of Confucius: Gongye Chang*.
127. *Mo-tse: Preparing the Ladder*.
128. [Czech Republic] Comenius. *The Great Didactic*, trans. Fu Rengan, p. 51. (Beijing: People's Educational Press, 1984).
129. Hu Yuan. *Learning Records of Confucianism in Songzi*.
130. *Chronicles of Mr. Yan Xizhai*, volume 2.
131. *The Analects of Confucius: Shu Er*.
132. *The Analects of Confucius: Li Ren*.
133. *Annotations of The Four Books: Annotations of the Doctrine of the Mean*.

Chapter 7

1. Yang Xianjiang. "Theory of Reading Methods," in *Student Magazine*, volume 13, no. 1, 1926.
2. *The Essence of Life Principles*.
3. *School Regulations of Bailudong Academy*.
4. Wei Zhengtong. *The Wisdom of the Chinese: Comparisons Between Great Chinese and Western Ideas*, pp. 133–139. (Changchun: Jilin Literature and History Press, 1988).
5. *The Analects of Zhuzi*, volume 8.
6. *Collection of Mr. Hui'an: Duke Wen of Zhu—Answer to Minister Wang*.
7. *The Analects of Zhuzi*, volume 10.
8. *Collection of Mr. Hui'an: Duke Wen of Zhu—Answer to Zhang Yuande*.
9. Ibid.
10. *The Analects of Zhuzi*, volume 10.
11. Ibid.
12. Ibid.
13. *The Analects of Zhuzi*, volume 8.
14. *The Analects of Zhuzi*, volume 10.
15. *The Analects of Zhuzi*, volume 11.
16. *The Analects of Zhuzi*, volume 10.
17. Ibid.
18. *Reading Methods of Zhu Xi*.
19. *The Analects of Zhuzi*, volume 10.
20. *Reading Methods of Zhu Xi*.
21. *The Analects of Zhuzi*, volume 11.
22. *The Analects of Zhuzi*, volume 119.
23. Ibid.
24. *Collection of Mr. Hui'an: Duke Wen of Zhu—The Essential of Reading*.
25. Ibid.
26. *The Analects of Zhuzi*, volume 104.
27. *The Analects of Zhuzi*, volume 90.
28. *The Analects of Zhuzi*, volume 116.
29. *The Analects of Zhuzi*, volume 11.
30. Ibid.

31. Ibid.
32. *Collection of Mr. Hui'an: Duke Wen of Zhu—Answer to Hu Jisui.*
33. *The Analects of Zhuzi*, volume 35.
34. *The Sequel of the Records of Thinking on Surrounding Matters*, volume 2.
35. *The Category of School Rules.*
36. *The Analects of Zhuzi*, volume 1.
37. *The Analects of Zhuzi*, volume 19.
38. *The Category of School Rules.*
39. *The Analects of Zhuzi*, volume 19.
40. *The Analects of Zhuzi*, volume 11.
41. *The Analects of Zhuzi*, volume 8.
42. *The Analects of Zhuzi*, volume 13.
43. *The Analects of Zhuzi*, volume 11.
44. *The Category of School Rules.*
45. *The Analects of Zhuzi*, volume 11.
46. *Reading Methods of Zhu Xi.*
47. *The Whole Collection of Marx and Engels*, volume 44, p. 24. (Beijing: People's Press, 2001).
48. *The Analects of Zhuzi*, volume 8.
49. *The Analects of Zhuzi*, volume 10.
50. *The Analects of Zhuzi*, volume 8.
51. Ibid.
52. *The Analects of Zhuzi*, volume 10.
53. Ibid.
54. *The Analects of Zhuzi*, volume 8.
55. Ibid.
56. *Collection of Mr. Hui'an: Duke Wen of Zhu—Answer to Sun Jingfu 3.*
57. *The Analects of Zhuzi*, volume 8.
58. *The Analects of Zhuzi*, volume 19.
59. [Russia] Konstantin Ushinski. *Humanity Is the Object of Education*, volume 1, trans. Li Zizhuo, p. 218. (Beijing: Science Press, 1959).
60. Yan Guocai. *Intelligence and Learning*, p. 127. (Beijing: Education and Science Press, 1982).
61. *The Analects of Zhuzi*, volume 5.
62. Chen Chun. *Principles of The Four Books*, volume 1.
63. Zhang Boxing. *Series of the Analects of Zhuzi.*
64. *The Analects of Zhuzi*, volume 11.
65. *The Analects of Zhuzi*, volume 12.
66. *Collected Annotations of The Analects of Confucius: On Politics and Governing.*
67. *The Analects of Zhuzi*, volume 12.
68. *The Analects of Zhuzi*, volume 10.
69. *The Analects of Zhuzi*, volume 12.
70. *The Analects of Zhuzi*, volume 19.
71. *The Analects of Zhuzi*, volume 10.
72. *The Analects of Zhuzi*, volume 19.
73. Ibid.
74. Li Guangdi. *Collection of Banyan*, quoted in Zhou Yongnian, *Reading Tactics of Excellent Ministers in Previous Dynasties.*
75. *Collection of Su Dongpo: Replying to the Five Schools Again.*
76. *The Whole Collection of Zheng Banqiao: The Script Foreword of The Four Books.*
77. Ibid.
78. *The Whole Collection of Zheng Banqiao: The First Letter to My Younger Brother Zheng Mo from the Governmental Office in Wei County.*
79. *The Whole Collection of Zheng Banqiao: The Poem Collection of Hunting and the Poem Collection of the Flower Hall.*
80. *The Whole Collection of Zheng Banqiao: A Gift to My Younger Brother Hou Jia, an Educational Officer in The Imperial Academy.*
81. *The Whole Collection of Zheng Banqiao: Painting: Orchid.*
82. *The Whole Collection of Zheng Banqiao: The First Letter to My Younger Brother Zheng Mo from the Governmental Office in Wei County.*
83. *The Whole Collection of Zheng Banqiao: The Poem Collection of Hunting and the Poem Collection of the Flower Hall.*
84. *The Whole Collection of Zheng Banqiao: The Foreword of the Collection of the Tang Poetry.*

85. Li Guangdi. *The Collected Works of Rongcun* (another name for Li Guangdi). Quoted in *Recipe of Effective Reading by Ancient Wise Men*, ed. Zhou Yongnian.
86. Li Xu. *An Abundance of Jottings by Old Mr. Chieh-An.*
87. Lu Longqi. *The Analogy of San Yu Tang*, volume 6: *To My Eldest Son Dingzheng.*
88. *Mencius: Jin Xin II.*
89. *Lun Heng: Shuxu (On Balance: Falsehoods in Books).*
90. *The Collection of Zhang Zai: The Study of Classics and Principles—Connotation of Classics.*
91. *The Collected Works of Lu Jiuyuan*, volume 32, *Shi Yi.*
92. *The Analects of Zhuzi*, volume 10.
93. *Ji Yun: Notes Written in Yuewei Cottage.*
94. *The Collection of Zhang Zai: The Study of Classics and Principles—Connotation of Classics.*
95. Ibid.
96. *The Collected Works of Lu Jiuyuan*, volume 34: *Analects.*
97. Ibid.
98. *The Collected Works of Lu Jiuyuan*, volume 35: *Analects.*
99. *The Collected Works of Lu Jiuyuan*, volume 7: *To Shao Zhongfu.*
100. *Recipe of Effective Reading by Ancient Wise Men*, ed. Zhou Yongnian.
101. *The Collection of Zhang Zai: The Study of Classics and Principles—Connotation of Classics.*
102. Ibid.
103. *The Collected Works of Lu Jiuyuan*, volume 35, *Analects.*
104. Yan Tuizhi. *Admonitions for the Yan Clan: Encouraging Learning.*
105. *The Collected Works of Lu Jiuyuan*, volume 10: *To Zeng Zhaizhi.*
106. Yan Tuizhi. *Admonitions for the Yan Clan*, volume 3: *Encouraging Learning.*
107. *The Collected Works of Chen Que: To My Two Sons.*
108. *Cun Xue Bian (Writings on Learning).*

Chapter 8

1. Jin Zheng. *The Imperial Examination System and Chinese Culture*, p. 1. (Shanghai: Shanghai People's Publishing House, 1990).
2. Gu Shusen said, "The enrollment in the Civil Palace Examination in the Sui Dynasty put an end to the local recommendation and examination system and became the origin of the later imperial examination system that lasted for 1,300 years." [*The Educational System in Chinese History*, p. 105. (Nangjing: Jiangsu People's Publishing Ltd., 1981).] Mao Lirui and Shen Guanqun also stated, "The imperial examination system originated in the Sui Dynasty." [*A General History of China's Education*, volume 2, p. 492. (Jinan: Shandong Education Press, 1986).]
3. Jin Zheng. *The Imperial Examination System and Chinese Culture*, p. 46. (Shanghai: Shanghai People's Publishing House, 1990).
4. *Rites of Zhou: Grand Minister.*
5. *Book of Rites: She Yi (On Archery).*
6. *Book of Han: Annals of Emperor Gaozu.*
7. Ibid.
8. Essay examinations are similar to today's written examinations, namely, propositional composition, testing strategies of policy. The method of extracting questioning is similar to today's oral or written examinations, through drawing questions at random, mainly focused on passages, sentences, and exegesis of Confucian classics.
9. Ye Mengde. *Analects of Shilin*, volume 9.
10. Ge Hong. *Baopuzi: Mingshi (Name and Reality).*
11. *Baopuzi: Shenju (Examining Promotions).*
12. *Book of Jin: Biography of Liu Yi.*
13. *Book of Han: Annals of Emperor Gaozu.*
14. *Book of Sui: Annals of Emperor Yang.*
15. Ibid.
16. Jin Zheng. *The Imperial Examination System and Chinese Culture*, p. 48. (Shanghai: Shanghai People's Publishing House, 1990).
17. *The Collection of Tang's Imperial Edicts*, volume 102.
18. *The Collection of Tang Novels*, volume 1.
19. *The New Book of Tang: Treatises on Official Selection.*
20. *Tong Dian (Comprehensive Institutions): Official Selection III—Ancient Laws and Regulations.*
21. Ibid.
22. Ibid.
23. Ibid.
24. *The Collection of Tang Novels*, volume 15.

25. "Xing Juan" referred to the offering of the best poems and articles from candidates to well-known people, officials, elites, and personages to raise one's profile and appreciation so that the candidates would be recommended to the chief examiner.
26. *The New Book of Tang: Treatises on Official Selection.*
27. Rulers of the Song Dynasties promoted gaining an official position through the imperial examination to the fullest, like Emperor Zhenzong of Song said in *Encouraging Learning*: "To be better off, you need not invest in fertile lands, for books will promise a bumper harvest. To own a home, you need not collect huge logs, for books will build a luxurious mansion at your feet. To find a wife, you need not seek a professional matchmaker, for books will pair you with the fairest. To travel, you need not anticipate being a lonely traveler, for books will arrange an impressive parade of entourages and carriages like a moving forest. If one wishes to realize these life goals, he had better pore over Confucian books with great interest." Sima Guang also stated in his poem "Encouraging Learning": "Once you succeed in the imperial examination, your social status will be elevated and your elders and ancestors will be honored. If you have no marital connection, there will be a fair lady to be your match. In summary, the imperial examination system can satisfy all the needs of intellectuals."
28. *History of the Yuan Dynasty: Records of the Imperial Examination.*
29. *History of the Ming Dynasty: Records of the Imperial Examination.*
30. Gu Yanwu. *Ri Zhi Lu (Notes of Everyday Learning Through the Years)*, volume 16: *Topic Setting.*
31. *Selected Records of Educational History*, ed. Lian Jiansheng and Liu Zhan, pp. 195–196. (Nanjing: Jiangsu Education Press, 1989).
32. *Comparison of Civil Servant Systems*, compiled by Guo Yongxian and Huang Weiping, p. 234. (Guangzhou: Guangdong Higher Education Press, 1991).
33. [Italy] Matteo Ricci and Jin Nige (Nicolas Trigault). *Matteo Ricci's China Journal (De Christiana expeditione apud Sinas)*, volume 1, Chapter 6, trans. He Gaoji, p. 59. (Beijing: Zhonghua Book Company, 1983).
34. Jin Zheng. *The Imperial Examination System and Chinese Culture*, p. 4. (Shanghai: Shanghai People's Publishing House, 1990).
35. Ibid.
36. Yan Yu of the Song Dynasty remarked in *Canglang Poetry Talks: Poetry Reviews*, "Officials in the Tang Dynasty were largely selected according to poems. Thus, there emerged specialized studies in the Tang Dynasty, and our dynasty was dwarfed." Emperor Kangxi of the Qing Dynasty said in the *Preface to Complete Tang Poems* that "At the beginning of the Tang Dynasty, officials were selected based on poems. Almost all the talents and intellectuals were dedicated to the study of Liu Yi (六 乂, Feng, Ya, Song, Fu, Bi, Xing) and regarded it as a ladder to a political career. So these people became diligent specialists."
37. Li Bai. *Ancient Customs.*
38. Feng Guifen. *Humble Suggestions Written in Xiaobin Cottage: On the Reform of the Imperial Examination System.*
39. Yuan Mei. *Talks on Poetry at Suiyuan*, volume 12.
40. Fan Zhongyan. *Shang Shi Shi Zi (Ten Suggestions on Reform).*
41. *Sequel Compilation of Treatises on Dealing with Affairs*, volume 65: *Li Zheng (Governing) V, Academy II.*
42. *Ri Zhi Lu (Academic Records of Days)*, volume 16.
43. *The Collected Works of Li Dazhao II*, p. 105. (Beijing: People's Publishing House, 1984).

Chapter 9

1. Zhang Zhengfan. *A Study on the Chinese Academy System*, p. 1. (Nanjing: Jiangsu Education Press, 1995).
2. Mao Zedong. *Organization Outline of the Hunan Self-Study University.*
3. Yuan Mei. *Essays at Suiyuan*, volume 14.
4. *The Academy System in Ancient China*, compiled by Chen Yuanhui, pp. 5–6. (Shanghai: Shanghai Education Press, 1981).
5. Wang Jingdi. "General Characteristics of Academies," in *Collected Essays on National Studies*, volume 1, no. 1, 1927.
6. *Picture Book of Jie Ren Yi (A Novel)*, volume 1.
7. *Records on the School-Owned Fields of Chong'an County, Jianning Province.*
8. Sun Yanmin. "A Study of the Academy System of the Song Dynasty," in Zhang Zhengfan. *A Study on the Chinese Academy System*, p. 12. (Nanjing: Jiangsu Education Press, 1985).
9. *History of the Yuan Dynasty: Records of the Imperial Examination.*
10. *Sequel to The General Study of Documents*, volume 50.

11. Huang Zongxi. *History of Chinese Thought in the Ming Dynasty*, volume 37.
12. *Sequel to The General Study of Documents*, volume 50.
13. Ibid.
14. *The Collection of Zhang Taiyue*, volume 29: *A Reply to Tu Pingshi, the Nan Si Cheng* (an official position in ancient China) *on Learning*.
15. *History of the Ming Dynasty as a Mirror*.
16. In 1652, the ninth year of the Shunzhi Period, the Qing government ordered that "supervisors should urge and lead instructors and scholars to abide by and practice the lessons and moral principles learned from the classics. It was forbidden to privately establish academies, bring together clans, and call together local villains to indulge in empty talk." (*Collections of Ancient and Modern Books: Class of Election—Department of Academy*.)
17. *A General Study of the Qing Dynasty*, volume 70.
18. *The Academy System in Ancient China*, compiled by Chen Yuanhui, p. 97. (Shanghai: Shanghai Education Press, 1981).
19. Ibid., pp. 101–108.
20. *Six Codes of the Tang Dynasty*.
21. Li Caidong. "A Brief Study of the Bailudong Academy," in *Journal of Jiangxi Educational School*, p. 17, 1985.
22. Yang Shenchu. *A Brief History of Yuelu Academy*, pp. 136–137. (Changsha: Yuelu Publishing House, 1986).
23. *The Analects of Zhuzi*, volume 8.
24. *The Analects of Zhuzi*, volume 11.
25. *The Analects of Zhuzi*, volume 10.
26. *The Academy System in Ancient China*, compiled by Chen Yuanhui, p. 159. (Shanghai: Shanghai Education Press, 1981).
27. Zhang Zhengfan. *A Study on the Chinese Academy System*, p. 65. (Nanjing: Jiangsu Education Press, 1985).
28. Guo Rencheng. "On the Patriotic Tradition of Yuelu Academy I," in *The Collected Works of Studies on the History of Academy Culture II*, ed. Yuelu Academy Cultural Research Institute of Hunan University, pp. 12–27. (Changsha: Hunan University Press, 1998).
29. *Annals of Jinkui County in Wuxi*.
30. Cf. *The Academy System in Ancient China*, compiled by Chen Yuanhui, p. 151. (Shanghai: Shanghai Education Press, 1981).
31. *The Collected Works of Lu Jiuyuan: Chronicles*.
32. *The Collected Works of Lu Jiuyuan: Analects I*.
33. Ibid.
34. Ibid.
35. *The Collected Works of Lu Jiuyuan: Chronicles*.
36. *History of Chinese Thought in the Ming Dynasty*, volume 11.
37. Li Caidong. "The Value of Studying Academies in Ancient China and Their Characteristics," in *Education Studies*, volume 10, 1985.
38. *Collection of Mr. Hui'an: Duke Wen of Zhu*, volume 69.
39. *The Chronicle of Zhuzi*, volume 2.
40. *The Chronicle of Zhuzi*, volume 4.
41. *The Analects of Zhuzi*, volume 106.
42. *Chronicles of the Song Dynasty*, volume 80: *The Merits and Demerits of the Doctrines*.
43. *History of Chinese Thought in the Ming Dynasty*, volume 34.
44. Yang Shenchu. *A Brief History of Yuelu Academy*, p. 155. (Changsha: Yuelu Publishing House, 1986).
45. Liu Yizheng. *The First Draft of the Records of Jiangsu Academy*.

Chapter 10

1. Xu Zi and Wang Xuemei. "Traditional Elementary Instructional Materials of China: An Overview," in *Poetry of Elementary Education*, p. 1. (Taiyuan: Shanxi Education Press, 1991).
2. *Methods for Teaching Young Children*, ed. Wang Jun.
3. *Lessons for Young Children*, ed. Cui Xuegu. *On Children's Education*, edited by Lu Shiyi in the Qing Dynasty, states, "Most children, when reaching the age of 5 or 6, know the changing rules of things. Two years later, they begin to enter primary school. And even though they have their father's instruction and their teacher's seriousness, it takes

much time and energy to teach them well. And how can the instruction of their fathers and brothers always follow the ancient laws? Therefore, nowadays, children should enter primary school at age 5 or 6."

4. [Great Britain] John Locke. *Thoughts on Education*, trans. Fu Rengan, p. 4. (Beijing: People's Education Press, 1957).

5. *Selected Works of the Schools of Thought of Modern Western Bourgeois Education*, ed. and trans. Education Department of Eastern Normal University and Hangzhou University, p. 106. (Beijing: People's Educational Press, 1980).

6. *Admonitions for the Yan Clan: Encouraging Learning*.

7. *Civilized Social Contracts: The Contract of Elementary Schools*.

8. The *History of the Han Dynasty: Records of Literature* states, "The *History of Zhou* was a book used by historiographers in the Zhou Dynasty....The seven chapters of the book *Cang Jie* (a book of characters) were written by Li Si, a prime minister (in the Qin dynasty of ancient China); the six chapters of *Yuan Li* (a book for the teaching of characters) were written by Zhao Gao, a minister in the Qin Dynasty; the seven chapters of the book *Bo Xue* (*Learning*) were written by Hu Mujing, an imperial astronomer, most of whose characters were selected from *The History of Zhou*." Because the book had been missing for a long time, we could not infer its contents, but it was considered as being written in four-word sentences by historian official Zhou in the time of King Xuan of Zhou, and this has been universally acknowledged.

9. Wang Chong in the Han Dynasty described his studying in the library: "I was born in the third year in the year of Jian Wu. When I was young, I played with my peer Lun without any indecent behaviors....I began to go to school at the age of 6. I was respectful, submissive, polite, restrained, and quiet, with the aspiration of becoming a minister. My father never punished me physically, and my mother never blamed me. People in my hometown were friendly to me. At the age of 8, I graduated from the library. There were more than 100 children in the library, all of whom were blamed for their faults or beaten because of their ugly handwriting. I made a great improvement in my calligraphy and made no mistakes." (*On Balance: Self-Discipline*).

10. According to the statistics of *Traditional Booklist for the Elementary Education of China* (first draft). Cf. *Critical Points of Elementary Education*, ed. Xu Zi and Wang Xuemei, pp. 230–338. (Taiyuan: Shanxi Education Press, 1991).

11. *The Whole Collection of Duke Wang Wencheng: Teaching Contract of Children's Education*.

12. Xu Zi and Wang Xuemei, eds. *Poetry of Elementary Education*, p. 245. (Taiyuan: Shanxi Education Press, 1991).

13. *Poetry of Elementary Education*, ed. Xu Zi and Wang Xuemei, p. 206. (Taiyuan: Shanxi Education Press, 1991).

14. Lu Xun. *How Do We Educate Children? The Collected Works of Lu Xun*, volume 5, pp. 255–256. (Beijing: People's Literature Publishing House, 1981).

15. *Bao Pu Zi: The Supplementary Chapter—Encourage Learning*.

16. *Collections of the Two Cheng Brothers: Records Left*, volume 2.

17. *The Compilation for Children's Cultivation*, volume 2: *Children's Education*, ed. Zhang Boxing.

18. Ibid.

19. *Views on Reading: Zi Zhitongjian* (*History as a Mirror*), volume 10.

20. *New Book of Jiazi: Antenatal Training*.

21. Wang Chong said, "Deafness, physical disability, and blindness are caused by damage to the fetus in the mother's uterus. If the character of such individuals is influenced by external factors, when they grow up, they will appear to have been born with a goat's tongue and a wolf's voice, as well as an evil character, and then they will die of disaster when grown. When in their mothers' bellies, they tended to suffer like Danzhu and Shangjun. Life lies in the fundamental, and therefore there is the method of "antenatal training" recorded in *The Book of Rites*." (*On Balance: Fate*). Yan Zhitui said, "In ancient times, the king had the method of 'antenatal training': when women had been pregnant for three months, they did not move from one place to another and remained calm with music and food, avoiding seeing or hearing evil things." (*Admonitions for the Yan Clan: Education of Children*). Zhang Hua (*The Record of Nature*). says, "When women become pregnant, they should avoid seeing ugly things, such as peculiar birds and beasts; touching abnormally smelling things; seeing beasts like bears or tigers; eating cattle heart, dog's meat, and carp's head; sitting sidelong and eating on a mat; and seeing or hearing evil things. Children born in this way will be virtuous, good-looking, and long-living. This is the antenatal training method for mothers."

Sun Simiao said in *Valuable Prescription: The Nourishing of the Fetus*, "It was said that when women had been pregnant for three months, the child changed gradually; their aptitude did not form at first. Therefore, when they have been pregnant for three months, mothers were supposed to see the rare elephants and beasts, as well as jewelry; they were supposed to see virtuous men, moral masters, listen to ritual music, and use sacrificial utensils; they were supposed to burn valuable incense and read poems and precepts; they were supposed to live peacefully and avoid sitting sidelong and eating on a mat; and they were supposed to play musical instruments to keep their mood peaceful. In this circumstance, the baby they gave birth to was benignant, loyal, clever, and healthy in body. This was the antenatal training of King Wen." Wan Jin said in *Gynaecology: Antenatal Training*, "When women become pregnant, they should pay attention to their emotions. They should be careful of joy, anger, meditation, worry, and panic, all which have a negative influence on pregnant women's physical bodies. If pregnant mothers are hurt by their emotions, their unborn children will also be hurt."

22. Cf. Wu Jie and Cai Dingwen. "Comment on Psychological Thoughts in the Ancient Times of China," in *Academic Journal of Jiangxi Normal University*, volume 1, 1984.
23. *Abstract Records of Critical Thoughts*, ed. Lu Shiyi.
24. Sun Qifeng. *Admonitions of Xiaoyoutang*.
25. *Abstract Records of Critical Thoughts*, ed. Lu Shiyi.
26. *Abstract Records of Critical Thoughts*, volume 10, ed. Lu Shiyi.
27. *Collection of Mr. Yang Yuan*, volume 26.
28. *Admonitions for the Yan Clan: Regulating Family*.
29. *Admonitions for the Yan Clan: Teaching Children*.
30. Zhang Boxing. *The Forming of Sound Habits*, volume 2: *Children's Education*.
31. Friedrich Engels. *The Origin of the Family, Private Property and the State, Collection of Marx and Engels*, volume 4, p. 72. (Beijing: People's Press, 1995).
32. Zhang Boxing. *The Collected Annotations of Children's Learning: Edited Theories of Children's Learning*.
33. Ibid.
34. *Ya Shu* (a book of Wang Yangming's philosophical ideas), Chapter 1.
35. *The Whole Collection of Duke Wang Wencheng: General Ideas of Children's Education After Reading the Work of Liu Bosong and Others*.
36. Zhang Xingjian. *Articles Written in the Xiaosun Room: Anecdotes on the Private School*.
37. *Measures of Teaching Children*.
38. *Collected Works of Tanji: Children's Education*.
39. *The Whole Collection of Mr. Yang Yuan*, volume 39.
40. Tang Biao. *Persuading Ways of the Father and Teacher*.
41. *Collected Works of Tanji: Children's Education*.
42. *Measures of Teaching Children*.
43. *Persuading Ways of the Father and Teacher*.
44. *Collected Works of Tanji: Children's Education*.
45. Ibid.
46. *Measures of Teaching Children*.
47. Cf. Yan Guocai. *Study of Psychological Thought in the Ming and Qing Dynasties*, p. 422. (Changsha: Hunan People's Publishing House, 1988).
48. *Measures of Teaching Children*.
49. Ibid.
50. *Persuading Ways of the Father and Teacher*.
51. Ibid.
52. Ibid.
53. *Measures of Teaching Children*.
54. *Articles Written in the Xiaosun Room: Anecdotes on the Private School*.

References

B

Bai Xinliang. *Developmental History of Ancient Chinese Academies.* (Tianjin: Tianjin University Press, 1995).

Bi Cheng. *The Turnover of Confucianism: Research on the Educational Thought of Yangming School.* (Beijing: Science and Education Press, 1992).

C

Cai Fanglu. *Cheng Hao, Cheng Yi and Chinese Culture.* (Guiyang: Guizhou People's Press, 1996).

Cao Xiren. *Introduction of the Comparison Between Chinese and Western Culture: Reviewing the Choice of Chinese Culture.* (Beijing: China Youth Press, 1992).

Chang Xiaozhen. *Essays on the Thought of Ancient Chinese Talents.* (Lanzhou: Gansu People's Press, 1986).

Chen Dongyuan. *Education in the Chinese Imperial Examination Era.* (Beijing: The Commercial Press, 1934).

Chen Guangzhong, trans. and annot. *Translation and Annotation of Huainanzi.* (Changchun: Jilin Literature and History Press, 1990).

Chen Liang. *The Collection of Chen Liang.* (Beijing: Zhonghua Book Company, 1987).

Chen Qiyou, checked and annot. *Annotations of the Collection of Hanfei.* (Shanghai: Shanghai People's Press, 1974).

Chen Qiyun. *A Historical Analysis of Ancient Chinese Thought and Culture.* (Beijing: Peking University Press, 2001).

Chen Que. *The Collection of Chen Que.* (Beijing: Zhonghua Book Company, 1979).

Cheng Hao and Cheng Yi. *The Collection of Cheng Hao and Cheng Yi.* Punctuated and collated by Wang Xiaoyu. (Beijing: Zhonghua Book Company, 1981).

D

Dai Zheng. *The Collection of Dai Zheng.* (Shanghai: Shanghai Classics Publishing House, 1980).

The Department of Education of Shanghai Normal University, ed. *Materials of Law School's Educational Thought in the Pre-Qin Dynasty.* (Shanghai: Shanghai People's Press, 1976).

Ding Gang and Liu Qi. *Ancient Academies and Chinese Culture.* (Shanghai: Shanghai Education Press, 1992).

Dong Zhongshu. *Book Chunqiu Fanlu: Four Essential Classics.*

E

Editorial Committee of Chinese Culture Academy, ed. *Lecture Records in Chinese Culture Academy.* (Beijing: SDX Joint Publishing Company, 1988).

The Educational Department of Beijing Normal University, ed. *An Overview of the Struggle Between Confucianism and Legalism in Educational History.* (Beijing: People's Education Press, 1975).

Mabel Emerson. *The Evolution of the Educational Ideal.* Zheng Mengxun, trans. (Beijing: The Commercial Press, 1924).

F

Feng Tianyu and Zhou Jiming. *The Mystery of Ancient Chinese Culture.* (Wuhan: Hubei People's Press, 1986).

G

Gao Shiliang. *China's Education History (the Ancient Part)*. (Beijing: Science and Education Press, 1991).

Ge Zhaoguang. *Taoism and Chinese Culture*. (Shanghai: Shanghai People's Press, 1987).

Gu Chun. *The Three Educational Theories of Lu Jiuyuan: Origin, Argument, Feature*. (Beijing: Science and Education Press, 2003).

Gu Fang. *Han Fei and Chinese Culture*. (Guiyang: Guizhou People's Press, 1996).

Gu Shusen, ed. *The Analects of Ancient Chinese Educators*. (Shanghai: Shanghai Education Press, 1962).

Guo Qingfan, ed. *Annotations of Chuang Tse Collection*. (Beijing: Zhonghua Book Company, 1982).

H

Han Yu. *The Collection of Han Yu*. Printed by Hanfen Library according to the Edition of Dong Yangtang.

Huang Shuguang. *Educational Thought of Natural Science and Chinese Culture*. (Shanghai: Shanghai Education Press, 1993).

Hui Jixing. *Xuncius and Chinese Culture*. (Guiyang: Guizhou People's Press, 1996).

J

Jiang Guanghui. *Natural Science and Chinese Culture*. (Shanghai: Shanghai People's Press, 1994).

Jin Liangnian. *Annotations of the Analects of Confucius*. (Shanghai: Shanghai Classics Publishing House, 1995).

Jin Liangnian. *Annotations of the Analects Mencius*. (Shanghai: Shanghai Classics Publishing House, 1995).

Jin Zheng. *The Imperial Examination System and Chinese Culture*. (Shanghai: Shanghai People's Press, 1990).

K

Kang Youwei. *Great Harmony*. (Beijing: Zhonghua Book Company, 1959).

L

Li Jinde, ed. *The Analects of Zhuzi (Zhu Xi)*. Punctuated and collated by Wang Xingxian. (Beijing: Zhonghua Book Company, 1986).

Li Qing. *The Human Concept in Chinese Culture*. (Shanghai: Xuelin Publishing House, 1996).

Li Weixiong. *Exploration of the Essence of Chinese Culture*. (Taipei: Liming Cultural Enterprises Co. Ltd., 1985).

Liang Qixiong. *Annotations of the Book of Xuncius*. (Beijing: Zhonghua Book Company, 1983).

Liang Shuming. *The Essence of Chinese Culture*. (Shanghai: Xuelin Publishing House, 1987).

Liao Qifa. *The Theory of Human Nature in the Pre-Qin and Han Dynasties and Research on Educational Thought*. (Chongqing: Chongqing Publishing House, 1999).

Liu Dai, ed. *New Theory of Chinese Culture: The Root*. (Beijing: SDX Joint Publishing Company, 1991).

Liu Dai, ed. *New Theory of Chinese Culture: The Thought*. (Beijing: SDX Joint Publishing Company, 1991).

Liu Dai, ed. *New Theory of Chinese Culture: The Learning*. (Beijing: SDX Joint Publishing Company, 1991).

Liu Shao. *Records of Personages* (the third edition of *An Outlook of Literary Sketches*). (Chengdu: Emerging Publishing House Co., Ltd., 1981).

Liu Xiaofeng, ed. *Traits of Chinese Culture*. (Beijing: SDX Joint Publishing Company, 1990).

Lu Jiuyuan. *The Collection of Lu Jiuyuan*. Punctuated and collated by Zhong Zhe. (Beijing: Zhonghua Book Company, 1980).

Lu Zhongfa, Lin Jiali, and Jiang Xing, annot. *Highlights of Children's Enlightenment Education (fully annotated)*. (Hangzhou: Zhejiang Ancient Books Publishing House, 1991).

Lv Tao, ed. *Confucius, the Great Educator*. (Shenyang: Liaoning Education Press, 1987).

M

Mao Lirui, Qu Junong, and Shao Heting, eds. *History of China's Ancient Education.* (Beijing: People's Education Press, 1983).

Mao Lirui and Shen Guanqun, eds. *The General History of Chinese Education (Volumes 1–6).* (Jinan: Shangdong Education Press, 1985–1989).

Q

Qiu Chun. *Essays on Ancient Educational Thought.* (Beijing: Beijing Normal University Press, 1985).

R

Ren Jiyu, *A New Interpretation of Lao Tz (revised).* (Shanghai: Shanghai Classics Publishing House, 1985).

S

Shen Guanqun. *Ancient Chinese Education and Educational Thought.* (Wuhan: Hubei People's Press, 1956).

Sheng Langxi, ed. *China's Academy System.* (Beijing: Zhonghua Book Company, 1934).

Shi Xuanyuan, Lin Yaochen, and Xu Liyan, eds. *The Mystery of Chinese Culture.* (Shanghai: Xuelin Publishing House, 1985).

Shi Xuanyuan, ed. *The Eternal Mystery: 500 Mysteries of Chinese Cultural History.* (Zhengzhou: Zhongzhou Ancient Books Publishing House, 1989).

Song Bencheng and Deng Yong, eds. *Review of Ancient Chinese Educators' Thoughts on Education and Teaching.* (Hohhot: Inner Mongolia Education Press, 1985).

T

Tan Jiefu, ed. *Annotations of Classified Mojing.* (Beijing: Zhonghua Book Company, 1981).

Tang Deyang, ed. *The Source of Chinese Culture.* (Jinan: Shandong People's Press, 1993).

Tao Yuchuan. *Comparative Study of Chinese Education History (Ancient Volume).* (Jinan: Shandong Education Press, 1985).

W

Wang Anshi. *The Collection of Duke Wen of Wang* (Wang Anshi). Punctuated and collated by Tang Wu. (Shanghai: Shanghai People's Press, 1974).

Wang Chong. *On Balance (Volume Seven of The Collected Works of Major Schools in Ancient China).* (Shanghai: Shanghai Store, 1986).

Wang Fuzhi. *Reflections on the Four Books.* (Beijing: Zhonghua Book Company, 1975).

Wang Fuzhi. *The Annotations of Shang Shu.* (Beijing: Zhonghua Book Company, 1976).

Wang Fuzhi. *The Annotations of the Cultivation of the Children of Zhang Zai.* (Beijing: Zhonghua Book Company, 1975).

Wang Fuzhi. *Supplement to the Book of Changes.* (Beijing: Zhonghua Book Company, 1977).

Wang Fuzhi. *Shi Guang Zhuan (Essays and Reviews on The Book of Poetry).* (Beijing: Zhonghua Book Company, 1964).

Wang Fuzhi. *Records of Thoughts and Questions: Waiting to Be Understood.* (Beijing: Zhonghua Book Company, 1956).

Wang Jingui. *Classics on Chinese Culture: The Book of Han and the History of the Later Han Dynasty.* (Beijing: Beijing People's Press, 1987).

Wang Jun. *The Methods of Teaching Children (Chapter One of the Collection of Lin Jian Ge).* (Yuanhe Jiang Printed Edition, 1895, in the Qing Dynasty).

Wang Shishun. *Annotations of The Book of Zhuangzi.* (Jinan: Shandong Education Press, 1984).

Wang Shouren. *The Complete Collection of Duke Wencheng of Wang (The Whole Collection of the Basic Knowledge of Chinese Ancient Civilization).* (Beijing: The Commercial Press, 1934).

Wang Tao. *Letters in Tao Garden.* (Beijing: Zhonghua Book Company, 1959).

Wang Yihong, *The Trend of Educational Thought in Ancient China.* (Beijing: The Commercial Press, 1931).

Wang Yongxiang. *The History of Unity Thought in Ancient China.* (Jinan: Qi Lu Press, 1991).
Writing Team of *Annotations of Shangzi* from Shandong University, ed. *Annotations of Shangzi.* (Jinan: Qi Lu Press, 1982).
Wu Enbo. *Annotations of The Four Books.* (Changchun: Jilin Literature and History Press, 1990).
Wu Xiangzhen, Dai Xuwei, and Li Dingkai, eds. *Chinese Educators' Views on Moral Education.* (Chengdu: Sichuan Education Press, 198s7).
Wuyishan Zhu Xi Research Center, ed. *Zhuxi and Chinese Culture.* (Shanghai: Xuelin Press, 1989).

X

Xia Yulong, ed. *A Favorable Turn of the Development of Chinese Culture.* (Beijing: Knowledge Press, 1989).
Xu Zi and Wang Xuemei, eds. *Readings for Enlightenment Education.* (Taiyuan: Shanxi Education Press, 1991).
Xu Zi and Wang Xuemei, eds. *Poetry for Enlightenment Education.* (Taiyuan: Shanxi Education Press, 1991).
Xu Zi and Wang Xuemei, eds. *Instruction of Enlightenment Education.* (Taiyuan: Shanxi Education Press, 1991).
Xu Shu'an. *An Overview of Ancient Talent Selection and the Imperial Examination System.* (Tianjin: Tianjin People's Press, 1985).
Xu Zi and Wang Xuemei, eds. *The Essence of Enlightenment Education.* (Taiyuan: Shanxi Education Press, 1991).

Y

Yan Yuan. *The Collection of Yan Yuan.* (Beijing: Zhonghua Book Company, 1987).
Yang Bojun, trans. and annot. *Annotations of The Analects of Confucius.* (Beijing: Zhonghua Book Company, 1980).
Yang Bojun, trans. and annot.. *Annotations of The Book of Mencius.* (Beijing: Zhonghua Book Company, 1960).
Yang Xiangkui. *Research on Ancient Chinese Society and Thought.* (Beijing: People's Publishing House, 1962).
Ye Shi. *Preface of Records in Learning.* (Beijing: Zhonghua Book Company, 1977).
Ye Shi. *The Collection of Ye Shi.* (Beijing: Zhonghua Book Company, 1961).
Yu Yingshi. *Shi and Chinese Culture.* (Shanghai: Shanghai People's Press, 1987).

Z

Zhang Fangyan, ed. *Annotations of the Classics of Confucianism, Taoism and Buddhism.* (Wuhan: Hubei Education Press, 1993).
Zhang Jue. *Annotations on the Book of Xunzi.* (Shanghai: Shanghai Classics Publishing House, 1995).
Zhang Mingqi. *Research on Dong Zhongshu's Educational Thought.* (Beijing: People's Education Press, 2000).
Zhang Zai. *The Collection of Zhang Zai.* (Beijing: Zhonghua Book Company, 1978).
Zhang Zhengfan. *Research on the Chinese Academy System.* (Nanjing: Jiangsu Education Press, 1985).
Zhang Zhiyan. *Laozi and Chinese Culture.* (Guiyang: Guizhou People's Press, 1996).
Zhang Liuquan. *The Utilitarianism School in the Southern Song Dynasty and Its Educational Thought.* (Beijing: Science and Education Press, 1984).
Zhang Liuquan. *The History of Chinese Academies: The Evolutions and Contents of Academies from the Song to the Qing Dynasties.* (Beijing: Science and Education Press, 1981).
Zhao Ming. *The Thought of Taoism and Chinese Culture.* (Chang Chun: Jilin University Press, 1986).
Zheng Guanying. *Golden Age Prophecy.* (Beijing: Hua Xia Press, 2002).
Zhu Xi. *Collection of Mr. Hui'an: Duke Wen of Zhu—Four Essential Classics.*
Zhu Xi. *Collected Annotations of The Four Books.* (Beijing: Zhonghua Book Company, 1983).

Index

About the Author

Zhu Yongxin was born in August 1958 in Dafeng, Jiangsu Province. He is a member of the Eleventh National People's Congress (NPC) Standing Committee and the Health Committee of the United Nations Educational, Scientific and Cultural Organization (UNESCO). Currently, he is vice chairman of the Central Committee of the China Association for Promoting Democracy (CAPD) and the deputy secretary general of the Twelfth National Chinese People's Political Consultative Conference (CPPCC) and a member of the Standing Committee. He is also vice president of the China Education Society, the Tao Xingzhi Study Association of China, a professor and doctoral tutor at Soochow University, and a part-time professor at Peking University, Beijing Normal University, Tongji University, and other universities. He is an initiator of the New Educational Experiment. He is primarily engaged in the study of the history of educational thought and educational policy. He has authored more than 40 books, including *Zhu Yongxin's Educational Works* (16 volumes), *The History of Chinese Educational Thoughts*, and *The Dream of New Education*. His works have been translated into English, Japanese, Korean, Arabic, and other languages. He has published more than 400 papers on education in China, the United States, Britain, Japan, and other countries. He has also been editor-in-chief of more than 30 works, including the *Contemporary Japanese Education Series*, *New Century Education Library*, and *New Educational Library*.

Among these works, *100 Proposals for China's Education*, a collection of thoughts regarding participation in political consultation and democratic supervision, was named one of the *50 Favorite Books of Ordinary People* by the Press and Publication Administration of China in 2011 and won the nomination for the fourth Outstanding Publication Award of China. He has participated in research projects commissioned by UNESCO, the National Natural Science Foundation, and the National Social Science Fund, among other organizations.

In 2000, he initiated the New Educational Experiment. By 2014, more than 200 million teachers and students from more than 2,224 experimental schools in 28 provinces, municipalities, and autonomous regions nationwide had participated in the experiment, which is changing Chinese education through action. The New Educational Experiment became one of 15 project finalists for the 2014 World Education Innovation Award organized by the Qatar Foundation.

Among his awards, Zhu Yongxin has been named one of "China's Top Ten People of Educational Excellence," China's "Educator of the Year in the 30 Years of the Reform and Opening Up," one of "China's Top Ten Wise People," Central China Television's "Moving China" candidate, the Press and Publication Administration of China's "National Reading Spokesperson," and For the Public Interest's "Person of the Year" for *South Reviews*.

CPSIA information can be obtained at www.ICGtesting.com
Printed in the USA
BVOW08*0458100215

387039BV00008B/82/P